Living on the Edge

Studies in Medieval and Early Modern Culture

LXXXIII

Living on the Edge

Transgression, Exclusion, and Persecution
in the Middle Ages

Edited by
Delfi I. Nieto-Isabel and Laura Miquel Milian

DE GRUYTER

ISBN 978-1-5015-2307-6
e-ISBN (PDF) 978-1-5015-1486-9
e-ISBN (EPUB) 978-1-5015-1488-3
ISSN 0085-6878

Library of Congress Control Number: 2022938893

Bibliographic information published by the Deutsche Nationalbibliothek
The Deutsche Nationalbibliothek lists this publication in the Deutsche Nationalbibliografie; detailed bibliographic data are available on the internet at http://dnb.dnb.de.

© 2024 Walter de Gruyter GmbH, Berlin/Boston
This volume is text- and page-identical with the hardback published in 2022.
Cover image: 'Cathars' expelled from Carcassonne, *Grandes Chroniques de France*, Cotton MS Nero E II, folio 20verso © The British Library

www.degruyter.com

To the transgressors, the excluded, and the persecuted of all time

To all the people who live on the edge

Acknowledgements

This book was first conceived in 2017, when the Graduate Students' Association of the University of Barcelona (UB), ARDIT *Cultures Medievals*, held its 3rd International Congress, which brought together an exceptional crowd of PhD students and Early Career Scholars. Their ideas, commitment, and love for what they do have imbued each and every one of the following pages. The final result has become the beloved child of two mothers who have seen it grow, fail, succeed, and are now finally sending it into the world to try its wings. This has been a long and eventful journey that has carried us through two completed dissertations, the birth of a little baby daughter, a host of postdoctoral applications—some of them successful—moments of joy, moments of grief, and even a pandemic. We would not have made it without the help of so many, too many to count; after all, it takes a village. Our deepest gratitude goes to them all.

Needless to say, ARDIT deserves a special mention; we thank its board members, and the Congress's organising and scientific committees, who thought that transgression, exclusion, and persecution in the Middle Ages were topics worth discussing. We are also indebted to the Master's Degree and Doctoral programme in Medieval Cultures of the UB, and the Institute for Research on Medieval Cultures (IRCVM), without whose constant support the congress itself would not have been possible in the first place. But, most of all, we must thank the true heart of this endeavour, the authors who have generously contributed their work, entrusted us with it, and supported us throughout this project. While completing their dissertations, struggling with applying for their first postdoctoral fellowship, or looking for a permanent position, twelve young scholars from ten different institutions and seven countries have joined forces, sharing their most recent research results, and their enthusiasm. We are sure that they are as grateful as we are for the work of the twenty-five reviewers who have devoted their time and expertise to make this book better. Even if their names must remain confidential, they have been most generous under difficult circumstances, and have shown, once again, that Medieval Studies is a welcoming and ever-expanding field, where collaboration and exchange are key. We would also like to thank Dr. Justine Trombley, one of the keynote speakers at the 2017 conference; now a Leverhulme Early Career Fellow at the University of Nottingham, she eagerly accepted writing the Foreword that follows. This book would never have seen the light of day without the exceptional work and kindness of Shannon Cunningham (Medieval Institute Publications) and Christine Henschel (De Gruyter) and the dedication of Laura Kopp, a fantastic copy editor; for that we are most grateful.

Finally, we would like to thank our friends and family, who have stood at our side even during the most trying of times, as we all grasped what living on the edge meant.

Table of Contents

Justine L. Trombley
Foreword —— 1

Delfi I. Nieto-Isabel
Introduction
All but Marginal: The Co-Constructions of Otherness in the Middle Ages —— 3

Part I: **The Fundamental Edge**

Sergi Sancho Fibla
Chapter 1
Reading in Community, Writing a Community: Douceline's *Vida* and the Beguines of Roubaud —— 23

Courtney A. Krolikoski
Chapter 2
"No More Horrified by Them": Royal Holy Women and Lepers in Twelfth- and Thirteenth-Century Hagiography —— 59

Mireia Comas-Via
Chapter 3
Exclusion and Marginalization of Widows in Late Medieval Barcelona —— 75

Laura Cayrol-Bernardo
Chapter 4
Ageing Women, (In)Visible Bodies: Iconographies on the Edge in Late-Medieval Iberia (Thirteenth to Fifteenth Centuries) —— 93

Part II: **The Religious Edge**

Rachel Ernst
Chapter 5
Catharistae in Question: A Case of Rupture in the Manichaean Sect —— 119

Marta Fernández Lahosa
Chapter 6
Art, Iconography, and Orthodoxy between the Fourth and Fifth Centuries: The Case of the Ascension —— 141

Stamatia Noutsou
Chapter 7
The Early Cistercian Order and the Persecution of Heresy: Bernard of Clairvaux's and Geoffrey of Auxerre's Attitudes Towards the Violent Persecution of Heretics —— 159

Jordi Casals i Parés
Chapter 8
From Persecution to Exile: Jewish Views on Christians and Christianity in the Late Medieval Crown of Aragon —— 177

Part III: **The Edge of Society**

Ivan Armenteros-Martínez
Chapter 9
Social Domination and Resistance: Slavery in the Medieval Christian Western Mediterranean —— 201

Anna M. Peterson
Chapter 10
Diverging Views of the "Leper" in Legal, Literary, and Doctrinal Texts from Thirteenth-Century Western Europe —— 221

Angana Moitra
Chapter 11
On the Margins of Society: Exclusion through Exile as a Structuring Motif in *Sir Orfeo* —— 237

Estela Estévez Benítez
Chapter 12
Defying Containment: The Use of the Frame in Depictions of Monstrous Peoples in Monte Cassino Rhabanus Maurus Codex —— 251

Notes on Contributors —— 267

Index —— 271

Justine L. Trombley
Foreword

I had the great privilege of participating in the conference that gave rise to this volume, which was held in Barcelona in 2017. I work on "the edge" as a historian of Western Christian heresy and inquisition. Up to that point, most of my encounters with other scholars at conferences had been with those who also worked on that part of the edge, or within the circles that feed into it. But what this conference did so excellently was to allow me for the first time to connect in a really meaningful way with scholars who worked on those marginalized in medieval society within disciplines that I rarely got to encounter in any depth: health, ageing, poetry, art history. It was a diverse program, yet it melded together easily—not always a simple feat when bringing a conference to fruition. The organizers had meticulously put together a program that effortlessly bridged gaps and brought out comparisons in a broad range of areas. But it also revealed instructive differences, showing that marginalization and transgression was not a uniform experience, but something that could also be shaped by status, affiliation, and various other attributes, and that there could be margins within margins; even the marginalized could transgress in the eyes of others on the margins. It was, like most things in historical study, simultaneously connected and splintered, which meant it was satisfyingly thought-provoking. The conference was an incredible opportunity to see what "the edge" in the Middle Ages looked like on a grand scale, and to see connections between fields and eras which previously had seemed remote or only tangentially connected to one another.

This volume now brings those successes to a wider audience. It, like the conference, asks: What does it mean to "live on the edge"? One could make the joke that anyone who has ever been an early career academic knows exactly what it means. Perhaps it is fitting, then, that this volume is mostly put together by and made up of pieces written by early career academics. Working at one kind of "edge" themselves, the authors and editors explore various other edges of the Middle Ages. The times in which such a volume has come together are also fitting. I am writing this foreword while in lockdown during the 2020 coronavirus pandemic. Rarely does one event so clearly present to us what "the edge" looks like in all its various forms: the edge of health and sickness, or the edge of life and death; those who once felt secure now on the edge of unemployment and financial collapse; the edge of what one can bear and tolerate; and those groups who, already occupying the edges and the margins, or teetering on the brink, now find themselves pushed further and further into the margins and see little space left there. This has, of course, been preceded by years of a seemingly never-ending stream of efforts by those in power to exclude, to demonize, to punish, and (thankfully not literally) to "burn" transgressors. It is, in other words, a time that demands examination of "the edge" and its attendant transgressions more than ever.

Each of the above issues can also be found in this volume, both explicitly and implicitly, in the lives and representations of lepers, widows, religious and ethnic minorities, even of imaginary "monstrous" races. It asks: What does it mean to occupy "the edge"? How is it created? What happens when those who were previously far from the edge are pushed into it? How did people defy it? It also interrogates transgression: Who is allowed to say what? Where is the line of transgression, and who gets to define that line? How or why does someone commit a transgression? These are questions which transcend historical periods, and which are of course still being asked now. But, as most scholars know, pursuing the stories of these figures is not merely a question of documenting victimhood, but of discovering the ways people negotiated, accepted, or pushed against their marginalization. Some might not have considered themselves to *be* on the margins. The complexities and contradictions in these figures' lives and treatment reinforce the variation, not uniformity, of medieval society and thought. There was no one view or experience of "the leper" or "the heretic" just as there was no one view or experience of "women."

But the volume also takes a multi-faceted, not singular, view of the topic. To paraphrase Barbara Newman on the subject of heresy, the edge does not exist in a vacuum. Someone has to create it, someone has to push people towards, into, or over it. Therefore, the volume does not merely chronicle the narratives of outcasts or defiant transgressors, but it also interrogates the persecutors and those in power. This, too, comes with still-urgent questions: How did such people create the edge? Why did they do so? How did they define and maintain it? How did they portray and treat those occupying the edge? Again, this reveals some surprising and complex histories. It is not just a question of power or a question of belief, but a question of both simultaneously and of how they collided with other forces swirled into the mix. The "problems" those in power saw with those they marginalized might not always be the ones we might expect. And those doing the marginalization might not be *who* we expect, either. Persecutors and excluders could often be just as divided and diverse as those whom they pushed aside. They, too, had different experiences with "the edge."

It is almost a cliché now among historians of heresy that there was no clear line between heresy and orthodoxy. This volume brings that not-quite-cliché to the broader field of marginalization in the Middle Ages. It shows, with nuance and skill, that the edge then, as now, was both easy and difficult to define.

Delfi I. Nieto-Isabel
Introduction
All but Marginal: The Co-Constructions of Otherness in the Middle Ages

> It was so much easier to blame it on Them. It was bleakly depressing that They were Us. If it was Them, then nothing was anyone's fault. If it was Us, what did that make Me? After all, I'm one of Us. I must be. I've certainly never thought of myself as one of Them. No one ever thinks of themselves as one of Them. We are always one of Us. It's Them that do the bad things.
>
> Terry Pratchett, *Jingo*

This is a book about Us and Them; or rather, it is a book about the boundaries that set the two apart, about who establishes those boundaries, and who is left out in the cold. It is also a reflection on individual and collective identities, on their exclusive nature and their construction. But most of all, this book is a glimpse into the edge of medieval society and the people that lived on its margins, either by choice or by force.

The history of transgression and the studies focused on hitherto overlooked groups in medieval Europe are rapidly expanding fields of research. Scholars devoted to the history of disabilities, queer history, the history of medicine, and the history of ageing have joined heresiologists, experts in medieval transgressive literature, and in religious and ethnic minorities to provide an increasingly complex image of a diverse medieval period in which differences were at the same time abhorred and sought after.[1] This volume aims to contribute to this discus-

---

[1] To cite but a few examples, see Richard H. Godden and Asa Simon Mittman, eds., *Monstrosity, Disability, and the Posthuman in the Medieval and Early Modern World* (New York: Palgrave Macmillan, 2019); Will Rogers and Christopher Michael Roman, eds., *Medieval Futurity: Essays for the Future of a Queer Medieval Studies* (Berlin: De Gruyter; Kalamazoo: Medieval Institute Publications, 2020); Glenn Burger and Steven F. Kruger, eds., *Queering the Middle Ages* (Minneapolis: University of Minnesota Press, 2001); Elma Brenner and François-Olivier Touati, eds., *Leprosy and Identity in the Middle Ages: From England to the Mediterranean* (Manchester: Manchester University Press, 2021); Greg Eghigian, ed., *The Routledge History of Madness and Mental Health* (Abingdon: Routledge 2017); Sue Niebrzydowski, ed., *Middle-Aged Women in the Middle Ages* (Woodbridge, UK and Rochester, NY: Boydell & Brewer, 2011); Albrecht Classen, ed., *Old Age in the Middle Ages and the Renaissance: Interdisciplinary Approaches to a Neglected Topic* (Berlin and New York: De Gruyter, 2007); Rebecca Merkelbach and Gwendolyne Knight, eds., *Margins, Monsters, Deviants: Alterities in Old Norse Literature and Culture* (Turnhout: Brepols, 2020); Rebecca Merkelbach, *Monsters in Society: Alterity, Transgression, and the Use of the Past in Medieval Iceland* (Berlin: De Gruyter; Kalamazoo: Medieval Institute Publications,

https://doi.org/10.1515/9781501514869-003

sion by offering a range of approaches to the subject that cover a wide variety of medieval European regions and their neighbouring areas—from North Africa and the Mediterranean, to the British Isles and northern Europe—across the period between the last decades of Late Antiquity and the early years of the Renaissance.

The chapters that follow deal with some of the many faces of alterity in the Middle Ages and the way in which medieval society reacted to it, most times by "othering" individuals and groups that were considered different. Back then, much as it is now, "otherness" was a way of defining social, moral, religious, intellectual, and behavioural boundaries. In this sense, throughout this volume, "otherness" is understood as inextricably intertwined with power, for only those who held some measure of power were capable of successfully "othering" differences and placing them outside the edge of what was accepted, of what was normative.[2] The resulting liminalities were co-constructed frameworks rooted in the interplay between identity and context. Exploring those liminalities, where alterity was "othered" and marginalised but also embraced, is the main goal of this book. Its conclusions lend new strength to the understanding of medieval Europe as a vivid mosaic of identities and mindsets that could not be contained within fixed boundaries. Were women considered the fundamental "other" that was to be safely kept under control, or were gender edges porous? Were religious edges clear-cut and impregnable, or were they a permanent work in progress? Did societal egdes leave outside the sick, the poor, the enslaved, and the transgressor, or was forced inclusion the means to steamroll difference? These are the overarching questions that underlie this volume. Their answers point towards the existence of fluid margins that kept changing, and speak of the attempts of power to tame difference either by suppressing it or by pushing the different over the edge and "othering" them. However, as I shall endeavour to show in the following pages, these attempts were not always successful. In particular, I will focus on religious dissent and the way in which its supporters

---

2019); Geraldine Heng, *The Invention of Race in the Middle Ages* (Cambridge: Cambridge University Press, 2018); and Ann E. Zimo, Tiffany D. Vann Sprecher, Kathryn Reyerson, and Debra Blumenthal, eds., *Rethinking Medieval Margins and Marginality*, Studies in Medieval History and Culture (Abingdon, UK and New York: Routledge, 2020).

2 For a more detailed analysis of these problematic notions and the differences between "otherness" and "alterity," see, among others, Rebecca Merkelbach and Gwendolyne Knight, "Introduction: Old Norse Alterities in Contemporary Context," in *Margins, Monsters, Deviants: Alterities in Old Norse Literature and Culture*, ed. Rebecca Merkelbach and Gwendolyne Knight (Turnhout: Brepols, 2020), 9–23. I thank Dr. Merkelbach for generously sharing with me her views on the subject.

went from being Us to becoming Them, that is, from being members of the Christian community to becoming the "religious other."

On 11 August 1244, Arnauda de la Mota, a woman from Montauban—a village two days north from Toulouse—testified before the Dominican Friar Ferrer.[3] The standard inquisitorial formula of the time compelled her to say the truth "about herself and others, both living and dead, on the crime of heresy and Waldensianism."[4] Thirty years later, on 30 June 1273, a certain Burgundian man named Michel de Pech-Rodil also deposed under a similar formula, "sworn as a witness and questioned about the matter of heresy and Waldensianism."[5] Although the term "heresy" had never lost its more general meaning, in these examples it was used, as was common in thirteenth-century Languedoc, to describe a very specific religious group, the so-called Cathars.[6] By the early fourteenth cen-

---

[3] Between 1229 and 1247, Friar Ferrer, known as "the Catalan," acted first as episcopal inquisitor in Narbonne and later as papal inquisitor; he excommunicated Count Raimon VII of Toulouse in June 1242, and, according to his fellow Dominican Bernard Gui, his name was still feared in the early fourteenth century: "Nomen eius qualiter gladiosum in auribus hereticalium resonat usque hodie." See Célestin Douais, *Documents pour servir à l'histoire de l'inquisition dans le Languedoc* (Paris: Librairie Renouard and Société de l'Histoire de France, 1900), cxxxviii–cxliii. For a biographical account of Friar Ferrer, see Walter L. Wakefield, "Friar Ferrier, Inquisition at Caunes, and Escapes from Prison at Carcassonne," *Catholic Historical Review* 58, no. 2 (1972): 220–37. On his inquisitorial activities, see Yves Dossat, *Les crises de l'Inquisition Toulousaine au XIIIe siècle (1233–1273)* (Bordeaux: Imprimerie Bière, 1959), 222–25.

[4] Bibliothèque nationale de France, Collection Doat, MS 23, fol. 2v: "de se et de aliis vivis et mortuis super crimine haeresis et Valdensis." All volumes of the Collection Doat will hereinafter be simply referred to as "Doat" followed by manuscript number.

[5] Doat 25, fol. 10r: "testis iuratus et interrogatus super facto hæresis et Valdenciæ." Doat 25 and 26 have been recently edited and translated into English in Peter Biller, Caterina Bruschi, and Shelagh Sneddon, eds., *Inquisitors and Heretics in Thirteenth-Century Languedoc: Edition and Translation of Toulouse Inquisition Depositions, 1273–1282* (Leiden and Boston: Brill, 2011); however, all the citations from the manuscripts of the Collection Doat included in this chapter are based on the original manuscripts kept in the Bibliothèque nationale de France, transcribed and translated by the author.

[6] See Jean Duvernoy, "L'acception: 'haereticus' (iretge) = 'parfait cathare' en Languedoc au XIIIe siècle," in *The Concept of Heresy in the Middle Ages (11th–13th C.): Proceedings of the International Conference, Louvain, May 13–16, 1973*, ed. W. Lourdaux and D. Verhelst (Leuven: Leuven University Press, 1983), 198–210. In this paper, Duvernoy also makes a case for the term "heretic" being used to refer to a member of the sacerdotal elite of this group. However, these "heretics" were rarely called "Cathars," a word by which they have come to be known but whose usage was mostly restricted to Italian groups and some ecclesiastical sources. Pope Alexander III used the term in the Third Lateran Council (1179); Rainier Sacconi, a Dominican inquisitor and former heretic, used it in 1250 in his *Summa de Cathari*; and Pope Alexander IV included the word "Catharos" in his papal bull of 25 May 1260, copied in Doat 31, fols. 273r–276r. There are many interesting contributions to the debate on the use of the term

tury, the inquisitor Bernard Gui called these religious dissenters "modern Manicheans" in his renowned inquisitorial manual, *Practica inquisitionis heretice pravitatis*, but "heretic" was still used to refer to them throughout the *Liber sententiarum inquisitionis Tholosanae*, which recorded the sentences pronounced by Gui during his tenure as inquisitor, between 1307 and 1323.[7] For instance, one of the recipients of these sentences, a married woman named Galharda Fabre who lived in a farmstead near Buzet-sur-Tarn with her husband Peire, testified on 15 December 1305 that she had seen two men in her home who she knew were "of those that they call heretics."[8]

However, in the same *Book of sentences* the term also acquired a broader sense. In the General Sermon held on 7 March 1316, another Burgundian man called Johan of Breyssan was handed over to the secular arm to be burned at the stake for belonging to "that heresy that is called sect of the Waldensians or Poor of Lyon";[9] and Bernat de Na Jacma, a Franciscan tertiary from Belpech, was sentenced to life imprisonment in July 1322 for his adherence to spiritual Franciscans and Beguins who had been imposed penances "for being involved in the crime of heresy."[10] In fact, in the early fourteenth century, this generalised use of "heresy" and "heretics" to describe all religious groups that fell outside the pale of orthodoxy was not exclusive to Gui, as shown, among many others, by the case of a certain Jacma Lauret, a married woman who had to testify before the Bishop of Lodève in 1320 "as a suspect of the heresy and errors of the Beguins."[11] Thus, between the thirteenth and the early fourteenth century, the notions of "heresy" and "heretic" evolved in order to encompass an ever-increasing number of religious expressions. This evolution reflected a change not only in inquisitorial views but also in the way in which the Church responded to religious dissent. Heresy was ultimately a category created by orthodoxy, but in

---

"Cathars" to describe the Languedocian groups discussed here. I particularly agree with the arguments presented in Claire Taylor, "Looking for the 'Good Men' in the Languedoc: An Alternative to 'Cathars'?," in *Cathars in Question*, ed. Antonio Sennis (Woodbridge: York Medieval Press, 2016), 242–55.

[7] See Guillaume Mollat, ed., *Manuel de l'inquisiteur Bernard Gui*, 2 vols. (Paris: Les Belles Lettres, 1964), 10 ff.: "De Manicheis moderni temporis." The sentences that resulted from the inquisitions conducted by Bernard Gui are extant in Add. MS 4697 British Museum, edited in Annette Pales-Gobilliard, ed., *Le livre des sentences de l'inquisiteur Bernard Gui (1308–1323)*, 2 vols. (Paris: CNRS, 2002).

[8] Pales-Gobilliard, *Le livre des sentences*, 716: "de illis qui vocantur heretici."

[9] Ibid., 952: "in illa heresi que dicitur secta Valdensium seu Pauperum de Lugduno."

[10] Ibid., 1330: "pro hiis que conmiserant in crimine heresis."

[11] Doat 28, fol. 13r: "tanquam suspecta de haeresi et erroribus Begguinorum."

fact, both were conventions that developed together in a complex bilateral co-construction of the "heretical other."

The key factor of "heresy"—a word which, as is well known, derives from the Greek *haíresis*, that is, choice—is the deliberate decision to disobey the established orthodoxy. However, the establishment of such orthodoxy was indeed a long and arduous process, and the first centuries of Christianity were a period of struggle within the Church. As Paul had forewarned, the appearance of heresies was to be expected as an almost necessary means to sort the wheat from the chaff, "for there must be also heresies among you, that they which are approved may be made manifest among you" (1 Cor 11:19). This early period witnessed the return of a series of topoi linking the spiritual expressions that evolved outside the institutional framework of orthodoxy with an unbridled amoral sexual and vicious behaviour, thus perpetuating old cultural stereotypes that had also been used against early Christians before the Edict of Milan endowed Christianity with a legal status in 313.[12] Regularly used by early Christian authorities to defame competing religions, these formulas are spotlighted by Rachel Ernst's daring contribution to the present volume. Ernst puts forward the possibility that certain groups accepted these formulas, albeit reluctantly, as identity markers; labelled as the "abhorrent and depraved other," they would have embraced their "otherness" and turned it into a distinctive feature that singled them out for salvation.[13]

At any rate, from Late Antiquity to the Early Middle Ages, when the development of ecclesiastical structures and regulations was still very much under way, the main concerns of the Church were not heresies, but conversion and the consolidation of the most basic Christian practices and doctrines.[14] In fact, Marta Fernández Lahosa's chapter shows how despite stark contrasts, it is uncertain whether the newly established Nicene orthodoxy launched a campaign to advance its dogmatic agenda as distinct from that of the officially defeated and politically charged Arianism.[15] It was not until the eleventh century that the so-called popular heresies appeared, posing a major problem for the Church and

---

[12] See Bernard McGinn, *The Harvest of Mysticism in Medieval Germany* (New York: Crossroad, 2005), 53–54.
[13] See Chapter 5 below, Rachel Ernst, "*Catharistae* in Question: A Case of Rupture in the Manichaean Sect."
[14] See Jennifer Kolpacoff Deane, *A History of Medieval Heresy and Inquisition* (Plymouth: Rowman & Littlefield Publishers, 2011), 8–23 for a brief but comprehensive overview of the development of the ecclesiastical framework in the first centuries of the Middle Ages.
[15] See Chapter 6 below, Marta Fernández Lahosa, "Art, Iconography, and Orthodoxy between the Fourth and Fifth Centuries: The Case of the Ascension."

forcing it to urgent action.¹⁶ The most outstanding conclusion of Robert Moore's seminal *The Origins of European Dissent* was that the main expression of dissent in the Middle Ages was precisely related to the spread of popular heresies in this period.¹⁷ The ecclesiastical hierarchy, seeking ways to respond to the threat these groups posed, looked back to the Church fathers—especially Augustine and Jerome—and thus perceived the movements of the eleventh and early twelfth centuries as new outbreaks of the "heretical plagues" already known to early Christianity. The reaction of the Church evolved from a few undirected actions to organised preaching campaigns against heresy led by figures such as Bernard of Clairvaux and Geoffrey of Auxerre, whose stance on the issue and on the ways to combat it is the focus of the chapter by Stamatia Noutsou. Noutsou argues that while these two authors did not dismiss the use of violence against heretics out of hand, they did capitalise on the "heretical other" in order to enforce their own Cistercian ecclesiological agenda.¹⁸ In general, however, the backbone of ecclesiastical views on "heretical" groups remained the same during this period, as these were seen as the result of a gullible laity corrupted by an external factor: a charismatic and usually literate leader, the heresiarch or master of heretics.¹⁹

The image of the heretic outsider that threatened the passive community denied all agency to said community and was largely based on the prejudices of a literate ecclesiastical elite. Despite this commonly accepted premise, most scholars, from Norman Cohn in his classic work *The Pursuit of the Millennium*, to Moore, and more recently Andrew Roach—to name but a few—associate the re-

---

16 See the illustrative exchange of arguments between Robert Moore and Richard Landes about the appearance of popular heresies somewhat earlier, around the year 1000, in Richard Landes, "The Birth of Popular Heresy: A Millennial Phenomenon," *Journal of Religious History* 24, no. 1 (2000): 26–43; and Robert I. Moore, "The Birth of Popular Heresy: A Millennial Phenomenon?" *Journal of Religious History* 24, no. 1 (2000): 8–25. Whereas Landes suggests that these movements were related to the advent of the millennium and the apocalyptic expectations associated with it, Moore claims that, in this early period, the accusation of heresy was commonly used both as a rhetorical resource and a political weapon, which does not mean that there was actual popular religious unrest.
17 The book was originally published as Robert I. Moore, *The Origins of European Dissent* (Bristol: Allen Lane, 1977).
18 See Chapter 7 below, Stamatia Noutsou, "The Early Cistercian Order and the Persecution of Heresy: Bernard of Clairvaux and Geoffrey of Auxerre's Attitudes Towards the Violent Persecution of Heretics."
19 See John H. Arnold, *Inquisition and Power: Catharism and the Confessing Subject in Medieval Languedoc* (University Park: Pennsylvania State University Press, 2001), 19–48, for a detailed analysis of the evolution of ecclesiastical views on the composition of dissident movements and the corresponding response to them.

surgence of popular religious dissent in one way or another with the Gregorian reforms, which would have to some extent prompted it.[20] This establishment of a causal relationship between both phenomena denies the initiative and a degree of agency to popular movements; instead they should be addressed as reactions to shared concerns about an apparent decline of spiritual commitment and the perceived relaxation of the hierarchy. This slackening of discipline soon distanced the members of the ecclesiastical elite from the image of how "good Christians" should behave that prevailed among the laity, and therefore, in practice, rendered this elite unfit to serve as reference. This is especially significant given that these popular reactions would, in turn, pave the way for the apostolic awakening—the *imitatio apostolorum*—of the twelfth and thirteenth centuries, when, as Herbert Grundmann noted in his classical work *Religiöse Bewegungen im Mittelalter*, both the groups that ended up as fully institutionalised orthodox religious expressions and those that became dissidents were based on the same spiritual references, further blurring the boundaries between orthodoxy and heresy.[21]

From the second half of the twelfth century onwards, in connection with the search for new references, the relationship of some of these groups with the Scriptures—the traditional source of divine authority—changed. The official approach did not satisfy them any more, and this brought about the effective end of the ecclesiastical Latin monopoly. Sacred texts were gradually translated into the vernacular language outside of the institutional framework of orthodoxy and, in a society centred around orality, where passive reading was the norm and literacy was mostly based on memorisation, translations facilitated the spread of texts and beliefs. This climate of intertextuality and secularisation of sacred texts fostered the appearance of what Brian Stock described as "textual communities."[22] These communities, formed by literate and mostly illiterate people,

---

[20] See Norman Cohn, *The Pursuit of the Millennium: Revolutionary Millenarians and Mystical Anarchists of the Middle Ages* (New York: Oxford University Press, 1970); and Andrew P. Roach, *The Devil's World: Heresy and Society 1100–1300* (London and New York: Routledge, 2005), 10–33.
[21] Herbert Grundmann, *Religiöse Bewegungen im Mittelalter* (Berlin: Ebering, 1935), trans. as *Religious Movements in the Middle Ages* by Steven Rowan (Notre Dame: University of Notre Dame Press, 1995). The German edition was republished in 1961 and 1975; I refer here to Herbert Grundmann, *Religiöse Bewegungen im Mittelalter: Untersuchungen über die geschichtlichen Zusammenhänge zwischen der Ketserei, den Bettelorden und der religiösen Frauenbewegung im 12. und 13. Jahrhundert und über die Grundlagen der deutschen Mystik* (Hildesheim: Olms, 1961). It was also translated into Italian in 1980 by Mulino Bianco (Bologna).
[22] See Brian Stock, *The Implications of Literacy: Written Language and Models of Interpretation in the Eleventh and Twelfth Centuries* (Princeton: Princeton University Press, 1983), esp. 140–58.

were organised around the common understanding of a text, which was generally provided by one literate member, the *interpres*, who disseminated its message among the rest of the group. Thus, wanting to reconnect with a new, in a way, more literal, interpretation of the texts, these spiritually committed communities based their way of life, their beliefs, and therefore their religious identity, on a specific view on the sacred textual corpus. At the same time, while from the twelfth century onwards the Church sought to formalise the inferiority of women, the "female other," the boundaries of this "otherness" were blurred within the groups of religious dissenters.[23] Although it would be grossly inaccurate to talk about gender equality, it is clear that non-mainstream religious communities crossed gender boundaries, as is characteristic of clandestine and persecuted groups where social customs become less important than the survival of the group as such.

The twelfth century also witnessed the introduction of a key concept that had especially important effects on the spiritual sphere: the development of the self. In 1215, *Omnis utriusque sexus*, Canon 21 of the Fourth Lateran Council, commanded every Christian to confess all their sins at least once a year, thus reflecting and also enabling this development by imposing self-examination, and furthering the creation of a new discourse of the self.[24] This new sensibility pervaded literary expressions, with the emergence of the distinct figure of the author and the heroic characters who fought for their personal motivations and interests. Although written much later, the fourteenth-century Middle English romance *Sir Orfeo*, which is the subject of Angana Moitra's contribution to this volume, perfectly exemplifies this evolution. As Moitra discusses, the self-imposed exile of the hero, while removing him to the margins of society, is crucial to his psychological maturation. Furthermore, the associations drawn from Scripture

---

For the relationship between passive literacy and the circulation of beliefs in the case of religious dissenters see, especially, Robert I. Moore, "Literacy and the Making of Heresy, ca. 1000 – ca. 1150," in *Heresy and Literacy, 1000 – 1530*, ed. Peter Biller and Anne Hudson (Cambridge: Cambridge University Press, 1994), 19 – 37, and Alexander Patchovsky, "The Literacy of Waldensianism from Valdes to ca. 1400", in ibid., 112 – 36. For a discussion of this crucial moment in the history of written texts and the appearance of a new kind of reading as the highest expression of social activity, see Ivan Illich, *In the Vineyard of the Text: A Commentary to Hugh's Didascalicon* (Chicago: University of Chicago Press, 1993).

23 On this topic see Shulamith Shahar, *Women in a Medieval Heretical Sect: Agnes and Huguette the Waldensians* (Woodbridge: Boydell & Brewer, 2001), 46 – 65.

24 For a comprehensive overview of the sacrament of penance in the Middle Ages, see Thomas N. Tentler, *Sin and Confession on the Eve of the Reformation* (Princeton: Princeton University Press, 1977); for a more recent state-of-the-art on this subject, see Peter Biller and A. J. Minnis, eds., *Handling Sin: Confession in the Middle Ages* (Woodbridge: York Medieval Press, 1998).

and Christian theology in connection with the exile of Sir Orfeo reinforce the spiritual significance of his journey of self-improvement.[25]

However, neither this turn inwards nor the gradual shift from the *imitatio apostolorum* to the *imitatio Christi* that took place between the twelfth and thirteenth centuries, evolved "at the expense of corporate awareness," but rather alongside an increasing concern with the differentiation of groups from each other, with setting the boundaries between different communities, and with processes of belonging.[26] These boundaries were set in place both to define collective identities and to protect them from external and potentially disruptive influences that in turn ended up confined to the sphere of that which was "other."[27] Anna M. Peterson's contribution, focused on the conceptualisation of lepers as a group in a variety of legal texts from France, Italy, and the Iberian Peninsula, shows how even when the boundaries of "otherness" were made outwardly evident by a disfiguring disease such as leprosy, legal and social norms were still needed to regulate the definition of "the sick other" and their interaction with the rest of the community.[28] This exclusive nature of identities is also manifest in the chapter by Estela Estévez Benítez, where she argues that the extreme otherness of the so-called "monstrous peoples" needed to be contained even in manuscript depictions in order to buttress the idea of the barrier between Them and Us.[29]

For the thirteenth and early fourteenth centuries, the notion of textual community seems to fall short of describing the dynamics of the groups of religious dissenters and needs to be replaced with a more nuanced idea: the interpretive community. This controversial concept of literary theory, first proposed by Stanley Fish in 1976, is based on the principles of reader-response criticism, and claims that the different readings of a text are in fact a cultural construct that

---

[25] See Chapter 11 below, Angana Moitra, "On the Margins of Society: Exclusion through Exile as a Structuring Motif in *Sir Orfeo*."

[26] Caroline Walker Bynum, "Did the Twelfth Century Discover the Individual?," in *Jesus as Mother: Studies in the Spirituality of the High Middle Ages* (London: University of California Press, 1982), 85.

[27] The concept of collective identity has been extensively addressed by sociologists since the last decades of the twentieth century. I am using it here as defined by Alberto Melucci, that is, as a process that is negotiated over time through the definition of a shared framework, active relationships between actors, and, finally, emotional recognition. See, among others, Alberto Melucci, "The Process of Collective Identity," in *Social Movements and Culture*, ed. Hank Johnston and Bert Klandermans (Minneapolis: University of Minnesota Press, 1995), 41–63.

[28] See Chapter 10 below, Anna M. Peterson, "Diverging Views of the 'Leper' in Legal, Literary, and Doctrinal Texts from Thirteenth-Century Western Europe."

[29] See Chapter 12 below, Estela Estévez Benítez, "Defying Containment: The Use of the Frame in Depictions of Monstrous Peoples in Monte Cassino Rhabanus Maurus Codex."

depends on the cultural references of the reader.[30] It is necessary to note that, according to Fish's theoretical concept, it is impossible to escape one's own interpretive community, and, more importantly, to define its limits, for doing so would imply verbal communication, and thus, a new process of interpretation by another individual. In other words, perceived self-identity and, in turn, "otherness," pervade every cultural and intellectual sphere, establishing insurmountable boundaries that, once set, hinder communication between the groups on both sides of this interpretive divide. It is also possible to describe the community of interpretation as a group whose members are active agents who complete the meaning of the text through a specific interpretation, which, in itself, defines the limits of their specific community. As Sergi Sancho Fibla rightly remarks in his chapter, this ability of texts to define and legitimise identities is apparent in the case of the beguines of Roubaud and their production of a *Life* of their foundress.[31] Readers, active and passive, engage with the text creating a hierarchy of authority within communities. Likewise, the different groups of late medieval spiritual dissenters shared some of the same textual references—mainly, the Scriptures—but belonged to clearly distinct communities of interpretation, which, at the same time, set them apart from what the Church defined as orthodoxy. As noted above, vernacular linguistic diversity was crucial for the appearance of these groups. Moreover, the proliferation of unofficial translations, lacking the uniformity of Latin, restricted these new texts to very specific communities and fostered the appearance of new concepts, while also enhancing the significance of passive reading for their members, who could now fully engage in the discussion of sacred texts and beliefs.[32]

The new relationship established between spiritual groups and sacred texts, unmediated by the Church, reflected the widespread search for new spiritual references and new mediators with the divine, and the response of the Church evolved accordingly. In the thirteenth century, the papacy, in the midst of a process of ecclesiastical institutionalisation, resorted to direct violence—the Albigensian Crusade—and set the foundations of the Inquisition, which would result in the formulation and refinement of repression mechanisms over the following two centuries. The old trope of the illiterate laity being swayed by the literate outsider that had defined the ways of fighting heresy gradually changed between

---

30 Stanley E. Fish, "Interpreting the 'Variorum'," *Critical Inquiry* 2, no. 3 (1976): 465–85.
31 See Chapter 1 below, Sergi Sancho Fibla, "Reading in Community, Writing a Community: Douceline's *Vida* and the Beguines of Roubaud."
32 For a reflection on the dialogue between Latin and vernacular expressions of spirituality and the significance of the latter, see, among others, Bernard McGinn, *The Flowering of Mysticism: Men and Women in the New Mysticism, 1200–1350* (New York: Crossroad, 1998), esp. 19–24.

the thirteenth and the fourteenth century. However, establishing causal relationships between the construction of the self and the progressive individuation of spiritual dissenters, characteristic of the ecclesiastical legislation of the time, would again mean placing all agency on just one side of the equation. Both processes belong to, and are the result of, the same complex cultural framework, and as such, should be jointly analysed. For instance, the individual engagement that sacramental penance demanded was at the same time a driving force and a by-product of this context, and the same could be said about the ecclesiastical approach to the issue of heresy.

From the mid-thirteenth century onwards, the legislation issued by provincial councils struggled with the creation of a variety of categories of transgression, and, despite the new more individuated ways of perceiving dissenters, the difference between *fautores* and *credentes*, between supporters and true believers, was still determined on the basis of literacy. This was not without consequence, as *fautores* could leave their "heretical otherness" behind and be safely brought back to the fold—albeit with some caution. In contrast, *credentes* were in general too far gone and automatically excluded from the community of Christians: they needed to be persecuted and weeded out to prevent their "otherness" from spreading. As I have noted above, the illiterate were allegedly more gullible and likely to sympathise with "heretical movements," but, at the same time, they were deemed incapable of fully comprehending their beliefs. Thus, in a way, this lack of understanding was the last standing barrier between potentially reversible transgression and full-blown exclusion.

Accordingly, in the 1240s, most deponents interrogated by inquisitorial courts were first asked about their practices and the circumstances under which they had come into contact with "heretics," and later classified into the corresponding transgressive categories. The main innovation of this approach was the acknowledgement of a certain degree of agency on the part of the deponent, who was no longer an undifferentiated member of a faceless ignorant mass but increasingly considered as an autonomous subject.[33] As the thirteenth century progressed, the aforementioned transgressive categories soon led to a path of no return. Associated with a series of gestures and attitudes that turned them into collective identities set in stone, they became the embodiment of "heretical otherness." Actually, this was the most important kind of alterity for inquisitors, for even the fundamental "inner otherness" of women was overlooked

---

[33] See Arnold, *Inquisition and Power*, 74–110 for a detailed discussion of the process of individuation of repressing and controlling mechanisms and the construction of the "confessing subject" over the thirteenth century.

in favour of it, as is apparent in inquisitorial interrogations and punishments, which regularly crossed conventional gender boundaries. This is relevant, because these gender boundaries seemed to be otherwise all-pervading, as shown in the chapter by Mireia Comas-Via, which focuses on the dramatic changes that widowhood entailed for women who were unable to marshal social help from relatives and connections. These widows ended up marginalised, either living in poverty or being forced to adopt precarious lifestyles that frequently transgressed social norms and resulted in de facto social exclusion.[34] Likewise, the contribution of Laura Cayrol-Bernardo reveals how social gender boundaries also extended beyond female inner otherness, translating into a physical otherness that valued preconceived ideas of female beauty and systematically devalued and deprecated the ageing female body.[35]

In the 1320s, Bernard Gui devoted most of his *Practica* to listing the beliefs of the different "heretical sects" of his time.[36] According to him, these sets of beliefs formed several different creeds, the adherence to which determined the extent of the involvement of any given deponent. On the one hand, Gui's stance reflects the evolution of the concept of belief as seen by inquisitors, and, on the other, it reveals the expansion of the categories of transgression that not only helped classify the implication of individuals into specific groups, but were also needed to establish distinctions between the different groups. Gui still maintained some of the prejudices characteristic of the literate elite, for he warned his fellow inquisitors that, for instance, "some among these Beguins have heard or know most of the aforementioned erroneous articles and errors, while others only know a few, given that some among them are more educated or convinced than others."[37] However, his claim was nuanced by his acknowledgement that literacy was not the only reason for the different degrees of belief, for conviction also played a part; and, at the same time, he did not deny the capability of any given suspect to eventually—*paulatim*—become a true believer, whose transgression would lead them to a kind of "heretical otherness" that could only be tackled through persecution and exclusion. But the fact is that beliefs are a complex subject. Beliefs changed over time and were constantly tested. Moreover, dissi-

---

34 See Chapter 3 below, Mireia Comas-Via, "Exclusion and Marginalization of Widows in Late Medieval Barcelona."
35 See Chapter 4 below, Laura Cayrol-Bernardo, "Ageing Women, (In)Visible Bodies: Iconographies on the Edge in Late-Medieval Iberia (Thirteenth to Fifteenth Centuries)."
36 On the date of composition of the *Practica*, see Mollat, *Manuel de l'inquisiteur*, vol. 1, xi–xv.
37 Mollat, *Manuel de l'inquisiteur*, vol. 1, 154: "quod quidam ex ipsis Bequinis plura de predictis articulis erroneis et erroribus didiscerunt et sciunt et alii pauciora, sicut magis et minus eruditi seu imbuti sunt in eisdem."

dent communities maintained, at the same time, different sets of beliefs that, from the perspective of inquisitors, were mutually exclusive. In fact, beliefs pose a methodological problem for the analysis of inquisitorial sources, because in order to define the boundaries of a spiritual community it is first necessary to define the degree of involvement required for deponents to cross the gap between "selfness" and "otherness." Proposing a blanket approach to this issue would in a way mirror the solution adopted by inquisitors, creating a system of categories into which suspected heretics could be neatly classified according to our own views instead of their own experience.

Furthermore, these communities were not only based on beliefs, on a specific doctrine, but also, and more importantly, on a series of devotional practices and rituals that allowed them to bond as a community and were in fact the source of their identity and self-awareness as a group.[38] The extreme ascetic habits of the *bons omes* and *bonas femnas*—commonly referred to as "Cathars"—regarding food and sex, the material poverty and preachings of the Poor of Lyon, and the adherence to spiritual poverty and apocalyptic expectations of the Beguins of Languedoc were some of the ways of setting themselves apart from the rest, of defining an identity of their own. Thus, it could also be said that these distinctive practices were used to delimit boundaries by opposition, for those who chose to engage in them were willingly presenting themselves as "other." This was precisely the case of the royal holy women whose pious practices are the focus of the chapter by Courtney Krolikoski. By actively seeking to interact with lepers, they differentiated themselves from other Christians, to the point that these relations laid the basis for a new model of sanctity.[39] This variety of strategies to embrace "religious otherness" was especially important in a context of struggle both between dissenters and the Church and between the different groups of dissenters, for all of them, in one way or another, staked their claim on apostolic succession and the symbols and conduct of the "true Church."[40]

---

38 For a discussion on how religious experience created boundaries between communities of the same denomination, see Sari Katajala-Peltomaa and Raisa Maria Toivo, "Religion as Experience," in *Lived Religion and the Long Reformation in Northern Europe, ca. 1300–1700*, ed. Sari Katajala-Peltomaa and Raisa Maria Toivo (Leiden and Boston: Brill, 2016), 1–18.
39 See Chapter 2 below, Courtney A. Krolikoski, "'No More Horrified by Them': Royal Holy Women and Lepers in Twelfth- and Thirteenth-Century Hagiography."
40 Part of this struggle is the "semiotic warfare" to which Arnold refers following Gábor Klaniczay's concept in Gábor Klaniczay, *The Uses of Supernatural Power: The Transformation of Popular Religion in Medieval and Early-Modern Europe*, trans. S. Singerman (Princeton: Princeton University Press, 1990), 52; cf. Arnold, *Inquisition and Power*, 63–71.

Material gestures—such as forfeiting excesses and embracing a simple life—and spiritual attitudes—displays of piety and devotional practices—were shared by all of these groups, and as much as the Church tried to impose its authority and legitimacy, the only deviations from orthodoxy that could be presented and justified as such were doctrinal. Despite its privileged position as the approved source of religious knowledge, when it came to lived religion, the Church found itself on an equal footing with those it accused of heresy.[41] Thus, it was easy to draw a line between the established dogma and "religious otherness" in cases such as that of a certain Peire Garcias, who confided to his relative Guilhem Garcias—a Franciscan friar who lived in the convent of Toulouse—that there were two gods, and that John the Baptist was one of the greatest devils ever;[42] and the same could be said of the admission of the aforementioned Bernat de Na Jacma that he had believed that the Church of Rome was the great prostitute of the Book of Revelation.[43] However, it was harder to explain why Bernat Fenàs, by all accounts a simple man from the village of Albi, was wrong to show his respect for two men who he believed were good and led a good life, even if it was by genuflecting before them and asking for their blessing.[44] The practices of these groups became heretical only to the extent that their participants were considered heretics themselves. Their religious collective identity was the result of a process of co-construction of "otherness" that involved both their own religious experience and the way in which this was perceived by orthodoxy. That is to say, gestures hitherto deemed acceptable became markers of alterity because of the perceived "otherness" of the individuals who made them.

"Heretic" was only one among the many names that were used in the inquisitorial registers to name the groups of religious dissenters such as, for instance, the *bons omes* and *bonas femnas*, the Poor of Lyon, and the Beguins of Languedoc, but it is clear that none of them ever described themselves as such. The identity of the "heretic" was defined in opposition to a self-granted authority;

---

41 Lived religion is understood here as the embodied and enacted spirituality of everyday life, in accordance with the definition in Nancy T. Ammerman, "Finding Religion in Everyday Life", *Sociology of Religion* 75, no. 2 (2014): 189–207.
42 Doat 22, fols. 89r–90v: "Petrus dixit ad requisitionem praedicti fratri Guillelmi quod due die erant." Ibid., fol. 90v: "Item dixit quod beatus Johannes Baptista erat unum de maioribus diabolis qui unquam fuissent." It was his relative Guilhem, together with some of Guilhem's brethren, who denounced Peire and deposed before the inquisitor.
43 Pales-Gobilliard, *Le livre des sentences*, 1336: "Item dixit se credidisse quod ecclesia Romana [...] sit illa Babilon, meretrix magna, de qua dicitur in Apocalipsi quod sedebat super bestiam habentem capita VII et cornua X."
44 Doat 27, fol. 33r: "visitavit et modo quo supra flexis genibus adoravit dictos hereticos, credidit esse bonos homines et tenere bonam vitam."

that is, in Pratchett's words, it was always Them that were the "heretics," never Us, even if Them happened to be the Church of Rome. For instance, the same Bernat de Na Jacma confessed that he was not sure whether Pope John XXII was simply wrong or a heretic himself, and Bernat was only one among the many who maintained such opinions.[45] These communities transgressed the established norm, but they did believe in their own legitimacy to do so, which moved them to try to reform the ecclesiastical hierarchy that defined this norm, and even to overthrow it when found lacking. Their alterity, translated into exclusion and persecution, was precisely the source of their authority, for they modelled their own experience after Christ, who had endured suffering and persecution at the hands of Jewish and Roman authorities. Opposing their own use of terms such as "just," "righteous," "holy," and "good" to the adjectives that accompanied the description of heretics in inquisitorial sources, such as "nefarious," "pestilential," and "wicked," these groups subverted the narrative of the persecuting authorities and constructed their own.[46] However, in order to grasp the structure and performance of the spiritual networks they formed, it is necessary to acknowledge the fact that, in many cases, the only extant evidence of their dissidence is provided by documents that were created and codified by these authorities. As Jordi Casals i Parés argues in his contribution to this volume, that is also often the case with regard to the study of medieval Jewish communities, especially around the period when their persecution gained momentum in the fourteenth century.[47] To counter this one-sided view, Casals takes on the analysis of Hebrew sources produced in the late medieval Crown of Aragon, bringing to light some of the ways in which Jews transgressed the boundaries set up for them by the all-pervading Christian society, and delving into Jewish views on the persecution they had to endure and on Christianity as a whole.

In a similar way, the terminological shift from "heresy" and "heretics" to "dissent" and "dissidents" that can be found in these pages is meant to symbolise the change in perspective necessarily involved in any interpretation of historical data that aims to be inclusive. Analytical categories need to be defined as

---

[45] Pales-Gobilliard, *Le livre des sentences*, 1332: "nescit tamen si credidit quod erraret in fide vel quod hereticus esset."

[46] For a more detailed discussion on this construction of opposing narratives, see Delfi I. Nieto-Isabel and Carlos López-Arenillas, "From Inquisition to Inquiry: Inquisitorial Records as a Source for Social Network Analysis," in *Digital Humanities and Christianity: An Introduction*, Introductions to Digital Humanities—Religion 4, ed. Claire Clivaz and Tim Hutchings (Berlin: De Gruyter, 2021), 195–212.

[47] See Chapter 8 below, Jordi Casals i Parés, "From Persecution to Exile: Jewish Views on Christians and Christianity in the Late Medieval Crown of Aragon."

clearly as possible but with enough flexibility to encompass the dynamic realities the sources reveal.[48] This flexibility is manifest in the chapter by Ivan Armenteros-Martínez, which, focusing on the models of social integration of enslaved people in the medieval Mediterranean, questions the alleged social death of slaves and instead presents it as a sort of social resurrection that resulted in a multifaceted process of socialisation.[49] It could therefore be said that the ways in which society dealt with alterity led to changes in the social makeup, and the same goes for the established religious norm and its interaction with those who are seen as "other." Thus, religious persecution and exclusion breed clandestinity, but they also reinforce the persecuted groups' inclination to believe that they are the chosen ones, thus feeding into the process of construction of collective identities.

The accusation of heresy in thirteenth- and fourteenth-century Languedoc subsumed a wide variety of activities and categories. The different groups of religious dissenters were fully integrated into the spiritual landscape of the period long before inquisitorial action was launched against them. Despite the efforts of the persecuting authorities, most Christians did not see these groups as dangerous, and, more importantly, they did not perceive them as "other" either, but rather as men and women who led a life of commitment.[50] In contrast, inquisitors gradually understood the need to systematise heresy in order to effectively repress it; while maintaining a rather binary perspective—heretical/non-heretical—they evolved towards a nuanced concept that allowed for different degrees of transgression. As noted above, common gestures more rooted in tradition, courtesy, and charitable practices than in doctrinal displays were perceived as heretical when their recipients were labelled as heretics. In sum, all those who had contact with people suspected of doctrinal deviance were in turn likely to be "infected" and thus became suspects themselves. Modern scholarship has struggled to stay away from these and other unhelpful binaries with uneven degrees of success, but however misleading inquisitorial categorisations have proved for

---

48 This is a common enough problem for historical research that nonetheless seems in need of further clarification in the field of historical sociology; see Karen V. Hansen and Cameron L. Macdonald, "Surveying the Dead Informant: Quantitative Analysis and Historical Interpretation," *Qualitative Sociology* 18, no. 2 (1995): 227–36 at 227–29.
49 See Chapter 9 below, Ivan Armenteros-Martínez, "Social Domination and Resistance: Slavery in the Medieval Christian Western Mediterranean."
50 See Julien Théry-Astruc, "L'hérésie des bons hommes: Comment nommer la dissidence religieuse non vaudoise ni béguine en Languedoc (XIIe–début du XIVe siècle)?," *Heresis* 36–37 (2002): 75–117, at 97–98, for a discussion on the imposition of the concept of *heretica pravitas* (heretical depravity) and "la normalité de la dissidence des bons hommes" [the normality of the dissidence of the *bons omes*].

the assessment of heretical activity and of the actual dimensions and organisation patterns of these movements, they played a major part in the process of social co-construction of heretical identities. Thus, it could be said that religious dissenters ended up as "heretics" both due to the varying demands, constraints, and deficiencies of orthodoxy and through their own process of radicalisation.[51] Identity, and in particular, collective identity is exclusive in nature. Its very construction is based on the process of definition of distinct features that separate the self from the "other," a process that often brings about a certain degree of marginalisation. In fact, despite a shared disregard for ecclesiastical authorities, medieval "heretical" groups mostly showed no interest in changing the social system as a whole but rather withdrew to its margins imbued with a sense of collective religious responsibility as the last bastion of Christianity.[52]

---

51 For an in-depth discussion of this interplay and its consequences for the development of vernacular theology, see Nicholas Watson, "Censorship and Cultural Change in Late-Medieval England: Vernacular Theology, the Oxford Translation Debate, and Arundel's Constitutions of 1409," *Speculum* 70 (1995): 822–64.
52 For instance, see the discussion on this point for the case of Waldensians in Shulamith Shahar, *Women in a Medieval Heretical Sect: Agnes and Huguette the Waldensians* (Woodbridge: Boydell & Brewer, 2001), 21–22.

Part I: **The Fundamental Edge**

Sergi Sancho Fibla
Chapter 1
Reading in Community, Writing a Community: Douceline's *Vida* and the Beguines of Roubaud

For some decades now, researchers devoted to the history of Christianity have turned their attention to narratives frequently overlooked by traditional scholarship. Eminent figures, such as popes, bishops, and saints undoubtedly had a hand in shaping the past, but their stories have overshadowed the masses of religious and lay people who dwelled on the margins of church institutions.[1] This scenario is best exemplified by the communities of lay religious women, namely tertiaries, penitents, recluses, and beguines. Such communities should not be understood as a counterweight in permanent conflict with the Church, but as religious centres that built a way of life of great social impact beyond what we could call the institutional edge. Their connections with the hegemonic centres of religious life, or their lack thereof, must be considered separately in every case, as these depended on a great variety of social, economic, political, and theological aspects. However, besides circumstantial agreements and disagreements, this chapter will show how the decentralised nature of these female communities was not only central to their way of life, but also apparent in the type of memorial documents that the community produced and transmitted.

The *Vida de la benaurada Sancta Doucelina mayre de las donnas de Robaut* is the most important source for the study of the two beguine communities known to have existed in the territory of Provence in the medieval period.[2] In ad-

---

[1] Miri Rubin and Walter Simons, eds., *The Cambridge History of Christianity, Vol. 4: Christianity in Western Europe ca. 1100–ca. 1500* (Cambridge: Cambridge University Press, 2009), 309–23.
[2] This title is taken from the first sentence of the manuscript, which reads: "En nom de nostre senhor acomensa li vida de la benaurada" [In the name of Our Lord, here begins the life of the Blessed (Doucelina)] (fol. 1, lines 1–4). Unless otherwise indicated, all translations by the author. The manuscript, hereinafter referred to as the *Life*, was first edited by Joseph-Hyacinthe Albanès in 1879 and then by Raoul Gout in 1927: *La vie de sainte Douceline, fondatrice des béguines de Marseille composée en langue provençale, publiée pour la première fois avec la traduction en français et une introduction critique et historique*, ed. Joseph-Hyacinthe Albanès (Marseille: Étienne Camoin, 1879); *La vie de sainte Douceline, texte provençal du XIIIe siècle*, ed. Raoul Gout (Paris: Bloud et Gay, 1927). Throughout this chapter I will directly quote the manuscript, available in Open Access at https://gallica.bnf.fr/ark:/12148/btv1b9061385d/f1.item. In order to facil-

dition, Salimbene de Adam's (d. 1288) *Cronica* and several notarial documents provide a different angle that also needs to be taken into account when approaching the study of these groups.[3] However, the main objective of this essay is to provide an in-depth analysis of Manuscript fr. 13503 of the Bibliothèque nationale de France (hereinafter, BnF), which contains the *Life* and an appendix with a formula for religious vows and a hymn.[4] Specifically, my aim is to explore the reasons why such a document was made and to put forward some hypotheses about its use. To this end, I will discuss the construction of the holiness of Douceline and the identity of the community within the political and spiritual context of the period. Building on previous literature on this subject, I will propose a new reading of the causes that led to the composition of the *Life* and also of the ways in which it was used within the community.

The volume in question is a 104-folio manuscript, written in large, easy-to-read Gothic script. From the *Life* of the foundress to the last page, where we find a formula for the vows and a hymn added to the upper and inner margins of folio 103v, its entire content seems to be related to the aforementioned beguine communities. The *Life* was written by a single hand between the very end of the thirteenth century and the early fourteenth, the formula for the vows was written by another hand a little later, and finally, the hymn, was the work of a third, later hand. The manuscript measures 16.7 x 12 cm, which makes it easy to handle and read, either individually or collectively.

The *Life* tells us that Douceline was born into a merchant family. After the early loss of her mother, Douceline, dedicated her life to charitable works along with her father and brother, caring for the sick and the poor. Her father died a few years later and her brother Hugues (d. 1256), one of the great Franciscan intellectuals of his time, moved to Paris. During Hugues's absence, Douceline entered different convents, among them the Poor Clares of Genoa, but it

---

itate direct consultation of the manuscript, in each quotation I will indicate not only the folio, but also the lines quoted (folio, lines). Abbreviations will be written in italics/Roman and letters added in superscript or in the margin, in brackets.

3 Salimbene, who was a friend of Douceline's brother, travelled to Marseille in 1248 and wrote his chronicle around 1284. Salimbene de Adam, *Cronica*, ed. Giuseppe Scalia (Parma: Monte Università Parma, 2007) http://www.alim.dfll.univr.it/alim/letteratura.nsf/(cercaVolumi)/79639A883D5C4E9CC1256D4F004126CF?OpenDocument. Due to the closure of the libraries during the coronavirus crisis, I chose to quote sources and bibliography available in Open Access, except for the documents kept in the Archives départementales des Bouches-du-Rhône (hereinafter, ADBdR) and the manuscript containing the *Life*, which I had the occasion to photograph myself.

4 Although most scholars allude to the first of these texts as a "formula of profession" (probably following Albanès), it is worth noting that it is rather a "formula for taking vows."

seems that she was never professed, and upon her brother's return, she told him that she wanted to found a beguinage. Thus, with Hugues's support, she founded the first community in Hyères between 1240 and 1242 and a second one in Marseille in 1257.[5] According to the *Life*, Douceline was the active foundress and prioress of both communities, carrying out both the instruction and correction of the novices and the management of the houses herself. Beyond such prosaic aspects, the text places special emphasis on her ascetic practices and the ecstatic episodes she underwent. As regards the former, we find fasting and self-mortification; as for the latter, we are told she received visions, experienced incorporations of the divinity, made prophecies, and even levitated. This whole series of prodigies earned Douceline a reputation for holiness across Provence and beyond, and even though she did not have the same prominence as other female saints of the region, such as Roseline de Villeneuve and Delphine de Puimichel, it seems that her cult managed to survive for some time, as her relics were still venerated in the Early Modern period.[6]

Yet, as some scholars have pointed out, the *Life* is not only a hagiography of Douceline, but also a memorial of the community of beguines of Roubaud—so called because of the proximity of the house of Hyères to the river Roubaud. This was a text that constructed a model of sanctity, while outlining other behavioural patterns between the individual and the collective.

---

5 There could also have been a community in Aix-en-Provence, although probably not institutionalised. Actually, the *Life* says that some women were already following Douceline before the first beguinage was established (fol. 5r, 21–25), which means that some of them might have been following her example in other villages, either in community or individually. Two pieces of evidence point to the existence of a community in Aix-en-Provence. First, the presence of this city in the praises that appear at the end of the manuscript. There we find blessings extended to three cities: *Ieras, Aics,* and *Marsella,* in this order (fol. 101v, 2–10). Secondly, in her will, Cecilia de Volta, a beguine from Marseille, alludes to a beguinage in Puyloubier, established by people of Aix-en-Provence, and also to a beguine from this city: "Item, lego dominabus beguinis de Podio Luperio, Aquis degentibus [...] domine Sparrone, beguine de Aquis." 28 August 1341, first published in Albanès, "Pièces justificatives," in *La vie de sainte Douceline,* 282. Current code: ADBdR. MS 391 E 15, fol. 52.

6 Not belonging to an order undoubtedly affected the memory of Douceline negatively. She is only sometimes mentioned in Franciscan chronicles and martyrologia from the sixteenth century onwards; see, for instance, Didaco de Lequile, *Hierarchia Franciscana in quatuor facies historice distributa: quarum singulae quatuor facies patefacient. Cuius hierarcha cruciformis Christi fungens legationem, cum suo Dominico consodali lectissimo monarchiam ecclesiasticam stellis duabus noviter, ac feliciter exorientibus, columna Romana firmiter patrocinante, ac protegente, inseparabiliter reparat, sustinetque,* vol. 1 (Rome: Iacobi Dragondelli, 1664), 274.

The Construction of a *sancta maire*

As in many other hagiographies of the time, the construction of Douceline's sanctity starts by portraying an exemplary kinship and childhood. Right from the beginning, the text claims that Douceline and Hugues owed their holiness to their parents, since "it is a good root that makes a good tree and good fruit."[7] However, the only information it provides about them is that they were both good people and that the father was a merchant. These qualities were passed on to Douceline, as, besides being a living saint, she is called on one occasion a "good merchant,"[8] an association that is far from trivial. In thirteenth-century accounts of female religious establishments—and in some later ones— the socio-economic status of their members showed a divide between aristocratic nuns and those who did not have a noble origin.[9] Most of the saintly founders of convents usually belonged to the first of these groups, but this was not the case with Douceline, although it must be noted that the institution she created was not a female monastery, but a house of lay religious life. The weight of her family's bourgeois merchant origin needs to be placed in this context. It was the virtuous life their parents led that left seeds in both Douceline and Hugues.

After the episode devoted to her childhood, the text carries out the construction of Douceline's sanctity by assimilation to various reference figures, especially the Virgin Mary and St. Francis. In fact, the Virgin appears as a kind of shadow that underlies each of the actions of the beguine and serves as a model for the whole community. In what we could call her first "vocational" vision, we are told that Douceline, accompanied by three other women, was returning from serving in a hospital. For a long time, she had been asking God to reveal the religious order and way of living that would best suit her.[10] Then, two women and a little

---

7 Fol. 1r, 25–1v, 2: "De bo/na razis ieis bons albres, e tuh li fruc son bon. Car li pairon eran verai, li en/fant foron bon e drechurier e sant" [A good root gives birth to a good tree. Since their parents were honourable, the children were good and honest and holy].

8 Fol. 15r, 18–19: "Li bona merca/diera" [The good (female) merchant].

9 On this dichotomy, see André Vauchez, *La sainteté en Occident aux derniers siècles du Moyen Age* (Rome: École Française de Rome, 1988), 204–23 and 324–28. On nobility and sanctity, see André Vauchez, *Santi, profeti e visionari: Il soprannaturale nel medioevo* (Bologna: Il Mulino, 2000), 69–80.

10 Fol. 5r, 25–5v, 17: "Et un jorn qu'illi am/tres autras venia dun espital ques [5v] az ieras .i. pauc foras lo castell, et a/via dezirat lonc temps e quist a nos/tre senhor de tot son cor que li lais/ses trobar orde e maniera de vieure que mais plagues a dieu, e la mezes en aquell estament que plus li pla/zeria" [And one day, she and three other women were on their way back from a hospital that was in Hyères, just outside the castle. For a long time, she had yearned and asked

girl appeared on the road, all three dressed in black and wearing a white veil.[11] In this scene, we can already perceive the communal character of the hagiography, which starts not from an inner personal experience, but from a collective one. It was Douceline who broke the silence and asked these women who they were and to what order they belonged, as the habit they wore was not known to her and her companions. The women answered: "we belong to the order that pleases God" and, pointing to their veils, they added: "take this and follow us."

Douceline identified that new order by its most evident signs: the habit and the veil. We find this emphasis on clothing in different passages. For example, when she donned the habit for the first time, in a solemn scene, she put on the veil as a sign of Christ's Passion, imitating Mary, who, Douceline claimed, wore it all her life.[12] Thus, since clothing was seen as the primary aspect of the identity of beguines, not only Douceline, but the entire community followed the example of the weeping Mary.[13] The references are many, but this connection reached its highest degree of representation at the moment of Douceline's death, which, although it occured on 1 September, was a process that began precisely

---

Our Lord with all her heart to allow her to find the order and way of life that would be most pleasing to God; and to place her in the estate [*estament*] that would be most pleasing to Him].
11 It is possible that the veil was not simply white, but also transparent (*clars*) (fol. 5v, 16). In this way, they would cover their faces with it (16–17), and we could understand why they had to raise it in order to speak (6r, 1–2). The clothing of beguines is an aspect I would like to look into in future studies.
12 Fol. 7r, 16–25: "Pauzet lo mantel sus lo cap en senhal de la passion de ihesu crist. e portet pueis tostemps lo mantel sus lo cap. en reverencia et as heissemple de la mai/re de dieu. que segon quilli dizia apres la passion del fil portet tostz temps lo mantel sus lo cap" [She covered her head with the mantle as a sign of the Passion of Jesus Christ and wore it all the time out of reverence and following the example of the mother of God who, according to her, always wore it on her head after the Passion]. As this is an apocryphal passage, the text indicates that she knew this through revelation: "la qual cauza crezem: quilli saupes per reve/lacion de nostre senhor" [Which thing we believe that she knew by revelation of our Lord]. The scene of a habit spiritually offered by the Virgin or Christ is quite common in the *vitae* of founders.
13 Fol. 7v, 4–8: "Li sancta femena de tot cant poc si conformet az ella et azordenet tota sa vida segon aquella de nos/tra dona et az eissemple della illi si reglet. ab consell de son fraire" [The saintly woman adapted herself to her, and ordered her whole life according to that of Our Lady; and heeding the advice of her brother, she structured her life after her example]. The three women she saw could also be related to the Three Marys, main characters of the Passion. See also Douceline imitating the Virgin just like Francis imitated Christ in fol. 17r, 21–25: "As eissemple e per l'amor de la paura maire de Ihesu Crist, de la qual del sieus vestirs ill s'era revestida, a/issi cant sant Frances si revesti dels vestirs del Senhor" [As an example and for the love of the poor mother of Jesus Christ, with whose clothes she had dressed herself; just as St. Francis dressed himself with the clothes of the Lord].

on the day of the feast of Mary's Assumption, 15 August. At vespers on the vigil of the feast, Douceline had received communion in the church of the Franciscans and so she spent the whole day in ecstasy. In the evening, the friars were getting ready to sing the Vespers of the Virgin, beginning with the antiphony *Assumpta est Maria*, when suddenly Douceline was taken up towards heaven in front of the friars and beguines. Full of terror, they pounced on her body to hold her down and not allow her to leave too soon.[14] Although throughout the *Life* we are told of different cases of levitation, the parallelism between Mary's Assumption and that of the saint is evident here.

Douceline's experiences also recall episodes in the life of several male figures, especially Christ and St. Francis. On the one hand, a process of *imitatio Christi* is explicit not only in Douceline's evangelical mission, charity work, her embrace of a life of poverty, and the performance of miracles by contact, but also, even more evidently, by the adoption of the form of the cross in some of her ecstasies. On the other hand, she is usually associated with the phenomenon of stigmata, although this is only indirectly mentioned in the text, and always in relation to St. Francis.[15] Douceline, and probably the other beguines,

---

14 Fol. 74r, 19–26; fol. 74v, 1–17: "E con ill fos adoncs plus aondozamens que non solia absorbida tota en Dieu en aquell raubiment cant venc la hora que li fraire comenseron ves/pras de la benaurada maire de Dieu ell capellans entonet la premiera antifena que dis Asumpta est Maria [74v] in celum gaudent angeli soptamen[s] illi s'eslevet adoncs sus en l'aer tan aut que quals semblet s'en volgue[s] pujar sus, tan autamens fon rau/bida en Dieu la qual cauza senti/ron fort las filhas que li eran en/torn que cant la viron enassi montar sus tan vertuozamens dopteron fort que le sieus esperitz s'en annessa a Dieu, e lur pauzes lo cors. Adoncs totas ensemps s'abriveron ves ella cridant per retenir la car tenramens l'amavan e temian la mot perdre" [And as she was completely absorbed in God in that ecstasy, more than she used to be, when the hour came for the friars to begin the Vespers of the blessed Mother of God, the priest intoned the first antiphon which says, "Assumpta est Maria in caelum gaudent angeli," suddenly she rose in the air so high that it seemed as if she wanted to ascend. This was felt by her daughters, who were around her, and who, when they saw her rising so virtuously, were afraid that her soul would go with God and they rushed together to her, crying out to hold her, for they loved her tenderly and dearly feared losing her].

15 See fol. 36r, 1–26; fol. 36v, 1–8: "Mais cant il si senti moguda per aquellas parau/las que li fraire dizian denfra lo man/tell, com non ho connogues. afligia si mezesma estant mot humilmens. Si que pueis li trobet hom los blava/irols els grans tors en las mans. e/n aissi las s'avia tormentadas. per tal que si tolguessa aquell gran senti/ment que non ho entendessa. E anc per tot aquo non remas. car les sieus [36v] esperitz era trop abrazatz que nulla afliccion aquella ardor non li podia esteinher. Az aquellas paraulas li sancta contemplairis de dieu si va fort enflamar. soptamens e ill'estet rau/bida. E cant le comps ho vi. ac mot gran gauch. car adoncs ac consegut so que tant dezirava" [But when she felt moved by those words that the friar said, under her habit, as if hiding it, she hurt herself very humbly. So much so that bruises and contusions appeared on her hands, from how much she had tormented them trying

knew about this episode, as we are told that she had read the *Life* of the saint of Assisi and, moreover, people seemed to link her to Francis's experience.[16]

The ecstatic episodes linked to the stigmata show that, beyond the hyperbole characteristic of hagiographic accounts, Douceline had gained a certain saintly reputation and was the object of popular devotion, as shown by the passage in which the reader of the Franciscan convent of Paris visited her, "since the fame of her sanctity had spread far and wide."[17] Moreover, besides nobles and clerics, commoners also seemed to be drawn to this saintly woman. We are told about the fervour that people felt for Douceline throughout her lifetime, especially with regard to her ecstasies,[18] but such displays of fervour reached their peak during her funeral. In the morning following her death, people arrived "am gran abrivament" [with great enthusiasm] to see and touch her body. Since everyone understood that she was or would soon be a saint, they took something from her "to make relics." Faced with such a scene and fearing that the crowd would end up desecrating the corpse, the friars decided to call in the *viguier* and ask for armed reinforcements.[19] The latter arrived with all the secular au-

---

to shake off that feeling and not heed it. But all this was of no avail to her, for her spirit was too inflamed for affliction to quench her fire. The holy contemplator of God was strongly inflamed and quickly went into ecstasy. And when the count saw it, he was filled with great joy, for he had obtained what he had desired so much].

16 See fol. 36r, 1–16: "E preron a parlar de las nafras de mon seinnhor sant Fran/ces al qual illi avia sobeirana amor e d'aquell dous parlament [que fon] entrel Se/raph e mon seinnher sant Frances cant li donet sas plagas" [And they began to speak of the wounds of our Lord Francis, for whom she had a sovereign love, and about that sweet conversation the seraph and Our Lord St. Francis had when he gave him the wounds].

17 Fol. 34r, 15–17: "Car lueinh s'era espandi/da li odors e li fama de la sieu sancti/tat." For the whole passage, see 34r, 10–34v, 26.

18 Right in this passage the copyist even corrects the text to add more intensity to the description: "E abrivavan si tan fort la[s] gens ves ella *per* tocar [...] car tan grans era li devocions quel pobols [hi] avia que non si poiria dire que neis li peccador s'en convertian a Di/eu. tan gran cambiament de cor pre/nia hom esgardant la en aquel tira/ment" [And the people rushed so violently to touch her [...] for their devotion was so great that one could not express it even sinners were converted to God] (fol. 32v, 2–22).

19 Fol. 77v, 1–26: "E qui que pogues penre ren que d'ella fos prennian per far relequias. e gitavan lurs pa*ter* nosters e lur anels. e li autri lur capions, sobr'ella. E venian a*m* coutels *per* trenquar entr'els la rau/ba. e tot cant podian d'ella prenni/an am gran devocion. e agron gran paor lo cors santz destruissessan. e que entier de la maizon de Robaut no*n* lo poguessan traire. Car tot son vestir tallavan que *per* ren que fe/zessan li fraire no*n* ho podian defen/dre. si que am pauc uns fraires no*n* hi *per*det lo bras car la lur defen/dia. E en aissi no*n* la podian sebelir per la prieissa dell pobol e adoncs pre/ron consell li fraire entr'els. que tra/mezessan al viguier. qu'ell fezes gardar lo sant cors" [And whoever could take something from her, did so to make relics; and they threw their *pater nosters* [similar to rosaries] and their rings and others threw

thorities to pay homage to the saint, and so they proceeded to solemnly transfer the body in a procession, with candles and torches. However, people continued to pounce on the body with such ardour that not even the armed men were able to prevent her clothes from being torn and passed around on up to three occasions.[20] The altercations flared up again on the first anniversary of her death and during the subsequent transfer of the bodies of Douceline and her brother Hugues, which took place three years later, on 17 October 1278.[21]

The cult of Douceline did not wane after her death; quite the opposite. According to the *Life*, her tomb was frequented by the sick in search of miracles,[22] while two wills dating from 1288 and 1341, respectively, include the offering of masses, and candles and lamps for the shrine.[23] Furthermore, the memory of the saint was not limited to her tomb, nor, as we will see later, to the beguinage, but was also preserved in Hyères and Marseille. Shortly after Douceline passed away, we are told that the beguines had in their possession relics of the saint, especially a finger—or maybe a hand—with which they used to work miracles inside and outside the house. That they would decide to keep that specific part of Douceline's body is only to be expected, given that, as the text remarks, the miracles she performed during her life were all by touch. Thus, after her death, her finger continued to amaze people, either through direct contact or through the water in which the finger had been submerged.[24] All this, in short, attests to the construction of a model of holiness and a model of venera-

---

their caps onto her. And they came with knives to tear her clothes and take from her everything they could, with great devotion. And they [the friars and the beguines] had great fear that they would destroy the holy body and that they would not be able to take it out of the house of Robaut, for all her clothes were torn, and no matter how much they did, the friars could not defend her. A friar almost lost an arm defending her. And so, they could not bury her because of the pressure of the people and then the friars decided to go to look for the *viguier* to guard the holy body].

20 See fol. 78r, 1–25.

21 On the anniversary, see fols. 79v, 11–80r, 12. On the translation of the bodies, see fols. 87v, 6–88r, 6. Claude Carozzi notes briefly but lucidly how such events follow the narrative of Bonaventura's *Legenda maior*: Claude Carozzi, "Une béguine joachimite: Douceline, soeur d'Hugues de Digne," in *Franciscains d'Oc: Les "Spirituels" (ca. 1280–1324)* (Toulouse: Privat, 1975), 169–201, esp. 171.

22 Fols. 79r, 23–26; 79v, 3–9; and 96v–97r.

23 See "Tali videlicet [...] Dulceline, ejus sororis"; and "lampadi [...] quondam, .x. sol." See Bartholomea's donation: 16 February 1288, in Albanès, "Pièces justificatives," 261; and Cecilia de Volta's will: 28 August 1341, ADBdR MS 391 E 15, fol. 52.

24 Following the traditional idea of major and minor relics, it seems that the convent reserved the possession of the former, while they lent the latter and the water to the population, see fols. 91v, 10–14; 92v, 13–17; 92v, 23–25; 93; and 95r, 26–95v, 6.

tion for the community. The beguines saw and identified in the text the exemplary attitude of the saintly woman as well as a memorial to their own history and identity.

Orde and *estament*

Salimbene portrays Douceline as a pious woman who never entered any order but led a religious life.[25] However, it should be noted that we are told that Douceline lived for some time with the Poor Clares of Genoa and was received in other female monasteries.[26] These temporary stays were not enough for Douceline to commit herself to the cloistered life; quite the opposite, in fact. It was precisely after that period that she asked Hugues to provide her with a way of living as a beguine. Scholars have repeatedly pointed to her brother as the promoter of such a vocation,[27] but the *Life* makes it clear that the initiative came from her and from the vision mentioned above.[28]

It is difficult to picture how Hugues and Douceline understood the beguine life. Northern European beguines and those portrayed in the *Life* had some aspects in common, such as vows of chastity (or virginity) and obedience, life in community, and works of charity. However, it is also true that in recent decades several studies have shown that this movement displayed many variants and that the attributes just mentioned could be applied to many other religious communities of lay and penitential life. One of these were the *Fratres Saccati* or Friars of the Sack, who provide an interesting case for comparison, given that their creation was precisely attributed to Hugues.[29] In Salimbene's chronicle

---

25 Salimbene de Adam, *Cronica*, 806: "Hec nunquam aliquam religionem intravit, sed semper in seculo caste et religiose vixit" [She never entered any order [religion], but always lived chastely and religiously in the world].
26 Fol. 6v, 3–10: "En aquel temps le sans homs sos fray/res. frayre hugo de dinha fon an/natz a paris. e fes la recebre a las sor/res menors de Jenoa. iassi aisso quilli fos receupuda en prohensa en mota[s] autras partz en monestiers de mone/guas" [At that time the holy man, her brother, Friar Hugo de Dinha, had gone to Paris and had her admitted into the convent of Franciscan nuns of Genoa, although she was also admitted into many other convents in Provence].
27 See, among many others, Geneviève Brunel-Lobrichon, "Existe-t-il un christianisme meridional? L'exemple de Douceline: Le béguinage provençal," *Heresis* 11 (1988): 41–51.
28 Fol. 6v, 22–26: "E cant le sans fraire hu/go. ac auzit della et entendut dili/gentmentz. sauput quez ac tot son entendement. no[n] vole prezes autre ordre" [And when holy brother Hugo had diligently listened to her and heard her, and knew what her will was, he did not want her to take any other order].
29 See Salimbene de Adam, *Cronica*, 367.

we are told that this movement originated with a group of lay, bourgeois, and learned men from Hyères who, around 1248, listened to Hugues's sermons.[30] Some of them asked him to help them enter the Franciscan order, which he refused, telling them that they should live a life of penance instead.[31] Once this kind of penitential novitiate had been completed in the countryside, these "brothers of the sack" settled on the outskirts of the city and from there spread across Europe.[32] This is how Salimbene explains it, although evidence suggests that such groups actually started out some years earlier with a novice who had been expelled from a community of Franciscans.[33]

Salimbene claims that the Friars of the Sack led a lay religious life that was not well received by Franciscans and Dominicans. Hence the attempts of the ecclesiastical authorities to gradually incorporate them into the framework of regulated religious orders. It is in this context that we understand the celebration of the General Chapter of this community in Marseille on 12 May 1251, during which most of the existing groups of these so-called friars met and were asked by the bishops of Marseille and Toulon to choose an approved rule. From 1255 onwards, these communities became increasingly institutionalised and saw a rapid expansion outside Provence. If we look at the donations they received in Marseille in the 1270s, we can infer that they had an exceptional reputation and popularity, even though in 1274 they were to all intents and purposes condemned to a sort of slow death. In fact, the Second Council of Lyon, in its Canon 23, *Religionum diversitatem*, decreed the suppression of all religious groups that had appeared after the Fourth Council of the Lateran (1215) and had not been sanctioned by the Pope. In addition to Franciscans and Dominicans, who were considered to be special cases, those who had received such sanction could continue to operate on the condition that they did not admit any more professions nor found any more communities. This was to be the case of the Friars of the Sack. In Marseille, the community endured some years of economic and institutional struggle, and most of its estate was sold from the last decade of the thirteenth century onwards. In 1320, John XXII directly asked the Bishop of Marseille to sell all the properties and goods the community had in the city. At the same time, the Pope had the beguines of Hyères installed in the houses where the friars had

---

30 On the origins of the community, see Isabelle Rava-Cordier, "L'expansion d'un ordre mendiant originaire de Provence: Les frères sachets," *Provence Historique* 55 (2005): 3–26 at 1–2.
31 See Salimbene de Adam, *Cronica*, 367.
32 See Salimbene de Adam, *Cronica*, 366, 368.
33 This is how it appears in Thomas Eccleston's chronicle and other documentary sources: Rava-Cordier, "L'expansion d'un ordre mendiant," 8.

lived, and defended the whole beguine community of Roubaud in three separate bulls.[34]

The way of life of the Friars of the Sack was far removed from the beguines' lifestyle, and the causes that brought about their disappearance were also different from those that resulted in the community of beguines dying out. However, I find it useful to underline the parallelism between these two groups because of their links to Hugues de Digne, and also because they exemplify the consequences of maintaining good—or bad—relations with the mendicant orders. Indeed, whereas the beguines of Roubaud were always welcomed by Provençal Franciscans, the Friars of the Sack experienced significant difficulties because of the intense competition between them and male mendicants.

In contrast, the community of beguines underwent other kinds of institutional conflicts that have been extensively studied in recent years. It is not my aim to analyse these in depth here, although it is necessary to bring up two texts that influenced the writing of the bulls that John XXII issued in defence of the beguines of Roubaud, which can probably shed light on their integration into the political-religious scene of Provence at the beginning of the fourteenth century.

Beguines were placed under scrutiny at the Second Council of Lyon, and the decretal *Periculoso*, issued in 1298, concerned them directly, as it imposed strict enclosure on all women religious. However, it was the Council of Vienne (1311–1312) that dealt a significant, albeit not final, blow to their way of life.[35] This moment was only one stage in a long process that began in the thirteenth century and did not culminate until the Council of Trent (1545–1563). In this sense, as Elizabeth Makowski points out, when Boniface VIII issued his constitution *Nuper ad audientiam* (1303), which aimed to combat the danger that some women posed for orthodoxy, he might already have had beguine communities in mind.[36] Yet, the pontiff's spurn of the wandering or preaching practices of women religious was due not only to a personal antipathy, but also to the fact that these were perceived as an institutional challenge to the hierarchy of the

---

34 *Lettres secrètes et curiales du Pape Jean XXII (1316–1334), relatives à la France*, ed. Auguste Coulon and Suzanne Clémencet (Paris: De Boceard, 1961), vol. 1, col. g71, no. 1155.

35 Jennifer Deane, "'Beguines' Reconsidered: Historiographical Problems and New Directions," *Monastic Matrix*, Commentaria 3461 (2008), https://monasticmatrix.osu.edu/commentaria/beguines-reconsidered-historiographical-problems-and-new-directions.

36 Elizabeth Makowski, *Canon Law and Cloistered Women: Periculoso and Its Commentators, 1298–1545*, Studies in Medieval and Early Modern Canon Law 5 (Washington DC: Catholic University of America Press, 1997), 24, 27.

Church.[37] This is apparent in the decree *Cum de quibusdam*, which is usually considered the founding text for the persecution of the beguine movement. Although the text says "with the approval of the council," we cannot really know if it was a result of the Council of Vienne, as in 1312 Clement V ordered the copies of the canons of the council that were already in circulation to be destroyed, and his death soon after delayed the dissemination of new copies. John XXII did not promulgate these canons until 1317, but according to the canonist Giovanni di Andrea (d. 1348), he did so by making some changes and corrections to the text.[38] For some time, scholarship has used these modifications to explain the apparently contradictory message of this decree. The inconsistency relates to the existence of a sort of "escape clause" at the end of the text that seems to override the condemnation with which it begins.[39] However, was this really a contradiction? Unlike in the case of *Ad Nostrum* (Clem. 5.3.3), which explicitly condemned German beguines and beghards and was issued at the same time as *Cum de quibusdam*, the latter does not mention any concrete doctrinal errors, nor does it include any allusion to a *quaedam abominabilis* sect. In fact, *Cum de quibusdam* only speaks in a rather vague manner about women who lead a quasi-religious life, do not follow the patterns of regulated religious orders, and preach.[40] The aforementioned "escape clause" warns that the decree should not be understood to prohibit any pious woman who lives honestly from making penance and serving God in humility, regardless of whether she has made a vow of chastity or not.[41]

Jacqueline Tarrant notes that long before the escape clause, the text already contains aspects that nuance the initial ban. The expressions *earum alique*, or

---

[37] Makowski, *Canon Law and Cloistered Women*, 40.
[38] Elizabeth Makowski, *A Pernicious Sort of Woman: Quasi-Religious Women and Canon Lawyers in the Later Middle Ages* (Washington DC: Catholic University of America, 2005), 25.
[39] Ernest W. McDonnell, *The Beguines and Beghards in Medieval Culture: With Special Emphasis on the Belgian Scene* (New Brunswick, NJ: Rutgers University Press, 1954), 529.
[40] In fact, Tarrant rightly insists that *Cum de quibusdam* and *Ad nostrum* are aimed at two completely different groups, even though they both use the "beguine" label. However, the latter also includes their male counterparts, while *Cum de Quibusdam* focuses only on female communities. Jacqueline Tarrant, "The Clementine Decrees on the Beguines: Conciliar and Papal Versions," *Archivum historiae pontificae* 12 (1974): 300–308. For the difference between the texts, see also Walter Simons, "In Praise of Faithful Women: Count Robert of Flanders's Defense of Beguines Against the Clementine Decree *Cum de quibusdam mulieribus* (ca. 1318–1320)," in *Christianity and Culture in the Middle Ages: Essays to Honor John Van Engen*, ed. David Mengel and Lisa Wolverton (Notre Dame, IN: University of Notre Dame Press, 2014), 331–57.
[41] *Corpus juris canonici*, ed. Émile Friedberg, vol. 2 (Leipzig: B. Tauchnitz, 1879–1881), 71. Open access version in http://www.columbia.edu/cu/lweb/digital/collections/cul/texts/ldpd_6029936_002/index.html.

quibusdam mulieribus, imply that not all groups of lay women were under suspicion. According to her, the final clause does not depart from the message of the rest of the decree, but merely adds a safeguard for those women who could be considered "orthodox beguines."[42] Makowski also claims that Clement V did not intend to ban all beguine communities without exception. However, she admits that *Cum de quibusdam* caused great confusion within the ecclesiastical institution, as it sometimes came to be understood as a total condemnation of beguines and other similar groups.[43]

Indeed, if the latest studies on European beguines have shown us anything, it is the vast variety of such communities and of the responses they received from the hierarchy. The question of the heterodoxy of beguines has attracted the attention of many researchers over the last decades, but it is evident that this issue has often been simultaneously magnified and oversimplified.[44] As we will see in the case studies provided below, the boundaries between institution and heterodoxy are difficult to determine. The beguines of Roubaud were, according to the *Life*, criticised and threatened to the point that, especially from the end of the thirteenth century onwards, they lived in fear, as is evident in the text. Some scholars have put forward the possibility that the community was dissolved or that a dissolution sentence was at least issued at some point. Personally, I do not think menaces went that far, but I believe the community certainly felt in peril, particularly before the city council of Marseille spoke in their defence and John XXII issued three bulls endorsing their way of life (1320, 1323, and 1325). These documents are fundamental to understanding this period, as they seem to make direct mention of the escape clause of *Cum de quibusdam*; that is, they seem to portray Roubaud's *donnas* as *fideles aliquae mulieres*. In his three aforementioned bulls, John XXII proceeded in a rather vague manner, avoiding legal terminology that could compromise his defence and alluding to these beguines as "simple and honest women, who frequent the churches and do not get involved in disputes or theological errors."[45] Thus, it seems evident that the Pope was clearly linking *Cum de quibusdam* and *Ad Nostrum*, claiming not only that these women lived honestly, simply, and chastely in their community, but also that they did not get involved in preaching or theology. Moreover, in the third of these bulls, he began by explicitly quoting *Cum de quibusdam*, pointing out the reasons why the way of life of certain beguines had been forbid-

---

42 Jacqueline Tarrant, "The Clementine Decrees," 306.
43 Makowski, *A Pernicious Sort of Woman*, 27.
44 Deane, "'Beguines' Reconsidered."
45 Bull of 18 December 1323. Albanès, "Pièces justificatives," 276–77.

den, and afterwards reiterating the aforementioned defence of the women religious of Provence: "honeste vivebant, devote frequentabant ecclesias," etc.⁴⁶ In the first of these bulls he also differentiated this community from other problematic groups, specifically the German beguines and beghards who had been condemned in *Ad Nostrum*.⁴⁷

How did the petitions of the beguines manage to reach the pontifical see? The support of Sança de Mallorca (d. 1345), Queen of Naples, may have proved crucial. Her assistance is mentioned in the first of the bulls, which was addressed to the Bishop of Toulon and singled out the beguines of Hyères. In the second and third bulls, related to the community of Marseille, Sança is not mentioned, but we can find references to her institutional support in another document from 1323. This is the record of a meeting of the city council of Marseille, where the beguines begged for the queen's intervention three months before the second bull was issued.⁴⁸

The fact that the community needed papal confirmation and that the bull concerning the community of Marseille had to be issued twice could make us infer a possible climate of hostility towards the beguines of Roubaud. However, there is no evidence to suggest any doctrinal conflicts, but rather a question of institutional legitimacy. These difficulties were probably caused by the various condemnations of the time against non-regulated religious ways of life. As I mentioned above, it is not clear whether the community of Roubaud suffered any actual condemnation during this period or was threatened by local or external secular or ecclesiastical authorities. What is clear, however, is that this period represents a critical moment for the community and is roughly the moment in which the *Life* could have been written.

Some studies have raised the possibility that the threat of which the text speaks might have been related to a doctrinal issue; that is, a possible adhesion to Joachimite views or proximity to spiritual Franciscans. It is evident that these beguines had a close relationship with the friars. They attended some of the offices in their church, they had friars as confessors, they claimed St. Francis as a protective figure, and Douceline was considered to be a reflection of Francis him-

---

46 Bull of 16 February 1325. Albanès, "Pièces justificatives," 277–80 at 279.
47 Bull of 22 November 1320. Albanès, "Pièces justificatives," 299–300.
48 This document also shows the involvement of the prelate of Marseille in the defense of the beguines. Council of the city of 7 September 1323, Archives municipales de Marseille, BB 13, fol. 91r. Sança de Mallorca is known for her great support not only of Franciscans and Poor Clares, but also of lay religious communities. See Matthew Clear, "Piety and Patronage in the Mediterranean: Sancia of Majorca (1286–1345) Queen of Sicily, Provence and Jerusalem" (PhD diss., University of Sussex, 2000).

self and even the saint's spiritual daughter.⁴⁹ Likewise, Hugues de Digne and John of Parma, renowned followers of Joachim of Fiore, are prominently featured in the *Life*. Even Josselin d'Orange, to whom Douceline promised obedience, could be considered a Joachimite.⁵⁰ The truth is, however, that the *Life* contains little or no explicit reference to doctrine.⁵¹ It should also be noted that the text was probably written immediately before John XXII issued the aforementioned three bulls, and it would have made little sense for the pontiff to encourage the existence of a group likely to stir spiritual agitation so close to the court of Avignon.⁵² In fact, as Jean-Paul Boyer states, the relationship between the Franciscans of Marseille and Pope John XXII was much more ambiguous than historians of heresy have long assumed.⁵³ Therefore, it stands to reason that

---

49 Fol. 78v, 24–25: "Veraia fi/lha de mon seinnhor sant Frances" [She was the true daughter of St. Francis].
50 Fol. 13r, 30–34: "Volc aver una donna p*er* prioressa, a cui illi humil/mens obezis e promes li hobedien/cia am gran devocion, p*er* so que tos/temps ill fos obediens p*er* amor dell senhor. Vodet atressi obediencia a fraire Jaucelin homs santz ques e/ra menistres des fraires menors *en* Prohensa" [She wanted to have a woman as prioress, whom she could humbly obey and promise her obedience with great devotion, and thus, being always obedient for the love of the Lord. She also made a vow of obedience to Friar Jaucelin, a holy man who was minister of the Friars Minor in Provence].
51 The three most relevant points in this sense are Douceline's absolute poverty, the warlike image of St. Francis—who is called the "standard-bearer of Christ" and "the leader of the Lord's knights" in fols. 38r and 60v—and Douceline's evocation of the New Jerusalem during an ecstatic paraliturgic performance (fol. 44r–v). Despite this, and despite Claude Carozzi's hesitations on the matter, most scholars continue to consider Douceline a follower of Joachimite doctrines. See Renate Blumenfeld-Kosinski, "French Holy Lives: A Survey," in *Medieval Holy Women in the Christian Tradition c.1100–c.1500*, ed. Alastair Minnis and Rosalynn Voaden (Turnhout: Brepols, 2010), 241–65, esp. 245–46; Kathryn Kerby-Fulton, "When Women Preached: An Introduction to Female Homiletic, Sacramental, and Liturgical Roles in the Late Middle Ages," in *Voices in Dialogue: Reading Women in the Middle Ages*, ed. Linda Olson and Kathryn Kerby-Fulton (Notre Dame: University of Notre Dame Press, 2005), 33–51, esp. 43; Marie-Rose Bonnet, "Douceline et le Christ, ou la fenêtre ouverte," in *Par la fenestre: Études de littérature et de civilisation médiévales*, ed. Chantal Connochie-Bourgne (Aix-en-Provence: Presses Universitaires de Provence, 2003), 43–55, https://books.openedition.org/pup/2183?lang=fr. On Carozzi's doubts, see Carozzi, "Une béguine joachimite."
52 Claude Carozzi, "L'estament de sainte Douceline," *Provence historique* 93/94 (1973): 270–79 at 279.
53 Jean-Paul Boyer, "Prêcher Marseille: Paroles franciscaines à l'aube du XIVe siècle," in *La Provence et Fréjus sous la première maison d'Anjou 1246–1382*, ed. Jean-Paul Boyer and Thierry Pécout (Aix-en-Provence: Presses Universitaires de Provence, 2010), 135–70. The relationship between the Pope and the Franciscans of Marseille was as good as his relationship with the Provençal Inquisition, which at the beginning of the fourteenth century was under the control of the friars. In 1308, Hugonette Bertrande made the inquisitors of Provence her residual heirs on the

the names that appear in the *Life* were in no way chosen to align the community with a specific spiritual tendency, but rather as figures of authority who would legitimise the order, the *estament*.[54] It is in this sense that we should understand the account of the intimate relationship between Douceline and the Count of Provence, a relationship that benefitted both sides: on the one hand, the beguines availed themselves of influential political support—which later materialised in Queen Sança's mediation—and on the other, Douceline played a part in the policy of divine legitimation carried out by the Capetians.[55] Evidence seems to suggest that the threats the beguines faced could have had more to do with their status than with the doctrines they adhered to.

Monega non est? Looking for an Identity

As noted above, not only does the *Life* concern Douceline's experiences, but it also conveys a rich picture of the life of the community. Thus, in the period following Douceline's death, we are told that a beguine from the house of Hyères had a vision. In it she saw how the soul of a companion who had died a few days earlier was already in heaven. The text then goes on to describe how all the saints came to her and, since they did not know her, asked her who she was, to what order (*estament*) she belonged and what habit she wore. She answered that she had lived under the hand of St. Francis. But the saints insisted:

---

condition that the Holy Office remained under Franciscan control; see Huguonette Bertrand's will, Archives municipales, MS 1, II 45, fol. 91v.

54 As Sean Field points out, it is also possible that, although these beguines did not claim to be related to the doctrines of Franciscan Spirituals, the society of the time saw them as being close to the friars because of the label they shared with the lay supporters of the latter and because of their connection with John of Parma and Hugues de Digne. He adds that this could be one of the reasons why Douceline's cult "slipped into semiobscurity." Sean L. Field, *Courting Sanctity: Holy Women and the Capetians* (Ithaca: Cornell University Press, 2019), 219.

55 See Field, *Courting Sanctity*; Jean-Pierre Attard, "Religion, sainteté et pouvoir en Provence angevine, première maison d'Anjou, modèle et miroir du monde angevin (1246–1382)" (PhD diss., Aix-Marseille Université, 2015). A document from 1272 proves that the intimate relationship between Douceline and the Count the hagiography conveys was indeed real: *Actes et lettres de Charles 1er roi de Sicile concernant la France, 1257–1284*, ed. Alain de Boüard (Paris: Éditions de Boccard, 1926), no. 582 [5–6 November 1271—*Aversas. De registrate et rupte*, Reg. 15, fol. 73v]. Republished in Damien Ruiz, "Louis d'Anjou et le milieu spirituel Marseillais: Une histoire de famille," in *Da Ludovico d'Angiò a san Ludovico di Tolosa: I testi e le immagini. Atti del Convegno internazionale di studio per il VII centenario della canonizzazione (1317–2017)*, ed. Teresa D'Urso, Alessandra Perriccioli Saggese, and Daniele Solvi (Spoleto: Fondazione Centro italiano di studi sull'alto Medioevo, 2017), 67–94, esp. 73; and Field, *Courting Sanctity*, 60, n. 17.

"why then do you not wear the Franciscan habit, nor that of the Poor Clares, nor that of any other order [*relegions*]? Who are you and to what order [*estament*] do you belong?"⁵⁶

This is an unusual vision for a hagiography and can only be understood in the context of the community of Roubaud and the institutionally complex moment they lived in during the early fourteenth century. The "dispute" between the visionary beguine and the saints was resolved with the coming of Christ, but not before two more references to the bewilderment of the saints at seeing the habit she wore: "la quall no*n* connois/sem ni sabem de qual estament si/ a, ni connoissem son abiti" [[She], whom we do not know, nor do we know her order or her habit] and "ni monega no*n* est, ni non sabem qui sia" [She is not a nun, and we do not know who she is].⁵⁷ Jesus Christ then confirmed what the beguine had told them, adding that she belonged to an order (*estament*) that was dear to him and that he oversaw personally.⁵⁸

---

56 Fols. 85v, 18–86r, 15: "El covent d'leras s'esdevenc que una donna de Robaut mori. E un'autra estant a si mezesma en sa oracion va si re/pauzar. E fon li semblant qu'illi fos en un luoc on aquill arma era e vi la estar mot humilmens az u/na part, e era li semblant degues esser paradis terrenal. E vezia totz [86r] los Santz *per* orde e venian tut az a/quest arma e demandavan li qui era ni de qual estament ni de qui era l'abiti que portava que no*n* lo conoissian. E illi respondet que sotz la man de sant Frances s'era regida. E aisso dizia mot humilmens. E li Sant li dizian retornant sa respos/ta sotz la man de sant Frances ti est regida. E tu con no*n* portas lo sieu abiti, ni l'abiti de sancta Clara, ni de las autras relegions. Qui ies'tu que sotz la man de sant Frances ti sies regida, e no*n* portes son abiti? Qu*i* iest tu ni de qual estament?" [A woman died in the convent of Hyères. And another woman, who was in prayer, went to rest. And it seemed to her that she was in a place where the soul [of the dead woman] was. She saw her in a corner, very humbly, and it seemed to her that that place was the earthly Paradise. And she saw all the saints in order, and they all went to that soul and asked her who she was, of what order, and what was the habit she wore, which they did not know. And she answered that she had lived under the hand of St. Francis. This she said very humbly. And the saints questioned her answer: "You have lived under the hand of St. Francis, yet you do not wear his habit, nor the habit of St. Clare, nor of the other orders. Who are you who has lived under the hand of St. Francis and yet does not wear his habit? Who are you and to what order do you belong?"].
57 Fol. 86r, 26–86v, 1.
58 Fol. 86r, 15–26, 86v, 1–9: "El Seinnhers dousamens respon/det am benigna cara hieu la con/nosc, illh es so dis d'un estament qu'ieu ami, lo qual ai en ma gar/da e le quals si regihis desotz la ma*n* de sant Frances. E ben dis ver que sotz la man sieua man s'es regida mais no*n* porta son abiti. E ieu sai qui es" [The Lord answered sweetly with a benign face, "I know her. She is, I say it, of an order for which I have affection and which I take care of, and they live under the hand of St. Francis. And it is true that she has lived under his hand, although she does not wear his habit. I know who she is"]. This heterodox conception of nuns is in line with Hugues de Digne's idea of female religious life: "Sebbene Douceline e le sue compagne non fossero considerate monache, secondo l'opinione comune lo erano secondo la definizione da lui data poco oltre

Indeed, the beguines portrayed in the *Life* were not *monegas*—that is, nuns—but they were close enough. Not only did they wear their own specific habit, but they also took vows, allegedly followed a rule, celebrated the liturgy, had novices among them, and probably instructed young girls. It is true that they lived in the world, but the degree of regulation imposed on them was considerable, or at least this is what the *Life* suggests. Thus, besides venerating the holy foundress, it is likely that the aim of the text was also to provide a more institutionalised image of the community. In fact, as Francine Michaud notes, in 1327, in the will of Guillaume de Montolieu, his legatee and daughter Marita, a beguine, is described as *monialis seu soror de Robaudo*. Michaud points out that these beguines could have been institutionalised after the conflicts resulting from the Council of Vienne.[59]

However, it is important to remark right from the outset that this process of institutionalisation should in no way be understood as a denial of the beguine status on the part of the community, but rather as a desire for legitimacy. In fact, despite the risk of being mistaken for the so-called "béguins du Midi"—persecuted as heretics in the early fourteenth century—the "beguine" label was used as another identity hallmark by the women religious of Roubaud.[60] According to the text, upon taking her vows, Douceline called herself *beguina*.[61] Also, in

---

'omnes autem mulieres communiter viventes et regularem observantiam canonice profitentes, monache dici possunt'." Alessandra Sisto, *Figure del primo francescanesimo in Provenza: Ugo e Douceline di Digne* (Florence: Leo S. Olschki Editore, 1971), 138.

59 30 December 1327; ADBdR, MS 381 E 33, fol. 72v. Quoted in Francine Michaud, "Le pauvre transformé: Les hommes, les femmes et la charité à Marseille, du XIIIe siècle jusqu'à la Peste noire," *Revue historique* 650 (2008): 243–90, esp. note 7. On the basis of notarial sources, Michaud argues that the main concern of the beguines shifted from a willingness to engage in charity work to their own preservation. This scholar refers, in fact, to the clauses present in various wills that required legatees to remain in the *estament*, which were published by Albanès in the "Pièces justificatives." Francine Michaud, "The Pilgrim, the Priest, and the Beguine: Ascetic Tradition vs. Christian Humanism in Late Medieval Religious Practices," *Pecia: Ressources en médiévistique* 1 (2002): 157–80, esp. 180.

60 See Walter Simons, "Beginnings: Naming Beguines in the Southern Low Countries, 1200–1250," in *Labels and Libels: Naming Beguines in Northern Medieval Europe*, ed. Letha Böhringer, Jennifer Deane, and Hildo van Engen (Turnhout: Brepols, 2014), 9–52, esp. 35–36; and Sean L. Field, "Being a Beguine in France ca. 1300," in *Labels and Libels*, 117–33.

61 Fol. 7v, 24–25: "El s*ancta* maire volc esser apellada beguina" [The holy mother wanted to be called "beguina"]. Although in southern France the terms *beguin* and *beguine* were also used to describe the followers of Petrus Iohannis Olivi, it must be said that we have no evidence of any doctrinal link between them and the beguines of Provence. See David Burr, *The Spiritual Franciscans: From Protest to Persecution in the Century After Saint Francis* (University Park: Pennsylvania State University Press, 2001) and Louisa Burnham, *So Great a Light, So Great a Smoke: The*

the final part of the *Life* we find a series of praises that ends with, "Gauch a totas cellas ques an pres lo sant nom de beguina" [Be blessed all those who have taken the holy name of beguine].⁶²

The choice of the term by Douceline and her contemporaries is interesting above all because the *Life* placed the emphasis on the novelty of such a label in the region. At the beginning of the account of her religious life, the text focuses on how there were no communities of beguines in Provence, and how, in fact, such a word had never even been heard in the area before. Furthermore, the foundational vision in which Douceline saw two beguines and a little girl—which, in a way, anticipated what would happen in the vision received by the beguine from the house of Hyères mentioned above—demonstrated that Douceline had never seen such a habit, and shortly afterwards, the text explicitly claims that she was indeed the first beguine in Provence.⁶³ It is therefore not surprising that the saints appeared bewildered in the *monega non est* vision when they saw a beguine coming, because they could not identify her habit, a key element of this episode. Actually, the *Life* already describes the habit of beguines in detail in the account of Douceline's very first vision, and later on, it narrates the moment when she finally donned the habit in a solemn way, as if it were the scene in which St. Francis stripped off his clothes—that is, the beginning of a new life.⁶⁴ In essence, she was donning the mantle of the *Mater Dolorosa*, the veil that Mary wore after the Passion of her son.

Beguin Heretics of Languedoc (Ithaca: Cornell University Press, 2008). It is true that a close connection between Franciscans and the beguine movement in general was apparent across the region, but perhaps the traditional distinction between an orthodox phenomenon in the north and a dissident equivalent in the south should be nuanced.

62 Fol. 101v, 15–17.

63 Fol. 5r, 14–17: "En aquel temps non era estament de begui/nas, ni en Proensa non las auzian men/taure" [At that time there were no communities of beguines in Provence, nor was there any mention of them]; fol. 6r, 20–22: "Negun temps aquel abiti de donnas non avian mais vist, ni la ma/niera de la lur honestat" [They had never seen women donning that habit, nor their honest lifestyle]; fol. 8r, 1–2: "Nostra do/na fon li premiera beguina" [Our Lady was the first Beguine].

64 Fol. 7r, 6–18: "Dezamparet tan/tost los vestirs que portava. am gran ardor e vesti si de negre, la co/lor e la forma del habiti que porta/van las donas que avia vist. Et am meravillos alegrier desperit bendet si en aquella maniera quellas eran bendadas. E près lo vel am gran de/vocion et am gran gauch de sarma e pueis am gran fervor et am gran sentiment de nostre senhor pauzet lo mantel sus lo cap en senhal de la passion de Ih[es]u crist" [She took off all the clothes she wore and, with great ardour, dressed herself in black, the color and shape of the habit worn by the women she had seen. And with marvelous joy of spirit she covered her head in the manner in which they were covered. And she took the veil with great devotion and with great joy in her soul. Then, with great fervour and with great feeling for Christ, she put the veil on her head as a sign of the passion of Jesus Christ]. Damien Boquet briefly compared such a passage

The verses added at the end of the manuscript, in fol. 103v, can be understood in this sense. This is the hymn *Imperatrix clemencie*, a plea to the Virgin to share her anguish and the suffering of her son, which can be found in so many other manuscripts of the time, always in a penitential context or in connection with the Passion of Christ. It was a prayer that could be sung and that was included in the Office of the Sorrows of the Virgin attributed sometimes either to John XXII or to Bonaventura of Bagnoreggio (d. 1274). We find this office, for example, in an early fifteenth-century manuscript from Santa Maria de Bélem and in the contemporary Brunet Psalter. In the latter, the prayer is headed precisely by a depiction of the Entombment of Christ, with the figure of the *virgo lacrimosa* in the centre, and the text contains numerous repetitions alluding to prayers on the Passion.[65]

The beguines of Roubaud also had some of the elements that characterised any other religious community, such as a rule (or "way of living") and vows. Regarding the former, the *Life* explains that when Douceline decided to found the first community, she intended to write a rule, but asked her brother for advice first.[66] We do not know if such a document was ever written, as later the foundress tried to calm the doubts and fears of her companions by telling them: "Be united in the unity of God's love, since he has gathered you with his love [*caritat*]. The other orders maintain a strong bond with their rule, you are united only by the love of God [*caritat*]."[67] Although Douceline added that their ethereal

---

to this emblematic episode of Francis's life, but a thorough comparative study remains to be made, especially regarding the parallelism between this scene in Douceline's hagiography and in the *Life* of Delphine de Puimichel. Damien Boquet, "Écrire et représenter la dénudation de François d'Assise au XIIIe siècle," *Rives méditerranéennes* 30 (2008): 39–63 at 62.

65 University of Aberdeen, Burnet Psalter, Aul ms. 25. The office is found in fols. 288v–300, and the hymn in fol. 288v: https://www.abdn.ac.uk/burnet-psalter/text/288v.htm. The Portuguese manuscript, made in Bruges in the early fifteenth centuury, is known as *Horas de D. Duarte*, and is kept in Lisbon, Arquivio Nacional da Torre do Tombo, Ordem de São Jerónimo, Mosteiro de Santa Maria de Belém, liv. 65.; fols. 217v–234r (the hymn is in fol. 218v).

66 Fol. 9r, 7–12: "Volc es/crieure a si et a ssas filhas via e mani/era de vieure, la qual cauza plus fi/zelmens a far e plus veraia volc illi aver per lo dechat el conseill dell sant paire" [She wanted to write for herself and her daughters a rule and way of life. She wanted to do this in the most faithful and just way, and so she asked the holy father [Hugues] for advice].

67 Fols. 55v, 15–26 and 56r, 1: "Estas, filhas, en unitat en l'amor dell Sein/nhor, car en l'amor de Crist est aissi a/campadas e Crist vos a liadas en la sieu caritat. Tut li autri sant orde an fort liam de regla, mai vos au/tras, sa dis, non est a plus liadas mai sol a caritat. Aquist pauca cordeta, li caritatz de Crist, vos a en si liadas per qu'es plus fort liams que negun [56r] autra regla" [Daughters, you are united in the love of the Lord, for in the love of Christ you have been gathered, and Christ has bound you with his love [*caritat*]. All the other holy orders have a strong bond with the rule, but you, she said, are bound only by love [*caritat*]. This little rope, the love of Christ,

bond was stronger than any rule, the fact is that she called it *cordeta* (little string), which shows her awareness of the fragility of her community. If there had really been some kind of document similar to a rule or a *propositum*, we would most likely have found it inserted in the formula for the vows included at the end of the manuscript.⁶⁸ Like the text of the *Life*, this formula was written between the aforementioned period of threats to the community—probably at the end of the thirteenth century—and the issue of John XXII's bulls. In fact, papal protection is explicitly quoted in the last sentence: "segon que papa Johan l'a confermat." The formula is brief and simply refers to the vows of virginity and obedience, and whereas the vow of virginity was taken before God and Our Lady, the vow of obedience was to be taken before the founding brothers and the prioress.⁶⁹

---

has bound you because it is a stronger bond than any rule]. The allusion to *caritas* might be linked to the singing of the antiphone "Ubi caritas et amor," since right after this speech the *Life* says they celebrated the *mandatum*.

68 In the sixteenth-century Franciscan chronicle by Marcos de Lisboa, special emphasis is placed on the fact that Hugues provided them with "rules and constitutions." It would be interesting to know what sources the author used, as there are significant differences between his account and that of the *Life* even regarding Douceline's visions: "[...] ajuntãdose a ella muitas matronas honradas et virgens perpetuamente se dedicarão ao serviço de Deos, com algumas regras et constituiçoes que lhes ordenou Frey Ugo pera mais devota et ordenadamente viverem" [many honest matrons and virgins joined her and devoted themselves for life to the service of God, with certain rules and constitutions that Brother Hugues provided for them so that they could lead a devout and ordered life]. Marcos de Lisboa, *Chronicas da ordem dos frades menores, e das outras ordems segunda e terceira, instituidas na Igreja per o sanctissimo Padre Sam Francisco* (Lisboa: Pedro Crasbeeck, 1615 [1562]), vol. 2, book 5, chap. 1, 133.

69 Fol. 102v: "Ieu, aitals per nom, vodi e prome/ti [...]e doni de tot mon cor a Dieu e a ma donna Santa Maria Ve[r]ge e a ~~nostre sant paire e a nostra santa maire~~ e a tota la cort celestial ma verge/nitat de *conser*var e de gardar de tot mon poder e de tota ma forsa totz los temps de ma vida e non jamais venir en contra | E prec a vos donna e a totas quantas est | que m'en sias garentia davant la cara de Dieu | al jorn del jusii.—Per aqui mesesme vodi e promiti a Nostre Seinhor e a Nostra Donna, e a nos/tre sant paire e a nostra santa ma/ire e a totz los santz. e a vos donna—obediencia e fermamens e sinpla esser obediens a vos donna, e a totas aquellas que apre vos *p*riorissas seran de gardar e obs*erv*ar l'estament de Robaut de Massella. segon que papa Johan l'a confermat" [I, whose name is X, vow and promise [...] and I, with my whole heart, vow to God and to Our Lady, Holy Mary Virgin, ~~and to our holy Father, and to our holy Mother,~~ and to all the heavenly court, that I will keep and guard my virginity with all my will and all my strength for as long as I live, and I will never turn back | And I beg you, Lady, and all those who are here | to be my guarantee before the face of God | on the day of the final judgment.—Therefore, I vow and promise to Our Lord and to Our Lady, and to our holy Father and our holy Mother, and to all the saints and to you, Lady—obedience. And [I vow] firmly and simply to be obedient to you, Lady, and to all those who after you will be prioresses, to keep and observe the *estament* of Roubaud and Marseille, as Pope John has confirmed it]. One may wonder if the

Once again, this suggests a turn towards a monastic spirit. In fact, at the beginning of the *estament*, the *Life* mentions both the vows of chastity and virginity as part of a sermon delivered by Douceline's brother, Hugues de Digne, which makes sense given that notarial documents show that there were widows in the community.[70] However, after receiving papal confirmation, only the vow of virginity made it into the formula.[71] Douceline also took a vow of obedience, not only to the prioress of the community but also to Josselin d'Orange, Minister Provincial of the Friars Minor of Provence. Finally, the third characteristic monastic vow, the vow of poverty, is missing from the formula, but it is hinted at, albeit vaguely, in the hagiographic text. Douceline (and only her) promised a form of total poverty before her brother, a vow similar to that of the most radical Franciscanism of her time that the text directly relates to the example of Francis.[72] In contrast, Hugues seems to have refused to let the other beguines lead a life of absolute poverty, recommending instead a *mejana paupertat*.

To sum up, at first the vows included an approximation of virginity—chastity —and obedience. Then Douceline made a private vow of absolute poverty. Finally, the formula only considered virginity. On the one hand, virginity involved chastity, but on the other, it contributed to the construction of an image of beguines close to that of monastic nuns. However, at no time was the vow of poverty established as necessary; instead, they committed to a life of *mejana paupertat*. It is difficult to clarify what they meant by "medium poverty," but it surely implied an idea of moderation, and it was not a full vow, rather a behaviour guideline. The beguines of Roubaud could keep their goods and properties but

---

phrase "segon que papa Johan l'a confermat" could refer to a constitution (or rule) made in accordance with the confirmation of the Pope.

70 Fols. 8v, 24–9r, 2: "Motas autras per volon/tat de dieu: verges e vezoas, e neis cellas queran en matremoni dezam [9r] paravan lur senhors els enfans e venian sen az ella" [Many others, by the will of God, virgins and widows, and those who were bound in marriage left their husbands and children and went with her]. See the wills of several widowed beguines quoted in Antoine de Ruffi, *Histoire de Marseille* (Marseille: Henri Martel, 1696), no. 1, LXI.

71 According to Michaud, Douceline had insisted on chastity, being aware of the appeal her project held for widows, but soon after her death, in 1274, young women started to join the community. Michaud argues that this seems to be a trend, as in 1337 none of the beguines had been married: "among the eleven beguines who left wills between 1280 and 1407, four were widows." The insistence on virginity could result either from a shift to a monastic ideal or from a need to recruit younger women. Michaud, "The Pilgrim, the Priest," 175.

72 Fol. 15v, 13–17: "E vodet en las mans del sant pai/re fraire Hugo de Dinnha la sancta pau/pertat de Ihesu Crist am gran ardor gar/dar, tot en aissi cant sant Frances la tenc e la donet" [And in the hands of the holy father Hugo de Dinha, she made the vow to keep the holy poverty of Christ with ardour, as St. Francis had done and given to others].

the wealthier ones were to help the poorer.⁷³ We know about the intense economic activity of these beguines,⁷⁴ and Felipa Porcelleta herself, *grans rica femena* (a very rich woman),⁷⁵ bought the houses with which they extended the beguinage when she was already a member of the community.⁷⁶ One explanation for the absence of the vow of "medium poverty" in the formula would be the desire to distance themselves from Douceline's model of exceptional holiness, and at the same time not to enter into any of the theological controversies of the time about poverty and religious life, particularly the one surrounding the so-called "burned béguins" of Languedoc.⁷⁷

Finally, the *Life* also recounts that, like any other religious community, the group had a general prioress who was the head of both houses, of the *donnas* and of the novices. Also, like other convents, they had personnel at their service: an *infirmarer*,⁷⁸ a doorkeeper, and so on. The hagiography insists on the instructive role that Douceline had as prioress and teacher of the younger women.⁷⁹ She

---

73 Fol. 18r, 3–7 and 18v, 1–3: "E adoncs li s*an*cta mai/re *per* consell de[l] sant paire, volc que elegissan mejana pau*per*tat. Que po/gueissan aver lurs ops, e lur neces/sitat pauramens e atempradame*n*s" [And so the holy mother, on the advice of the holy father, wanted them to choose moderate poverty. That they could provide for their needs in a poor but balanced way]. The adjective *mejana* is used to allude to something that is moderate or well-tempered (21v, 16–25).
74 See Michaud, "The Pilgrim, the Priest," 172; Louis Blancard, *Documents inédits sur le commerce de Marseille au Moyen Âge* (Marseille: Barlatier-Feissat, 1884–1885), 372–80; Kathryn L. Reyerson, "Un exemple de microcrédit féminin entre ville et campagne. Montpellier et ses alentours au début du XIVe siècle," in *La fabrique des sociétés médiévales méditerranéennes*, ed. Marie Dejoux and Diane Chamboduc de Saint Pulgent (Paris: Éditions de la Sorbonne, 2018), 223–31, esp. note 35.
75 Fol. 16v, 8.
76 See "Achat de cens par Philippine de Porcellet," 22 October 1297; cf. "Inventaire des cens échus au couvent des franciscains," of 14 March 1390, where such buildings no longer appear. Albanès, "Pièces justificatives," 265–67, 289–91.
77 See David Burr, *Olivi and Franciscan Poverty: The Origins of the* Usus Pauper *Controversy* (Philadelphia: University of Pennsylvania Press, 1989).
78 Douce Vivaud's will: February 1348, ADBdR, MS 381 E 76 fol. 80v.
79 Fol. 19v, 12–14. In the will of another Felipa Porcelleta, who was not the prioress but the daughter of Bertrand Porcellet, we find the expression, "esse impuberem," 20 April 1292, in Albanès, "Pièces justificatives," 263–64. Also, in 1291 Agnès Vigouroux seems to have joined the community very young, since she needed a legal authorisation to do so; see "Reception of a beguine," 20 April 1292, in Albanès, "Pièces justificatives," 264–65. According to Francine Michaud, "no doubt the beguinage served also as a refuge for girls unsuitable for marriage," a claim that she supports with the example of the sister of Durante Borda, who placed the girl in Roubaud with a substantial pension because of family solidarity. Durante's sister was *fortius invalestati* (had a severe physical disability) and the money allocation was made on condition

was in charge of the education of the beguines, she passed on to them moral teachings, but also spiritual and ritual instructions, including the divine office, prayer, chanting, and liturgy.[80] This is in contrast to the passage were we are told that the saint did not want her beguines to have "edifici d'esglesia *ni* sutileza de letras," that is, neither liturgical-clerical education nor access to formal learning. According to the text, this attitude was motivated by her desire to keep them away from vainglory.[81] This expression must be understood within the context of the hagiographic genre, as the *Life* makes an effort to convey the image of an illiterate Douceline and a community of honest and non-educated women. The alleged interdiction not only contradicts numerous passages of the *Life* itself, but also other documents that attest to the learned background of some of the beguines of Roubaud. Thus, the text seems to focus on providing a virtuous account of the honest life of the community. In addition, a whole chapter is devoted to the duties of the prioress, in this case Douceline, which included controlling the younger girls and offering them moral guidance.[82] This explains the

---

that she remained in the community. 22 January 1285, ADBdR, MS 6 G 26, quoted in Michaud, "The Pilgrim, the Priest," 174.

80 See fols. 8r, 12–13; 9v, 13–14; and 10r, 8.

81 Fol. 11v, 11–24: "No*n* podia sufrir que res s'agi/nolles azella, neis dun enfant que enans qu'illi si fossan clinatz, ill sera a/ginollada. Sobre totas cauzas s'estudi/et en aquesta vertut a fondar si me/zesma e tot son estament. Aquesta v*er*/tut mandava fort gardar a totas sas fiihas, aissi cant fundament de tot so*n* estament, e *per* aisso illi no*n* volc sufrir quellas aguessan edifici d'egleisa ni autras dignitatz, ni aguessan so/tileza de letras. ni cantessan l'ufici, ni volia aguessan neguna cauza *per* que trop s'eslevessan" [She could not bear to have anyone kneel before her, not even a child. Before anyone bowed, she had already knelt. She applied herself much to this virtue, more than to any other, and founded on it her very life and that of the order [*estament*]. She commanded that her daughters should diligently observe this virtue as the foundation of all her order [*estament*], and therefore she never wished to allow them to have a church, or other dignities, nor to have the subtlety of letters, nor to sing in the office, nor to have anything that would make them boast].

82 Fol. 18v, 11–22: "E car li s*an*cta maire era caps e maistra de totas las autra[s] covenia qu'illi lur fes heis/semples en totas v*er*tutz, q*ue* no*n* solamens era caps e regeiris d'a/quellas de Robaut qu'eran en sa ho/bediencia, de las cals era maires, ans era atressi capdels e maistra d'aquellas que *per* lo sieu heissemple s'eran enbeguinidas en la carriera estant pres de Robaut, a Massella, e/n aissi con az Ieras" [And since the holy mother was chief and master of all the others, it was necessary that they all take her as an example of virtue, for she was not only chief and regent of those of Robaut who were under her obedience and of whom she was the mother, but also of those who, following her example, had become beguines in the street near Robaut, in Marseilles and in Hyères]. It would be interesting to look into the differences in the status of the beguines of the community: the text speaks of *donnas*, *fillas*, young women, and those who had been *enbeguinidas*. It might be crucial to know whether these labels represented real distinctions and, if so, if they were similar to the monastic groups of choir nuns, lay people, *donnés*, etc.

emphasis the text places, for example, on the harsh discipline she imposed on young women.⁸³

The Book of the House: A Book for the House

Following Joseph-Hyacinthe Albanès, most scholars have regarded the *Life* as a second version of an earlier text.⁸⁴ Albanès based his thesis on the passage dated "when [the Life] was first written."⁸⁵ However, this sentence should be taken with great caution, for although it could refer to a first manuscript identical to the one we have—indicating that the same text was copied in different volumes—the words are vague enough to allow for other interpretations. For instance, it could be alluding to a completely different text written by one or several different "authors," so that there would be no filiation between the two versions. There is also the possibility that the sentence refers to the compilation of preliminary notes or the preparation of the contents, so that *escricha* (written) would then refer to the action of planning or conceiving the work. Obviously, we could even think that the text places the writing of the *Life* at an earlier moment just to legitimise it, making it closer to Douceline's time.

Thus, the date of composition is the key to solve many of the enigmas that surround this beguine community. Although Paul Meyer had placed this composition in the last quarter of the thirteenth century,⁸⁶ Albanès established two distinct dates for each of the alleged versions, namely 1297 and 1315. These dates have been taken at face value by scholars dealing with this manuscript.⁸⁷ Al-

---

83 There are many passages that display this kind of scene. See, for example, fol. 19v, 15–17: "E cant li *sancta* maire ho sa/up. batet la mot duramens. en tant quel sancs li corria *per* las costas" [And when the holy mother learned about it, she hit her hard, so hard that blood trickled down her sides].
84 According to Albanès: "Pour nous faire bien comprendre, nous dirons que le texte que nous possédons est une seconde édition, dans laquelle il y a des choses qui n'étaient pas dans la première." Joseph-Hyacinthe Albanès, "Prolégomènes," in *La vie de sainte Douceline*, xxi. On the reception, "La première ayant disparu, c'est la seconde qui a fait l'objet des éditions successives de Joseph-Hyacinthe Albanés et Raymond Gout." Attard, "Religion, sainteté et pouvoir," 131.
85 "Cant fon premieramens escri/cha" (fol. 80r, 20–21).
86 Paul Meyer, "Les derniers troubadours de Provence, d'après le chansonnier donné à la Bibliothèque impériale par Mr Ch. Giraud," *Bibliothèque de l'école des Chartes* 30 (1869): 245–97, esp. 263.
87 Carozzi, "L'estament de sainte Douceline," 270; Michaud, "The Pilgrim, the Priest," 174; Attard, "Religion, sainteté et pouvoir," 131. Sean Field has revised the dates, accepting the first one but hesitating between 1312 and 1320 for the second. As for the differences between the two alleged versions, he points out: "It is not clear what textual modifications, if any, were made to the

banès dated it so precisely on the basis of the miraculous episode of Maragda Porcelleta, which the text placed on a Saturday, the eve of the anniversary of Douceline's death. As it seems that she died on 1 September, the only years in which the anniversary fell on a Sunday were 1286 and 1297, "si l'on ne veut redescendre jusqu'au quatorzième siècle." Albanès rejected 1286 because of two reasons: first, it was too early for the text to mention the captivity of Charles II, and secondly, two characters that appear in the *Life*, Maragda Porcelleta and Pellegrin Repelin, would be too young to perform the actions attributed to them.[88] Likewise, Albanès establishes the second date based on the fact that Felipa Porcelleta, whom he considered to be the author, died in 1317. According to Albanès, as the text does not refer to her death, it must have been written just before, around 1315. Finally, the historian also argues that the second version may have been corrected or extended due to the way in which the Franciscan Pellegrin Repelin was presented: "for he had been a priest and preacher of the order for a long time."[89] As Repelin was a novice in 1288, Albanès claimed that ten years were not enough to say that he had been "for a long time in the order," a reference that he estimated implied approximately thirty years.

Therefore, the dates proposed by Albanès and most of the subsequent scholarship are based on rather weak arguments. For instance, we are told that Felipa's death was important enough to be mentioned in the *Life*, and that Felipa was the author of the text. Although Albanès's work is undoubtedly praiseworthy, these theoretical cornerstones seem too unstable not to raise questions. In my view, we cannot pinpoint the exact dates in which the writing of the *Life* was carried out. Taking into account the paleographic analysis of the text, as well as the script and the events mentioned in it, I am inclined to situate the composition between the last years of the thirteenth century and 1320–1322. As we shall see below, it does not seem accurate to speak of Felipa as the author or even to consider that her death would have necessarily been recorded in the hagiography of the foundress. However, it is quite clear that the profession of vows was added later and that mentioning papal approval in the text made perfect sense in that context. A more specialised paleographic study and the analysis of new documents could help us determine the composition period more accurately.

Life at this point, but probably the new copy was intended to emphasize the orthodoxy of Douceline's foundations in the uncertain atmosphere for beguines after the Council of Vienne." Field, *Courting Sanctity*, 219.
88 Albanès, "Prolégomènes," xxi–xxii.
89 "Que sos fils era capellans e predicaires en l'orde de sant Fran/ces" [That his son was a priest and preacher in the order of St. Francis] (fol. 71v, 4–6).

As noted above, Felipa Porcelleta has traditionally been considered the author of the *Life* since the publication of Albanès's pioneering study and edition.⁹⁰ As a matter of fact, we have much more information about Felipa than about Douceline. Many notarial documents have survived about her family, one of the most powerful and wealthiest lineages of medieval Provence both on a religious and a political level, as it had a close relationship with the court of Charles of Anjou. After her marriage, Felipa moved to Barjols, probably Douceline's hometown, where she had two daughters, Mabila and Douceline. She was widowed at the age of twenty-one, and then, around 1274, she joined the beguinage in Marseille and became its prioress.⁹¹ Documents show that she was one of the main sources of funds for the house,⁹² and several other of her kinswomen also became beguines.⁹³ The date of her death seems to be a source of debate among historians, although we know that it could not have been before March 1317.⁹⁴

From the critical perspective of the twenty-first century, it is worth asking to what extent the question of determining the authorship of the text is truly important. Not only did this work originate in a manuscript culture prior to the modern views on literary creation, but it was also the fruit of a cultural and religious environment in which reading and writing practices did not need a fixed and unmovable text to legitimise a message. In fact, the content of the text, especially in its less plausible passages, that is, the miracles, is supported by arguments of

---

90 Albanès, "Prolegomènes," xxxiv–xxxv. See, among others, Jean-Paul Boyer, "De force ou de gré: La Provence et ses rois de Sicile," in *Les princes angevins du XIIIe au XVe siècle: Un destin européen*, ed. Élisabeth Verry and Noël-Yves Tonnerre (Rennes: Presses Universitaires de Rennes, 2003), 23–59, esp. 43; Martin Aurell i Cardona, *Une famille de la noblesse provençale au Moyen Âge: Les Porcelet* (Avignon: Aubanel, 1986), 165, n. 56; *The Life of Saint Douceline, a Beguine of Provence*, ed. and trans. Kathleen Garay and Madeleine Jeay (Cambridge: D. S. Brewer, 2001), 16; Madeleine Jeay, "La Vie de sainte Douceline par Felipa Porcelet: Les mobiles d'une hagiographe du XIIIe siècle," in *Dix ans de recherche sur les femmes écrivains de l'ancien régime: Influences et confluences. Mélanges offerts à Hannah Fournier*, ed. Guy Poirier (Québec: Les Presses de l'Université de Laval, 2008), 17–36; Sean L. Field, "Agnes of Harcourt, Felipa of Porcelet, and Marguerite of Oingt: Women Writing about Women at the End of the Thirteenth Century," *Church History* 76 (2007): 298–329.
91 Both the *Life* and the wills prove this. See fol. 84v, 10–12: "Ma donna Feli/pa Porcelleta ques era majers prio/ressa de l'estament" [My Lady Felipa, who was the (main) prioress of the order [*estament*]]. See also Albanès, "Pièces justificatives," 269, 282, 286 ff.
92 See Albanès, "Pièces justificatives," 265–68; and Martin Aurell i Cardona, *Actes de la famille Porcelet d'Arles (972–1320)* (Paris: CTHS, 2001), nos. 464, 520, 536, 539–40, 548–50, 558–59, 567–68, 578, 591, 607, 617–18, and 620.
93 We know that at least Felipa and Maragda, daughters of her nephew Bertrand, joined the community. Aurell i Cardona, *Actes de la famille*, 262–63.
94 Aurell i Cardona, *Actes de la famille*, nos. 617–18.

authority typical of medieval culture: the power of the prioress (for a text created within the community) and the testimonies of eyewitnesses.

But, at the same time, the need to attribute authorship to a single person is understandable in the context in which Albanès lived. For this purpose, the Provençal historian put forward a hypothesis based on somewhat debatable premises. Albanès argued that the *Life* provided intimate information about the saint that only one person in the community could have known.[95] If someone from the inside had written it, Albanès maintained that the author could only have been the next prioress.[96] Admittedly, if the text was indeed written within the walls of Roubaud, the prioress would have had to be involved, but we know that the only surviving manuscript was the work of a copyist named *Jacobi peccatoris*.[97] However, it is also true that there are some clues that suggest that the enterprise of writing the *Life* could have been the result of the cooperation of the community of beguines, who would have contributed to its conception, patronage, writing, and/or dictation. One of the details that points in this direction is the use of pronouns. Most of the text resorts to the impersonal *hom* or the third person plural pronoun to refer to the community, not only in the account of events of Douceline's time, but also when alluding to the composition of the manuscript.[98] Towards the end of the text though, the first person plural pronoun appears on several occasions. Whereas in some cases it applies to those who had written or rather conceived the work—whether they were the beguines or not[99]—in others,

---

[95] It must be said, however, that the same text sometimes alludes to the confessor as an external source of information.
[96] "Philippine de porcellet, pensons-nous, mit elle-même en oeuvre les nombreux matériaux qu'elle possédait, sans qu'elle eût à recourir à la coopération d'un autre." Albanès, "Prolegomènes," xxxv. See also xxvi–xxvii and xxxiv–xxxv.
[97] "Obsecro vos qui hoc legeritis, ut Jacobi peccatoris in orationibus vestris memineritis" [I beseech you who read this, that you will remember Jacobi the sinner in your prayers] (fol. 102r).
[98] Fols. 65v, 24–26; 66r, 1: "E li benaura/da maire era adoncs en aquel co/vent, el luoc on estan ara present/mens" [And then the blessed mother was in that convent, right in the place where they are now].
[99] Fol. 99r, 1–9: "Aguem per sagrament per que ren non hi dupti que so que n'es escrich, es dich per veritat. Car gan ren d'autres miracles n'avem lais/satz estar quels aviam per las propri/as personas, car non aviam pron fer/meza de garentias ho sagrament non los avem escritz" [So that no one may doubt what is written, we swear that we tell the truth. We have said nothing of other miracles that people have told us directly, since we did not have sufficient guarantee by testimony or by oath, and that is why we have not written them down].

the use of "we" directly refers to the community: "nos prometia, nos fermava ... nos salvariam / nos confermet."¹⁰⁰

Besides linguistic evidence, the most revealing detail can be found at the end of the *Life*, in the account of the problems that arose in the convent of Marseille after the death of Douceline due to disagreements about what should be included in the narration of the life of the foundress. It seems that some of the members of the community argued that a certain praise (*lauzor*) or, most probably, a certain anecdote related to Douceline had no place in the work. As I have mentioned above, according to the text, this is precisely the moment when the first version was written, "cant fon premieramens escri/cha" [when it was first written].¹⁰¹ The doubts of these beguines stemmed from fear, but, unfortunately, we do not know which praise or anecdote motivated this reaction. The important point about this short passage is that it shows a collegial decision, an act of sharing and discussing the contents that were to be integrated into the *Life*. Regardless of the veracity of this specific episode, it does convey the image of a community of beguines planning a text by themselves.

Moreover, the narration makes it clear that the passage was finally included, as we are then told that it was the devil who instilled such fear into the sceptical beguines, to the point that they even came to doubt the sanctity of Douceline: "si li S*ancta* no*n* fora s*ancta*, que non fos ~~sancta~~ digna de lauzor" [if the saintly woman were not saintly, she would not be ~~a saint~~ worthy of praise].¹⁰² One of them received a visit from the spirit of the saint in the middle of the night. Another one, a young novice, saw Douceline attending matins and, although the holy woman was wearing the habit of a beguine, the novice did not understand what she was doing there, as she did not know her. Thus, just like the saints in the *monega non est* vision, the novice asked her who she was. Douceline answered: "Dulcelina hec de Digna, sede polorum est digna, inter sacras virgines" [This is Douceline of Digne, who deserves a place in Heaven among the holy virgins].¹⁰³ It should be noted that the fact that the novice was not able to physically recognise the saint could be alluding to a problem of generational relay, as young women were precisely the ones who would have to project and spread the memory of Douceline in the future. The text ends the account of this anecdote by adding that the spirit stayed to sing during the office, and so the final

---

100 Fols. 86v, 16–26; 87r, 1–4. After this passage, which corresponds to the vision of the saints in Paradise ("monega non est"), the references change back to the third person. We also find it in fol. 87r–v.
101 Fol. 80v, 1–5.
102 Fol. 80v, 7–8.
103 Fol. 82r, 23–25.

scene is one of total cohesion: their hearts were tied together so that each one felt what the others felt. Thus, the dispute and the threat of separation, which we are told Douceline so feared, ended up settled by the presence and commemoration of her memory.[104] Right after that, the text explains that something similar happened in Hyères during the celebration of the saint's anniversary.[105]

Therefore, it is quite likely that the beguines of Roubaud did have an active role in shaping the *Life*. Were they also its main readers? Everything seems to indicate that they were. For example, in the will of Cecilia de Volta we find a breviary that this beguine bequeathed to two other companions and which she called *Librum sanctae matris nostrae*. Upon the death of these two women, the book was to pass on to the niece of one of them—provided she was a beguine in Roubaud—and, later, at the death of the latter, it was to be returned to the community. The use of the verb *devolvo* might either imply that the manuscript was used by the community even if it belonged to Cecilia, or that it was originally made within the beguinage and had to be returned there. We do not know if the volume cited by Cecilia is the one in our hands today; in all likelihood, it was but one among several copies, as it stands to reason that each house would have had one.[106]

---

104 Fol. 83v, 1–7: "E a/doncs fon nusa e aperta li concien/cia de l'una a l'autra. E acorderon si az un acordi en lur bon pensament, car ho vezian l'una el cor de l'autra aissi con en lo sieu, que li *sancta* maire era aqui presens" [And then the consciousness of one was read and opened to the other. And they agreed on the same thought, since they saw that the holy mother was present, and they saw it in the heart of the other, just as they saw it in their own hearts].

105 Fol. 84v, 19–21: "Semblant cauza s'estalvet en l'autre covent d'Ieras, l'an apres ques aisso fon agut" [The same thing happened in the other convent of Hyères the following year].

106 Albanès outlines the journey of the manuscript. His is an excellent work but the timeline it provides is, somewhat inevitably, full of gaps. It is assumed that after the suppression of the community of beguines, the manuscript passed on to the Franciscans and when the convent of Saint-Louis was destroyed in 1524, it would have been moved to the convent of La Guiche en Charolais, which would explain the seventeenth-century note: "Ex bibliotheca Minimorum" (fol. 1). Albanès, "Prolegomènes," xiii–xvii. It is not certain, however, that the volume Cecilia de Volta speaks of is the same as that found in possession of the Franciscans, so Albanès's linear narrative could be inaccurate. It is also interesting to note that for a time, probably during the eighteenth century and up to the mid-nineteenth, the community of Roubaud was thought to be in Spain, and the manuscript was thought to be written in Catalan or Valencian. This is what a note still extant on the second cover of the manuscript and probably dating from the eighteenth century indicates. A work from 1844 bears witness to this: "Hay un papelillo pegado con una obléa, y en él se lee lo siguiente, escrito en letra como del siglo pasado: 'Vie de madame de Doncelline ou Doncellemio, fondatrice de l'ordre des Dames de Robeau en Espagne'." Eugenio de Ochoa, *Catálogo razonado de los manuscritos españoles existentes en la Biblioteca Real de París* (Paris: Imprenta Real, 1844), 23.

Other details hint at some of the possible uses of the volume. To begin with, its size, which made it easily manageable—hence Cecilia's description of the volume as a *breviari* in her will—and also the fact that the formula and the hymn were later added to it. Along these lines, one should also consider the presence, albeit implicit, of a liturgical programme that the beguines probably followed. In fact, the *Life* describes the rites performed by the community on the most important feasts of the year. During each of them, Douceline experienced a rapture in connection with the liturgy of the day, as is usual in the hagiographies of the time. But the *Life* takes this topos one step further, as it also describes the foundational act of what could have been a sort of paraliturgy exclusive to this community of beguines: a procession that Douceline performed, while in a trance, in the dormitory—as they did not yet have an oratory—and which was related to the veneration of certain relics that they kept in that space.[107] Moreover, such passages are accompanied by the proclamation of Latin quotations from the offices that the *Life* translates into the vernacular. Therefore, there is also the possibility that it was used as an instructive text for novices, for whom it would provide basic formation in the Latin of the office, the liturgy, and also, as noted above, in the moral code of the house.

Again, the text includes a passage that could explicitly corroborate such hypotheses. The passage in question, already mentioned above, explains that Maragda Porcelleta, niece of Felipa, lost her voice just before the commemoration of Douceline's day, that is, most probably, the anniversary of her death.[108] That was "the day they were to hear her *Life* read again while they were at the table."[109]

---

107 Fol. 43v, 8–23: "Illi si va le/var e messi premiera, comenset s'en a/nar tota drecha e tendu-da *per* aquel raubiment a ques era fort tirada los huols fermatz al cel, e tot le cor tirat sus meravillozamens. Mais cant intret el dormidor, tantost cant fon desotz las reliquias ques estavan al som, car no*n* avian an/quars oratori azordenat on po/guessan estar, estant raubida, illi si va aginollar, e fes lur reverencia. E pueis ill si levet e apres comenset a cantar, annant *per* dormidor, de l'un cap tro a l'autre, tot en aissi con si se/guis procession ... [etc.]" [She rose and went all straight and stiff from the ecstasy she was experiencing, with her eyes heavenward and her whole heart wonderfully leaning upward. But when she entered the dormitory, as soon as she was under the relics that were at the back (for they did not yet have a decent oratory to place them), being thus ecstatic, she knelt down and paid obeisance to them. And then she rose and began to sing, going about the dormitory, from one side to the other, as if in procession ... [etc.]].

108 The celebration of such a "day of remembrance" can be found at different points in the *Life*, as well as in the will of Cecilia de Volta, ADBdR MS 391 E 15, fol. 52. In the *Life*, see fols. 79v, 22–80r, 2; 84v, 22–26; and 90r, 19–21.

109 Fol. 94r, 18–26: "Ab tant, e una dis quals tota enpaciens: "Veramens, gloriosa maire, non en serai pagada si davant la lesson de la taula deman illi no*n* a parlat *per* tal que plus alegramens pus/cam, so dis, auzir legir la vostra vida, ques aquel jorn si devia le/gir de novell en cov-

The number of miracles that, according to the hagiography, happened on that day could lead to the conclusion that the work proposes to conceive the act of reading it as a performative practice whose objective was the manifestation of the sacred—in particular, the intercession of the saint. Perhaps the act was carried out as part of a specific paraliturgy, a dramatised reading, chanting, or some kind of veneration of her relics, since, as we have noted above, some of them were in the possession of the community.[110]

Conclusions

The *Life* is a multifaceted source whose writing most probably responded to several reasons and whose uses could also have been most varied. In my opinion, this work cannot be understood as a hagiography that sought the canonisation of Douceline as a saint. Neither can it be conceived as a text for the silent and individual reading characteristic of modern literacy practices. First and foremost, it is a text that outlines a model of holiness that, in itself, contains a construction of the collective identity of the community of beguines. In other words, it conveys not only the ideal construction of the image of the saint, but also the practices that the community carried out, including those related to the creation and use of the text itself. Furthermore, this work responds to a period of danger or fear for the survival of the community, fears that the text explicitly states, leading to the introduction of pillars of authority that support the existence of this group of beguines. Finally, it is also a work that projects itself into the future, proposing a message of solid legitimacy, a well-defined identity, and a way to build and venerate the past to the new generations of beguines. All these aspects are certainly not exceptional among medieval and modern hagiographies, but I believe that the presence of all of them and the density with which we find such references in the text make it a particularly telling example.

This work, in fact, urges new and future beguines to continue their project as a community, recalling the great dangers the beguines encountered after the deaths of Hugues and Douceline. The text might have also been written close to Felipa's death—shortly before or after. Felipa was not only the general prioress of the community, but also an economic supporter and a main political pillar for the order. Thus, Douceline's response when she was advised to leave such a frag-

---

ent" [However, a woman said very impatiently, "Truly, glorious mother, I will not forgive you if, before the lesson of the table tomorrow, she has not been able to speak, so that we can hear your life read in a more joyful way," for on that day it was to be read again for the community].
110 See the miracle of the young girl, and that of the blind woman in fol. 90r–v.

ile community and to choose another order after the death of her brother, was proposed as a model of behaviour for any beguine who, after the death of Felipa or that of any other important pillar of the community, was tempted in the same way.[111] The dangers that arose after the death of Hugues were overcome thanks to several different measures: the protection of John of Parma, the institutional cohesion of both houses with the creation of the position of general prioress,[112] and the divine protection of the Trinity. At the same time, the dangers that threatened the community after Douceline's passing were warded off thanks to miracles and her popular acceptance as a saint, with visions that legitimised the beguine identity,[113] and her intercession with St. Francis, the Trinity, and Christ for the protection of the group.[114] These actions, however, were to be renewed, either through the liturgy dedicated to the Trinity, or through the reading of the *Life*.[115] The last sentences of the *Life* are once again revealing. After blessing the cities that housed the community, the beguines, and their holy mother, the author wished eternal happiness to those who would "persevere."[116]

---

[111] Fol. 53r, 8–25: "En aquell temps [que] le sans paires fraire Hu/go fon passatz d'aquest segle, li s*anct*a maire remas desconsolada e en mot gran treball. Don illi si tornava a la maire de gra*ci*a. aissi con a refuch qu'il/li la capdelles. e que fos garda de si e de sas filhas. [...] car alcunas *per*sonas s'esforceron de desfar so que le Sans ni illi avia*n* fach d'aquell sant estament, dizent que *p*er ren no*n* podia durar aquell estame*nt* freol. e consellavan li que prezessa au*-*tr'orde" [At that time when the holy father Friar Hugo died, the holy mother was disconsolate and with much grief. Hence she turned to the Mother of Grace as a refuge to take care of her and her daughters [...] because some people were trying to undo what the saint and she had made of that order [*estament*], saying that it was impossible for that fragile order [*estament*] to last and they advised her to take another order [*orde*]]. Notice the explicit difference between *estament* and *orde* in this passage.
[112] Just then, concerned about the future, she decided to create the figure of the Prioress General, to "maintain unity" ("tengues en unitat aquell sant estament," fol. 58r, 1–2).
[113] See fols. 86v, 21–87r, 4; and 87r, 11–7.
[114] On her deathbed, Douceline left the succession of the order and the care of her beguines in the hands of Christ, St. Francis, and the Holy Spirit (fol. 76v).
[115] After the death of her brother, Douceline had a vision of Jacob's staircase in which she saw the Trinity and was reassured that it was watching over them. She then ordered both convents to sing an antiphon devoted to the Holy Trinity every day at the end of matins (fol. 55r, 24–55v, 1).
[116] Fols. 101v, 25–102r, 6: "Pas, fermeza e segurtat, a la maison de Robaut d'Ieras e de Mar[102r]sella, car *per* aquesta maire lur s*anct*a benediccion confermamens e graci/a lur es donada e gloria de dieu, am benauransa eternal, a totas cellas que *per*severaran fizelmens" [Peace, endurance and safety for the house of Robaut of Hyères and Marseille, for thanks to this mother, her blessing was confirmed and grace is given to them. And the glory of God, with His everlasting blessing, to all those who will persevere faithfully]. This fear for the future of the community is also apparent in the wills and substantial bequests to community members, which increasing-

As we have seen, the question of the exact date of the composition of the *Life* is crucial. If it was indeed written before 1317, it could have been a reaction to the decrees of the Council of Vienne, surely in circulation before that date.[117] This would explain the emphasis on the monastic nature of the community as well as on the fact that the habit had been received from divine revelation. However, if this were the case, they could not have known the exact text of *Cum de quibusdam*, which would also explain why they decided to include the stress on the novelty of the beguine identity. In contrast, if the *Life* was written after 1317, the text would have been, to the letter, a direct response to the decree, but this would make the allusions to novelty hard to understand as a political strategy.

In any case, the fears of which the *Life* speaks materialised less than a century later, when the community disappeared. The donation made by Marguerite d'Alon in 1407 shows that she was the only surviving beguine: "ipsa domina Margherita unica, sola et singularis remansit usque nunc in dicto collegio, et nulla est alia beguina que succedere valeat in bonis dicti collegii." However, the memory of the foundress remained alive, for Marguerite bequeathed a sum for the celebration of the anniversary of *Beate Dulsaline* in the church of the Friars Minor.[118]

In order to study the spirituality of lay religious groups like the beguines, it seems necessary to reassess the permeability of boundaries that have traditionally been considered as immovable, such as the one between regulated and non-regulated women religious, between works in Latin and in the vernacular, and between literate and illiterate communities, among others. To this we must add the deconstruction of the stories of the most visible figures, which, in some cases, prevent us from grasping the collective character of medieval spirituality. As Marie-Rose Bonnet pointed out, Douceline "disappears" in the second part of the *Life*, melting into the group of beguines.[119] Thus, we can actually see her *Life* as a "Book of the house," which does not deny the hagiographic character of the text, for we can find similar examples in other cases, such as the later *Libro de la casa* of Juana de la Cruz.[120] This collective aspect is apparent

---

ly included the condition of remaining in the *estament*. See the aforementioned wills of Felipa Porcelleta, Cecilia de Volta, and Douce Vivaud.
117 Simons, "In Praise of Faithful Women," 335.
118 "Retento etiam et reservato [...] qua celebratur sollempnitas et commemoratio beate Dulsaline." Donation of Marguerite d'Alon: 1 April 1407, in Albanès, "Pièces justificatives," 296–97.
119 Bonnet, "Douceline et le Christ."
120 See, *Libro de la Casa y Monasterio de Nuestra Señora de la Cruz*, ed. María Luego Balbás and Fructuoso Atencia Requena. Catálogo de Santas Vivas, online: http://cata

once again in the *Life*, when Douceline appeared, accompanied by the whole first generation of beguines, to a woman whose children had all died as newborns. The figures in the apparition were "about thirteen," as if the beguines were Douceline's apostles, and the ailing woman was healed, not without first asking the saint: "who are you?"[121] A question that becomes a mantra that seems to haunt the *donnas* of Roubaud throughout all the narration.

Therefore, the *Life* does not seem to respond so much to problems of heresy or doctrinal heterodoxy, as to identity conflicts derived from the unclear status of beguines within the institutional system of the Church. This text, sponsored and used by the beguines themselves, was born from the desire to propose both an ideal model of conduct, that of Douceline, and an exemplary collective model, that of the community. Whereas the ideal model is not to be imitated, but revered, the second model must be brought into practice through a code of conduct, moral standards, liturgical practices, and a re-enactment of the memory of the foundress and the first generation of beguines. Although the construction of a communal identity model was already hinted at by some of the scholars who have studied the text of the *Life*, the present chapter proposes a new interpretation of the community production of this work and, especially, of the possible uses that the beguines made of it. Such aspects allow us to further explore the study of non-regulated communities, beyond the history of their great figures and the dichotomies that have traditionally characterised it.

---

logodesantasvivas.visionarias.es/index.php/Juana_de_la_Cruz#Vida_de_Juana_de_la_Cruz:_Libro_de_la_Casa_y_Monasterio_de_Nuestra_Se.C3.B1ora_de_la_Cruz.

121 Fol. 89v, 19 – 24: "Adoncs li fe/mena li demandet qui era. Ieu, sa dis li *Sancta*, sui Doucelina de Dinnha, beguina de Robaut e sorre de Fraire Hugo de Dinnha" [Then the woman asked her who she was. "I am Doucelina de Dinnha," said the saint, "a beguine from Robaut and sister of Friar Hugo de Dinnha"].

Courtney A. Krolikoski
Chapter 2
"No More Horrified by Them": Royal Holy Women and Lepers in Twelfth- and Thirteenth-Century Hagiography

In the mid-sixth century, the Frankish queen Radegund welcomed a group of lepers into the Abbey of the Holy Cross at Poitiers, the Benedictine female monastery she had founded in 552. Radegund

> had a table laid with dishes, spoons, little knives, cups and goblets, and wine and she went in herself secretly that none might see her. Seizing some of the leprous women in her embrace, her heart full of love, she kissed their faces. Then, while they were seated at the table, she washed their faces and hands with warm water and treated their sores with fresh unguents and fed each one. When they were leaving, she offered small gifts of gold and clothing. To this there was scarcely a single witness, but the attendant presumed to chide her softly: "Most holy lady, when you have embraced lepers, who will kiss you?" Pleasantly, she answered: "Really if you won't kiss me, it's no concern of mine."[1]

Although this episode from the *Vita Sanctae Radegundis* composed by Venantius Fortunatus dates from before the period explored by this study, it is an early example of the relationship between royal holy women and lepers in the Middle Ages. Radegund's intimate interaction with these lepers emphasized her piety, charity, and humility—elements that both Christian saints and royal women were expected to embody—while simultaneously placing the lepers in a position worthy of horror and disgust. Like Fortunatus, we are meant to ask, "doesn't this make one shudder, this thing she did so sweetly?"[2]

Note: I would like to thank Faith Wallis, Anna M. Peterson, Claire Phillips, Vivian Mills, Juliana Amorim Goskes, and Christine Morgan for their help with this paper, from its earliest drafts to what you now hold. My work is better because of this community of talented and generous women.

1 *Monumenta Germaniae Historica: Scriptores Rerum Merovingicarum*, ed. Bruno Krusch, vol. 2 (1888), 370–71; translated in: Venantius Fortunatus, "The Life of the Holy Radegund," in *Sainted Women of the Dark Ages*, ed. Jo Ann McNamara, John E. Halborg, and E. Gordon Whatley (Durham: Duke University Press, 1992), 70–86 at 78.
2 Venantius Fortunatus, "Life of the Holy," 78.

This chapter examines the intersection of female sanctity, royal status, and leprosy in twelfth- and thirteenth-century hagiographic texts to highlight how the use of exclusionary language regarding lepers helped to both legitimize royal female sanctity and mark lepers as worthy recipients of charity. Through an analysis of the *vitae* of Matilda of Scotland (d. 1118), St. Hedwig of Silesia (d. 1243), and St. Elizabeth of Hungary (d. 1231), I argue that the exclusionary and grotesque language used to describe lepers in twelfth- and thirteenth-century hagiographies helped to further shape the image of both lay royal holy women and leprosy sufferers in medieval society. While this type of language, as we will see, seems to cast the leper in the role of the unwanted and abhorred "other," the actions of saintly women towards them instead marked them as worthy of charitable donations and care. Numerous holy figures—male and female, royal and common, religious and lay—provided care, compassion, or alms to lepers throughout the Middle Ages, but it was lay royal holy women who formed an enduring bond with them, hallmarked by a particularly physical and female form of piety. And while hagiographies of non-royal women also include interactions with lepers, the intersection of religiosity and royal status provides a unique and intriguing avenue of analysis. Although the *vitae* of Matilda, Hedwig, and Elizabeth span a period of over one hundred years, they are still worth comparing as all three women occupied a similar position in their respective societies and cultures. Furthermore, the early twelfth to the early thirteenth century was a time of growing urbanization and secular education. A comparison of how both the holy women and their leprous contacts were enshrined in hagiography over this period of societal change provides a clearer and more nuanced understanding of how the disease was understood and treated in literature for a more diverse and changing type of audience.

It is important to emphasize that this chapter will not be looking at lepers as historical actors. Instead, within hagiographies, lepers must be understood as a *topos*—a literary convention used by hagiographers to emphasize the exceptional nature of their subjects. This distinction is crucial, as there has been considerable discussion in recent decades about the use and misuse of the term "leper" in both historical research and everyday language. Though I firmly believe that the use of "leper" in modern discourse often serves to perpetuate and prolong the stigma surrounding those suffering from Hansen's Disease, I hold that its use is merited, albeit with caution and care, in certain historical contexts. Recent work on leprosy in the Middle Ages overturned a longstanding myth surrounding lepers in medieval society. Prior to the 1980s, historiography defined lepers as the ultimate social outcasts, but thanks to the work of scholars like François-Olivier Touati, Luke Demaitre, and Carole Rawcliffe, we now understand that lepers were integrated into the social fabric, receiving charity and alms from lay and clerical sources, participating in markets and fairs, and regularly interacting with healthy members of society.³ It might, then, seem contrary to current understandings to look at lepers once again through exclusionary terms that have become taboo. Yet, the lepers within these hagiographies are indeed presented as "miserable," "contemptible," and "offensive"—to use some of the language we will encounter. We must remember, and indeed be vigilant in this, that the figure of the leper presented in these episodes was a means to demonstrate the extreme piety and heroic actions of the women who cared for them. Similarly, it is important to note that, while the term "leper" and its derivatives are controversial, their use in this paper is meant to reflect the language of the original sources.

Within hagiography we see a striking importance given to the moments when lay royal holy women engaged with lepers. Though many hagiographies for both sexes included lepers, providing intimate, physical care to the leprous poor became an outstanding mark of female piety. The language used in these narratives emphasizes the lepers' excessively distorted, disfigured, and disturbing appearance as well as their disabled bodies. This is then juxtaposed with the excessively pleasant appearance and the outstanding humility of the royal holy women. This contrast in appearance and composure is used to highlight what ultimately made them saintly—their real, lived charity and compassion for those whom their hagiographers often described as the most "miserable of persons."

Sanctity, Status, and Gender

Saints and holy figures are, in many ways, socially constructed. It does not matter if we speak of officially designated saints or of those venerated locally; as Caroline Walker Bynum has said, there is "no saint without an audience."⁴ For this reason, Anneke B. Mulder-Bakker's double typology of royal holy women—

---

3 See: Luke Demaitre, *Leprosy in Premodern Medicine: A Malady of the Whole Body* (Baltimore: The Johns Hopkins University Press, 2007); Carole Rawcliffe, *Leprosy in Medieval England* (Rochester: Boydell Press, 2006); François-Olivier Touati, *Maladie et société au moyen age: La lèpre, les lépreux et les léproseries dans la province ecclésiastique de Sens jusqu'au milieu du XIVe siècle* (Paris: De Boeck & Larcier, 1998).
4 Caroline Walker Bynum, "Foreword," in *Gendered Voices: Medieval Saints and Their Interpreters*, ed. Catherine M. Mooney (Philadelphia: University of Pennsylvania Press, 2016), ix–xii at ix.

namely, canonized and uncanonized—is useful as it recognizes this difference.⁵ Both groups of women were seen by their societies, and in many cases churchmen, as holy, yet only a small percentage gained official canonization. The hagiographic texts of many royal holy women have survived, in fact, largely due to learned churchmen who wanted to record their legacy. Therefore, if we "define sanctity on the basis of the religious experience of medieval communities" neither group can be omitted from our discussion.⁶ Together these two types of holy royal women represent the on-the-ground perspective of holiness of the societies from which they emerged. For this reason, whether or not they were ever canonized, I have elected to use the *vitae* of both types of royal holy women in this essay.

Royal women, especially queens, shared in royal power, wielding influence over both their country and their husbands. They were essential to the ability of a medieval government to function. They ruled as regents while their spouses were on military campaigns or during their son's minority, controlled magnates, and held sway over the decisions—both secular and spiritual—made by their husbands. A queen was responsible, alongside her king, for the *fortuna atque mores* of her people and it was her responsibility, as the nexus between the king and his subjects, to intercede on their behalf when the king's actions or demands might interfere with their well-being.⁷ Her proximity to the king made her a useful ally as well as a powerful individual. As such, she was often perceived as a maternal figure whose advice was sought after and whose words and actions carried political and social weight.⁸

Hagiographic texts were meant not only for presenting the sanctity of an individual, but also to serve as models of imitation for other Christians. Repeated encounters with these texts inspired the faithful to "emulate the example [of the saint] and become themselves exemplary Christians for other believers in their surroundings."⁹ Monastics, clerics, aspiring saints, and the common lay faithful

---

5 Anneke B. Mulder-Bekker, "Introduction," in *Sanctity and Motherhood: Essays on Holy Mothers in the Middle Ages*, ed. Anneke B. Mulder-Bekker (New York: Garland Publishing, Inc., 1995), 3–30 at 17.
6 Mulder-Bekker, "Introduction," 17.
7 Martin Homza, *Mulieres suadentes—Persuasive Women: Female Royal Saints in Medieval East Central and Eastern Europe*, trans. Martina Fedorová et al. (Leiden: Brill, 2017), 2; Theresa Earenfight, *Queenship in Medieval Europe* (New York: Palgrave Macmillan, 2013), 6.
8 Lois L. Huneycutt, "Intercession and the High-Medieval Queen: The Esther Topos," in *Power of the Weak: Studies on Medieval Women*, ed. Jennifer Carpenter and Sally-Beth MacLean (Urbana: University of Illinois Press, 1995), 126–46 at 126.
9 Anneke Mulder-Bakker, "General Introduction: Holy Laywomen and their Biographers in the Thirteenth Century," in *Living Saints of the Thirteenth Century: The Lives of Yvette, Anchoress of*

could all find inspiration within these *vitae*, which allowed them to strive for Christian perfection within themselves—either by entering into convents or abbeys in the Early Middle Ages, or through newfound experiences of lay devotion and sanctity in the Later Middle Ages. By the thirteenth century faith had become a communal affair. People gathered together to worship, most often at the local parish church, and discussed texts and lessons. Acting in many ways similarly to the physical relics of saints, *vitae* allowed the faithful to engage with the holiness of royal holy women. Indeed, as Kenneth Baxter Wolf notes, *vitae* offered "tangibly human representations of spiritual concepts that might have otherwise eluded" their audiences.[10] They provided women with role models—but only if their actions were not considered too extreme for the average woman.[11] However, the use of hagiography for examining the relationship between royal holy women and lepers is intriguing as we will never know whether any of the women included in this study ever actually met or interacted with a leper. As hagiographic texts were often created and authenticated in a complex process that sought to adhere to clerical tradition and also to spread the potential saint's virtuous reputation, the holy woman herself is often blurred or lost in the process.[12] Yet, as we will see, the hagiographers of the women included in this study included stories of intimate moments between holy women and lepers in their texts for a reason.

The royal holy women presented in this chapter behaved largely as royal women were expected to. Indeed, as most medieval holy women are known to us through texts written by male clerics, depictions of these women might tell us more about medieval men's notions of women and female sanctity than about the holy women themselves.[13] They were presented as obedient daughters, submissive and loyal wives, and good mothers who used their power and relationship with the king wisely and effectively. As prominent Christians they were seen to be living pious lives, performing works of charity, and encouraging their families to follow suit. Yet, while their memory and hagiographic traditions emphasize that they were obedient and holy figures, worthy of emulation and

---

Huy; Juliana of Cornillon, Author of the Corpus Christi Feast; and Margaret the Lame, Anchoress of Magdeburg, ed. Anneke Mulder-Bakker (Turnhout: Brepols, 2011), 1–42 at 42.
10 Kenneth Baxter Wolf, *The Life and Afterlife of St. Elizabeth of Hungary: Testimony from Her Canonization Hearings* (Oxford: Oxford University Press, 2011), 44.
11 Jane Tibbetts Schulenburg, *Forgetful of Their Sex: Female Sanctity and Society ca. 500–1100* (Chicago: The University of Chicago Press, 1998), 1–2.
12 Bynum, "Foreword," ix.
13 Catherine M. Mooney, "Voice, Gender, and the Portrayal of Sanctity," in *Gendered Voices*, ed. Mooney, 1–15 at 3.

adoration, we will see that these royal holy women were also "transgressors, rule-breakers, flouters of boundaries."[14] It is this contradictory combination of obedience and transgression that makes the interaction between royal holy women and lepers so important for both groups.

All the More Wonderful: Contrasting Images of Holiness and Leprosy

According to André Vauchez, one of the most obvious signs of a saint's virtue was their appearance.[15] Their body and their comportment were seen as a reflection of the soul, so a beautiful appearance, humble composure, or acts of extreme bodily asceticism might be read as a mark of inner virtue. Similarly, grand acts of charity or religious devotion were recorded to emphasize the place of a holy person within the Christian tradition. It is through such descriptions that a hagiographer manipulated the canon to present a specific image of their aspiring saint. We will see how these virtuous descriptions both provide the background and present a counterpoint to the description of the lepers. Moreover, I argue that such descriptions help to strengthen their royal subject's claim to sanctity. Lepers, with their overtly physical and highly visible manifestation of disease, often served as a generalized symbol of physical sickness. This became increasingly important after the turn of the twelfth century when the Church began to place new emphasis on the seven corporal works of mercy as an outlet for devotional expression.[16] Descriptions of the physical aspects of women's piety—including washing, kissing, and otherwise caring for lepers—became an integral representation of their holiness.[17]

Like her mother St. Margaret of Scotland (d. 1093), Matilda of Scotland (d. 1118), Queen of England, was known for her charity and compassion for the suffering of the sick and the poor. One episode from Matilda's life that was repeated by a number of chroniclers throughout the twelfth and thirteenth

---

14 Elizabeth Petroff, *Body and Soul: Essays on Medieval Women and Mysticism* (New York: Oxford University Press, 1994), 161.
15 André Vauchez, *Sainthood in the Later Middle Ages*, trans. Jean Birrell (Cambridge: Cambridge University Press, 1997), 435.
16 See: Luke Demaitre, *Leprosy in Premodern Medicine: A Malady of the Whole Body* (Baltimore: Johns Hopkins University Press, 2007), 82; Julie Orlemanski, "How to Kiss a Leper," *Postmedieval* 3/2 (2012): 142–57 at 150.
17 John Coakley, *Women, Men, and Spiritual Power: Female Saints and their Male Collaborators* (New York: Columbia University Press, 2006), 10.

centuries took place at an Easter court gathering in 1105.[18] In this story, Matilda invited a group of lepers into her chambers, where she washed their feet and kissed them. One of the earliest medieval versions of this story is included by Aelred of Rievaulx in the twelfth-century *Genealogia regum anglorum* and is told through the voice of Matilda's younger brother, David. He explains that he "went up to the queen's apartments when [he] was summoned by the queen herself. And, behold! The place was full of lepers, and there was the queen standing in the middle of them. And taking off a linen cloth she had wrapped around her waist, she put it into a water basin, and began to wash and dry their feet and to kiss them most devoutly while she was washing them with her hands."[19] When Matilda called for David to bear witness to her pious and charitable act, David objected by saying "My lady! What are you doing? Surely if the king knew about this he would never deign to kiss you with his lips after you had been so polluted by the putrefied feet of lepers!"[20] Matilda replies "under a smile" that "who does not know that the feet of the eternal king are to be preferred over the lips of a king who is going to die?"[21]

This episode in Matilda's life is a direct act of *imitatio Christi:* washing the feet of the lepers imitates Christ who humbled himself by washing the feet of his disciples.[22] Further, Christ was depicted multiple times in the New Testament as ministering to and healing lepers.[23] The combination of these two Christ-like acts makes Matilda's ministrations towards the lepers in her bedchamber that much more striking. By physically transcending the boundary between healthy and sick, her proximity to the leprous body becomes its own sort of suffering for her to accept and, ultimately, overcome. It is likely that Matilda's actions were also meant to imitate her parents' Lenten devotions, wherein King Malcom and Queen Margaret would daily feed and wash the feet of several hundred paupers.[24] Indeed, if Matilda had heard about these actions from the *Vita Margaretae* written in 1104, the imitation of her parents was likely a conscious decision. However, while her parents annually fulfilled their religious duty to feed and humble themselves before the poor, Matilda's actions with the lepers were far

---

18 Lois L. Huneycutt, *Matilda of Scotland: A Study in Medieval Queenship* (Rochester: Boydell Press, 2003), 104.
19 Aelred of Rievaulx, *De genealogia regum Anglorum* (PL CXCV, col. 736). Translated in: Huneycutt, *Matilda of Scotland*, 104.
20 Huneycutt, *Matilda of Scotland*, 104.
21 Huneycutt, *Matilda of Scotland*, 104.
22 Jn 13:1–17.
23 Mt 8:1–4; Mk 1:40–45; Lk 5:12–16; Lk 17:11–19.
24 Huneycutt, *Matilda of Scotland*, 105.

more striking. As Lois L. Huneycutt notes, based on the number of times this story was repeated, it "deeply impressed her contemporaries."[25] By bringing the lepers into her chambers Matilda both humbles herself and clearly and strikingly demonstrates her devotion. With a rebellious and overt disregard for the possible repercussions of her actions, Matilda transgresses the border between sick and healthy in order to be Christ-like and, indeed, engages in a moment of self-transformation.

Also interesting in this story of Matilda's interactions with the lepers in her chambers is that she takes off part of her own royal garments to tend to their wounds. As this episode was said to have taken place during an Easter gathering, it is likely that her dress was quite sumptuous, which was the norm for festive or ceremonial occasions for royalty.[26] This act of removing the linen cloth that had been wrapped around her waist to tend to their wounds and sores makes this act even more personal and intimate, further humbling her before the lepers in her care. While this episode was only one story in her life, Matilda showed enduring concern and support of lepers in her kingdom. For example, she founded a hospital dedicated to St. Giles that, until the Dissolution in 1539, provided care to fourteen lepers.[27] Further, she was a benefactor to the leprosarium at Chichester and potentially patronized the hospital of St. James in Westminster that housed and cared for "thirteen diseased women."[28] Matilda's piety and devotion could not be ignored and, as a result, was an example to both the royal court and the subjects of her kingdom.

The second woman we turn to in this study is Hedwig of Silesia (d. 1243), a duchess who was known for her humility and charity. Hedwig was related to much of the Eastern and Central European aristocracy and was a popular figure among both religious and lay communities. While her hagiography has garnered limited attention outside of Germany and Poland, Hedwig was one of Eastern Europe's most important medieval saints. When she was five years old, she was sent to live in a Cistercian abbey and remained there until 1203 when she married the Duke of Silesia, with whom she had six children. Despite her secular life and devotion to her family, Hedwig remained committed to a religious lifestyle. She is often described as engaging in physical acts of bodily mortification as a result of her piety. For example, Hedwig often would go walking barefoot in win-

---

25 Huneycutt, *Matilda of Scotland*, 105.
26 Julie Ann Smith, "Queen-Making and Queenship in Early Medieval England and Francia" (PhD diss., University of York, 1993), 202.
27 Huneycutt, *Matilda of Scotland*, 105.
28 Huneycutt, *Matilda of Scotland*, 106.

ter, an act that she tried to keep concealed from her husband.[29] Further, she was so devoted to penitence that she would kiss the places in the choir where the nuns placed their feet, dunk her head in the dirty water that they had used to wash themselves, and even washed her grandchildren in that same water.[30] As the duchess of Silesia, she supported Cistercian houses, Franciscan friars, and several other religious institutions. In 1203 she founded a women's hospital at Neumarkt which catered specifically to the care of lepers.[31] Hedwig is said to have paid special attention to this hospital, giving generous donations for its upkeep, and cared for the residents "as for her very own daughters."[32]

In one episode of Hedwig's life recorded by Caesarius of Heisterbach in 1225, we are told that Hedwig may have contracted leprosy herself.[33] While she is not explicitly named, the reference to *de ducissa leprosa que sanata est* (the duchess with leprosy who was healed) is understood to refer to Hedwig, as her husband Henry is also named; moreover, the scene takes place in Poland, where they resided.[34] In this episode, one night after being diagnosed with leprosy, Hedwig was advised by Christ in a dream to establish a church and dedicate it to the Virgin Mary and St. Bartholomew the Apostle.[35] Christ explained that, should she follow his command, she would be cured of the disease. When she woke, she told her husband about the dream and they immediately set out to have the

---

29 Dyan Elliott, *Spiritual Marriage: Sexual Abstinence in Medieval Wedlock* (Princeton: Princeton University Press, 1993), 232.
30 Elliott, *Spiritual Marriage*, 245.
31 Gábor Klaniczay, *Holy Rulers and Blessed Princesses. Dynastic Cults in Medieval Central Europe*, trans. Éva Pálmai (Cambridge: Cambridge University Press, 2000), 240.
32 "Unde leprosas quasdam feminas insimul habitantes prope oppidum, quod dicitu Novum forum, sic in suam receperat curam, ut eis aliquociens in ebdomada mitteret pecunias, carnes et ferinas ac in vestibus et aliis vite necessariis largiter providebat esidem procurabatque ipsas in ómnibus tanquam filias speciales." "Vita sanctae Hedvigis ducissae Silesiae (Vita maior, vita minor, genealogia)," in *Monumenta Poloniae Historica IV*, ed. Aleksander Szemkowicz (Warsaw: Państwowe Wydawnictwo Naukowe, 1960–61), 501–655 at 546–47.
33 "Dominus Deus, qui multus modis electos suos probat, ducis huius uxorem, feminam per omnia laudabilem, lepra percussit." "Die beiden ersten Bücher der Libri VIII miraculorum," in *Die Wundergeschichten des Caesarius von Heisterbach*, ed. Alfons Hilka, vol. 3 (Bonn: Hanstein, 1937), 1–222 at 84–85.
34 Klaniczay, *Holy Rulers*, 240.
35 "Pro cuius emundatione cum dux, utpote uxoris unice dilecte, tam per se quam per alios religiosos Domino incessanter supplicaret multasque elemosinas erogaret, Christus, qui 'multum est sisericors' (ps. 120,8), ostendere volens, quantum matrem, de qua carnem suscipere dignatus est, diligeret, leprosam ducissam quadam nocte his cerbis alloquitur dicens: 'Si oratorium edificaveris beate virgini Marie et sancto Bartholomeo apostolo, a lepra tua sanaberis'." "Die beiden ersten Bücher," 84.

church built and dedicated. Also in hopes of curing her from leprosy, Hedwig and her husband founded a Cistercian abbey in Trebnitz.[36] According to Caesarius, these two actions were appealing enough to God for Hedwig to be cured of leprosy and, ultimately, led the duchess to devote herself to an ascetic religious life.[37] This episode, though only preserved in one source, provides another example of the relationship between leprosy, royal holy women, and the mortification of the body. Becoming leprous could be read as the ultimate form of bodily mortification for a royal holy woman, as the physical devastation to the body could be a slow and sometimes agonizing process. However, some medieval understandings of leprosy might see the disease as a manifestation of sin. Indeed, thirteenth-century preachers like Jacques de Vitry sometimes used leprosy as a metaphor for sin in their sermons in order to emphasize the shame and revulsion one should associate with those who have sinned.[38] That Hedwig is only healed after providing a sizable charitable foundation to care for the leprous poor makes this episode in her life all the more complex. Either way it is read, it highlights the link between the disease, charity, and royal holy women and clearly conveys to its readers that charity is something essential to Christian life and, ultimately, benefits the giver.

One episode from the *Vita Maior Beate Hedwigis* written by Simon of Trebnitz in 1353 describes a time when she washed and dried the feet of a group of lepers and kissed their feet and hands. After she had finished bathing them, she provided the lepers with new, clean clothing.[39] Here we are to understand that Hedwig was imitating the actions of Christ, humbling herself by washing the gathered lepers and providing them with alms. Where other royal holy women kissed the hands and faces of the lepers they cared for, or, as we will

---

[36] "Quod cum duci indicasset, ille sicut homo fidelis, sperans non sine causa huiusmodi vocem ad eam fuisse delatam, sub omni festinatione ecclesiam edificari iussit, in qua et conventum sanctimonialium Cysterciensis ordinis instituit, et ut amplius Domino eorum devotion placeret, propriam filiam illic locavit, omnia eis de suis prediis ordinans necessaria." "Die beiden ersten Bücher," 84–85.

[37] "Et ecce! Mirum in modum, mox ut Deus ibidem laudari cepit, laudantis virtus infirmam sanavit et factum est Gaudium magnum in terra illa, omnibus Deum glorificantibus, qui tanta eis ostendere dignatus est mirabilia." "Die beiden ersten Bücher," 85.

[38] Jessalynn Bird, "Medicine for Body and Soul: Jacques de Vitry's Sermons to Hospitallers and their Charges," in *Religion and Medicine in the Middle Ages*, ed. Peter Biller and Joseph Ziegler (Woodbridge: York Medieval Press, 2001), 91–108 at 92; Touati, *Maladie et société au moyen age*, 105–8.

[39] "Lotis autem pedibus et extersis lintheo, deosculabatur humiliter non solum pedes sed et manus eorum ipsoque pauperes data elemosina studebat semper dimittere consolatos." "Vita sanctae Hedvigis," 522.

see later with Elizabeth, kissed them in the "most ulcerous and disgusting of places," Hedwig is identified as having specifically kissed their feet. Though seemingly slight, the location of her kiss is important, as she is presented as having humbled herself twofold—not only did she kiss their wounds, but she also physically lowered herself to kiss their feet. The latter is indeed an act of extreme humility, and perhaps even extreme bodily mortification, for a holy woman to perform. As with Matilda, this action closely echoes those of Christ tending to his disciples. However, where Matilda's hagiography only says that she kissed the lepers, Hedwig's indicates that she specifically kissed their hands and feet—the locations where the sores and ulcerations could not be hidden by the leper's clothing. This makes Hedwig's physical transgression of the boundaries between healthy and sick potentially even more jarring.

The last woman that we will turn to is Elizabeth of Hungary, born in 1207, daughter of King Andrew of Hungary and Hedwig's niece. Betrothed at the age of four to Ludwig IV, Landgrave of Thuringia, Elizabeth spent her childhood in his court at Wartburg Castle. By all extant accounts, Elizabeth loved her husband and her three children and was otherwise happy in her marriage. She was, however, disdainful of the life of privilege and found the clothing, food, and money to be at odds with her lifelong desire for a spiritual life. In her canonization process, Isentrud, one of Elizabeth's handmaids, noted that Elizabeth was always "religious, humble, very charitable, and extremely intent on her prayers."[40] Many events in her *vitae* highlight these qualities and show how, from her youth, she was deeply devoted to God. For example, on Rogation Days, as well as on other occasions, Elizabeth would follow the procession of the cross "barefoot and dressed in wool."[41] In 1226, Conrad of Marburg, preacher and inquisitor, was appointed to be Elizabeth's confessor and, in 1227, after Ludwig's death, he assumed absolute control over her life and actions. He was a notoriously controlling and harsh man, fanatically devoted to shaping Elizabeth's life into that of a saint—often prioritizing her spiritual goals above her physical health. He dictated the food she ate, the clothing she wore, and even required that she be beaten nightly by her handmaids as an act of penance during her prayers.[42]

---

[40] "Quod semper vidit eam etiam vivente marito religiosam, humilem et valde karitativam et multum oration intentam." *Dicta quatuor ancillarum*, in *Quellenstudien zur Geschichte der hl. Elisabeth: Landgräfin von Thüringen*, ed. Albert Huyskens (Marburg: N. G. Elwert'sche, 1908), 114. Translated in Wolf, *Life and Afterlife*, 193–216 at 195.
[41] "Cum alie matrone in gloria multa comitatus et vestibus preciosis ad ecclesiam venire consueverunt, ipsa in laneis, nudis pedibus." *Dicta*, 117. Translated in Wolf, *Life and Afterlife*, 198.
[42] Elliott, *Proving Woman: Female Spirituality and Inquisitional Culture in the Later Middle Ages* (Princeton: Princeton University Press 2004), 94.

In the *Summa vitae*, written in 1232 and sent to Pope Gregory IX, Conrad highlights how Elizabeth's devotion manifested through her body and actions. He notes that religious men and women, seeing her after her prayers, would remark that her face was "shining wonderfully as if rays of sun were emanating from her eyes."[43] He then notes that Elizabeth used her widow's inheritance to found a hospital for the "sick and the weak," after Conrad refused to let her beg like a pauper.[44] At the hospital, she "placed the most miserable and contemptible people at her table."[45] In another episode, Elizabeth cared for a leprous girl she had hidden in her quarters by "laying her down, washing her, and even removing her shoes."[46] Though Conrad reprimanded and punished her severely for these actions, Elizabeth "like a prudent woman ... called [his] attention to the life that she lived before, saying that it was necessary for her to cure one extreme with its opposite in just this manner."[47] Here we can see that she understood that embracing lepers would help her counteract her life of privilege in the court and, in turn, allow her to become more Christ-like.

In the *Libellus de dictis quatuor ancillarum*, a compilation of depositions taken from Elizabeth's closest companions before the papal commission in January 1235, we see how important lepers were to her religious life. In one story we learn that, even before Ludwig's death, on Maundy Thursday, Elizabeth "gathered many lepers, washed their feet and hands, and then, after prostrating herself most humbly at their feet, kissed them in the most ulcerous and disgusting places. Wherever she found lepers, she sat next to them, consoling them and exhorting them to patience—no more horrified by them than she was by healthy

---

43 "Quod raro vidi mulierem magis contemplativam, quia quedam et quidam religiosi ipsa a secreto orationis veniente frequentius viderunt faciem eius mirabiliter fulgentem et quasi soli radios ex oculis eius procedentes." Conrad of Marburg, *Summa vitae* (1232), in *Quellenstudien zur Geschichte der hl. Elisabeth: Landgräfin von Thüringen*, ed. Albert Huyskens (Marburg: N. G. Elwert'sche, 1908), 159. Translated in Wolf, *Life and Afterlife*, 91–95 at 94.
44 "Ibi in opido construxit quoddam hospitale, infirmos et debiles recolligens." Conrad, *Summa vitae*, 158. Translated in Wolf, *Life and Afterlife*, 93.
45 "Miserabiliores et magis despectos mense sue apposuit." Conrad, *Summa vitae*, 158. Translated in Wolf, *Life and Afterlife*, 93.
46 "Quo mortuo virginem sibi leprosam me nesciente assumpsit procurandam et in domo sua abscondit, omne humanitatis officium sibi inpendens, it aquod non solum ad cibandam et ei sternendum, lavandam, sed etiam ad discalciandam se humilivit, specialiter sue supplicans familie, ne super his offenderetur." Conrad, *Summa vitae*, 158–59. Translated in Wolf, *Life and Afterlife*, 94.
47 "Super quo dum eam reprehenderm, respondit se ab eis singularem recipere gratiam et humilitatem, et quasi mulier indubitanter prudentissima vitam suam anteactam michi recolligens dixit, sibi necesse esse taliter contraria contrariis curare." Conrad, *Summa vitae*, 158. Translated in Wolf, *Life and Afterlife*, 94.

people—and donating many things to them."⁴⁸ In another instance Elizabeth "took care of a certain woman who was fetid, leprous, and covered with sores and pus, whom anyone else would have abhorred even from a distance"; Elizabeth bathed her and "tied strips of cloth on her sores, nurturing her with treatments" and "trimmed the nails on her hands and feet and touched her ulcerous face with her hand."⁴⁹ These descriptions of the lepers that Elizabeth cared for emphasize their physical deformities and the expected negative reaction to their presence. We are told that "others" would have been repulsed by their appearance, not driven to provide them with charity or care. Yet, Elizabeth was "no more horrified by them than she was by healthy people," despite the fact that they were described by Conrad as being quite horrifying. This is a common phrase in the five major sources on her life and miracles, meant to contrast Elizabeth's pious reaction with the rest of lay society—even the readers of her hagiography. Therefore, when Elizabeth kissed them—these "horrifying" lepers—we must understand that this is meant to highlight her extreme humility and compassion. Again, we are reminded that the people that Elizabeth was most ardent about welcoming into her hospital and leprosarium were the people that society was most likely to turn from, "even from a distance." In this instance, the woman whom Elizabeth cared for was "fetid, leprous, and covered with sores and pus"— a description clearly meant to incite the audience's revulsion and, at the same time, to serve as a vaulting point to demonstrate Elizabeth's piousness.

The descriptions of these three women, coupled with their actions, legitimized these sorts of interactions both for royal holy women and other aspirant holy women. This is because within each of these *vitae* we are presented with a woman who is acting in a way not considered to be acceptable for their sex or status. These women cared for lepers in a way that was physical, personal, and intimate, and while this might have been seen as improper for a woman of their station, they were acts expected of a saint. Indeed, Christians in the High and Later Middle Ages "acted on the belief that intimate care for the physi-

---

48 "In quadam autem cena Domini collegit multos leprosos, eorum pedes lavans et manus, ipsa loca magis ulcerosa et horrenda deosculabatur humillime pedibus eorum provoluta. Et postea, ubicumque reperit leprosos, sedit iuxta eos consolans et exhortan seos ad patientiam, nec plus horrebat eos, quam sanos, multa eis largiens." *Dicta*, 120–21. Translated in Wolf, *Life and Afterlife*, 201.

49 "Dixit etiam, quod quandam fedidissimam leprosam et plenam ulceribus et sanie in hospital procuravit, quam quilibet a longe videre abhorrebat, quam beata Elizabet levabat, tegebat et ulcera eius pannis ligabot et medicamentis fovebat et se prosternens coram illa corrigias calciamentorum eius solvit et voluit tollere calcios illius, sed non permisit. Ungues manuum et pedum eius precidit et manu faciem eius ulcerosam tangebat et convenienter sanata fuit ad tempus." *Dicta*, 128–29. Translated in Wolf, *Life and Afterlife*, 201.

cally infirm" was an act of "religious devotion and an opportunity for spiritual transformation."⁵⁰ To touch, kiss, and personally care for lepers was a unique sign of their holiness.

Conclusion

Royal holy women in the Middle Ages formed an increasingly pronounced and enduring bond with lepers. Though interactions between lepers and saints were not uniquely female, we see a physical, personal, and intimate relationship develop between these two groups in the hagiography of royal holy women. Interestingly, while the hagiographers emphasized and, increasingly, exaggerated the disgust towards leprous bodies felt by those in attendance, Margaret, Hedwig, and Elizabeth never reacted negatively to the lepers in their care. In providing care for those in need, these women fulfilled the scriptural promise that whoever "shows charity to his neighbor applies that charity to God" (Matt 25:35). This physical contact between royal holy women and lepers was intended to elicit a visceral response from future readers or listeners. We are meant to be both horrified and impressed by their heroic actions.

In the years between 1130 and 1260 Western Europe went through what has come to be known by historians as the "Charitable Revolution." This period saw a sudden, widespread, and noticeable increase in charitable donations and pious works done by the laity.⁵¹ As a result, providing charity and care to the sick and the poor was understood to be a pious act that impacted the giver as much as the recipient, if not more. This was largely reflected in the devotional practices and habits of the time which, as we have seen, became more focused on the humanity of Christ and the potential for living in *imitatio Christi*.⁵² We can see this reflected in a sermon by Jacques de Vitry, where he emphasized the importance of personally providing care for the sick and afflicted by saying that "services of humility greatly provoke compassion and the recognition of your own weakness."⁵³ In his *Historia occidentalis*, Jacques also noted that hospital

---

50 Orlemanski, "How to Kiss a Leper," 143.
51 André Vauchez, "Assistance et charité en occident, XIIIe – XVe siècle," in *Domanda e consumi: Livelli e strutture nei secoli XIII – XVIII*, ed. Vera Bargagli Bagnoli (Florence: Olschki, 1978), 151–62 at 152–53.
52 Vauchez, "Assistance et charité," 152.
53 BNF, ms. lat. 3284, fol. 103v. Transcribed: Sharon Farmer, "The Leper in the Master Bedroom: Thinking Through a Thirteenth-Century Exemplum," in *Framing the Family: Narrative and Representation in the Medieval and Early Modern Periods*, ed. Rosalynn Voaden and Diane Wolfthal

workers were like martyrs because they "endured so great and so many impurities of the sick, and such intolerable stench, bringing violence upon themselves."[54]

With this in mind, we can interpret the intimate care provided to lepers by royal holy women in two ways. First, the hands-on care could be interpreted as an act of self-mortification. By putting their bodies in contact with the disfigured bodies of the lepers, these women "endured a metaphorical martyrdom."[55] Much in the same way that Elizabeth was beaten during her nightly prayers, interactions with leprous bodies were meant to be read as a way in which these women mortified their flesh for the sake of their souls. Second, the actions of these women towards the lepers in their care point to an act of holy rebellion. Margaret and Elizabeth directly disobey the wishes and commands of the men in their lives. Margaret ignores her brother's rebuke for her intimate care of lepers and Elizabeth routinely disobeys Conrad to care for lepers, even though she knows her actions will result in severe punishments. An important overlap in these hagiographies concerns their location. Matilda, Hedwig, and Elizabeth all engaged with lepers in private, intimate locations where they could minister to their wounds and needs alone with only one witness present to be able to verify and recount their actions. Instead of performing a public and visible act of charity, these royal women chose to act in private. The setting here is important because it was a sin to overtly display one's piety. However, it was also important for their actions and experiences to be passed on to their community and to future generations for the benefit of their souls.

The actions of these female saints towards lepers served as model of piety for lay women in the medieval world. Though most lay people could not afford to found a hospital or leprosarium, they could donate their money or service to these assistive institutions. Lepers were, according to the examined texts, worthy recipients of care and compassion. Particularly in the Later Middle Ages, when the practice of charity was focused on the quality and deserving nature of the recipients, lepers represented the ideal. While the episode within Hedwig's *vita* is brief, the descriptions of the lepers do tell us that they were visibly afflicted by their disease. Matilda's and Elizabeth's hagiographies provide us with longer, more graphic depictions of the lepers, contrasting their visible illness with the piousness of the royal holy women. Though the language used to describe the

---

(Tempe: Arizona Center for Medieval and Renaissance Studies, 2005), 79–100 at 94. Translated: Orlemanski, "How to Kiss a Leper," 150.
54 Jacques de Vitry, *The Historia Occidentalis of Jacques de Vitry*, ed. John Frederick, Hinnebusch, Spicilegium Friburgense 17 (Fribourg: University Press, 1972), 148.
55 Farmer, "The Leper in the Master Bedroom," 84.

lepers seems exclusionary and grotesque, it is through this contrast with the holy women who cared for them that they were, in fact, highlighted to medieval society as worthy of such care. They were not meant to be "abhorred from a distance." Instead, Matilda, Hedwig, and Elizabeth's *vitae* serve to convey an important message often repeated in these hagiographies, that people should not "be offended by such things."[56]

---

[56] "Specialiter sue supplicans familie, ne super his offenderetur." Conrad, *Summa vitae*, 158–59. Translated in Wolf, *Life and Afterlife*, 94.

Mireia Comas-Via
Chapter 3
Exclusion and Marginalization of Widows in Late Medieval Barcelona

Medieval widows were generally regarded as poor and even destitute both in the collective mind and in the formality of documents, and this description was, most often, unfortunately fitting.[1] The reason why medieval sources described

---

Note: The research supporting this chapter falls within the framework of the project "La sociedad urbana medieval frente al envejecimiento: prácticas de subsidio, acogida, asistencia y salud (Cataluña, s. XIII–XV) (PID2019-110823GA-I00)," funded by the Spanish Ministry of Economy and Competitiveness, and of the Consolidated Research Group "MAHPA. Research Group on Medieval Art, History, Paleography, and Archaeology" (2014 SGR 794), accredited by the Government of Catalonia.

[1] Female widowhood in the Middle Ages has long aroused the interest of academia, especially thanks to contributions from British, American, and French scholars. In the 1990s, several compilations of articles were published on this subject, including *Upon My Husband's Death: Widows in the Literature and Histories of Medieval Europe*, ed. Louise Mirrer (Ann Arbor: The University of Michigan Press, 1992); *Wife and Widow in Medieval England*, ed. Sue Sheridan Walker (Ann Arbor: The University of Michigan Press, 1993); *Veuves et veuvage dans le haut Moyen Age*, ed. Michel Parisse (Paris: Picard, 1993); *Widowhood in Medieval and Early Modern Europe*, ed. Sandra Cavallo and Lyndan Warner (London: Longman, 1999); *Constructions of Widowhood and Virginity in the Middle Ages*, ed. Cindy L. Carlson and Angela Jane Weisl (New York: St. Martin's Press, 1999). As for the historiographic production in Catalan and Spanish, there is a scarcity of specific studies devoted to medieval female widowhood, with remarkable exceptions in the works of Teresa Vinyoles, María del Carmen García Herrero, María Isabel Pérez de Tudela, and the Broida Team: Teresa Vinyoles Vidal, "Dones protagonistes de relacions i convivències en el pas de l'Edat Mitjana al Renaixement," *Revista Pedralbes* 23 (2003): 317–36; Teresa Vinyoles Vidal, *Història de les dones a la Catalunya medieval* (Lleida-Vic: Pagès-Eumo, 2005); María del Carmen García Herrero, "Viudedad foral y viudas aragonesas a finales de la Edad Media," *Hispania: Revista española de historia* 53 (1993): 431–50; María del Carmen García Herrero, *Las mujeres en Zaragoza en el siglo XV*, 2nd ed. (Zaragoza: Prensas Universitarias de Zaragoza, 2006); María Isabel Pérez de Tudela y Velasco, "La condición de la viuda en el Medievo castellano-leonés," in *Las mujeres en las ciudades medievales: Actas de las III Jornadas de investigación interdisciplinaria*, ed. Cristina Segura Graiño (Madrid: Universidad Autónoma de Madrid, 1984), 87–101; María Isabel Pérez de Tudela y Velasco, "Ancianidad, viudedad ... El hombre medieval en su edad postrera," in *La familia en la Edad Media: XI Semana de Estudios Medievales, Nájera, del 31 de julio al 4 de agosto de 2000*, ed. José Ignacio de la Iglesia Duarte (Logroño: Instituto de Estudios Riojanos, 2001), 285–316; Broida Team, "La viudez ¿triste o feliz estado? (Las últimas voluntades de los barceloneses en torno al 1400)," in *Las mujeres en las ciudades medi-*

widows as weak individuals who needed help is that they lived without the apparent protection of a man. Not having a husband undoubtedly stressed the alterity of widows, even among other women. In the eyes of their contemporaries, this situation made them more vulnerable not only to sexual assault, but also to economic marginalization and social exclusion.[2] However, being a widow involved a wide variety of personal situations. Widowhood indeed brought about an important transformation in the lives of medieval women, insofar as the death of their husband resulted in a change in their social standing. In addition to what the law stipulated regarding widowhood, documents[3] show that the daily life of widows was full of struggles, including economic, legal, judicial, and social difficulties.[4] Some widows benefitted from a peaceful widowhood and were able to take charge of their lives by running their own businesses or

---

evales, ed. Cristina Segura Graíño (Madrid: Universidad Autónoma de Madrid, 1984), 27–41. I have also made some contributions to this topic, such as Mireia Comas-Via, *Entre la solitud i la llibertat: Vídues barcelonines a finals de l'Edat Mitjana* (Roma: Viella, 2015); Mireia Comas-Via, "Widowhood and Economic Difficulties in Medieval Barcelona," *Historical Reflections/Réflexions Historiques* 43/1 (2017): 93–103; Mireia Comas-Via, "Looking for a Way to Survive: Community and Institutional Assistance to Widows in Medieval Barcelona," in *Women and Community in Medieval and Early Modern Iberia*, ed. Michelle Armstrong-Partida, Alexandra Guerson, and Dana Wessell Lightfoot (Lincoln: University of Nebraska Press, 2020), 177–94.

2 The medieval imaginary conveyed, through literature, several widow stereotypes, namely, the impoverished widow, the pious widow, the well-to-do and independent widow, the easily comforted widow, and the treacherous and evil widow. Real life, however, offered even greater variety, as widowhood could entail suffering and isolation, but also power, independence, remarriage and becoming a positive role model for other women just as easily as a negative stereotype. In fact, widowhood often resulted from a combination of all these features and many others (Comas-Via, *Entre la solitud*, 56–76).

3 This study is mainly based on municipal documentation kept in the Historical Archive of the City of Barcelona (hereinafter AHCB), procedural documentation, and notarial sources, mostly from the Historical Archive of Protocols of Barcelona (hereinafter AHPB).

4 Clearly, not all widows had the same problems, as their initial social standings differed greatly. In a notarial injunction dated 13 August 1489, the widow Francina Morella complained about damages caused by the fact that Guillem Morató, innkeeper at the *Hostal del Bou* in Barcelona, had not paid two of the nine *lliures* (pounds) he owed for the rent of this establishment. On several occasions, the widow had claimed payment of the amounts due, but the innkeeper had ignored her. Therefore, Francina Morella declared herself to be a "miserable" widow because of these unsettled payments. Probably, this declaration was a reflection of Francina's distressing situation, but in other cases the use of similar expressions was a strategy or rhetorical device used in court (AHPB, Lluís Jorba Major, 238/15, loose document, 1489 August 13). On the discursive construction of the widow as a "poor and miserable person," see Susan McDonough, "Impoverished Mothers and Poor Widows: Negotiating Images of Poverty in Marseille's Courts," *Journal of Medieval History* 34 (2008): 64–78.

managing their late husband's estate,[5] but despite the differences between widows from different social backgrounds, it is clear that most of them did not have sufficient means to maintain their social and economic position after being widowed.[6] Widowhood impoverished women,[7] and for some of them it could become synonymous with destitution and even social exclusion.

The aim of this chapter is to analyze the circumstances that led to the marginalization and social exclusion of many widows in medieval Barcelona—that is, the reasons that led them to live between poverty and destitution, often on the margins of society and forced to break social norms in order to find a place for themselves and survive.[8] To this end, I will focus on the poorest widows of the city of Barcelona in the last medieval centuries, but also on those who, because of their moral transgressions and illicit sexual behaviour, were denied the protection of the community. Therefore, first of all, I shall discuss the causes of impoverishment linked to female widowhood and the lack of economic resources of these women. In this sense, it is essential to consider their legal status and the difficulties that many of them had in retrieving their dowry. Secondly, I will examine the presence of widows in the urban framework of Barcelona to define their degree of poverty. Finally, I will give some examples of widows who were victims of marginalization and social exclusion.

---

5 By way of example, see the biographies of several women whose widowhoods were not too financially challenging in Carme Batlle, "Noticias sobre la mujer catalana en el mundo de los negocios (siglo XIII)," in *El trabajo de las mujeres en la Edad Media Hispana*, ed. Cristina Segura Graíño and Ángela Muñoz Fernández (Madrid: Almudayna, 1988), 201–21; Eulàlia De Ahumada, *Hipòlita Roís de Liori (ca. 1479–1546)* (Madrid: Ediciones del Orto, 2005); Teresa Vinyoles Vidal, "L'amor i la mort al segle XIV: Cartes de dones," *Miscel·lània de Textos Medievals* 8 (1996): 111–98; Teresa Vinyoles Vidal, "La dama que va fer pintar el retaule de les santes Clara i Caterina de la catedral de Barcelona," in *Capitula facta et firmata: Inquietuds artístiques en el quatrecents*, ed. Maria Rosa Terés (Valls: Cossetània, 2011), 263–79.
6 For an in-depth analysis of the struggles of widows in late medieval Barcelona, see Comas-Via, "Widowhood and Economic Difficulties."
7 On the connection between gender and poverty, see also Sharon Farmer, *Surviving Poverty in Medieval Paris: Gender, Ideology and the Daily Lives of the Poor* (Ithaca and London: Cornell University Press, 2005), especially 136–64, and Luís Martínez García, "Pobres, pobreza y asistencia en la edad media hispana: Balance y perspectivas," *Medievalismo* 18 (2008): 67–107 at 73.
8 Coral Cuadrada, "Marginalidad y otredad en Cataluña (siglos XIV–XVI)," *En la España Medieval* 38 (2015): 57–97 at 60. On this same topic, see also Ricardo Córdoba de la Llave, "Los caminos de la exclusión medieval: Pecado, delito y represión. La península Ibérica (ss. XIII y XVI)," in *Los caminos de la exclusión en la sociedad medieval: Pecado, delito y represión*, ed. Esther López Ojeda (Logroño: Instituto de Estudios Riojanos, 2012), 13–50 at 21.

The Legal Situation: Difficulties in Recovering the Dowry

A few words must be said about the dowry and the difficulties that many widows had in recovering it after their husband's death.[9] The dowry had to be returned to the widow after a year of mourning, that is, one year after she was widowed.[10] However, this restitution was not always immediate or complete, for not all heirs could or wanted to divest themselves of part of the family estate in order to honour the widow's rights. As a result, many widows were placed in a difficult economic situation.

As the *ius commune* gradually spread, the dowry became a compulsory contribution the bride made to help bear the burdens of the marriage. The husband was in charge of the administration of the dowry during the marriage and also benefitted from its fruits and, therefore, could freely use it however he saw fit, as long as it was returned upon the event of his death. The fact that the widow could recover a certain amount of money after her husband's death, according to the provisions agreed upon in the marriage contract, meant that the dowry was generally considered as widowhood insurance. However, its restitution did not imply either an increase or an improvement, as the widow only received, at best, what she had contributed at the time of the marriage, even though its value may have decreased over time. Moreover, if the bride contributed clothes to the marriage, these were considered as amortized after ten years, as was the case with furniture after twenty-five years. Therefore, given the decrease in the value of the dowry and the difficulties in recovering it, in general, it did not provide sufficient economic support for all widows. Nevertheless, its significance lay not only in its basic economic value but also in the legal figure of the *tenuta*, which granted the widow rights over her husband's estate.[11] In this way, the

---

[9] These difficulties were not exclusive to Barcelona's widows but rather commonplace across medieval Europe. See, for example, the studies carried out for the cities of Florence and Venice by Isabelle Chabot and Stanley Chojnaki, respectively: Isabelle Chabot, *La Dette des familles: Femmes, lignage et patrimoine à Florence aux XIVe siècle* (Rome: École Française de Rome, 2011), 135–67; Stanley Chojacki, *Women and Men in Renaissance Venice: Twelve Essays on Patrician Society* (Baltimore: Johns Hopkins University Press, 2000), 95–111.

[10] *Recognoverunt proceres: Versión medieval catalana del privilegio así llamado* (Barcelona: Universitat de Barcelona, 1927), 4–6.

[11] The origin of the *tenuta* can be traced back to the law promulgated by King Pere IV of Aragon at the *Corts* of Perpignan in 1351, known as "Hac nostra": *Constitucions y altres drets de Catalunya compilats en virtut del capítol de cort LXXXII de las corts per la S. C. y R. Majestat del rey Don*

widow could live as a usufructuary until her dowry was fully returned, that is, she could live on her late husband's property until she recovered the amounts due. In contrast, failure to restore the dowry resulted in a large number of injunctions and lawsuits brought by widows who claimed their rights. In general, most problems arose when the husband's heirs were not the widow's children but rather stepchildren, siblings, or in-laws who thought that returning the dowry could result in the dismemberment of the inheritance they had received. Many of them tried to take advantage of the widow's vulnerability as a woman who was on her own—that is, without a man. However, it is clear that widows were aware of their rights and did not hesitate to use all the means at their disposal to defend them.[12]

Thus, a widow relied on her dowry—if it was ever returned—but also on whether her husband had made provisions in his will for her to become usufructuary of his property, which was not always the case. At any rate, neither dowry nor bequests always provided sufficient financial support to ensure a proper living, hence the economic and personal situation of each widow also depended on the wedding and household "paraphernalia" she might have,[13] as well as on her productive or working capacity.

Widows in the Urban Environment

We will focus on Barcelona's *Quarter de la Mar* (literally, Sea Quarter) to see how the widow population evolved in this part of the city, where most household heads were involved in activities related to the sea, textile production, and clothing. In fact, Santa Maria del Mar is the most representative of all quarters and the one that allows for the most generalizations. This is because, on the one hand, 30 percent of the inhabitants of the city lived there and, on the other, it was densely populated, as it only accounted for 13 percent of the total city area.[14] I have ana-

---

Philip IV. nostre Senyor celebradas en la ciutat de Barcelona any M. DCCII, ed. Josep Maria Pons i Guri, vol. 1 (Barcelona: Generalitat de Catalunya, 1995), Llib. 5, Tit. 3, Cons. 1.
12 On the difficulties of recovering the dowry and lawsuits brought by widows, see Comas-Via, *Entre la solitud*, 106–16.
13 Paraphernalia were the separate property of the wife, acquired before or during the marriage, and excluding her dowry.
14 Alberto García Espuche and Manuel Guàrdia Bassols, "La consolidació d'una estructura urbana, 1300–1516," in *Història de Barcelona, Vol. 3: La ciutat consolidada (segles XIV i XV)*, ed. Jaume Sobrequés i Callicó (Barcelona: Enciclopèdia Catalana-Ajuntament de Barcelona, 1992), 35–72 at 47, 71.

lyzed the *fogatjaments* or hearth tax rolls of 1363[15] and 1378[16] and two militia rolls, those of 1389[17] and 1399.[18] Although neither *fogatjaments* nor militia rolls are demographic records, but rather fiscal documents, the information they provide allows us to restore an image of the socio-spatial structure of the city's southeastern quadrant, which can then be transferred to the rest of medieval Barcelona.[19]

At first glance, the number of widows that appear in these sources is considerable, as they account for about 10 percent of the total hearths (Table 1).[20] In fact, most of the hearths listed as headed by women were headed by a widow, 60 percent on average according to the data from the four years with available documentation (Table 2).

Table 1: Percentage of hearths headed by widows over total number of hearths

Year	Hearths headed by widows (%)
1363	9.8
1378	13.6
1389	6.2
1399	10.0
Average	9.9

---

15 This analysis is based on Manuel Riu i Riu, "El barri barceloní de Santa Maria del Mar l'any 1363," *Acta historica et archaeologica mediaevalia* 26 (2005): 563–86.
16 AHCB, 1B. Consell de Cent, XIX. Fogatges, 2 (1378).
17 AHCB, 1B. Consell de Cent, XIX. Fogatges, 5 (1389).
18 AHCB, 1B. Consell de Cent, XIX. Fogatges, 6 (1399).
19 The figures offered by David Herlihy and Christiane Klapisch-Zuber for the city of Florence in relation to households made up of widows, orphans, and destitute people are not too far removed from the situation of medieval Barcelona. Thus, in the 1372 *catasto* this group represented 10.7% of the population, increasing to 11.5% in 1378. Data are quite similar in fifteenth-century hearth tax rolls: in 1427 the percentage of widows, orphans, and destitute people was 11.7%, and in 1470 it was 12.8%. David Herlihy and Christiane Klapisch-Zuber, *Les Toscans et leurs familles: Un étude du catasto florentin de 1427* (Paris: CNRS, 1978), 213.
20 It should be noted that the actual number of widows was likely to be higher than what these documents suggest. This is because women who were not named in relation to a man or clearly labelled as widows were probably not all single, as some were nicknamed after a man's name, and therefore could well be mistresses, married women, or widows. However, the percentages above only take into account widows that were labelled as such. Manuel Riu takes the same approach and believes that, even when widowhood is not specifically recorded, it is hard to believe that there were so many husbands who were away on business or for other reasons. Riu, "El barri barceloní," 571.

Table 2: Percentage of hearths headed by widows over total number of female-headed hearths

Year	Hearths headed by widows over total female-headed households (%)
1363	43.30
1378	70.10
1389	52.40
1399	77.60
Average	60.85

The image of the city provided by this type of documentation highlights another unfortunate circumstance: in accordance with the regulations regarding the year of mourning and usufruct, widows who lived alone were expelled from the marital house once this time had passed. That is, after having recovered their dowry, they were forced to leave their homes and needed to seek new housing. The solution was usually to rent a smaller house, a room or even a store or a workshop. Location, size, and comfort would naturally depend on the economic resources of each widow.

Another detail that we can draw from hearth tax and militia rolls is that there was a greater concentration of widows in certain blocks. This leads to the conclusion that these were dwellings that had been divided into apartments. In this way, independent lodgings were created within the same building that could be rented to several people who would live separately from the rest of the occupants. Thus, the space was optimized as much as possible in order to obtain a greater number of accommodations.[21] This was the case, for instance, with the property of Caterina, widow of Pere Vidal, house builder: she lived in one section of the building and rented the rest.[22] Undoubtedly, this system of compartmentalization of buildings entailed a very dense occupation, which is what we actually find in the *Quarter de la Mar*. Widows used to inhabit the most peripheral sectors of this neighbourhood, especially around the *Rec Com-*

---

21 Simone Roux, "L'Habitat urbain au Moyen Âge: Le quartier de l'Université de Paris," *Annales: Économies, sociétés, civilisations* 24 (1969): 1196–1219 at 1210–11.
22 AHPB, Joan Eiximenis, 29/59, fols. 100r–102r, 1394 May 5–1396 April 29. Another example is provided by Manuel Riu regarding a remarried woman who converted a house that had belonged to her father into seven separate lodgings. The woman made a downpayment of 350 *lliures* for the works, and earned an annual income of 252 *lliures*. Manuel Riu i Riu, "La financiación de la vivienda, propiedades horizontales y pisos de alquiler en la Barcelona del siglo XIV," *En la España medieval: La ciudad hispánica durante los siglos XIII al XVI (II)* 7 (1985): 1397–1406 at 1399–1401.

tal, the poorest area. However, in the central areas, which could be considered richer, we also locate a significant number of widows, both poor and relatively better off. Poorer widows in these central streets of the quarter lived in small houses, stores, or rooms that were mostly substandard housing, that is, spaces converted into homes with poor living conditions. Thus, extreme economic realities coexisted in the same place, from the greatest wealth to the most absolute poverty.[23]

It is important to bear in mind that this was a context of cyclical epidemics and crises.[24] The successive outbreaks led to a decrease in the population of the city, which resulted in many houses and workshops left unoccupied.[25] In 1391, the assault on the *Call*, the Jewish quarter, caused its destruction and abandonment and, later on, the disappearance of Barcelona's *aljama*.[26] This circumstance also contributed to the chaotic urban development of Barcelona during the decades following the Black Death of 1348. Documents show how some widows ended up living—or barely surviving—in abandoned stores and workshops. The lack of an owner made these spaces an interesting option for people with fewer resources.[27] A representative example of this situation can be found in the trial published a few years ago by Jaume Riera in his book *El cavaller i l'alcavota*.[28] Raimundeta, widow of the tanner Joan Nogués and grandmother of Úrsula, one of the girls raped by the knight Arnau Albertí, lived in the workshop underneath Albertí's house since Candlemas 1410. She testified to this when she was interrogated during the trial against the knight in the autumn of that same year. Another example is that of a woman named Rosa who, in an entry in the *Llibre del Bací dels pobres vergonyants* of the parish of Santa Maria del Pi in Barcelona in 1447, claimed to have lived in a store owned by Sança Ximenis

---

23 García and Guàrdia, "La consolidació d'una estructura," 48, 58.
24 Antoni Furió, "La corona de Aragón en la crisis del siglo XIV," in *La Corona de Aragón: Siglos XII–XVIII*, ed. Ernest Belenguer Cebrià and Felipe Vicente Garín Llombart (Valencia: Generalitat Valenciana-Ministerio de Cultura, 2006), 79–100.
25 For instance, documents record that the expansion of the cemetery of Santa Maria del Mar, which had become too small due to the numerous fatalities, was made possible by the fact that the houses around the church had been left uninhabited following the death of their owners. Jordi Günzberg i Moll, *Vida quotidiana a la ciutat de Barcelona durant la pesta negra (1348)* (Barcelona: Rafael Dalmau, 2002), 9.
26 An *aljama* was a self-governing community of Jews living in a city under Christian rule.
27 Riu, "La financiación de la vivienda," 1399.
28 Jaume Riera i Sans, *El Cavaller i l'alcavota: Un procés medieval* (Barcelona: Club Editor, 1973), 144–48.

de Cabrera, lady of Novalles.²⁹ The cases mentioned so far refer to elderly widows who were on their own,³⁰ but dwelling in places not intended for housing was not exclusive to them, as documents also point to other women who lived by themselves, such as freed and foreign women who lived in squalor in these marginal spaces. These were, in short, extremely poor women with very few resources.

Another option available to widows was to share a house or room, which was more affordable than maintaining and paying for a single-person dwelling.³¹ The 1374 trial against the weaver Guillem Rifà provides an example of widows sharing a house. This was a group who had met in Sassari, on the island of Sardinia, where they had lived for a while before emigrating to Barcelona. Caterina, Pere Garraf's widow, lived with Clara, widow of Guillem Comes, a house builder, and her daughter Blanca, who was raped by Guillem Rifà. Also living with them were Margarida, widow of the tailor Bartomeu Artigues, and Agnès, widow of Francesc Plaensa, Clara's cousin. They all lived together in a house that was next to Guillem Rifà's home, but later they moved to Petritxol Street and then to En Roset's Street, near the parish of Santa Maria del Pi, as they testified in the inquiry against the weaver.³²

---

29 See Jordina Camarasa, "Les dones en la documentació del Bací dels Pobres Vergonyants de la Parròquia de Santa Maria del Pi de Barcelona: Estudi i edició dels llibres dels anys 1441 i 1447" (Master's thesis, Universitat de Barcelona, 2016), 44: "Ítem a la dona na Rosa, stà en la botiga de la senyora de Novales, I sou VI." The *Bací dels Pobres Vergonyants*, which can be roughly translated as "collection plate for the deserving poor," was a charitable institution that relied on the parishes of Barcelona, although it was not exclusive to this city.
30 For a discussion on the connection between old age and widowhood for men and women, see Pérez de Tudela y Velasco, "Ancianidad, viudedad ...," 285–316.
31 Sharon Farmer analyzed the relationships between poor women who were on their own and emigrated to Paris on the basis of the life and miracles of Saint Louis. She gathers numerous examples of women, single or widowed, sharing rooms and even beds: Sharon Farmer, "Down and Out and Female in Thirteenth-Century Paris," *The American Historical Review* 103/2 (1998): 345–72.
32 ACA, Processos de la Reial Audiència, 1374. Document cited by Teresa Vinyoles Vidal and Mireia Comas Via, "Relacions de gènere en el marc de l'expansio catalano-aragonesa a Sardenya," in *XVIII Congrés d'Història de la Corona d'Aragó (València, 2004)*, vol. 2 (Valencia: Universitat de València-Fundació Jaume II el Just, 2005), 1755–65.

Living Under the Threat of Poverty

A significant number of women were described as poor or destitute in *fogatjaments* and militia rolls.[33] The hearths belonging to independent women, among whom there were also some widows, were the poorest. Specifically, almost a quarter of the widows identified as heads of households in the analyzed documents were poor.[34] This percentage could actually be somewhat higher, considering that these types of documents, either fiscal or military in nature, did not list the entire population, and excluded both those who were exempt from paying taxes because they belonged to privileged social groups, and those who were too poor to pay them.

The hearth tax roll of 1363 specifies the tax levied on each hearth according to its economic capacity, which allows us to determine the wealth of the widows listed in this source. Thus, the widows declared exempt from paying this tax were twenty-two (that is, 11.1 percent of the total number of widows) and represented 18 percent of the fiscal poor. Only in two cases is it indicated that these widows lived with their children.[35] Those with a medium to low economic level, and thus close to the poverty threshold, were 163 (81.9 percent of the total).[36] In contrast, only fourteen (7 percent of all widows) were considered to be rich. In fact, some of these wealthier widows were linked to the richest hearths in the entire *Quarter de la Mar*. Among these we find, for example, the widow of Jaume Solà, who had

---

33 The percentage of poor households listed in the 1363 *fogatjament* of Barcelona was 5.8%, while in 1378 poor households were 12.5% of the total; see Riu, "El barri barceloní," 566; AHCB, 1B. Consell de Cent, XIX. Fogatges, 2 (1378).
34 The study of fiscal documentation in places such as Paris, Lyon, Burgundy, and Florence shows how women who were heads of households were widely represented among the fiscal poor: Farmer, "Down and Out," 353–54. In the case of fifteenth-century Lyon, according to Nicole Gonthier's study, widows represented 5 percent of the fiscal poor of the city: Nicole Gonthier, *Lyon et ses pauvres au Moyen Âge (1350–1500)* (Lyon: L'Hermès, 1978), 57.
35 In the 1427 *catasto* of Florence, studied by Isabelle Chabot, some widows, who presented themselves as too poor to pay taxes, claimed to live on alms or to live for free in lodgings provided by friends and fellow widows: Isabelle Chabot, "Widowhood and Poverty in Late Medieval Florence," *Continuity and Change* 3 (1988): 291–311 at 304.
36 The minimum tax charged was six *diners* per month, that is, six *sous* per year: Riu, "El barri barceloní," 566. The Catalan coinage was based on the Carolingian *sou*, equivalent to twelve *diners* (pence) and one-twentieth of one *lliura* (pound). The city of Barcelona minted its own currency.

to pay an annual tax of thirty *lliures*, and the widows of Jaume Llull, Guillem Ferrer, and Bernardó Serra, who had to pay fifteen *lliures* per year each.[37]

In view of this data, it is worth asking what factors influenced the socioeconomic situation of widows. First, it is necessary to consider the social and economic group to which they belonged while their husbands were alive. Not all women faced widowhood from the same starting point, as there were widows who were very well placed within social structures. This circumstance was due to the fact that they had a considerable dowry, in addition to paraphernalia and the generosity of their husbands at the time of their respective deaths (usufruct, legacies, and so on). Women's economic independence could be supported by these resources in addition to their own capacity for work.

However, the dowry system could turn out to be insufficient. That is, even if the widow was able to retrieve her entire dowry—which was not always the case because husbands could, and sometimes did, spend it—this was not always enough to ensure her subsistence. It should be borne in mind that among *menestrals* (craftsmen or artisans) and the members of the *poble menut* (lower or common people), dowries were not very large. Thus, among low-skill artisans, dowries ranged between forty and eighty *lliures*, and among the lower classes, made up mainly of peasants and freedmen, between twenty and twenty-five *lliures*.[38] In addition, currency fluctuations often affected the value of the dowry, and other times the dowry consisted of clothing and movables, which, as indicated above, lost their value after some time. Furthermore, the restitution of the dowry did not imply any increase or improvement, for the woman was only owed what she had contributed at the time of her marriage. For all these reasons, although the dowry is often presented as widowhood insurance, this was not always the case.

Another factor determining the economic well-being of widows was the possibility of continuing the family business or of having a trade of their own to support themselves. However, many guild statutes prohibited this practice. With the rise of guild powers, women were excluded from certain professions to avoid competition in times of crisis. In the case of wool weavers, for example, if one of their members died without a male heir, the business had to be closed down. The most surprising fact is that the argument used to ban the incorpora-

---

[37] Manuel Riu considers that the wealthiest families of the *Quarter de la Mar* were those who had to pay a tax of more than ten *sous* per month, that is, more than six *lliures* per year. The household heads who had to meet these amounts in 1363 were 239 out of a total of 2,034 hearths. Riu, "El barri barceloní," 569–70.

[38] Teresa Vinyoles Vidal, *Les barcelonines a les darreries de l'Edat Mitjana (1370–1410)* (Barcelona: Fundació Salvador Vives Casajuana, 1976), 85.

tion of women into this sector was the alleged dishonour and infamy they could bring about:[39]

> Per esquivar deshonestedats e infàmia, que alcuna dona vídua qui sia estada muller de teixidor, o d'altra persona, estant vídua, no puxa ne gos tenir obrador del dit ofici de teixidor, si doncs no ha fill mascle d'edat de XII anys o més qui vulla ésser teixidor.[40]

This prohibition was carried out without any hesitation. In 1486, the leaders of the wool weavers' guild went to the house of a deceased guild member the day after his burial and tore the looms from the wall to prevent his widow from weaving. Thanks to the intervention of the City Council of Barcelona, the widow was given three months to continue her trade as a weaver while she found another way to make a living.[41] However, it must be said that having a paid job was not always enough to ensure a decent living. *Fogatjaments* show women professionals who were labelled as poor,[42] as do the records of the *Bací dels pobres vergonyants*,[43] which evinces that having a profession did not preclude them from falling into poverty.

Moreover, the existence of sons and daughters of the marriage and the age of these children at the time of the father's death must be taken into account, as these also affected the economic situation of widows. Furthermore, if illness hindered the widow's ability to work, there was little hope of escaping poverty in the absence of other resources. Elderly widows who did not have access to any source of income because they were too old to work were in this same situation. When illness and the deterioration of the body that comes with old age prevented them from working, they had to turn to the assistance and protection of their families or charitable institutions, such as the Hospital de la Santa Creu or the poor boxes of the parishes of Barcelona, and some were left helpless waiting

---

[39] Wool weavers were not the only ones to resort to these arguments. The statutes of the guild of tailors also referred to honour and reverence to God in order to prevent tailors' wives from becoming members of the guild: Próspero de Bofarull, *Procesos de las Cortes de Cataluña, Aragón y Valencia*, Colección de documentos inéditos de la Corona de Aragón, 1 (Barcelona: Establecimiento litográfico y tipográfico de José Eusebio Montfort, 1847), 297.

[40] [To avoid dishonesty and infamy, that no widow of a weaver, or of any other man, may or dare run a weaver's workshop as a widow, unless she has a son of 12 years of age or older who wants to be a weaver]. AHCB, Ordinacions, IV–4, fol. 37.

[41] Pierre Bonnassie, *La organización del trabajo en Barcelona a fines del siglo XV* (Barcelona: Consejo Superior de Investigaciones Científicas, 1975), 29.

[42] Mireia Comas-Via, Carme Muntaner Alsina, and Teresa Vinyoles Vidal, "Elles no només filaven: Producció i comerç en mans de dones a la Catalunya baixmedieval," *Recerques* 56 (2008): 19–45 at 25.

[43] Camarasa, "Les dones," 40.

for the imminent and inevitable end of their lives. However, in general, medieval society had sufficient strategies to assist people in need, either through institutionalized charity, or through other forms of unorganized welfare, such as networks of solidarity to which the most impoverished widows could turn in order to survive in the heart of urban society. Friends, neighbours, or simply other women in the same circumstances could make up for the lack of family ties in the city.[44]

In short, the combination of all these elements had a varying impact on the processes of impoverishment and deterioration of the social condition of widows, so that many of them inevitably went on to join the lower classes of society if they did not have the capacity to avoid this outcome. Royal Chancery records include a considerable number of letters from widows who petitioned the king for economic benefits and tax exemptions in order to address their difficult economic situation. This is the case of the widow of Joan Pere de Sentmenat, who, together with her four sons and five daughters, was exempted by Queen Juana Enríquez from paying the *lluïsme*[45] (laudemium or acknowledgement money) on the *lleuda of Mediona*,[46] half of which was owned by the king. Taking into account that the sale of her deceased husband's rights to the *lleuda* would mean an income of about thirty to thirty-two thousand florins, this royal grant saved the widow an amount of fifteen hundred florins. The letter she sent to the king also stated that this "noble household" was suffering much need and penury because of the many debts choking the family economy.[47] Another example is that of Caterina, widow of the wheat dealer Mateu Gual, who, with no earnings or income, had to support three young children. This case is documented thanks to the informative proceedings regarding the poverty of this widow that were initiated by Pere Falcó and Lluís Ribelles by commission of the regent of the Royal Chancery. Witnesses declared that they were amazed at how she could support her three children.[48]

The analysis of this and other documentation leads to the conclusion that part of Barcelona's widows were impoverished by the particular circumstances of their widowhood and not because they were born poor. In this same sense,

---

[44] For a more detailed discussion on this topic, see Comas-Via, "Looking for a Way."
[45] Sum paid to the owner of the direct domain when the land and possessions under lease were transferred.
[46] The *lleuda de Mediona* was a tax levied on the entry of goods into the city of Barcelona: Roser Salicrú, *El tràfic de mercaderies a Barcelona segons la lleuda de Mediona (febrer de 1434)* (Barcelona: Consejo Superior de Investigaciones Científicas, 1995).
[47] ACA, Cancelleria, reg. 3.498, fols. 165r–166r, 1462 May 13.
[48] ACA, Cancelleria, Processos en quart, 1484, 1484 September 20.

Teresa Vinyoles has verified, through the study of several *fogatjaments* of the city, that there were artisan families that paid their taxes while the husband was alive but, once the woman was widowed, were considered poor as they no longer could afford them.[49] Thus, this new situation pushed some widows to inevitably join the group of the deserving poor (*pobres vergonyants*), that is, those who were ashamed of their situation and deserving of compassion and assistance from the rest of medieval society, unlike the undeserving poor, for which begging was the principal means of support.[50]

Between Destitution and Social Exclusion

There is no doubt that, for all these reasons, the line between poverty and destitution was a very thin one. Laws protected the dignity of widows with special care, for as women without men, they were more vulnerable to defamation and assaults. To prevent dishonest abuses, King Pere IV of Aragon, known as the Ceremonious, enacted a law in 1344 prohibiting members of his retinue—family and household members alike—as well as members of the retinue of his brother and procurator general, the *infant* Jaume, from staying in the homes of married women, maidens, and young widows.[51] Despite the authorities' concern to safeguard widows from insults, assaults, and exploitation, many of them, especially the elderly, the poor, and those at risk of social marginalization, were victims of relatives, neighbours, and strangers.

Following up on the example of the aforementioned trial against Arnau Albertí, we find that the girls he raped were mostly the daughters of widows who declared that they lived in the most extreme poverty.[52] Moreover, Na Trialles, the

---

49 Teresa Vinyoles Vidal, "La violència marginal a les ciutats medievals (exemples a la Barcelona dels volts del 1400)," *Revista d'Història Medieval, Violència i marginació en la societat medieval* 1 (1990): 155–77 at 161.
50 On medieval poverty and the distinctions between different groups of poor people, see James Brodman, *Charity and Welfare: Hospitals and the Poor in Medieval Catalonia* (Philadelphia: University of Pennsylvania Press, 1998), 5–6.
51 Bofarull, *Procesos de las Cortes*, 252.
52 The protagonists of this story were the following girls: Úrsula, daughter of Joana, called the Valencian, widow of Joan de Climent, wood and stone illuminator, remarried to Joan de Córdoba, armourer of the Kingdom of Castile, inhabitant of Barcelona; Domenja and Agnès, daughters of Antònia, known as *la Begura*, widow from her first marriage to Ramon Cotxí, widow from her second marriage to Bernat Begura, and wife of Joan Albanell; Isabel, daughter of Francesca, known as *Na Mingueta* or *la de les tauletes*, widow of Minguet de Renda, royal hunter (Riera, *El Cavaller i l'alcavota*).

woman accused of procuring and providing the girls to Arnau Albertí, was an elderly widow herself.[53] Widows in the lower strata of society were much more vulnerable to all kinds of violence. Thus, in addition to suffering assaults, these assaults often turned them into victims of social exclusion, causing them to endure the punishment of social abandonment, poverty, and marginalization. Consequently, they were doubly victimized.[54] The following examples, this time from the city of Lleida, show the vulnerability that characterized destitute widows.

In the first case, the victim was a very old widow, named Sança, who was beaten and raped by a peasant. During the trial, the numerous bruises on Sança's face made her "moan loudly." Although the defendant was a repeat offender, the verdict was an acquittal.[55] In the second trial I have selected, the victim was a widow who prostituted herself. One night, a neighbour named Joan Peiró entered the woman's house and, despite her resistance, raped her. Her screams alerted a priest who entered the widow's house. During the interrogation, the clergyman, who had witnessed the scene, declared that he knew nothing about it and, furthermore, expressed his shock at the widow's assertion of such facts. The assailant, on his part, denied the accusations against him.[56] Both cases highlight the defenselessness of certain widows due to the precarious social situation in which they lived. These women who were alone, without help or support from any quarter, were always under suspicion, more so than the men accused of raping them, who managed to get away with their crimes.

Once widows fell into a spiral of marginality, their alternatives gradually dwindled, especially if all doors and windows were closed to them. At any moment, a widow in a desperate situation could end up opting for prostitution and procuring. These crimes were prosecuted by municipal by-laws and regulations to punish men and women who engaged in the sex trade and caused unrest within the community.[57] The edicts against procurers, procuresses, gamblers, and vagrants that threatened to expel them from the city often included the

---

53 Caterina Tarí, widow of Bernat Trialls and known as *Na Trialles*, was initially hired to care for the illegitimate brother of the knight during his illness (Riera, *El Cavaller i l'alcavota*).
54 Córdoba, "Los caminos de la exclusión," 34.
55 Municipal Archive of Lleida (hereinafter AML), reg. 805, fols. 85–106, 1412 August 15. Document cited by Manuel Camps Surroca and Manuel Camps Clemente, "Los delitos contra la libertad sexual en Lleida en el siglo XV," in *VII Jornadas de la Sociedad Española de Medicina Legal y Forense*, Vol. 2 (Lleida: Universitat de Lleida, 1995), Appendix 4.
56 AML, reg. 810, fols. 70–71, 1428 October 21–1428 November 18. Camps and Camps, "Los delitos contra," Appendix 5.
57 Córdoba, "Los caminos de la exclusión," 29.

name of some widow who had been sentenced to exile and, in some cases, had no hope of a pardon, such as Joana, widow of the labourer Joan Clapers. This widow was accused of procuring and sentenced to three years of exile, without possibility of obtaining a pardon from the authorities of Barcelona. Joana felt that she had been unjustly accused and, for this reason, she turned to the city councilors to have her sentence lifted.[58] However, we do not know if the council ruled in her favour or against her. Teresa Vinyoles also recalls the example of the widow Elisenda Cugada, who was forced to engage in procuring. In a letter sent to the city councilors, she asked for their help in selling a house she owned to the brothel. Elisenda, who claimed to be "vídua e misserable persona, e sens amichs alguns" (a destitute widow, with no friends whatsoever), intended to invest the money obtained from the sale so that she could live the rest of her life well and honestly.[59] It is interesting to point out how, besides presenting herself as a destitute widow, Elisenda highlighted the lack of family and friends to whom she could turn in the face of difficulties. All this suggests that, unless widows could resort to family, neighbourhood solidarity networks, or even to charitable institutions in case of need, the lack of support could bring some of them closer to high-risk situations. Undoubtedly, as Giuliana Albini states, the possibility of belonging to a supportive community allowed women to create a safety net that helped them meet their vital needs and escape marginalization.[60]

---

58 "Humilment ab aquella pus humil reverència e honor que pot, expon la dona na Johana, d'en Johan Clapers quòndam, brasser, ciutedà de Barchelona, dient que com per informació no reebuda de persones a ella malvolents, no tements Déu ne los seus Sants Manaments no advertents, sia stada publicada per la dita ciutat per alcavota e exel·lada de aquella a tres anys, sens esperança de vènia. E com la dita dona agreujada del dit exill, lo qual, ab tota honor parlant, li és stat fet contra justícia e per adversa informació, com ella sia quítia de tal vida e condició, de la qual és stada intitulada e, contra justícia, inculpada" [Humbly, with the most respectful reverence and honour she can manage, the woman Johana, widow of the late Johan Clapers, labourer, citizen of Barcelona, declares that because of information provided by persons who wished her ill, who did not fear God, nor kept His Holy Commandments, she was denounced as a procuress by the said city and exiled from it three years ago, without hope of pardon. And how the said woman is aggrieved by the said exile, which, speaking in all honour, was imposed upon her against justice and due to adverse information, as she is not guilty of such life and condition, for which she was accused and against justice, indicted]. AHCB, 1C. Consellers, V. Miscel·lània, 13, 1477 April 24–29.
59 AHCB, 1B. Consell de Cent, X. Lletres comunes originals, 2. Document cited by Vinyoles, "La violència marginal," 161–62.
60 Giuliana Albini, "Pauperismo e solidarietà femminile nell'Italia settentrionale (secoli XIII–XIV)," *Storia delle Donne* 13 (2017): 103–26 at 114.

Final Remarks

The link between poverty and marginalization was strong, especially in the case of female widowhood. But it should be noted that this was a gendered poverty, as it was the fact of being a woman without a man that reduced widows' social status to that of poor people. For widows without resources, who were sometimes even expelled from the conjugal home once the usufruct was over, widowhood could entail a long list of difficulties. It was precisely poverty and, in some cases, the resulting marginalization, which led them to social exclusion, especially elderly widows without economic resources and lacking any independence, whom this situation relegated to destitution. Among the most vulnerable widows, we should also include those who were newly arrived in the city and had no ties to the community that received them. The obvious signs of female poverty, however, could be somewhat alleviated thanks to the development of forms of assistance, both institutionalized and informal, to which the most needy widows could turn. Thus, some situations of marginalization might not have been permanent or might have been alleviated by a bequest or by the pious contributions of some charitable institution. In short, the city, despite being a space of undeniable marginalization and social exclusion, could also offer alternatives for these widows.

Laura Cayrol-Bernardo
Chapter 4
Ageing Women, (In)Visible Bodies: Iconographies on the Edge in Late-Medieval Iberia (Thirteenth to Fifteenth Centuries)

Over the last few decades, studies on the biological, economic, social, and cultural aspects of ageing have multiplied, as a result of the ongoing debates on demographic ageing and its impact on our societies. While biomedical accounts are often privileged over the social and cultural, the consolidation of Cultural Gerontology as a discipline since the beginning of the twenty-first century brought with it renewed considerations about cultural constructions of the human ageing body, drawing attention to the importance of the intersection between gender and age.[1] In this context, research on the presence of older women in contemporary art, literature, and popular culture has recently begun to flourish. Several studies consistently point to the under-representation of older women in contemporary culture and the lack of diversity among those who are more visible. It has been noted that older women's bodies often appear rejuvenated, concealed, or dissimulated, normative feminine beauty being systematically identified with youth.[2]

---

[1] Legal scholar Kimberlé Crenshaw coined the term "intersectionality" to refer to the way in which race and gender are interrelated and mutually shaped: Kimberlé W. Crenshaw, "Mapping the Margins: Intersectionality, Identity Politics, and Violence against Women of Color," *Stanford Law Review* 43/6 (1991): 1241–99. On intersectionality in age studies, see: Neal King, "The Lengthening List: Age Relations and the Feminist Study of Inequality," in *Age Matters: Re-Aligning Feminist Thinking*, ed. Toni M. Calasanti and Kathleen F. Slevin (New York: Routledge, 2006), 47–74; Toni Calasanti and Neal King, "Intersectionality and Age," in *The Routledge Handbook of Cultural Gerontology*, ed. Julia Twigg and Wendy Martin (London: Routledge, 2015), 193–200. On gender as an analytic category in Cultural Gerontology, see: Julia Twigg, "The Body, Gender, and Age: Feminist Insights in Social Gerontology," *Journal of Aging Studies* 18 (2004): 59–73 at 60–62; *The Routledge Handbook of Cultural Gerontology*, 1–9.

[2] These ideas were already pointed out in the pioneering works by Simone de Beauvoir, *Le deuxième sexe* (Paris: Gallimard, 1949) and Susan Sontag, "The Double Standard of Aging," *The Saturday Review*, 23 September 1972, 29–38. See also, among others: Kathleen Woodward, *Figuring Age: Women, Bodies, Generations: Theories of Contemporary Culture* (Bloomington and Indianapolis: Indiana University Press, 1999); Twigg, "The Body, Gender, and Age," 61–62; Laura

In the field of Medieval Studies, despite the publication of some trailblazing individual and collective works, the topic of old age has been met with a certain avoidance and still remains largely unexplored, both in regard to specific subtopics and to geographic areas.³ Regarding medieval older women, the existing studies are even more scarce, especially within the field of cultural history.⁴ As far as research in Art History is concerned, the evolution of this field of study has been slow and reluctant. The only comprehensive volume on old age in the arts that has been published to date does not include a single depiction of an old woman prior to the seventeenth century, and very few when addressing the following centuries.⁵ Some research has been carried out on the iconography of old age in Antiquity, while most historical studies on images of older people, including some that focus on women, concentrate on the sixteenth and seventeenth centuries.⁶ Regarding the Middle Ages, no study on the iconographies of ageing or old age has been published so far.

Hurd Clarke, *Facing Age: Women Growing Older in Anti-aging Culture* (Lanham, MD: Rowman & Littlefiel, 2011); Jeannette King, *Discourses of Ageing in Fiction and Feminism: The Invisible Woman* (London: Palgrave Macmillan, 2013); *Ageing Women in Literature and Visual Culture: Reflections, Refractions, Reimaginings*, ed. Cathy McGlynn, Margaret O'Neill, and Michaela Schrage-Früh (London: Palgrave Macmillan, 2017).
3 Georges Minois, *Histoire de la vieillesse en Occident: De l'Antiquité à la Renaissance* (Paris: Fayard, 1987); Marie-Thérèse Lorcin, "Vieillesse et vieillissement vus par les médecins du Moyen Âge," *Bulletin d'histoire économique et sociale de la région lyonnaise* 4 (1983): 5–22; Marie-Thérèse Lorcin, "Rides et cheveux gris dans les ouvrages de Roger Bacon," in *Les soins de beauté: Moyen Âge–début des Temps Modernes*, ed. Denis Menjot (Nice: Faculté des Lettres et Sciences Humaines de Nice, 1987), 253–59; *Vieillesse et vieillissement au Moyen-Âge* (Aix-en-Provence: Presses Universitaires de Provence, 1987); *Aging and the Aged in Medieval Europe*, ed. Michael M. Sheehan (Toronto: Pontifical Institute of Mediaeval Studies, 1990); Joel T. Rosenthal, *Old Age in Late Medieval England* (Philadelphia: University of Pennsylvania Press, 1996); Shulamith Shahar, *Growing Old in the Middle Ages: "Winter Clothes Us in Shadow and Pain"* (London: Routledge, 1997); Raquel Homet, *Los viejos y la vejez en la Edad Media: Sociedad e imaginario* (Rosario: Pontificia Universedad Católica Argentina, 1997); *Old Age in the Middle Ages and the Renaissance: Interdisciplinary Approaches to a Neglected Topic*, ed. Albrecht Classen (Berlin and New York: De Gruyter, 2007); Christian Krötzl and Katariina Mustakallio, *On Old Age: Approaching Death in Antiquity and the Middle Ages* (Turnhout: Brepols, 2011).
4 See the pioneering article by Jole Agrimi and Chiara Crisciani, "Savoir médical et anthropologie religieuse: Les représentations et les fonctions de la *vetula* (XIIIe–XVe siècle)," *Annales: Économies, Sociétés, Civilisations* 48/5 (1993): 1281–1308.
5 Mark Gregory D'Apuzzo, *I segni del tempo: Metamorfosi della vecchiaia nell'arte dell'Occidente* (Bologna: Editrice Compositori, 2006).
6 Because of their gender perspective, it is worth noting the publications by Caroline Schuster-Cordone, *Le crépuscule du corps: Images de la vieillesse féminine* (Fribourg: InFolio, 2009) and Lynn Botelho, "Images of Old Age in Early Modern Cheap Print: Women, Witches, and the Poi-

However, the process of ageing is a deeply visual phenomenon as it is indissoluble from the physical body and its appearance. Age is consequently an integral part of visual depictions of the human body, therefore the absence of ageing signs in certain characters can be as revealing as their presence. Images thus constitute key elements in the cultural construction of women's old age. In the light of the insights provided by previous studies concerned with contemporary culture, the present study aims at tracing the presence of older women in the visual arts and analysing the gender and age dynamics displayed through a selection of artworks executed in the Iberian Peninsula between the thirteenth and the fifteenth century. To do so, religious art will be prioritised. The source material is selected among the depictions of older women whose identity is known with certainty.[7] The corpus of images selected for this chapter is purposefully varied in terms of styles, geographical origins, and chronologies in order to highlight key ideas that were present in different areas over the centuries as well as innovations, continuities, and discontinuities.

Invisible Presence

From early on, older men were very present in Christian art. They are usually recognisable by their long beards, which are sometimes accompanied by other signs of ageing such as baldness or, at least from the twelfth century onwards, wrinkles. In a religious context, older men are most often depicted in an upright position and adopting a dignified body posture. They are mostly positive characters, full of wisdom and authority, or who enjoy a privileged relationship with God. Therefore, they do not display physical characteristics that show decrepitude or decline. They are, however, depicted as obviously old, their age not only being shown but often also emphasised. Moreover, the depiction of various stages of the life cycle was common, showing different degrees of ageing, making the process of biological ageing decodable for spectators. The Twenty-Four Elders of the Apocalypse are a particularly interesting example: as a group of individuals known under the generic name of "elders," their old age becomes their most distinctive and positive feature. Relevant biblical male characters such as

---

sonous Female Body," in *Old Age in Pre-Industrial Society*, ed. Susannah R. Ottaway, Lynn Botelho, and Katharine Kittredge (Westport, CT: Greenwood Press, 2002), 225–46.

7 In view of the need to limit the image catalogue I have chosen to focus on sculptures and wall and panel paintings. For an analysis based on a larger corpus that includes manuscripts and profane iconography, see Laura Cayrol-Bernardo, "Histoire d'une absence? Vieillir au féminin au Moyen Âge ibérique (XII–XV siècle)" (PhD diss., EHESS, 2021).

patriarchs, prophets, apostles, or even God the Father, as well as many saints, were also often depicted as old men.[8]

While men's old age is abundantly represented in religious works, at first sight older women seem to be absent. This could be partly due to the fact that older women are less obvious to identify than men: women's old age cannot be represented through beards and their hair is generally covered, as was prescribed for all married and widowed women. But this apparent absence does not seem to be simply due to technical difficulties. In fact, the earliest unambiguous depiction of an older woman that I have identified presents a woman with grey shoulder-length hair, only covered with overlapping narrow strips of cloth that leave much of her hair loose and on display. This headdress, known in Spanish as *toca de tipo almízar*, was common among Iberian women and coexisted with other more covering styles.[9] This image is located on folio 58r of the manuscript of the *Libro del acedrex, dados e tablas* (1252–1284) commissioned by King Alfonso X of Castile.[10] The woman, who is shown teaching a child how to play chess, not only has grey hair but also presents an obviously wrinkled face and neck.

Another example worth mentioning is the pictorial cycle dedicated to the life of Saint Mary of Egypt in the church of the Benedictine monastery of San Salvador de Oña (Burgos), dated between 1360 and 1380 (Fig. 1).[11] The episodes in the

---

[8] For an overview on this topic see D'Apuzzo, *I segni del tempo*, 93–188.

[9] On this type of headdress, see: Carmen Bernis Madrazo, *Indumentaria medieval española* (Madrid: CSIC, Instituto Diego Velázquez, 1956), 39; Gonzalo Menéndez Pidal, *La España del s. XIII leída en imágenes* (Madrid: Real Academia de la Historia, 1986), 87.

[10] Real Biblioteca del Monasterio de El Escorial, Ms. T-I-6. On this manuscript and its illuminations see, among others: Ana Rodríguez, "El Libro de los Juegos y la miniatura alfonsí," in *Alfonso X el Sabio, Libros del Ajedrez, Dados y Tablas*, vol. 2 (Madrid and Valencia: Vicent García Editores/Ediciones Poniente, 1987), 30–123; María Teresa López de Guereño Sanz, "Las miniaturas del *Libro del acedrex, dados y tablas* de Alfonso X el Sabio," in *Libro de los Juegos de Ajedrez, Dados y Tablas de Alfonso x el Sabio* (Valencia: Editorial Scriptorium, 2010), 19–67; Laura Fernández Fernández, *Arte y ciencia en el scriptorium de Alfonso x el Sabio* (Sevilla: Universidad de Sevilla, 2013); María Teresa López de Guereño Sanz, "Arte y gestualidad en el *Libro del acedrex, dados e tablas* de Alfonso X el Sabio," *Laboratorio de Arte* 29 (2017): 23–52.

[11] For a stylistic and iconographic analysis of these paintings, see Fernando Gutiérrez Baños, *Aportación al estudio de la pintura de estilo gótico lineal en Castilla y León: Precisiones cronológicas y corpus de pintura mural y sobre tabla*, vol. 2 (Madrid: Fundación Universitaria Española, 2005), 118–22; Fernando Gutiérrez Baños, "La imagen del ermitaño en el arte medieval hispano," in *El monacato espontáneo: Eremitas y eremitorios en el mundo medieval*, ed. José Ángel García de Cortázar and Ramón Teja (Aguilar de Campoo: Fundación Santa María la Real, Centro de Estudios del Románico, 2011), 186–90; Fernando Gutiérrez Baños, *El mural de Santa María Egipcíaca: Monasterio de San Salvador de Oña* (Oña: Asociación Amigos de San Salvador, 2016).

life of Mary of Egypt are deployed chronologically along two horizontal sections. The upper part is dedicated to the saint's youth and repentance and the lower to her penance, old age, and death. The character of Mary of Egypt has the particularity that several versions of her *vita* describe in detail her physical appearance when she was old, as the degradation of her body was seen as part of her self-mortification and her path to holiness.[12] At Oña, physical changes represented in Mary's body serve as markers of temporality that indicate that several decades had elapsed between one image and the next. On the scenes corresponding to her old age, the saint is depicted as a naked woman with grey hair, a wrinkled forehead, and sagging breasts. She shows obvious signs of ageing but is presented as a dignified character, with an upright body posture and without any sign of weakness or decrepitude. This iconography is of special interest since in medieval art older female naked bodies are rarely on display. Given that this is the only depiction of Mary of Egypt in medieval Iberian art that is currently preserved in which the saint can be identified in an unquestionable way, we cannot know for sure if this type of representation was common or an exception. We do know, however, that in other areas of Western Europe this saint was usually represented as a young woman covered in body hair or with long hair down to the ground, not as an older woman in the nude.[13]

---

12 For instance, according to the thirteenth-century Castilian poem *Vida de María Egipçíaca:* "Perdio las carnes & la color,/ que eran blancas como la flor;/ E los sus cabellos, que eran Ruuios,/ tornaron blancos & suzios./ [...] La faz, muy negra & arrugada,/ de frio viento & elada./ [...] En ssus pechos non auia tetas:/ como yo cuydo eran secas" (She lost the flesh and colour, that used to be white as a flower; and her hair that used to be blonde, became white and dirty. [...] Her face, very dark and wrinkled from cold wind and frost. [...] Her chest became so dry that she had no breasts.) Manuel Alvar, *Vida de santa María Egipciaca: Estudios, vocabulario, edición de los textos* (Madrid: CSIC, 1972). On the origins of Mary of Egypt's *vitae* and their dissemination in the Iberian Peninsula, see Joseph T. Snow, "Notes on the Fourteenth-Century Spanish Translation of Paul the Deacon's *Vita Sanctae Mariae Aegyptiacae, Meretricis*," in *Saints and their Authors: Studies in Medieval Hispanic Hagiography in Honor of John K. Walsh*, ed. Jane E. Connolly, Alan D. Deyermond, and Brian Dutton (Madison: Hispanic Seminary of Medieval Studies, 1990), 83–96; Connie L. Scarborough, "Santa María de Egipto: La vitalidad de la leyenda en castellano," in *Actas del XII Congreso de la Asociación Internacional de Hispanistas (1995): Medieval y Lingüística*, ed. Aengus M. Ward, vol. 1 (Birmingham: Department of Hispanic Studies, University of Birmingham, 1998), 302–10; Carina Zubilaga, "Pervivencia, traducción y resignificación de la leyenda de Santa María Egipcíaca en la literatura europea medieval: Estudio de las vidas francesa e hispánica de la santa frente a la tradición oriental previa," *exlibris (Investigación)* 3 (2014): 66–77.
13 Daniela Mariani, "La chevelure de sainte Marie l'Égyptienne d'après Rutebeuf: Contraste des sources et de la tradition iconographique," *Perspectives médiévales* 38 (2017), DOI: 10.4000/peme.12698.

Fig. 1: Saint Mary of Egypt lifted by angels in the presence of Abbot Zosimas. Detail from the mural paintings of the Life of Saint Mary of Egypt (ca. 1360–1380), Church of the Monastery of San Salvador de Oña (Burgos). Photo: Fernando Gutiérrez Baños.

Nevertheless, the previous two examples are exceptions: in thirteenth- and fourteenth-century art, older women usually seem to lack iconographic attributes that make their age visible. That is to say, it is often impossible to know a woman's approximate age when the character is not unequivocally identifiable through text or context. Therefore, in order to analyse how women's ageing was approached in late medieval Iberian religious art, I have chosen to focus on female saints who were explicitly described as old in their *vitae*. Medieval Christian hagiography refers to many women who, we know for certain, were not young. Among them are women who conceived their children—also saintly characters—at an unusually old age, such as the biblical characters of Sarah, Hannah, and Elizabeth, or Saint Anne, mother of the Virgin. Other saints are presented as venerable old women, like the prophetess Anna and hermit saints who lived long lives, as is the case of Mary Magdalene and Mary of Egypt. Finally, it is worth noting that textual sources also mention other women who were the mothers of adult men, such as Saint Helena, discoverer of the True Cross and mother of Emperor Constantine, or Saint Monica, mother of Saint Augustine, who could therefore not have been young girls. Not all of them have a rich iconographic tradition in the Iberian Peninsula but, in general, the existing representations follow similar parameters and chronological evolution as regards the depiction of the aged female body.[14] In this study I will prioritise the examples of Saint Elizabeth and Saint Anne. They are the two most abundantly depicted older female saints throughout the Late Middle Ages and therefore allow for a more detailed analysis of the iconographic attributes used to make their old age visible (or not).

The most frequently depicted older female character is Saint Elizabeth. The Gospel of Luke relates that, in the Annunciation, the archangel Gabriel told Mary that her cousin Elizabeth had conceived a child with her husband Zachary in her old age. Newly pregnant with Jesus, the Virgin then went to visit her relative. When Elizabeth heard Mary's salutation, the infant John the Baptist leaped in her womb.[15] From the earliest days of Christian iconography, the Visitation was often part of pictorial or sculptural cycles devoted to the Childhood of Christ, usually paired with the Annunciation. It was also a recurring theme in cycles depicting the life of the Virgin. Medieval iconography focuses mainly on the moment when the two women meet.[16]

---

14 I have addressed this topic more extensively in Cayrol-Bernardo, "Histoire d'une absence?," 101–11.
15 Lk 1:39–56.
16 On the iconographies of the Visitation, see Anne-Marie Velu, *La Visitation dans l'art: Orient et Occident Ve–XVIe siècle* (Paris: Cerf, 2012).

In Romanesque works, the age difference between Elizabeth and Mary is imperceptible. They are both dressed the same way, without making any distinction between the young virgin and the old married woman.[17] In paintings, such as the Catalan altar frontal from Santa Maria d'Avià (ca. 1200), Mary is only recognisable because she is dressed in blue.[18] The same can be said of the Visitation scenes sculpted on the Gothic tomb of the Infanta Berenguela at the Abbey of Las Huelgas (Burgos) and that of Urraca López de Haro in Vileña, both from the last third of the thirteenth century where Mary and Elizabeth are hardly distinguishable from one another.[19] Age, therefore, does not appear as a relevant element in these representations.

In the field of monumental sculpture, the same episode is represented on Saint John's Portal on the western façade of the cathedral of León, dated to around 1270 (Fig. 2). The thirteenth-century sculptures in León's cathedral closely follow French models and have been typologically related to the cathedrals of Reims and Amiens.[20] In the Visitation scene both women wear similar outfits, but Elizabeth wears a wimple covering her neck. Although she has a slightly thinner face than Mary's, she looks ageless; that is, her age cannot be determined from her physical appearance. Without knowing the story behind the scene, it is impossible to guess that one of the women was much older than the other.[21] The same portal includes several representations of men of different ages who are clearly distinguishable by features such as baldness or long beards. However, just like the women, in this case they have idealised faces with no wrinkles. In the Visitation represented in the Puerta del Reloj at the cathedral

---

[17] I have analysed a more extensive catalogue of examples from the twelfth and thirteenth centuries in Cayrol-Bernardo, "Histoire d'une absence?," 108–11.
[18] On this work, see Rosa Alcoy, "El frontal de Santa Maria d'Avià," in *Catalunya Romànica, XII: El Berguedà* (Barcelona: Enciclopèdia Catalana, 1986), 102–11; Rosa Alcoy, "Les taules pintades a Catalunya i els corrents anglesos a la fi del romànic," *Lambard: Estudis d'art medieval* 7 (1993–1994): 139–56.
[19] On the iconography of the Visitation in thirteenth-century funerary sculpture in Burgos, see Mª Jesús Gómez Bárcena, "La Visitación y el Nacimiento en los sepulcros góticos burgaleses," *Boletín de la Institución Fernán González* 2 (1982): 307–17.
[20] Ángela Franco Mata, *Escultura gótica en León y su provincia (1230–1530)* (León: Diputación de León, 1998), 128.
[21] It is interesting to note that the sculptures of the Visitation at Reims cathedral, dated before 1225, include a rather naturalistic representation of Saint Elizabeth, who is depicted unambiguously as an elderly woman. However, this type of depiction was unusual in thirteenth-century Île-de-France sculpture. Female characters with wrinkled faces did not become common until two centuries later. Jean Wirth, *L'image du corps au Moyen Âge* (Florence: Sismel, Edizioni del Galluzzo, 2013), 51.

Fig. 2: Scene of the Visitation. Detail from archivolt, Saint John's portal, western façade of León Cathedral (ca. 1270). Photo: Mercedes Pérez Vidal.

of Toledo, executed in the early fourteenth century, Mary wears her long hair on display while Elizabeth only partially hides hers with a veil. Their faces are still almost identical.[22]

From the first third of the fourteenth century, western clothing became increasingly gendered, a process that would culminate in the fifteenth century. In the case of women, this is expressed through more marked silhouettes and lower, wider necklines.[23] These changes also seem to lead to greater differentiation based on age. In Catalonia, the Italian-influenced Altarpiece of the Saints Johns by the Master of Santa Coloma de Queralt (ca. 1356), containing scenes from the lives of Saint John the Baptist and Saint John the Evangelist, includes

---

[22] Teresa Pérez Higuera, *La puerta del Reloj en la catedral de Toledo* (Toledo: Caja de Ahorros de Toledo, 1987), 56.

[23] Gil Bartholeyns, "L'enjeu du vêtement au Moyen Âge: De l'anthropologie ordinaire à la raison sociale (XIIIe–XIVe siècles)," in "Le corps et sa parure" issue, *Micrologus. Natura, Science e Società Medievali* 15 (2007): 219–57 at 236.

a panel with two depictions of Saint Elizabeth.²⁴ As in the previous cases, the first one was part of the scene of the Visitation. Elizabeth greets Mary at the door of her house, bowing to her. Mary, in turn, puts her hands on her older cousin's shoulders marking the hierarchy between them.²⁵ The second scene is the birth of Saint John the Baptist, in which Mary helps her cousin during labour. In both cases, Elizabeth's face is not very different from Mary's, but her head is entirely covered and she wears a white wimple, while the Virgin has her hair covered with a simpler veil and wears a low neckline. While wimples were popular among women of all ages and social groups during the twelfth and thirteenth centuries, from the mid-fourteenth century onwards they became associated with the poor, the elderly, widows, and religious women.²⁶ This process went hand in hand with a growing concern for making social identity visible through dress across Western Europe during this period.²⁷ It is, however, important to emphasise that physical signs of ageing remain completely absent from this image. The same altarpiece includes numerous representations of women and men of diverse appearances. While women present different clothing, hairstyles, and facial expressions, there is no unequivocal age-based distinction between the female characters. Yet, some of the male characters not only display features such as baldness or long grey beards, which cannot be found among women, but also have obviously aged faces with deep wrinkles.

The high altarpiece in the Old Cathedral of Salamanca, executed in International Gothic style of Italian influence, is dated around 1440 and attributed to the Tuscan painter Dello Delli.²⁸ Again, both women are characterised especially through their clothing. However, although not obviously aged, Elizabeth's face is

---

24 Rosa Alcoy, "El Mestre de Santa Coloma de Queralt i l'italianisme del segle XIV: El retaule dels sants Joans," *Recull (Associació Cultural Baixa Segarra)* 4 (1996): 7–26.
25 On this iconography, see Velu, *La Visitation*, 52–62.
26 José Guerrero Lovillo, *Las cantigas: Estudio arqueológico de sus miniaturas* (Madrid: CSIC, 1949), 203; Carmen Bernis Madrazo, *Trajes y modas en la España de los Reyes Católicos: I, Las mujeres* (Madrid: CSIC, 1975), 17; Roberta Miliken, *Ambiguous Locks: An Iconology of Hair in Medieval Art and Literature* (Jefferson, NC: McFarland & Company, 2012), 948; Nieves Fresneda González, *Moda y belleza femenina en la Corona de Castilla durante los siglos XIII y XIV* (Madrid: Dykinson, 2016), 313.
27 On the increased use of clothing as an indicator of social order in the thirteenth and fourteenth centuries, see Bartholeyns, "L'enjeu du vêtement," 219–57. During the same period, sumptuary laws regulating dress also proliferated. See: José Damián González Arce, *Apariencia y poder: La legislación suntuaria castellana en los siglos XIII–XV* (Jaén: Universidad de Jaén, 1998).
28 Carmen C. Bambach, "The Delli Brothers: Three Florentine Artists in Fifteenth-century Spain," *Apollo: The International Magazine of Arts* 517 (2005): 75–83.

more angular than Mary's. Thus, we can affirm that works of different aesthetics, origins, and qualities throughout an extended time period resorted to similar methods in their ways of visually representing the difference in age between Mary and Elizabeth, without giving the latter an appearance that corresponds to her age according to written sources.

The most relevant changes were brought about by Late Gothic art of Burgundian influence, characterised by a greater tendency to naturalism and a profusion of details. In this sense, one of the most notable examples is the altarpiece of the Visitation (ca. 1455–1460) currently kept in the Diocesan Museum of Segorbe.[29] In its central panel, Elizabeth is again depicted leaning towards Mary, who in turn places both hands on her shoulders. The substantial difference on this occasion is that Elizabeth is represented as a very old woman with a wrinkled face and stooped body posture. She is dressed in dark clothing and wears a white wimple, an outfit of Burgundian origin.[30] In contrast, the Virgin is portrayed as a young girl with partially uncovered hair and rich and more colourful clothing. In Castile, towards the end of the fifteenth century, the so-called Master of Miraflores also represented Elizabeth at both the Visitation and the Birth of Saint John the Baptist (ca. 1490)[31] (Fig. 3) as an obviously aged woman, although not as decrepit as in the previous case.

The second example I want to focus on is that of Saint Anne, mother of the Virgin Mary. Anne is not a biblical figure. She first appears in the second-century apocryphal gospel known as the *Protevangelium of James*. Her character was based on stories from the Old Testament about women who had children at an advanced age, such as Sarah, Hannah, and on Elizabeth herself.[32] In Anne's case, she and her husband Joachim conceived the Virgin after twenty years of childless marriage. After this first daughter, a long textual tradition attributes two other successive marriages to Anne—known as Anne's *trinubium*—which resulted in two other daughters, both called Mary.[33] Thus, if the saint

---

[29] On this work and its possible attribution, see Ximo Company, "Valencia and Late Gothic Painting," in *Late Gothic Painting in the Crown of Aragon and the Hispanic Kingdoms*, ed. Alberto Velasco and Francesc Fité (Leiden: Brill, 2018), 246, n. 97.
[30] Bernis Madrazo, *Indumentaria medieval*, 39.
[31] Pilar Silva Maroto, *Pintura hispano-flamenca castellana: Burgos y Palencia. Obras en tabla y sarga*, vol. 2 (Valladolid: Junta de Castilla y León, 1990), 645–67.
[32] See Milka Ventura Avanzinelli, "Sterilità e fecondità delle donne bibliche," *Storia delle donne* 1 (2005): 75–88.
[33] *Interpreting Cultural Symbols: Saint Anne in Late Medieval Society*, ed. Kathleen Ashley and Pamela Sheingorn (Athens and London: The University of Georgia Press, 1990), 6–43; Virginia Nixon, *Mary's Mother: Saint Anne in Late Medieval Europe* (University Park, PA: Penn State University Press, 2004), 16.

Fig. 3: Maestro de Miraflores, Visitation. Museo del Prado, Madrid (originally from Miraflores Charterhouse, Burgos). Oil, tempera on panel. Photo: Museo del Prado.

was no longer young at the time of her first pregnancy, she was much less so when the following pregnancies occurred. In medieval Iberian art, the scenes most frequently represented depict Anne meeting her husband at the Golden Gate of Jerusalem when the upcoming pregnancy had just been announced, and Anne holding her daughter and grandson, a composition known as *Santa Ana Triple* in Spanish or *Anna Selbdritt* in German. Some other images show Anne teaching her daughter how to read,[34] and the scene of the birth of the Virgin.[35]

In general terms, the progression in Anne's depictions from a complete absence of signs of ageing to evident old age follows a similar chronological framework to that regarding Elizabeth.[36] From the thirteenth century onwards, Anne was systematically depicted dressed in very covered-up clothing, which could be linked to her successive periods of widowhood. It is worth noting her depiction in the Portal of Saint Anne in the cathedral of Vitoria Gasteiz (fourteenth century), which, to my knowledge, is the earliest in the Iberian Peninsula dedicated to Mary's mother.[37] It is an unusual representation of the Virgin's extensive family, including her parents and husband. The sculptures are in a mediocre state of conservation which particularly affects the faces. However, the figure of Anne can easily be identified by her outfit. Widows, regardless of their age, were indeed expected to wear very modest and covering outfits, although this was not systematically applied.[38] Nevertheless, similar clothing can be seen in several images of Elizabeth, who was not a widow, as well as in images of Anne hugging her husband. Thus, in addition to a possible reference to widowhood, Anne's clothing (and that of other older women) seems to be a result of the

---

34 Pamela Sheingorn, "The Wise Mother: The Image of Saint Anne Teaching the Virgin Mary," *Gesta* 32/1 (1993): 69–80.
35 See José María Salvador González, "*Et vocavit nomen eius Mariam:* Aproximación iconográfica al Nacimiento de María en la pintura gótica española," *De Medio Aevo* 3/2 (2013): 121–52.
36 From the middle of the fifteenth century onwards, we find depictions of Saint Anne in which she is visibly aged, such as the Meeting at the Golden Gate represented in the altarpiece dedicated to her at Santa Ana de Fonz (Huesca). Alberto Velasco Gonzàlez, "El retablo gótico de Santa Ana de Fonz (Huesca): Un ejemplo de promoción episcopal en relación al inmaculismo," *Boletín del Museo e Instituto Camón Aznar* 90 (2003): 275–302.
37 Lucía Lahoz, "Contribución al estudio de la portada de Santa Ana: Catedral de Vitoria," *Boletín del Museo e Instituto Camón Aznar* 63 (1996): 79–104.
38 On widows' mourning attire, see: Françoise Piponnier and Perrine Mane, *Se vêtir au Moyen Âge* (Paris: Adam Biro, 1995), 138; Isabelle Chabot, "'La sposa in nero': La ritualizzazione del lutto delle vedove fiorentine (secoli XIV–XV)," *Quaderni storici* 86 (1994): 421–62; Mireia Comas-Via, *Entre la solitud i la llibertat: Vídues barcelonines a finals de l'Edat Mitjana* (Rome: Viella, 2015), 81–84.

phenomenon of "age ordering" as theorised by Julia Twigg; that is, structured expectations about what is appropriate or not according to an ordered and hierarchically arranged concept of age.[39] In the case of older women's clothes, this translates into features such as looser cuts, higher necklines, darker colours, and, generally, more covering and self-effacing styles. In fact, the distinction of female characters of different ages through dress in medieval Iberian art exceeds the scope of religious iconography. For example, Rocío Sánchez Ameijeiras has identified the use of longer clothes on the recumbent effigies of some women as a way of making their older age evident.[40]

On the one hand, this type of clothing could be intended to provide greater warmth to bodies that had become colder with age, one of the main consequences of physical ageing according to medieval physicians.[41] In addition, it may correspond to a common expectation that the elderly wear longer clothing because of their more static lifestyle, as expressed by Hernando de Talavera (1428–1507), confessor to Queen Isabel I of Castile, known as the Catholic.[42]

---

39 Julia Twigg, *Fashion and Age: Dress, the Body and Later Life* (London: Bloomsbury Academic, 2013), 25.
40 For instance, in the chapel of Santa María del Cabello in Quejana, Elvira López Salcedo is represented with a longer mantle than her daughter-in-law Leonor de Guzmán, the tombs of both having been carved in 1396. The same author points to a possible use of different headdresses for the same purpose in other cases. See Rocío Sánchez Ameijeiras, "Wool, Leather, Silk, and Gold: Religious and Secular Attire in Medieval Galicia," in *Con-fío en Galicia: Vestir Galicia, Vestir o Mundo*, ed. Miguel Anxo Seixas Seoane (Santiago de Compostela: Xunta de Galicia, 2016), 369–79 at 377.
41 On the idea of the human body losing heat as it ages, see: Lorcin, "Vieillesse et vieillissement," 12, 17; Lorcin, "Rides et cheveux gris," 256; Shahar, *Growing Old*, 39; Agrimi and Crisciani, "Savoir médical," 1298; Chiara Crisciani and Giovanna Ferrari, "Estudi introductori," in Arnau de Vilanova, *Tractatus de humido radicali*, ed. Michael R. McVaugh (Barcelona: Universitat de Barcelona / Fundació Noguera, 2010), 11–269 at 24–25.
42 "Porque comunmente las mugeres están y fueron hechas para estar encerradas e occupadas en sus casas y los varones para andar e procurar las cosas de fuera, por esso a donde quier que ay seso se vsa que ellos trayan roba corta y ellas ropa luenga. Ca para andar acá y allá por el poluo y por el lodo es menesteres ropa corta y hábito corto, y bien por esta causa los clérigos y los letrados, e los onbres ançianos y honrrados, en toda parte trahen y siempre traxeron hábitos largos." (Because women commonly are, and were made to be, enclosed and busy in their homes, and men were made to go about and deal with things outside [of the home], that is why wherever there is wisdom it is seen that [men] wear short clothes and [women] wear long clothes. To walk here and there in the dust and the mud, short clothes and short habits are necessary, and for this reason the clerics and the learned, and the elderly and the men of honour, everywhere wear and have always worn long garments.) Teresa de Castro, "El tratado sobre el vestir, calzar y comer del arzobispo Hernando de Talavera," *Espacio, Tiempo y Forma III* 14

However, when analysing this phenomenon it is important to take into account the negative cultural expectations towards postmenopausal women's bodies, pervasive in medieval textual sources. Lay and ecclesiastical authors convey a predominantly pejorative view of women's ageing bodies, both on a purely physiological level and with regard to physical appearance.[43] This narrative equates female ageing with decline and loss of attractiveness, a process that was thought to coincide in time with the end of fertility.[44] Older women were therefore expected to avoid showy outfits, tone down, and cover up. Those who exposed their bodies and dressed as was deemed appropriate for younger women were particularly ridiculed and deprecated. For instance, the archpriest of Talavera, Alfonso Martínez de Toledo (1398–1466), condemned those "devilish old women" who, according to him, looked like monkeys who instead of breasts had nothing but bones.[45] With this in mind, it is not surprising that venerable older women were visually represented in more modest clothing.

Returning to Anne, the *Ana Triple* iconography has a particularity that is worth emphasising. Until the very end of the Middle Ages, Anne is almost always represented as a young woman, her face being practically identical to that of her daughter. According to Virginia Nixon, this might be a way to highlight Anne's

---

(2001): 11–92 at 31–32. It should be noted that the author first refers to women in general and then, specifically, to older men, not to older women.

43 Agrimi and Crisciani, "Savoir médical"; Patrizia Betella, "Vecchiaia femminile nella poesia toscana del XV secolo," *Quaderni d'italianistica* 19/2 (1998): 7–23; Gretchen Mieszkowski, "Old Age and Medieval Misogyny," in *Old Age in the Middle Ages and the Renaissance*, ed. Albrecht Classen (Berlin and New York: De Gruyter, 2007), 299–320; Laura Cayrol-Bernardo, "De la luxure à la sorcellerie: Regards sur la vieillesse féminine dans le Spill de Jaume Roig (ca. 1460)," in *Masculinité(s) – Féminité(s) au Moyen Âge / Maskulinität(en) – Feminität(en) im Mittelalter*, ed. Constanze Buyken (Turnhout: Brepols, forthcoming).

44 For example, the *Speculum al Foder*, a fourteenth-century Catalan text halfway between medical and erotic literature, states that after menopause women become old and no man should desire them: "E aquella qui passa aquesta edat és vella e negú no la deu cobejar." *Speculum al foder*, ed. Anna Alberni (Bellcaire d'Empordà: Vitel·la, 2007), 80–81. The Valencian physician Jaume Roig conveyed the same idea when he wrote that an older woman "cannot give birth or give pleasure" ("No pot parir ni dar plaer") in his misogynist poem *Espill* (ca. 1460): Jaume Roig, *Espill*, ed. Antonia Carré (Barcelona: Editorial Barcino, 2014), 139.

45 "en las viejas endiabladas, y ¿para qué? que cuando la vieja está bien arreada e bien pelada y llepada parece mona desosada: míranse los pechos, y ¿pechos? ¡Ya guaya, arquibanco de huesos, digo yo!" (among the devilish old women, what for? When the old woman is well groomed and well shaved, she looks like an unbearing monkey: she looks at her breasts, and ... which breasts? Just bones, I say!). Alfonso Martínez de Toledo, *Arcipreste de Talavera o Corbacho*, ed. Michael Gerli (Madrid: Cátedra, 1979), 181–82.

fertility as a justification for her *trinubium*.⁴⁶ In Iberia, this is evidenced in the fourteenth-century sculpture from the Cistercian nunnery of Santa María de Vileña (Burgos), which is currently preserved at the Museum of Burgos (Fig. 4), or the six examples at the Museu Marès (Barcelona), from different origins within the Iberian area and chronologies that range between the fourteenth and the late fifteenth century. The early sixteenth-century sculpture by Alejo de Vahía at the Cathedral of Palencia (ca. 1510) still follows the same parameters.⁴⁷

Ageless Bodies

The greater interest in detail and individualisation of faces brought about by Burgundian-influenced art did not always translate into a greater interest in representing women's biological age in an accurate way. This is clearly evidenced in the sculptures of the altarpiece dedicated to Saint Anne promoted by Countess Mencía de Mendoza y Figueroa (ca. 1421–1499). The work was carried out by the Flemish sculptor Gil de Siloé. This piece occupies a privileged place within the funerary chapel dedicated to the Purification which Mencía ordered to be built in the cathedral of Burgos for her own burial and that of her husband, the first Constable of Castile Pedro Fernández de Velasco (ca. 1425–1492).⁴⁸ The largest part of the work was executed around 1498. It remained unfinished when the

---

46 Nixon, *Mary's Mother*, 148.
47 Clementina Julia Ara Gil, *En torno al escultor Alejo de Vahía (1490–1510)* (Valladolid: Universidad de Valladolid, 1974).
48 On the Purification Chapel at Burgos cathedral, see: Felipe Pereda Espeso and Alfonso Rodríguez G. De Ceballos, "*Coeli enarrant gloriam dei:* Arquitectura, iconografía y liturgia en la capilla de los Condestables de la Catedral de Burgos," *Annali di Architettura: Rivista del Centro Internazionale di Studi di Architettura "Andrea Palladio"* 9 (1997): 17–34; Isidro G. Bango Torviso, "Simón de Colonia y la ciudad de Burgos: Sobre la definición estilística de las segundas generaciones de familias de artistas extranjeros en los siglos XV y XVI," in *Actas del Congreso Internacional sobre Gil Siloe y la Escultura de su época* (Burgos: Centro Cultural "Casa del Cordón," 2001), 51–69; Elena Paulino Montero, "Patrocinio religioso, patrocinio artístico e identidad familiar a finales de la Edad Media: El caso de los Fernández de Velasco," *eHumanista: Journal of Iberian Studies* 24 (2013): 411–32 at 422–28; Elena Paulino Montero, "*Ea quae insignite fiunt sepulcra mortuorum:* La capilla de la Purificación de la catedral de Burgos y la creación de la memoria," in *Retórica artística en el tardogótico castellano: La capilla fúnebre de Álvaro de Luna en contexto*, ed. Olga Pérez Monzón, Matilde Miquel Juan, and María Martín Gil (Madrid: Sílex, 2018), 243–58.

Fig. 4: Santa Ana Triple, Monastery of Santa María de Vileña (Burgos), fourteenth century. Polychrome wood. Photo: Mercedes Pérez Vidal.

countess died and was resumed from 1522 by Diego de Siloé, Gil de Siloé's son, under the patronage of Mencía's grandson, the fourth Constable of Castile.[49]

One of the most outstanding characteristics of the altarpiece is that it is entirely composed of round sculptures of holy women. In the lower register we find the figures of Saint Dorothea and Saint Mary Magdalene; the upper register features Saint Barbara, Saint Catherine of Alexandria, and Saint Margaret, the latter added by Diego de Siloé in the sixteenth century. The central part of the altarpiece displays a sculpture of *Santa Ana Triple* flanked by Saint Elizabeth and Saint Helena, mother of the Emperor Constantine (Fig. 5). The main figures are surrounded by a multitude of tiny sculptures of unidentified female martyrs. This iconography, of great originality within Castilian imagery, was most likely chosen by the promoter herself and reflects her particular way of understanding the relationship between gender, memory, and lineage.[50] I will, however, exclusively focus on the way in which this design was materialised.

The three most visible figures of the altarpiece are sculptures of women who were over fifty years old. Elizabeth, as we have seen, was already an elderly woman when she conceived Saint John the Baptist. Helena, who died at the age of fifty-five, was the mother of an adult man and was credited with the discovery of the Holy Cross towards the end of her life.[51] Moreover, Anne is represented as a grandmother with the Virgin and Child. However, all three are depicted with the facial features of young women. Nevertheless, there is a willingness to show the importance of advanced age as an attribute of these saints in order to make them recognisable. Anne's head is covered with a veil and she wears a wimple around her neck, an outfit that could be linked to her widowhood. However, Elizabeth, who was an elderly woman but not a widow, wears exactly the

---

49 For an analysis of this altarpiece from a stylistic point of view, see Margarita Estella Marcos, *La imaginería de los retablos de la capilla del Condestable de la Catedral de Burgos* (Burgos: Aldecoa, 1995).

50 For an interpretation of the iconography in relation to Mencía de Mendoza, see Felipe Pereda Espeso, "Mencía de Mendoza (1500), mujer del I Condestable de Castilla: El significado del patronazgo femenino en la Castilla del siglo XV," in *Patronos y coleccionistas: Los Condestables de Castilla y el arte (siglos XV–XVII)*, ed. Begoña Alonso et al. (Valladolid: Universidad de Valladolid, 2005), 81–89.

51 The earliest accounts of Saint Helena's life do not mention her age or the precise date of her discovery of the True Cross. For the origins of Helena's legend, see: Jan Willem Drijvers, *Helena Augusta: The Mother of Constantine the Great and the Legend of Her Finding of the True Cross* (Leiden: Brill, 1992), 79–180. Neither does the *Legenda Aurea* by Jacopo da Varazze, which was widely disseminated during the Late Middle Ages: Jacopo da Varazze, *Legenda Aurea*, ed. Giovannni Paolo Maggioni, vol. 1 (Florence: Sismel, Edizioni del Galluzzo, 2007), 521–25.

Fig. 5: Saint Elizabeth, Santa Ana Triple and Saint Helena. Saint Anne Altarpiece, Purification Chapel, Burgos Cathedral (ca. 1498). Polychrome wood. Photo: Felipe Pereda Espeso.

same outfit and headdress. In this case, old age is clearly represented through clothing, while the women's physical appearances show no signs of ageing.

Helena wears a low-cut dress and a much thinner veil that reveals part of her hair. Despite being a middle-aged widowed woman, she is represented with the appearance of a young girl. In fact, Saint Helena was not often depicted as a mature woman. For instance, in the painted altarpiece of Saint John and Saint Catherine in Sigüenza Cathedral, dated in the first half of the fifteenth century and therefore much earlier than the one in Burgos, the saint appears next to the prophet Isaiah.[52] While the latter is obviously an old man, albeit idealised, and has a long white beard, Helena has a youthful appearance. She wears her hair partially covered with a crown and a sheer see-through veil. Helena is depicted as a queen, highlighting her status as the mother of an emperor, and carrying the Cross on her right shoulder. In the Crown of Aragon, the altarpiece of the Holy Cross at the church of Blesa (Teruel), also of Burgundian influence,

---

[52] Mª Teresa López de Guereño Sanz, "El patronazgo de los de La Cerda en la Catedral de Sigüenza: Su capilla funeraria y el retablo de San Juan y Santa Catalina," in *Imágenes y promotores en el arte medieval: Miscelánea en homenaje a Joaquín Yarza Luaces*, ed. Mª Luisa Melero Moneo et al. (Bellaterra: Universitat Autònoma de Barcelona, Servei de Publicacions, 2001), 485, 492.

which was executed by the painters Miguel Ximénez and Martín Bernat around 1481–1487,[53] shows Helena in three different scenes. Again, she is wearing a crown and a sheer veil, and her face does not exhibit any sign of ageing. Meanwhile, the various men depicted in the same paintings do have wrinkles, white or grey hair, and beards of different lengths.

Returning to the Burgos altarpiece, on the one hand, the disparate representation of the three women is possibly due to the fact that age played an important part in the construction of Anne's and Elizabeth's sainthood—in particular in their ability to conceive and bear children in older age—while it was irrelevant to Helena's. On the other hand, it is important to note that, unlike the other two saints, Helena was not an elderly woman. Nevertheless, the faces of the three women are practically identical to each other and to that of the Virgin Mary accompanying Saint Anne. The rest of the women in the altarpiece also present a youthful and barely individualised appearance. The whole reveals a complete lack of interest in women's bodies beyond an idealised, generic, and ageless form of normative femininity captured through youthful faces replicated in an almost serial fashion.[54] This idea of replication and repetition is reinforced by the presence of the numerous small figures of anonymous martyrs, all young and all alike, that surround the main sculptures.

Since this altarpiece only includes representations of female characters, the work itself does not supply any male figure with which to make a comparison. However, another slightly earlier work by Gil de Siloé, also consecrated to the mother of the Virgin and the Immaculate Conception, is preserved in the same cathedral. This piece features both men and women of different ages. It is located in the chapel of the Immaculate Conception, the burial place of Bishop Luis de Acuña who commissioned the work. The piece was executed between 1483 and 1492 by Gil de Siloé with the collaboration of the painter Diego de la Cruz, who was in charge of the polychromy.[55] Its iconography revolves around the representation of the Tree of Jesse and the Virgin Mary's ancestors. The centre of the altarpiece is occupied by the scene of Saint Joachim and Saint Anne meeting at the

---

53 Mª Carmen Lacarra Ducay, "El retablo mayor de la iglesia de la Santa Cruz de Blesa (Teruel) 1481–1487," in *Blesa: Patrimonio artístico*, ed. Antonio Beltrán, Mª Carmen Lacarra Ducay, and Concha Lomba Serrano (Blesa: Asociación Cultural El Hocino de Blesa, 2004), 47–93.

54 For a general reflection on the lack of individuality and presumed perpetual youthfulness of female figures in Western art, see the seminal work by Griselda Pollock, "The Grace of Time: Narrativity, Sexuality, and a Visual Encounter at the Virtual Feminist Museum," *Art History* 26/2 (2004): 174–213.

55 On this altarpiece, see Joaquín Yarza Luaces, *Gil Siloe: El retablo de la Concepción en la capilla del obispo Acuña* (Burgos: Asociación Amigos de la Catedral, 2000).

Golden Gate. Although Anne's age is difficult to determine from her physical appearance, she has a more expressive and mature face than in the previous case. She is depicted in the same type of outfit as in the example above. Nevertheless, she looks younger than her husband, who is clearly shown as an older man through his greying beard and the wrinkles on his forehead. Other sculptures in the altarpiece are even more revealing. For instance, the representation of Bishop Acuña surrounded by his relatives and canons is worth noting: all men's bodies show various degrees of ageing through wrinkles, beards, and hair of different lengths, and individualised and differentiated faces. The same can be said about the male characters included in the Virgin's genealogy and the Four Evangelists. Meanwhile, the female characters in the scene of the Holy Women before Christ's tomb, which is depicted at the bottom of the altarpiece, are only differentiated through dress: Mary Salome and the Virgin have their heads covered while Mary Magdalene has her long blond hair on display. As in the previous example, their faces are ageless and all very similar.

However, another collaboration between Gil de Siloé and Diego de la Cruz shows different features. The sculpture depicting Saint Elizabeth in the main altarpiece at the Cartuja de Miraflores,[56] also in Burgos and strictly contemporary to the works of the Purification Chapel (1496–1499) looks unambiguously like an older woman. Although it is a very idealised representation, Elizabeth's face shows obvious signs of ageing that contrast with the youth of Queen Isabel of Portugal, who appears in prayer next to her. This apparently random choice of iconographies to represent older female saints could be a consequence of the repetition of models and serial production that was prevalent at the time. This has been proven in relation to the sculpture of Saint Anne in the Purification Chapel that I have already analysed. This piece, which combines the iconography of Saint Anne teaching the Virgin and that of the *Santa Ana Triple*, closely follows a model from Mechelen of which at least five practically identical examples have been identified so far.[57] In any case, a lack of interest in consistently representing women's age in an accurate way is evident.

---

[56] Joaquín Yarza Luaces, "El retablo mayor de la Cartuja de Miraflores," in *Actas del Congreso Internacional sobre Gil Siloe y la Escultura de su época* (Burgos: Centro Cultural "Casa del Cordón," 2001), 207–38.

[57] Pereda Espeso, "Mencía de Mendoza," 87, n. 212. On the other five sculptures, see Ton Brandenbarg, *Heilige Anna, grote moeder: De cultus van de Heilige Moeder Anna en haar familie* (Uden: Uitverij Sun, Museum voor Religieuze Kunst, 1992), 147–48, 150. As Pereda Espeso points out, another example that seems to follow the same model can be found in Henk van Os, *The Art of Devotion in the Late Middle Ages in Europe 1300–1500* (Amsterdam: Rijksmuseum Amsterdam, 1995), 96. On mass production of altarpiece sculptures and serial repetition, see Lynn F.

Conclusions

The representation of older female characters was widespread in medieval Iberian religious art—albeit not as much as the depiction of their male counterparts—and they occupied places of maximum importance in pictorial and sculptural works. However, their old age was often not made visible or clearly decodable.

Age was visually expressed through a complex interplay between physical characteristics and dress. Generally the only body part on display in depictions of older women is their face. Thus, skin and facial features usually act as the only indicators of biological ageing in female characters, while hair and beards also played a crucial role in depictions of men. Although women's ageing bodies were almost invisible in medieval Iberian art until the fourteenth century—in most cases until well into the fifteenth—features such as more angular faces or wrinkles were gradually incorporated. Yet, unambiguously wrinkled faces did not become common until the second half of the fifteenth century. Even in some late fifteenth-century artworks such as the altarpiece dedicated to Saint Anne in the Purification Chapel of Burgos cathedral, women of different ages are represented with practically identical faces, choosing an idealised form of beauty that rests on the norm of youthfulness over individualisation and a plausible representation of age. This phenomenon contrasts with the way in which age is approached in representations of male characters, sometimes even in the same works, where bodily features corresponding to different stages of the life cycle are depicted explicitly and in detail from earlier chronologies. Men of diverse ages are clearly represented, if not through facial features, then at least using their hair and beard to differentiate them from each other.[58]

Dress, on the other hand, acts as the main visual indicator of age ordering among women. While in earlier images female characters of different ages are often absolutely indistinguishable, from the fourteenth century onwards they are increasingly differentiated through clothing, as shown by the depictions of Elizabeth and Mary in the scene of the Visitation. This is a consequence of significant changes concerning the role assigned to fashion in Western societies.

Jacobs, *Early Netherlandish Carved Altarpieces 1380–1550: Medieval Tastes and Mass Marketing* (Cambridge: Cambridge University Press, 1998), 166–91.

58 On this subject, although it comes from a different geographical and artistic context than the ones analysed in this study, it is interesting to note the reflection by the Late Gothic Italian painter Cennino Cennini (1370–ca. 1440), who distinguished three categories of human beings that could be depicted in artworks: young men, women, and old men, leaving women in a generic category in which age did not appear as a relevant factor. Cennino Cennini, *The Craftsman's Handbook: The Italian "Il libro dell'arte,"* ed. Daniel V. Thompson (New York: Dover, 1960), 123.

In iconography, until well into the fifteenth century, the result is most often a remarkable contrast between youthful, ageless faces and clothing that reveals the actual age of the woman depicted. Both the prevalence of covered-up clothing among older female characters and the rejuvenation of faces in their visual depictions need to be understood within the context of a cultural repertoire largely shaped by the "male gaze,"[59] in which the ageing female body is systematically devalued and deprecated.

---

[59] On the concept of male gaze in a medieval context, see the groundbreaking work by Madeline Caviness, *Visualizing Women in the Middle Ages: Sight, Spectacle, and Scopic Economy* (Philadelphia: University of Pennsylvania Press, 2001).

Part II: **The Religious Edge**

Rachel Ernst
Chapter 5
Catharistae in Question: A Case of Rupture in the Manichaean Sect

Scholars who specialize in the study of heresy in the High Middle Ages are in the midst of an historiographical dilemma. The traditional narrative which professed the existence of an organized heretical sect known as the "Cathars" during the twelfth through fourteenth centuries in Western Europe has been called into question, denounced, and even purported to have been fabricated. Multiple scholars have registered their skepticism regarding the existence of any cohesive dualist sect before the inquisitions that post-dated the Albigensian Crusade.[1] Providing a striking example of how deeply entrenched this skepticism has become, Mark Gregory Pegg begins his chapter in the 2016 publication, *Cathars in Question*, by stating, "Catharism was neither a Balkan heresy, a construct of the persecuting society, or, for that matter, even a medieval phenomenon, as it has never existed, except as an enduring tradition of late nineteenth-century scholars of religion and history."[2] He continues arguing against the use of the term "Cathar" to refer to heresy in the High Middle Ages, as, according to him, the epithet is burdened with the supposition of the existence of a cohesive sect of heretics.[3]

These statements illustrate our current predicament. The primary sources that informed the traditional narrative of an organized Cathar counter-church are almost exclusively written by their opponents, specifically Christian theologians, ecclesiastical authorities, and inquisitors. Therefore, a deconstruction of the accepted understanding of medieval heresy was as inevitable as it was necessary.[4] However, if I may take Lucy Sackville's remark in *Heresy and Heretics in*

---

[1] Robert I. Moore provides a summary of these views, as expressed at the conference held at the Warburg Institute at the University College London in April of 2013, in the chapter "Principles at Stake: The Debate of April 2013 in Retrospect," in *Cathars in Question*, ed. Antontio Sennis, Vol. 4 (York: York Medieval Press, 2016), 257–73.
[2] Mark Gregory Pegg, "The Paradigm of Catharism; or, the Historians' Illusion," in *Cathars in Question*, 21–52 at 21.
[3] Pegg, "The Paradigm of Catharism," 28–34.
[4] It should be noted that literature espousing the ideology associated with the Western European group known as "Cathar" in the High Middle Ages, while sparse when compared to the extensive repository of works written by their detractors, does exist. Examples include the commentary on the *Pater Noster* in MS 269 of the Mediaeval and Renaissance Latin Manuscripts

the Thirteenth Century, out of context, "[T]hat necessary deconstruction can, when taken to an extreme, lead to a complete unravelling of the construct or representation [...]."[5] Sackville wrote these words to caution scholars against disconnecting polemical constructions of heresy from the heretics themselves. They could have just as well have been a warning to historians. A "complete unravelling" of our own construct of heresy in the High Middle Ages is exactly the dilemma that we now face. The result is the proliferation of a kaleidoscope of perspectives on this subject, and a lack of a common narrative.

In order to mitigate the rising tide of historiographical plurality, collaborative projects have been created to facilitate communication and share information between scholars in the field. For example, the Medieval Heresy and Dissent Research Network (hereinafter, MHDRN) at the University of Nottingham has facilitated discussion by organizing local conferences, and sponsoring panels and sessions at the International Medieval Congress at Leeds.[6] The Dissident Networks Project hosted by Masaryk University has used information from inquisition documents to create social network analysis and geographic information science maps, allowing scholars open access to common data.[7]

Others have taken the initiative to coordinate with fellow scholars to delineate the points of contention and consent regarding the origin and existence of the Cathars. In April of 2013, scholars gathered at the Warburg Institute at University College London for a conference entitled "Catharism: Balkan Heresy or Construct of a Persecuting Society?" The papers presented at this event were then published by York Medieval Press under the title *Cathars in Question*. This volume is unequalled in its range of viewpoints on the question of dualist heresy in Western Europe, offering the academic perspectives of fourteen different scholars.[8] Within its pages, the reader is presented with the full spectrum of perspectives on medieval heretical thought: from the views of "traditionalists," who subscribe to the view that Cathars were a cohesive sect with dualist beliefs

---

Collection at Trinity College, Dublin; the dualist theological treatise *Liber de duobus principiis*; and the "Florence Ritual" found in MS J.II.44, held at the Biblioteca Nazionale Centrale in Florence. David Zbíral provides a detailed analysis of the contents and authors of MS J.II.44 in "Heretical Hands at Work: Reconsidering the Genesis of a Cathar Manuscript (Ms. *Firenze, Biblioteca Nazionale Centrale, conv. soppr.* J.II.44)," *Revue d'Histoire des Textes* 12 (2017): 261–88.

5 Lucy Sackville, *Heresy and Heretics in the Thirteenth Century: The Textual Representations* (York: York Medieval Press, 2011), 9.

6 University of Nottingham, "Medieval Heresy and Dissent Research Network," https://www.nottingham.ac.uk/research/groups/medieval-heresy-and-dissent/index.aspx.

7 Masaryk University's Centre for the Digital Research of Religion, "Dissident Networks Project," https://dissinet.cz/.

8 "Acknowledgements," in *Cathars in Question*, vii–viii at vii.

Chapter 5: *Catharistae* in Question: A Case of Rupture in the Manichaean Sect — 121

which may have originated from the Balkans, to those maintained by "deconstructionists" or "skeptics," who reject this view entirely, and those of the majority, whose ideas lie somewhere in the middle.

In his introductory chapter, editor Antonio Sennis writes, "This volume constitutes an attempt to move the debate forward, and also, hopefully, to be a source of ideas for future analysis."[9] While there are more points of agreement than anticipated between the authors in this volume, determined and occasionally hostile rhetoric betrays the intractable stance that these contributors continue to take when defending their arguments. As Robert Moore remarks, "It may seem churlish, even arrogant, so uncompromisingly to dismiss the possibility of a compromise [...]. But as to the main point at issue middle ground does not exist."[10] Perhaps he is correct. Perhaps there are some matters on which we should not compromise. However, within this field, the polarization of thought and unwillingness to compromise has led to a "complete unraveling" of any cohesive narrative. The problem we are now faced with is "where do we go from here?"

In July of 2019 at the International Medieval Congress at Leeds, the MHDRN hosted a roundtable discussion entitled "New Perspectives on Late Medieval Heresy: A Round Table Discussion." During this panel, the question of narrative when addressing heresy was posed. There are as few historians remaining who adhere to a strict, traditional narrative of the Cathars as there are who completely reject their existence. How are we to discuss the events and practices, not to mention beliefs of these individuals, when we have not even reached a consensus on what they should be called?[11] How are we to educate those who are entirely unfamiliar with this topic?

The question of how we are to frame discussion of this subject needs to be addressed if we are to have any "future analysis" and advance scholarship in this field. As it stands, an *apologia* for each author's stance in this "spectrum of interpretation" (or an explanation as to why they will be sidestepping the

---

9 Antonio Sennis, "Questions about the Cathars," in *Cathars in Question*, 1–20 at 19–20.
10 Moore, "Principles at Stake," 268.
11 Several scholars agree that referring to heretics of the High Middle Ages as "Cathar" is inaccurate, but a viable alternative has yet to be agreed upon. See: Uwe Brunn, *Des Contestataires aux "Cathares": Discours de réforme et propagande antihérétique dans le pays du Rhin et de la Meuse avant l'Inquisition* (Paris: Institut d'Études Augustiniennes, 2006); Pilar Jiménez-Sanchez, *Les catharismes: Modèles dissidents du christianisme medieval (XIIe–XIIIe siècles)* (Rennes: Presses Universitaires de Rennes, 2008); Rebecca Rist, "'Lupi rapaces in ovium vestimentis': Heretics and Heresy in Papal Correspondence," in *Cathars in Question*, 229–41; Claire Taylor, "Looking for 'Good Men' in the Languedoc: An Alternative to 'Cathars'?," in *Cathars in Question*, 242–56.

issue altogether) has become an expected inclusion in every publication written on medieval heresy. While this serves to orient the audience on the author's position in the historiography of the current debate, it has the undesired effect of either putting the reader on the offensive or priming them to agree with the author's conclusions before they have finished reading the introduction. An initiate wishing to learn more about this topic must first acclimate themselves to this dizzying spectrum of scholarship and even decide what views they subscribe to before engaging with the source material. This is a challenge endemic to the study of any field of history, but the lack of resources written by the hands of the subjects of study and the historically strong opinions present in secondary literature make this particular topic a difficult landscape to navigate for newcomers. In spite of the intrinsic, reductionist nature of using narratives to convey historical information, they are ultimately necessary to facilitate communication, to reach an audience of non-specialists, and to teach this subject to students at an undergraduate and graduate level. We need a fresh narrative in order to reach new audiences and to facilitate the exchange of ideas between one another. For a new narrative to emerge, we need a new strategy.

Our historiographical dilemma is rooted in an erroneous narrative that is nearly two centuries old. Each new academic contribution, consciously or not, seeks to undermine or enforce this narrative. We cannot break free from this narrative because it is the foundation of our field. We cannot compromise, because doing so would mean consciously dismissing what we believe to be true. However, this does not have to be the case for new scholars who are entering the field.

If we are to move forward, we must be willing to accept the limitations of established academic historiographical traditions and dare to embrace alternative methods of communication. I suggest that we put aside the traditional style of constructing a single historical argument when introducing new research, and instead present the information with an argument that allows for the possibility of two or more conclusions, each based on an established historiographical narrative. This model can be framed as an internal debate, a tactic that scholars often use for the sake of anticipating their detractors' rebuttal. The exception in this case is that one argument does not prevail over another. In lieu of a conclusion, the author summarizes the strengths and weaknesses of the evidence supporting an existing narrative and leaves the reader to arrive at their own conclusion.

This style of presentation necessitates that the authors consciously distance themselves from their previous biases and opinions. I am aware that, while theoretically possible, this is unlikely to be completely successful in practice. Any specialist will have an affinity for one interpretation of the information over another and this will be apparent as they, either consciously or unintentionally, argue one side with more passion and skill than the other. I hope, however, that the act of advocating for a position that one is disinclined to agree with will encourage research into resources, methods, and disciplines that scholars would not have considered previously, and allow us to acknowledge the merit of positions that we may have dismissed. My primary motivation in proposing this method is to allow new scholars to approach the material untethered to the narratives and counternarratives to which current academics find themselves shackled. By presenting two diametrically opposed historiographical arguments, the readers are introduced to the extant ideologies but are not pressed by the author to subscribe to one over the other, and are free to form their own opinion.

A multi-sided historical debate model is not practical for the presentation of all research. There are times when the evidence only supports one possible interpretation. The apparent lack of conviction when an author does not reach a definitive conclusion carries with it the risk that the work may not be perceived as having made a meaningful contribution. That possibility does not detract from the benefits that this method has to offer. Its purpose is to serve as a springboard for discussion and to promote further research.

In this article, I will apply this style to some of the issues that have proved so divisive by stepping back from the medieval period and focusing on the Manichaeans in the Western Mediterranean during the fifth century. The reader would not be remiss in thinking me timid for selecting a topic removed from the fraught historiographical battleground that is heresy in the High Middle Ages to demonstrate my proposed model. However, I would argue that the hesitancy that I feel in addressing medieval dissonance head-on is exactly why this approach is necessary. The academic atmosphere surrounding this material has become so polarized that it is prudent to use a topic that does not elicit an emotional reaction as a test case.

The case study I will discuss is that of a splinter sect of Manichaeans called the Catharists (*catharistae*). While many medievalists will recognize that Augustine of Hippo's treatises against this religion were used in polemics and rhetoric to denounce medieval dissidents, here, my interest lies in a particular group of Manichaeans discussed by Augustine. In his book, *Des Contestataires aux "Cathares,"* Uwe Brunn suggests that Eckbert of Schönau's choice of the name "Cathar" for the group of heretics, which he believed were descendants of the Manichaeans, was selected in order to associate them with the Catharists of Augustine's time.[12] Perhaps it was for the sake of instilling an additional sense

---

12 Brunn, *Des Contestataires aux "Cathares,"* 323–33.

of abhorrence in his audience that Eckbert appended the chapter on Manicheans from *De haeresibus* to his work from 1163, *Sermones contra catharos*.[13]

First reported at a tribunal in Carthage in the year 421, these deponents were accused of particularly unusual and graphic sexual practices that were echoed at other tribunals held later that decade.[14] I will present two possible explanations for these charges: either the leaders of the tribunals and/or Augustine fabricated or exaggerated these rituals to further vilify this sect, or the reports were genuine and those that partook in these rituals did so to create an oppositional identity in defiance of increased persecution.

Regarding the possibility of fabrication or false testimony, I will discuss the passage of *De haeresibus* in which Augustine gives this account, along with his communication with Quodvultdeus of Carthage. Augustine's earlier writings against the Manichaeans will be compared to Manichaean theological texts to establish his accuracy in reporting Manichaean doctrine. To explore the likelihood that the practices of the Catharists were an act of defiant, created identity, I will outline the policy of the Roman state's increased persecution of the sect as recorded in the *Theodosian Code*, discuss the prevalence of Church opposition to Manichaeans, and describe Manichaeism's unique survival strategies.

It is not my intent to conclusively persuade the reader of either the accuracy or falsehood of the accusations that were made against this Manichaean sect. I wish to demonstrate the merits and failings of both possibilities so that, by virtue of being removed from familiar content, readers who study medieval history will be able to weigh the issues of oppositional reliability and sociological theory more dispassionately and reassess preconceived opinions on both.

The *Catharistae*

The only direct mention of the dissident Manichaean sect that Augustine calls the Catharists exists in his catalogue of heresies, *De haeresibus*, written in 428.[15] Prior to this, Augustine had penned nine treatises denouncing Manichaeism, a religion that he had practiced in his young adulthood until his disillusionment with the group's lack of charity and inability to satisfy his theological quer-

---

13 Eckbert of Schönau, *Sermones contra Catharos* (PL CXCV, cols. 97–102).
14 Johannes Van Oort, "'Human Semen Eucharist' Among the Manichaeans? The Testimony of Augustine Reconsidered in Context," *Vigiliae Christianae* 70 (2016): 193–216 at 198.
15 Augustine of Hippo, *De haeresibus ad Quodvultdeum* (PL XLII, col. 56). English translations of this text have been taken from Johannes Van Oort's article in *Vigiliae Christianae*.

ies led him to abandon the faith.[16] Augustine penned the first book of *De haeresibus* intending it to be part one of a two-volume set. This book consists of a detailed list delineating the beliefs and practices of every heretical sect known to Augustine that had existed from the time of Christ, eighty-eight groups in total. The second volume was intended to contain refutations for each of these heresies; however, Augustine died before he could complete the second part.[17]

Twenty-four years had passed since he had written the last of his works against the Manichaean religion. Augustine received multiple letters from Quodvultdeus, Archdeacon of Carthage, imploring him to write a compendium of heresies and a refutation against them for the Latin-speaking clergy of the region, citing the multiple heresies and heterodox beliefs that plagued the city.[18] He initially declined, explaining that Epiphanius of Cyprus and Philastrius of Brescia had each composed similar works, and he did not believe that he had anything to add. Indeed, when he finally acquiesced to Quodvultdeus's requests and composed the *De haeresibus*, he borrowed heavily from the polemics of both of the aforementioned authors, as well as from Eusebius of Caesarea.[19]

Augustine's most original contribution to the genre of anti-heretical handbooks can be found in the longest section, chapter forty-six. In this chapter, Augustine educates his audience on the practices and beliefs of the Manichaeans. Not only did he distill his previous expositions on Manichaean doctrine into 1,600 words, he added new information that had come to his attention since the composition of his last anti-Manichaean treatise, *Contra Felicem manichaeum* in 404.[20] His source material was based on the confessions of three deponents from two different tribunals held in Carthage. The testimony of these individuals provided evidence of a disturbing, secret ritual and the emergence of a divergent sect within Manichaeism.

The first tribunal took place after a procurator named Ursus uncovered a Manichaean sect in the area. Augustine was among the bishops who were called

---

16 Augustine of Hippo, *Confessions* III–V, ed. and trans. Albert C. Outler (Louisville: Westminster John Knox, 1955).
17 Liguori G. Müller, "Introduction," in Augustine of Hippo, *De haeresibus: A Translation with an Introduction and Commentary*, ed. and trans. Liguori G. Müller (Washington DC: Catholic University of America Press, 1956), 1–53 at 8–9.
18 Quodvultdeus, "Letter 221," in *Corpus Scriptorum Ecclesiasticorum Latinorum*, ed. Alois Goldbacher, vol. 57 (Vienna: F. Temsky; Leipzig: G. Freytag, 1911), 443.
19 Augustine of Hippo, "Letters 222 and 224," in *Corpus Scriptorum Ecclesiasticorum*; Quodvultdeus, "Letters 221 and 223," in *Corpus Scriptorum Ecclesiasticorum*.
20 Augustine of Hippo, *De haeresibus ad Quodvultdeum* (PL XLII, col. 54–58); Augustine of Hippo, *De haeresibus: A Translation*, 3–9; J. Kevin Coyle, *Manichaeism and Its Legacy* (Leiden: Brill, 2009), 278; Van Oort, "'Human Semen Eucharist'," 3–4.

to interrogate the accused.[21] In *De haeresibus*, he explained that, during the course of the deposition, a girl named Margarita, who "was not yet twelve years old," revealed that she had been violated as part of a wicked rite, though he does not elucidate the details of this ritual in this section. Next, he wrote that, after initially denying it, a Manichaean "quasi-nun" called Eusebia, confessed that she too had taken part in this ritual. Her confession came after an examination by a midwife revealed that she was not a virgin, as she had originally claimed. Augustine took care to note that Eusebia had never been in Margarita's presence, indicating that their testimony had not been contaminated by collaboration.[22]

After this tribunal, several other deponents who were interrogated at subsequent hearings confessed to having participated in the same ritual. While Augustine was present at the tribunal where Margarita's and Eusebia's testimonies were given, he was not in attendance for the hearings that followed, and learned of the confessions in a record he calls *Gesta episcopalia*, which was given to him by Quodvultdeus.[23] One of these deponents was a man named Viator, who pro-

---

[21] Possidius, *Vita Sancti Aurelii Augustini, Hipponensis Episcopi* (PL XXXII, col. 46).

[22] "[U]bi puella nomine Margarita istam nefariam turpitdinem prodidit, quae cum esset annorum nondum duodecim, proprter hoc scelestum mysterium se dicebat esse vitatam. Tunc Eusebium quandam manichaeum quasi sanctimonialem, idipsum propter hoc ipsum passam, uix compluit confiteri, cum primo illa se asseruisset integram, atque ab obstetrice inspici postulasset. Quae inspecta et quid esset inventa, totum illud turpissimum scelus, ubi ad excipiendum et commiscendum semen farina substernitur, quod Margarita indicante absens non audierat similiter indicavit." Augustine of Hippo, *De haeresibus ad Quodvultdeum* (PL XLII, col. 56). [At this time a girl by the name of Margarita betrayed this monstrous ugliness and claimed, though she was not yet twelve years old, that she had been violated on account of this wicked rite. Then, with difficulty, he compelled Eusebia, some kind of Manichaean nun, to confess that she had undergone the same treatment because of this very same rite, though, at first, she maintained that she was intact and insisted on being examined by a midwife. When she was examined and when her true condition was discovered, she likewise gave information on that whole extremely ugly crime at which flour is sprinkled beneath a couple in sexual intercourse to receive and commingle with their seed. This she had not heard when Margarita gave her testimony, for she had not been present], Van Oort, "'Human Semen Eucharist'," 194–95.

[23] "Et recenti tempore nonnulli eorum reperti et ad ecclesiam ducti, sicut gesta episcopalia quae nobis misisti ostenunt, hoc non sacramentum sed exsecramentum sub diligenti interrogation confessi sunt." Augustine of Hippo, *De haeresibus ad Quodvultdeum* (PL XLII, col. 56). [Even in recent times several of them have been discovered and brought before ecclesiastical authority, as the Episcopal Acts which you have sent us show. Under careful examination, they confessed that this is no sacrament, but a sacrilege], Van Oort, "'Human Semen Eucharist' Among the Manichaeans?," 195.

vided his accusers with the name of the sect of Manichaeans who practiced this ritual, the Catharists.[24]

Following his description of the tribunal testimony, Augustine explained the etymology of this epithet by detailing the ritual and using his previous experience with Manichaean scripture to elucidate the reasoning behind it. He writes that this "sacrilegious" act involved two individuals copulating on top of a surface sprinkled with flour, the purpose of which was so that the seed from their union could be gathered by the Manichaeans, who would then consume it along with the flour. He explained that the intention of this ritual was that the Manichaeans could release the particles of divinity trapped within the semen, allowing it to be set free. The name *catharistae*, meaning "purifiers," referred to the belief that they were purifying the semen by ingesting it.[25]

Truth and Fiction in the Historical Record

Any student of the history of heresy would be wise to register skepticism upon hearing Augustine's description of this ritual and suspicion as to the manner in which the testimony was obtained. There are as many points that raise wariness in what is omitted from the record as there are in what is written. While inquisition documents taken from deponents during the thirteenth and fourteenth centuries present challenges when attempting to discern the accuracy of the be-

---

24 "Quorum unus nomine Viator eos qui ista faciunt proprie Catharistas vocari dicens." Augustine of Hippo, *De haeresibus ad Quodvultdeum* (PL XLII, col. 56). [One of them, whose name is Viator, claimed that those who commit such acts are properly called Catharists], Van Oort, "'Human Semen Eucharist' Among the Manichaeans?," 195.
25 "[D]ivinas enim virtutes quantum possunt imitari se putant ut purgent Dei sui partem; quam profecto, sicut in omnibus corporibus caelestibus et terrestribus atque in omnium rerum seminibus, ita et in hominis semine teneri existimant inquintatam. Ac per hoc sequitur eos, ut sic eam etiam de semine humano, quemadmodum de aliis seminibus quae in alimentis sumunt, debeant manducando purgare. Unde etian Catharistae appellantur, quasi purgatories, qui tanta eam purgantes diligentia ut se nec ab hac tam horrenda cibi turpitudine abstineant." Augustine of Hippo, *De haeresibus ad Quodvultdeum* (PL XLII, col. 56). [[T]hey are imitating divine powers as far as they can in order that they purge a part of their God, which they really believe is held befouled just as much in human seed as it is in all celestial and terrestrial bodies, and in the seeds of all things. And thus it follows that they are just as much obliged to purge from human seed by eating, as they are in reference to other seed which they consume in their food. This is the reason they are also called Catharists, as it were "purifiers" for they are so attentive to purifying this (part of their God) that they do not refrain even from the horrifying ugliness of such food], Van Oort, "'Human Semen Eucharist' Among the Manichaeans?," 195.

liefs of the accused,[26] they are plentiful, at the very least, and have garnered significant scholarly attention. In the case of the Catharists' trial, there is no record of the procedure or of the questions posed to those called before the tribunal. No transcript exists of their confessions, only a summary of their responses. We do not know what acts of coercion, if any, Eusebia endured between her initial testimony and her confession, other than the examination by the midwife (which, according to Augustine, was performed at Eusebia's request).

Moreover, as Augustine was not present at the tribunals that took place in "recent times," we have no way of knowing how these proceedings occurred. Though he makes a point of registering his disapproval of influencing deponents' confessions, if we are to take him at his word when he emphasizes the impossibility of communication between Margarita and Eusebia, even Augustine himself did not know if the ritual described at the initial hearing influenced the questions that were posed to deponents in the years that followed. Since Quodvultdeus was a correspondent of Augustine and was present at the more recent tribunals, we can assume that he, and likely other members of the clergy in Carthage, were aware of the accusations made at this infamous trial.

The entire existence of the Catharist sect can be interpreted as an invention of the Church that began when a child, who may well have been a victim of sexual trauma, was asked questions that led the tribunal to conclude that the nefarious Manichaeans were the culprits of the assault.

Following this supposition, Eusebia's testimony would have been coerced to substantiate the tribunal's suspicions, and the subsequent trials convicted Manichaeans of the same crime after they were subjected to questioning and coercion that fit the pattern that the members of the tribunal had created. Augustine's interpretation of these events completed the fabricated narrative by providing theological reasoning for why such a bizarre and sexualized ritual would have been practiced by a group of Manichaeans.

Accusations of esoteric, sexual rites are almost cliché when studying heresy, and most of these stories are dismissed as propaganda by modern historians. As common as such charges were in the medieval and Early Modern periods, they would not have been unfamiliar to those living in the fifth century. Before Christianity was legalized in the Roman Empire, Christians were accused of participating in unusual sexual practices in their clandestine meetings, of keeping multiple wives, and of having sexual relations with their mothers and sisters.[27] At the

---

26 James Given, *Inquisition and Medieval Society: Power, Discipline and Resistance in the Languedoc* (Ithaca, NY and London: Cornell University Press, 1997), 25–51.
27 Bart Wagemarkers, "Incest, Infanticide, and Cannibalism: Anti-Christian Imputations in the Roman Empire," *Greece & Rome* 57/2 (2010): 337–54 at 338.

same time, even Christian apologists, such as Hippolytus of Rome, accused other sects of Christians of practicing orgies in secret.[28] Allegations of sexual practices against heretical groups or individuals proliferated because they were effective in eliciting revulsion, since these acts subverted the perceived natural order and played on existing suspicions towards sects that were compelled to meet in secret due to persecution. The charge against the Catharists was especially effective in fomenting outrage since, in addition to the bizarreness of the sexual act and at least one instance that included the rape of a child, it also involved perverting the sacrament of the Eucharist.[29]

Whether based in truth or not, the legacy of this ritual and its power to invoke disgust towards dissidents outlived Augustine. Pope Leo I may have very well plagiarized *De haeresibus* in 443 in "Sermon XVI, On the Fast of the Tenth Month," when he related the following account that occurred during a deposition against the Manichaeans in Rome:

> And so with bishops and presbyters sitting beside me, and Christian nobles assembled in the same place, we ordered their elect men and women to be brought before us. And when they had made many disclosures concerning their perverse tenets and their mode of conducting festivals, they revealed this story of utter depravity also, which I blush to describe but which has been so carefully investigated that no grounds for doubt are left for the incredulous or for cavilers. For there were present all the persons by which the unutterable crime had been perpetrated, to wit a girl at most ten years old, and two women who had nursed her and prepared her for this outrage. There was also present the stripling who had outraged her, and the bishop, who had arranged their horrible crime. All these made one and the same confession, and a tale of such foul orgies was disclosed as our ears could scarcely bear.[30]

---

28 Hippolytus of Rome, "A Refutation of All Heresies," in *Ante-Nicene Fathers*, ed. Alexander Roberts, James Donaldson, and Arthur Cleveland Coxe, trans. John Henry MacMahon, vol. 5 (Buffalo: Christian Literature Publishing Co., 1886), chapter 1.

29 Although the primary witness in this tribunal was a child who testified that she was raped, possibly by multiple parties, the rape itself is only condemned in *De haeresibus* as the method by which the "wicked rite" was carried out (see fn. 39). Pope Leo I was far more preoccupied with the crime of rape, as is shown above.

30 Leo the Great, "Sermon XVI, On the Fast of the 10th Month," in *A Select Library of Nicene and Post-Nicene Fathers of the Christian Church: Leo the Great, Gregory the Great*, ed. Philip Schaff and Henry Wace (New York: The Christian Literature Company, 1895), 123–25 at 123. "Residentibus itasque mecum episcopis ac presbyteris, ac in eumdem conventum Christianis viris ac nobilibus congregatis, Electos et Electas eorum jussimus praesentari. Qui cum de perversitate dogmatis sui, et de festivitatum suarum consuetudine multa reserassent, illud quoque scelus, quod eloqui verecundum est, prodiderunt, quod tanta diligentia investigatum est, ut nihil minus credulis, nihil obtrectatoribus relinqueretur ambiguum. Aderant enim omnes personae, per quas infandum facinus fuerat perpetratum, puella scilicet ut multum decennis, et duae mulieres, quae

However, in spite of the incredulity we may feel upon reading Augustine's denunciation, there is no evidence that directly contradicts the truth of his claims. For the sake of argument, I would like to examine Augustine's history discussing the theology and practices of the Manichaeans in the Late Roman Empire to establish his record of accuracy. There are some other reports of Manichaean rituals that, while not identical to those described by Augustine, could allude to similar rites being carried out in other areas of the Empire.[31]

In addition, there are a set of sociological theories that have been applied to small dissident groups among dualist heretics in the medieval period, and at times, to the Cathar group as a whole, that could be applicable in this case as well. In his contribution to *Cathars in Question*, Julien Théry-Astruc mentions the "labeling theories" developed by a number of American sociologists in the twentieth century, along with the concept of "perverse implantation," formulated by Michel Foucault to explain the existence of genuine Cathar belief in the late thirteenth and early fourteenth centuries.[32] One of the implications of these theories is that individuals or groups of people who have been denounced as outsiders or deviants by a state, especially those who are persecuted by legal action, may adopt the labels, beliefs, and practices ascribed to them by their oppressors. This is not only an act of defiance, but a way to reclaim a social identity in a system of persecution. This has the potential to provide solidarity with other members of their society that have been likewise stigmatized.[33]

---

ipsam nutrierunt, et huic sceleri praepararant. Praesio erat etiam adolescentulus vitiator puellae, et episcopus ipsorum detestandi criminis ordinator. Horum omnium par fuit et una confessio, et patefactum est exsecramentum quod aures nostrae vix ferre potuerunt." Leo the Great, "Sermo XVI, De Jejunio decimi mensis" (PL LIV, col. 178).

31 For this, I rely heavily on the works of Johannes Van Oort, specifically his articles "'Human Semen Eucharist'" and "Another Case of the Human Semen Eucharist Among the Manichaeans? Notes on the 'Ceremony of the Fig' in Cyril of Jerusalem's *Catechesis* VI," *Vigiliae Christianae* 70 (2016): 430–40.

32 It is important to note that Théry does not believe that these theories are sufficient to explain the existence of genuine Cathar belief in light of the highly complex and fragmented nature of societal factors in play during this time. However, elements of what I will refer to as "constructed identity" theories are present in the works of many scholars who examine the inquisitions and the sociological changes they brought to the regions where they were imposed: Julien Théry-Astruc, "The Heretical Dissidence of the 'Good Men' in the Albigeois (1276–1329): Localism and Resistance to Roman Clericalism," in *Cathars in Question*, 79–111 at 81.

33 For the sake of brevity, I risk over-simplifying the complexities and variations within the aforementioned ideologies. For more on this topic, see Grado G. Merlo, *Eretici e inquisitori nella società piemontese del Trecento: Con l'edizione dei processi tenuti a Giaveno dall'inquisitore Alberto De Castellario (1335) e nelle Valli de Lanzo dall'inquisitore Tommaso Di Casasco (1373)* (Turin: Claudiana, 1977); and Julien Théry-Astruc, "L'hérésie des bons hommes: Comment

When we examine the extent of ecclesiastical and state persecution leveled against the Manichaeans in the Roman Empire in the fifth century, a picture emerges of a marginalized group that had been cut off from their co-religionists outside of the Empire and was facing extinction. There is no evidence that the Catharist ritual was practiced in Manichaeism outside of the Empire and the earliest report of a practice that resembles this rite dates to the 350s.[34] Therefore, it is reasonable to assume that if the Catharists existed, they innovated the ritual after decades of persecution. If we can accept that a sect that was subject to a persistent vilification by the state and ecclesiastical authorities might find a measure of solace in defying the established order by embracing the acts that they were accused of practicing, then Augustine's account of the Catharist ritual becomes more credible.[35]

Augustine and the Manichaeans

Augustine's personal relationship with Manichaeism began amicably. While living in Carthage in his late teens, Augustine became a hearer among the Manichaeans. In his autobiographical *Confessions*, he explains that his interest in the religion was rooted in the belief that he would have the opportunity to cultivate his understanding of the Christian Scriptures through their teachings.[36] He spent over a decade in their company, but abandoned the community after the Manichaean Bishop Faustus failed to provide satisfactory answers to his theological inquiries.[37] After his conversion to Christianity, Augustine penned nine treatises defending the faith against Manichaean doctrine, also condemning them in the *Confessions* and several letters of personal correspondence.

It is difficult to gauge his level of involvement in combatting the Manichaean sect after *Contra Felicem manichaeum* was written in 404. If we are to consider only his published works, it seems that they were no longer a source of preoccupation when Quodvultdeus contacted him in 427. However, his presence at the tribunal in 421 indicates he still had an interest in seeing that adherents of

---

nommer la dissidence religieuse non vaudoise ni beguine en Languedoc (XIIe–début du XIVe siècle)?," *Heresis* 36–37 (2002): 75–117.
34 Van Oort, "Another Case of the Human."
35 While the ritual itself may be explained by the construction of an oppositional identity, the criminal act of rape does not fit within this framework. See "Summary of Two Arguments" below.
36 Augustine of Hippo, *Confessions* III.
37 Augustine of Hippo, *Confessions* V.

the religion were either contained or converted to Christianity. His continued involvement in the conversion of reported Manichaeans is also supported by a letter to Quodvultdeus in which he requests, "Not to burden you, but I also charge you in writing back to me concerning the status in the Catholic faith of that Theodosius, by whom several Manichaeans were revealed, and likewise, of those persons exposed by him who we judged to be reformed."[38] The fact that his entry in *De haeresibus* on the Manichaeans far surpassed descriptions of other heresies in length and vitriol suggests that his loathing had not dissipated in his later years.

Collectively, the evidence indicates that Augustine was still vehement in his conviction that the Manichaean religion was subversive and that its practitioners needed to renounce their faith and embrace Christianity. To ascertain whether or not he exaggerated or constructed the narrative of the Catharists in *De haeresibus*, we should consider his record in reporting Manichaean doctrine. Augustine's account of Manichaean doctrine and practices can be verified as accurate when cross-referenced with their scripture in the nine treatises he composed prior to *De haeresibus*. For example, scholars originally considered Augustine's description of the Manichaean cosmogony to be an innovative piece of propaganda (understandably so, when one takes into account the highly convoluted nature of this myth, coupled with Augustine's derisive delivery). Then, a document written in Syriac by a Manichaean was unearthed at Turfan (China) at the end of the nineteenth century that corroborated his account.[39]

A specific excerpt from Augustine's creation story in *Contra Faustum*, applies to the theology that he uses to explain the Catharist ritual:

> When you represent your fabulous Christ, the son of your fabulous First Man [...] you say that he mingled with the principles of darkness in his conflict with the race of darkness, that by capturing these principles the world might be made out of the mixture. So that, by your profane fancies, Christ is not only mingled with heaven and all the stars, but conjoined and compounded with the earth and all its productions,—a Savior no more, but needing to be saved by you, by your eating and disgorging Him.[40]

---

[38] "Peto etiam mihi rescribere non graueris, quen ad modum sit in fide catholica ille Theodosius, per quem Manichaei nonnulli sunt prodit, et ipse, quos ab eo proditos putamus esse correctos." Augustine of Hippo, "Letter 222," in *Corpus Scriptorum Ecclesiasticorum*.

[39] Samuel N. C. Lieu, *Manichaeism in the Late Roman Empire and Medieval China: A Historical Survey* (Manchester: Manchester University Press, 1985), 8; Van Oort, "'Human Semen Eucharist'," 203–4.

[40] Augustine of Hippo, *Contra Faustum* II.V, in *The Works of Aurelius Augustine Bishop of Hippo: A New Translation*, ed. and trans. Marcus Dods (Edinburgh: T&T Clark, 1872), 145–499. "[C]um vos commentitium vestrum, filium commentitii primi hominis vestri [...] esse dicatis: quia videlicet pricipibus tenebrarum commixtum esse creditis in illo bello, quo ipse primus homo vester

Chapter 5: *Catharistae* in Question: A Case of Rupture in the Manichaean Sect — 133

Johannes Van Oort notes in his article "'Human Semen Eucharist' Among the Manichaeans?" that Augustine had access to at least a few Manichaean scriptural texts in Carthage and had suggested that something like the Catharist ritual might have been practiced long before the tribunal in 421. In *De natura boni contra manichaeos*, written in 399, he implied that since the Manichaeans believed that the God of Light was trapped in both seeds and in the impurity of human flesh, being liberated only when consumed by the members of the sect, it was natural to infer upon reading their scriptures that they practiced an "unspeakable error" in their zeal to liberate the God of Light.[41] Augustine adds that he had heard rumors of similar acts of "repulsiveness" among Manichaeans in Gaul and Paphlagonia.[42]

In conjunction with research into the Catharist ritual, Van Oort also re-examined a passage from the sixth volume of Cyril of Jerusalem's *Catechesis*, written in

---

cum tenebrarum gente pugnavit, ut de ipsis principibus tenebrarum tali commixtione captis mundus fabricaretur. Unde et ista sacrilga deliramenta vos cogunt, non soum in coelo atque in omnibus stellis, sed etiam in terra atque in omnibus quae nascuntur in ea, confixum et colligatum atque concretum Chrstium dicere, non jam Salvatorem vestrum, sed a vobis salvandum com ea manducatis atque ructatis." Augustine of Hippo, *Contra Faustum* (PL XLII, cols. 211–12).

This is part of a larger story called "The Seduction of the Archons," which Augustine discusses in the sixth book of this work: "In that battle, when the First Man ensnared the race of darkness by deceitful elements, princes of both sexes belonging to this race were taken. By means of these princes the world was constructed; and among those used in the formation of the heavenly bodies, were some pregnant females. When the sky began to rotate, the rapid circular motion made these females give birth to abortions, which, being of both sexes, fell on the earth, and lived, and grew, and came together, and produced offspring. Hence sprang all animal life in earth, air, and sea." Augustine of Hippo, *Contra Faustum* VI.8. In the text "On Mani's Teachings Concerning the Beginning of the World," from the Turfan cache, a comparable passage reads, "The Messenger [of Light] then revealed his forms, male and female, and was seen by all the Archons, the Sons of Darkness, males and females. And at the sight of the Messenger, who was beautiful in all of his forms, all the Archons became filled with lust for him [...] and in their lust they began to emit that light which they had swallowed from the Five Luminous Gods. And then that sin which was shut up in them mixed itself with [...] the light which came out of the Archons. [...] These Daughters of Darkness were previously pregnant of their own nature, and on seeing the beauty of the forms of the Messenger, their fetuses dropped and fell upon the earth and devoured the buds of trees." Theodore Bar Khoni, "On Mani's Teachings Concerning the Beginning of the World," in *Researches in Manichaeism, with Special Reference to the Turfan Fragments*, ed. and trans. Abraham Valentine Williams Jackson (New York: Columbia University Press, 1932), 244–45, 248. This is one of the more unusual accounts of Augustine regarding the Manichaean faith that was legitimized by the Turfan discovery. For the purposes of this article, it helps explain how particles of divine light became intermingled with tangible (Dark) things on earth.

41 Van Oort, "'Human Semen Eucharist'," 207–8.
42 Van Oort, "'Human Semen Eucharist'," 202.

the 350s, which described the beliefs of the Manichaeans in addition to other heresies. Among the list of their practices and beliefs is an allusion to a ritual which makes extensive use of the rhetorical device of declining to speak in specifics out of distaste for the subject matter, allowing the reader's imagination to run wild with speculation. He states, "I do not dare say in what they dip the fig they give to their wretched. I can indicate it only indirectly. Let men think of the delusive dreams and women of the menses."[43] Van Oort comments that while this has been typically dismissed as propaganda, Cyril's other works that mention the Manichaeans demonstrate that he has read the "Seduction of the Archons" legend. Furthermore, archaeological finds at Qocho, the former kingdom of the Manichaean Uyghur Turks, depict figs as being central to eucharistic meals.[44]

Augustine's composition of *Contra adversarium legis et prophetarum*, written ca. 420, provides us with insight into his capacity for restraint with the use of the "Manichaean" label. *Contra adversarium* was written to refute a heretical treatise that was read for the public in Carthage.[45] The treatise itself survives only in the quotations provided by Augustine. J. Kevin Coyle's description of this work in *Manichaeism and Its Legacy* reveals that the unknown author of the text espoused the belief that the God of the Old Testament was evil and the creator of the material world and of human flesh. Correlated to his beliefs in the diabolic origin of the flesh, the author denied the resurrection of the body. Yet, he proclaimed to be Christian, accepting the validity of the New Testament and the divinity of Jesus. As dualist and Manichean as these beliefs appeared, Augustine did not appear to believe that the author was a member of the sect. In *Contra adversarium*, he pointed out that many heretical groups believed that the God of the Old Testament was evil, and went on to state that the author's idea that the evil principle's existence was finite was an idea so ludicrous that even the Manichaeans would have dismissed it.[46] This treatise, composed only a year before the tribunal in Carthage, demonstrates that, in spite of his history of animosity towards the Manichaeans, he was still selective in his use of the term and does not appear to have been inclined to "create" adherents to the faith without evidence.

As compelling as these insights into Augustine's personal history and writings against the Manichaeans are, they are, ultimately, open to interpretation. Augustine's accuracy when reporting Manichaean theology, even when it appears bizarre or absurd, should allow for some suspension of disbelief when

---

[43] Van Oort, "Another Case of the Human," 431.
[44] Van Oort, "Another Case of the Human," 435–36.
[45] Coyle, *Manichaeism and Its Legacy*, 297.
[46] Coyle, *Manichaeism and Its Legacy*, 297–306.

considering the contents of *De haeresibus*. However, we should also take into account that this was the first treatise he had written against the sect in almost twenty-five years and we cannot know what factors influenced his testimony in those intervening years. Perhaps in trying to validate Augustine's account, we mimic the Church Fathers themselves in attempting to establish a pattern where there is only local custom and religious narrative applied to the crime (or crimes) of child rape. Perhaps upon hearing the testimony of Margarita at the tribunal in 421 and those that followed, Augustine crafted an explanation using elements of Manichaeism with which he was most familiar. Ultimately though, the choice to accept or dismiss Augustine's account lies in the reader's opinion of his character.

Constructed Identity

In the thirteenth and fourteenth centuries, entire communities in southern France that had endured the twenty years of war that comprised the Albigensian Crusade, were subjected to periodical bombardments of inquisition as papal legates and friar inquisitors sought to root out the dualist heretics that had been reported in pockets of Western Europe since the mid-twelfth century. While some historians vehemently oppose the idea that a cohesive organization of dualists existed prior to the Crusade, most agree that afterwards, there were at least some groups who genuinely professed beliefs that had been ascribed to the sect broadly known today as "Cathars."[47] One of the theories used to explain this ideological shift is that the deponents embraced the Cathar label and adhered to its beliefs (as described by inquisitors) in order to oppose the rise of an increasingly restrictive ecclesiastical order and the secular authorities that supported the inquisitions by carrying out their punishments. This explanation is convincing especially when applied to the diverse, opposing ideologies that flourished among smaller sects in the Italian Peninsula amidst the inquisitional activity in the late thirteenth and early fourteenth century.

If the unusual ritual of the Catharists was genuine, perhaps it can be understood as an act of defiance to a similar atmosphere of persecution. In the 420s in North Africa, when the tribunals took place, the deponents would have been living near the height of persecution of non-Christians in the Roman Empire. In 301, Diocletian commanded Julian, the Proconsul of Africa, to let the Manicheans be "consumed by the burning flames, along with their condemnable writ-

---

[47] Sennis, "Questions about the Cathars," 2–6.

ings."⁴⁸ The primary concern of the emperor was not the religious practices of the Manichaeans, but their Persian origin.⁴⁹ The passing of the Edict of Milan in 313 provided relief from the persecution and allowed the Manichaeans to practice their faith, but restrictions imposed by Valentinian I began to curtail their ability to proselytize and threatened their financial prosperity.⁵⁰

The first to be targeted were Manichaean teachers who were threatened with a vague "heavy punishment." This escalated with the passing of laws intended to cut off the community's finances by denying them the ability to inherit goods or property or receive gifts.⁵¹ By the reign of Theodosius I, laws that targeted Manichaeans and other heretics were issued for the purpose of purging the Roman Empire of those who did not adhere to Nicene Christianity. Laws were issued with increasing frequency and became stricter towards the end of the fourth century. With each new declaration, co-Emperors Theodosius I and Gratian widened the scope of restrictions on the Manichaeans' assembly. By 383, Manichaeans were not allowed to gather together in cities, villages, or even among the ascetic communities of Egypt. They could not attract converts or build places of worship. In 389, they were exiled from the city of Rome and their children lost the right to inherit property, even if they converted to Christianity. This nullified the exception to the law originally passed by Theodosius I in 381.⁵²

Perhaps the most significant change occurred in 382 when Theodosius I tasked Florus, Praetorian Prefect of the East, with appointing investigators to seek out informants who would testify against Manichaeans in open court. There was no statute of limitations imposed on the testimony that these informants provided. While not completely unprecedented (Constantine had used such methods to lead to the arrest of soothsayers in 319), bearing false or even unsub-

---

48 Peter Brown, "The Diffusion of Manichaeism in the Roman Empire," *The Journal of Roman Studies* 59 1/2 (1969): 92–103 at 92.
49 "They have sprung forth very recently like new and unexpected monstrosities among the race of the Persians—a nation still hostile to us—and have made their way into our empire where they are committing many outrages, disturbing the tranquility of the people and even inflicting grave damage to the civic communities; our fear is that, with the passage of time, they will endeavour, as usually happens, to infect the modest and tranquil Roman people of an innocent nature with the damnable customs and perverse laws of the Persians as with the poison of a malignant serpent." *Mos. et Rom. Leg. Coll.* xv, 4, 580–81, in Lieu, *Manichaeism in the Late*, 91–92.
50 Philip Tilden, "Religious Intolerance in the Later Roman Empire: The Evidence of the Theodosian Code" (PhD diss., University of Exeter, 2006), 127–28.
51 Coyle, *Manichaeism and Its Legacy*, 18–20.
52 Tilden, "Religious Intolerance in the Later," 170–73, 221–23.

stantiated witness in a Roman court was usually a crime in and of itself.[53] Allowing this "hearsay" testimony in court against heretics created a precedent for the inquisitions that would take place during the medieval period.[54]

Meanwhile, pressure from ecclesiastical authorities had been increasing steadily since the mid-fourth century. Following the composition of the *Acta Archelai* in the 330s, a fictional (and derogatory) account of Mani's life, multiple works against Manichaeans were written by Christian theologians all over the Empire.[55] While Augustine monopolized this intellectual war against the Manichaeans, Cyril of Jerusalem, Epiphanius, and Philastrius made their contributions as well.

When the Vandals attacked North Africa in 441, the Manichaeans remaining in Carthage fled to Rome. Pope Leo I went on the offensive, attempting to have them expelled from the area.[56] In addition to the sermon cited above, he also composed several letters to bishops in the Italian Peninsula, instructing them to attempt to convert any Manichaeans in their dioceses to the Christian faith. Those who would not repent and accept Christianity were to be "banished into perpetual exile by public judges."[57]

The assumption that secular authorities would assist the bishops demonstrates the level of cooperation between Church and state in their collective goal to rid these cities of Manichaeans. Furthermore, this alliance meant that the Manichaeans were pursued and persecuted by both primary authoritarian institutions of the Roman Empire. There was nowhere that they were safe, in public or private. Leo I's prediction of government cooperation was borne out in 444, when Emperor Valentinian III issued a decree which officially banned Manichaeans from Rome and the provinces.[58]

Between laws that increasingly restricted the assembly, proselytization, and the income of the Manichaean sect, and the open hostility from members of the Christian ecclesiastical hierarchy, being a practicing Manichaean became more dangerous with each passing year. Maintaining and openly professing their faith meant disinheriting their children, facing ominous non-specific punishments "according to the discretion of the judges," or being exiled. Even practic-

---

53 Tilden, "Religious Intolerance in the Later," 221–22.
54 Christine Caldwell Ames, "The Spiritual Foundations of Christian Heresy Inquisitions," in *A Companion to Heresy Inquisitions*, ed. Donald S. Prudlo (Leiden: Brill, 2019), 19–40.
55 Jan Willem Drijvers, *Cyril of Jerusalem: Bishop and City* (Leiden: Brill, 2004), 32.
56 Christine Caldwell Ames, *Medieval Heresies: Christianity, Judaism, and Islam* (Cambridge: Cambridge University Press, 2015), 40–41.
57 Leo the Great, "Letter VII: To the Bishops throughout Italy," in *A Select Library*, 6–7 at 6.
58 Ames, *Medieval Heresies*, 41.

ing their faith in secret was not safe, as they were not allowed to assemble in any context, and any one of their peers could have been an informant being encouraged to testify against them in court. This set of circumstances is the type of atmosphere in which oppositional social identities are created.

In addition to the context of oppression in the Roman Empire in the fourth and fifth centuries, another factor that allows for the potential of constructed identity is the history of the Manichaean faith itself. The Manichaeans originated in Mesopotamia in the third century under Parthian rule, when Zoroastrianism was not yet the mandatory state religion of Persia. It continued to flourish in the borderlands between Rome and Persia in Osrhoene and Armenia. In these regions, a plethora of sects that would have been heresy under a more restrictive state thrived, including Gnosticism, Gnostic Christianity, Elchasaites, and Marcionites. Some of these sects had complex hierarchies in which the adherents were inducted into the higher echelons through specific rites and rituals. Ideas passed between sects in this area, and so the idea of sacred, secret rituals among certain members of a religion would not have been foreign to the Manichaeans.[59]

When the Sassanids conquered Persia and instituted their militant brand of Zoroastrianism, the Manichaeans had already spread beyond its borders, establishing communities as far east as India and making inroads into the Roman Empire through Egypt. The religion proved to be a flexible one, adopting Buddhist practices and terminology in the East, incorporating Zoroastrian deities into their pantheon in Persia, and emphasizing the importance of Jesus and the Holy Spirit in their religion in the Roman Empire.[60] There was no centralized ecclesiastical authority that differentiated between orthodoxy and heresy. Only a few kingdoms ever adopted Manichaeism as a state religion. As a result, there was no expectation that doctrine, practice, or ecclesiology had to remain unchanged. For example, documents from the Turfan cache describe reverence of a highly stratified sacred hierarchy among the Sogdian Manichaeans in the eighth century for which there was no comparison among the Manichaeans in the Roman Empire.[61]

When one considers the persistent atmosphere of antagonism emanating from the Christian Church, the Roman state, and even their peers during the time of the tribunals in Carthage, the possibility that some Manichaeans constructed an identity centered around this Catharist ritual does not seem as improbable as originally reported. The flexible nature of the Manichaean faith

---

59 Lieu, *Manichaeism in the Late*, 29–38.
60 Lieu, *Manichaeism in the Late*, 25, 34–35.
61 Jes P. Asmussen, *Manichaean Literature: Representative Texts Chiefly from Middle Persian and Parthian Writings* (Delmar: Scholars' Facsimiles & Reprints, 1994), 26–36.

and its origins in border territories where so-called heresies thrived may have set a precedent that allowed for more acceptance of rites or initiation rituals that would have been abhorrently oversexualized to Roman Christians. Moreover, Augustine himself may hold at least some responsibility in the creation of this breakaway sect due to his success in publicizing the dietary practices of the Manichaeans and through his derisive commentary on the sexual overtones in the "Seduction of the Archons."

Summary of Two Arguments

Evidence for the existence of the Catharists and their notorious ritual rests almost exclusively on one mention in a single work. Furthermore, the accusations recorded by Augustine possess the same tone as countless other unproven claims of sexual impropriety lobbed at marginalized individuals or groups. The only element working in favor of the veracity of Augustine's statements is his history of proven accuracy in reporting the beliefs and acts of the Manichaean sect.

However, although there is no written evidence that directly references this ritual in either the Manichaean texts or in the works of other ecclesiastical writers, there is precedent for the idea that divine particles of Light were trapped in seeds and in human flesh, and for purifying rituals in the form of dietary practice. Given these established beliefs, the omnipresent persecution that could facilitate the construction of a defiant identity, and Manichaeism's esoteric origins and adaptable nature, Augustine's account of Catharist practices should not be wholly dismissed as a fabrication.

Complicating both of these arguments is the crime that instigated the necessity of the tribunal of 421, the alleged rape of the twelve-year-old girl, Margarita. Barring Leo I's suspiciously similar account from "Sermon XVI, On the Fast of the Tenth Month," there are no mentions of rape in the other allusions to the Catharist ritual, nor should we expect that there would be. This act of violence against a single individual, who we can safely assume had no ecclesiastical or political authority, does not fit with the narrative of a persecuted group constructing an oppositional identity. (Moreover, one would expect that, if systematic rape was being practiced by a sect of Manichaeans, it would hardly escape the attention of authorities.) However, neither does this crime fit with the argument that it was exaggerated or fabricated by Augustine, for the purpose of further vilifying the sect, as Margarita's trauma serves only as a springboard for Augustine's theological explanation and condemnation of the ritual itself. It is up to the reader to judge how this crime aligns with the argument by which they are most convinced, if it aligns at all.

The time and place in which this tribunal occurred lies outside the purview of traditional medieval scholarship, but the subject and its interpretations should not be unfamiliar to historians in this field. "Manichean" may have been a superficial and inaccurate label when applied to heretics in the medieval period, but Augustine and his peers created polemical treatises that served as templates that later theologians and inquisitors would use to condemn religious dissidents. Therefore, delving into this historical context is an exercise from which we can only benefit. I look forward to reading more research from other historians on this topic.

Marta Fernández Lahosa
Chapter 6
Art, Iconography, and Orthodoxy between the Fourth and Fifth Centuries: The Case of the Ascension

The development of an iconographic scene or element is obviously never due to a single reason, but chief among the hypotheses on the appearance of the Ascension of Christ lies its connection with the Christological and Trinitarian disputes of early Christianity. Following the scholarship on the meaning and possible functions of the image of the Ascension, authors such as Christe and Mathews have proposed that the emergence of this theme was the result of a deliberate attempt to combat Arian dissidence by giving the iconography of the Ascension the power to show the dual nature of Christ and his consubstantiality with the Father, which would align it with Nicene postulates.[1] On the basis of a study of the surviving and documented evidence, the following pages will question the extent to which these readings are well founded and examine the problems they present. Despite the fact that the boundaries of orthodoxy—and therefore the edge of dissent—were neither categorical nor fixed between the fourth and fifth centuries, hereinafter I will refer to Nicene Christianity as the nascent religious orthodoxy that gradually instigated the "othering" of Arianism and later Nestorianism, and will define the boundaries between them through the analysis of their respective Christological and Trinitarian interpretations.

Note: The conclusions presented here fall within the framework of my doctoral dissertation, which focuses on the origin of the iconography of the Ascension of Christ and its relationship with images of Roman imperial power. I would like to thank Dr. Carles Mancho and Dr. Carles Buenacasa for their help, as well as their revisions and feedback.

1 Yves Christe, *Les grands portails romans: Études sur l'iconologie des théophanies romanes* (Genoa: Librairie Droz, 1969); Thomas F. Mathews, *The Clash of Gods: A Reinterpretation of Early Christian Art* (Princeton: Princeton University Press, 1993).

The Iconography of the Ascension of Christ: A Brief Overview

The iconography of the Ascension of Christ appears within the universe of early Christian art between the end of the fourth century and the beginning of the fifth. The episode of Christ's ascension to heaven after his resurrection is featured in biblical literature in both canonical and apocryphal texts. Three of the four Gospels included in the New Testament capture the scene, with Matthew being the only one that neglects to mention it. In John's Gospel (Jn 20:17–18), the episode is recorded in the *Noli me tangere* passage with Mary Magdalene, and Mark (Mk 16:19–20) and Luke (Lk 24:50–52) briefly refer to Jesus's ascension to the right hand of the Father in the presence of the apostles. The most detailed New Testament description of the scene can be found in the Acts of the Apostles (Acts 1:3–11), the account that had the greatest impact on iconographic models. The text places the event in Jerusalem, forty days after Easter, specifying that Christ was carried up on a cloud as he spoke to the apostles of the coming of the Holy Spirit. The text also mentions the presence of two men dressed in white who announced that, just as the apostles had seen their master depart, one day he would return, which links the Ascension to Pentecost and the Parousia.

Several New Testament apocrypha, such as the Acts of Pilate and the Gospel of Peter, also provide an account of this episode. The Acts of Pilate, included in the so-called Gospel of Nicodemus since Carolingian times, narrate Christ's ascent to heaven in the context of the interrogation of three witnesses by Annas and Caiaphas. Their different variants describe how Christ ascended while he spoke to his disciples, and the Latin version details the presence of clouds and the expressiveness of the apostles who beheld the event.[2] In the Gospel of Peter, the ascension followed the resurrection, as Christ ascended to heaven accompanied by two men dressed in white in the presence of the guards of the tomb.[3]

However, it should be noted that the earliest surviving depictions of the Ascension do not match the main features portrayed in the aforementioned sources. The oldest examples, that is, the sarcophagi of Clermont and Servanes and, especially, the Reidersche Tafel, an ivory tablet preserved in the Bavarian

---

[2] Acts of Pilate, Version A, XIV; Acts of Pilate, Version A, XVI, 5–6. See Aurelio de Santos Otero, *Los evangelios apócrifos: Colección de textos griegos y latinos, versión crítica* (Madrid: Biblioteca de autores cristianos, 1999), 390–93, 432.
[3] Gospel of Peter, IX–X.

National Museum, in Munich, date from between the last third of the fourth century and the beginning of the fifth century, respectively, and show a very different image from the one narrated in Gospel accounts. Christ appears climbing a mountain with his right hand stretched out towards the sky, whence the *Dextera domini*, the Hand of God, emerges from the clouds about to receive him. This type of depiction of the Ascension of Christ, which we will henceforth refer to as the Western model, contrasts with portrayals from the fifth to the sixth century onwards in the Eastern part of the Roman Empire, which instead show a composition more in keeping with New Testament descriptions. The Monza ampullae and the Rabbula Gospels are the most outstanding examples of this Eastern model.[4]

Thus, in the fifth century, the polymorphic iconography of the Ascension established at the end of the fourth century seems to have "disappeared" to give way to a new composition, without any traces in the preserved artworks suggesting that these changes resulted from a typological evolution. In fact, the extant examples of the Eastern variant are scarce, at least before the sixth and seventh centuries, which makes it difficult to examine this question in depth. In any case, it is reasonable to assume that the Western model must have remained somewhere in the cultural background because, from the ninth century onwards, a new iconographic representation for the Ascension appeared that combined both types and whose most celebrated example is the Drogo Sacramentary.[5]

The iconography of the Ascension of Christ was not especially prominent between the late fourth and the early fifth century, at least no more than other con-

---

[4] On the debate on the types, nomenclature, and characteristics of these iconographic models, see Ernest T. Dewald, "The Iconography of the Ascension," *American Journal of Archeology* 19/3 (1915): 277–319; Sophie Helena Gutberlet, *Die Himmelfahrt Christi in der bildenden Kunst von den Anfängen bis ins hohe Mittelalter: Versuch zur geistesgeschichtlichen Erfassung einer ikonographischen Frage* (Strasbourg: Heitz & co, 1935); Gertrud Schiller, *Ikonographie der christlichen Kunst* (Gütersloher: Gütersloher Verlagshaus, 1966); Christe, *Les grands portails romans*; Victor M. Schmidt, "Ascensione," in *Enciclopedia dell'Arte Medievale*, vol. 2 (Rome: Instituto della Enciclopedia Italiana, 1991), 572–77; Louis Réau, "Ascensión," in *Iconografía del arte cristiano: Iconografía de la Biblia, Nuevo Testamento*, vol. 1/2 (Madrid: Ediciones del Serbal, 1996), 604–12; Magali Guenot, "Les Images de l'Ascension du Christ dans la Chrétienté latine entre le 9e et le 13e siècle" (PhD diss., Université de Lyon, 2016). See also my Master's thesis, Marta Fernández Lahosa, "Transmissió de models iconogràfics en l'art de la tardoantiguitat i l'alta edat mitjana: El cas de les apoteosis imperials i l'Ascensió de Crist (Segles I–VIII)" (Master's thesis, Universitat de Barcelona, 2015).

[5] Meyer Shapiro, *Estudios sobre el arte de la Antigüedad tardía, el Cristianismo primitivo y la Edad Media* (Madrid: Alianza, 1986); Robert Deshman, "Another Look at the Disappearing Christ: Corporeal and Spiritual Vision in Early Medieval Images," *The Art Bulletin* 79/3 (1997): 518–46; Guenot, "Les Images de l'Ascension."

temporary images such as the *Traditio Legis*,⁶ but several events that took place in this early period seem to have somehow promoted this episode of Christ's life. On the one hand, the feast of the Ascension of Christ, which until that moment was part of Pentecost festivities, developed as a separate celebration in the Christian liturgical calendar.⁷ On the other hand, a commemorative building was erected, apparently under imperial patronage, in the place from which Christ had supposedly ascended to heaven, thus creating a new pilgrimage site in the Holy City.⁸ Finally, the episode was incorporated into the Nicene Creed (325), later ratified and amended in the Constantinopolitan Creed, which was approved during the First Council of Constantinople in 381.⁹

The fact that the depiction of the Ascension first appeared after the different factions within the Church reached an agreement in the aforementioned councils has led some authors to see its incorporation into the Nicene Creed as the trigger for the emergence of this image in iconographic representations. Without direct evidence, Yves Christe proposes that the scene emerged just after the Council of Nicaea to vindicate the resulting Nicene Christological values against Arian positions.¹⁰ More generally, Thomas Mathews suggests that over a longer period of time, while the orthodox figure of Christ was being defined, these changes influ-

---

6 Robert Couzin, *The Traditio Legis: Anatomy of an Image* (Oxford: Archaeopress, 2015).
7 Christe, *Les grands portails romans*, 75; John Gordon Davis, "The Peregrinatio Egeriae and the Ascension," *Vigiliae Christianae* 8 1/2 (1954): 93–100 at 94; Gutberlet, *Die Himmelfahrt Christi*, 16. The sources that allow us to deduce that the feast became a separate celebration in this period are Egeria's pilgrimage to the Holy Land at the end of the fourth century (see Egeria, *Pilgrimage* XLII.1.1–8) and a fifth-century epistle by St. Augustine (see Augustine of Hippo, *Epistolae* LIV.1–2 (PL XXXIII, col. 200)).
8 Scholars disagree on this point; whereas some consider it a Constantinian undertaking on the basis of Eusebius de Caesarea, *Life of Constantine* III.41–43 (John Beckwith, *Arte paleocristiano y bizantino* (Madrid: Cátedra, 1997), 31, 64; Bernardino Llorca, *Historia de la Iglesia católica I. Edad Antigua: La Iglesia en el mundo grecorromano (1–750)*, (Madrid: Biblioteca de Autores Cristianos, 1950), 382), others attribute its promotion to the pilgrim Poimenia (Rosa María Cid López, "Egeria, peregrina y aventurera: Relato de un viaje a Tierra Santa en el siglo IV," *Arenal* 17/1 (2010): 5–31 at 25; André Grabar, *Martyrium: Recherche sur le culte des reliques et l'art chrétien antique*, vol. 3 (Paris: Collège de France, 1946), 288; Gutberlet, *Die Himmelfahrt Christi*, 18). For an overview of this debate, see Fernández Lahosa, "Transmissió de models iconogràfics," 64–66.
9 The original acts of the Council of Nicaea have not survived, but the Nicene Creed is extant in other sources. For a classic edition of the Greek text and its English translation, see John Norman Davidson Kelly, *Early Christian Creeds*, 3rd ed. (London and New York: Continuum, 2006). Kelly conducts a comparative study of the Nicene and Constantinopolitan Creeds and the Apostles' Creed.
10 Christe, *Les grands portails romans*, 75, 67.

enced artistic representations, so that some of the episodes of Christ's life were endowed with certain features to graphically support theological concepts. Mathews believes that scenes such as the entry of Jesus into Jerusalem (which first appears in the fourth century) and the Adoration of the Magi (present since the third century), as well as the Ascension, were used to emphasize the glory of Christ in an anti-Arian context, especially after the First Council of Constantinople. In opposition to Arian ideas, these were images where the divine character of Christ was publicly displayed.[11]

If we consider—rather reductively—that Arianism denies the divinity of Christ, his eternity and the consubstantiality of the three persons of the Trinity, a theophanic moment in the life of Christ such as the Ascension could have become an effective instrument to oppose Arian views; this could in turn be seen as evidence of the relationship between the Ascension and what we could call "Nicene art." However, the hypothesis that the image of the Ascension of Christ was one of the iconographies that served to express rejection of Arian ideas and to reinforce the divinity of Christ and his consubstantiality with the Father is far from proven, and the arguments supporting it do not provide a sound and conclusive answer. Let us see why.

Art, Ascension, and Arianism

To determine whether the Ascension was actually an iconographic programme born and/or used to serve Nicene postulates we should first examine whether this episode was only used by pro-Nicene proponents or by both sides; in other words, we should gauge the existence of iconographic differences between compositions. However, there are no extant depictions of the Ascension of Christ in Arian contexts, one possible reason being the scarce amount of preserved artistic expressions produced within the framework of this religious doctrine. The most famous Arian artworks featuring decoration that can serve as references are the Basilica of Sant'Apollinare Nuovo and the Baptistery of the Arians, in Ravenna, Sant'Agata dei Goti in Rome, and Sainte-Marie de la Daurade in Toulouse, all of which were promoted by Germanic leaders. Although there is no surviving Arian image of the Ascension, we believe that a brief overview of the decorations on these monuments will help us identify any features that may clearly differentiate them from pro-Nicene buildings.

---

11 Mathews, *The Clash of Gods*, 51–53.

There is ample evidence of Ostrogothic occupation in Ravenna, but few Arian buildings retain decoration dating from the time of the Ostrogothic King Theodoric.[12] The church of Christ the Saviour, today Sant'Apollinare Nuovo, is the result of a collage of interventions. Sponsored as a palace chapel by Theodoric between the late fifth and early sixth century, it underwent renovations when it was reconsecrated by the Catholic Bishop Agnellus in the mid-sixth century and renamed St. Martin. In the eighth century, the apse collapsed, and in the ninth century the church received the relics of St. Apollinaris—up until then kept in Classe—which earned it a new consecration that explains its current dedication.[13] The remaining Ostrogothic decoration can be seen on the walls of the central nave, and is divided into three levels. The upper band shows scenes from the life of Christ (his ministry, miracles and parables, and scenes of the Passion) alternating with panels depicting pavilions crested with pairs of doves, which, despite restorations, seem to belong to the original decoration.[14] In the second register we find saints and prophets, which can also be dated to the Ostrogothic period.[15] Finally, the lower register possibly contained scenes involving the king and his court, but it was greatly altered during Agnellus's time. All that remains of the original decoration is the representation of the port of Classe and the imperial palace, greatly altered, and an image of Mary with the Child among four angels that faces an image of Christ enthroned, also among angels. The row of female and male martyrs, as well as the three kings that were added to the enthroned Virgin to make up the scene of the Adoration of the Magi, date from a later period. Arthur Urbano argues that this alteration of the programme was more a *damnatio memoriae* than an action against specifically Arian scenes.[16]

---

[12] Giuseppe Bovini, *Edifici di culto d'età teodoriciana e giustinianea a Ravenna* (Bologna: Pàtron, 1970); Bryan Word-Perkins, "Where Is the Archeology and Iconography of Germanic Arianism?," in *Religious Diversity in Late Antiquity*, ed. David Gwynn and Susan Bager (Leiden: Brill, 2010), 265–89; Clementina Rizzardi, *Il mosaico a Ravenna: Ideologia e arte* (Bologna: Ante Quem, 2011).

[13] Arthur Urbano, "Donation, Dedication and Damnatio Memoriae: The Catholic Reconciliation of Ravenna and the Church of Sant'Apollinare Nuovo," *Journal of Early Christian Studies* 13/1 (2005): 71–110 at 90–95; Rizzardi, *Il mosaico a Ravenna*, 87.

[14] For a detailed description of the twenty-six scenes, see Bovini, *Edifici di culto*, 77–101; Rizzardi, *Il mosaico a Ravenna*, 90–98.

[15] These figures are difficult to recognize and have been identified as either prophets, apostles, or philosophers (Urbano, "Donation, Dedication and Damnatio," 76).

[16] Urbano, "Donation, Dedication and Damnatio," 95; Rizzardi, *Il mosaico a Ravenna*, 89. Additionally, Word-Perkins suggests that there could be different Arian saints and martyrs and that the Catholic restoration mainly consisted in replacing these with figures associated with orthodoxy (Word-Perkins, "Where Is the Archeology," 281). In these martyrs we can find a possible anti-Arian iconographic proposal, as the two rows are headed by St. Euphemia of Chalcedon

If this were the case, the changes in the iconographic programme, at least those that have been documented to date, would not have been extremely radical, as Arian iconography would have largely served as the basis for a Nicene decoration.¹⁷

As for the Arian Baptistery, it offers a very interesting case for comparison with the Baptistery of Neon, which is also called Orthodox Baptistery precisely to distinguish it from the former.¹⁸ However, the problems here are the same as in Sant'Apollinare, namely the lack of a complete decorative programme—as only the mosaics of the dome are extant—and successive restorations.¹⁹ The mosaics on the domes of both baptisteries are laid out in concentric registers around the central medallion depicting the baptism of Christ and featuring St. John the Baptist, a personification of the River Jordan, and the Holy Spirit in the form of a dove. A procession of apostles bearing crowns in their hands circles the dome among palm trees, meeting at an empty throne, or *hetoimasia*, in the case of the Arian Baptistery. In turn, the Orthodox Baptistery preserves the decoration of the lower register, lost in the Arian building, with a third band of aediculae framing empty thrones and plant elements alternating with pulpits with books on them.

The most remarkable differences between these two decorative programmes are the gilded colour of the Arian Baptistery, which contrasts with the blue back-

---

and St. Martin of Tours, respectively, both of whom were renowned for their fight against heresy and paganism (Deborah Mauskopf Deliyannis, "The Mosaics of Ravenna," in *The Routledge Handbook of Early Christian Art*, ed. Robin M. Jensen and Mark D. Ellison (London: Routledge, 2018), 347–63 at 360).

17 Word-Perkins, "Where Is the Archeology," 265; Urbano, "Donation, Dedication and Damnatio," 102–6. Dragos Mîrşanu argues that some images such as the Holy Supper can be interpreted in an Arian key: the lack of wine or glasses at the banquet leads the author to think that this is not a depiction of the New Testament episode but a ceremonial banquet associated with variants in the Arian cult (Dragos Mîrşanu, "Further Notes on the Aesthetic 'Shadow' of Gothic Arianism in Ravenna," *Studii Teologice* 4 (2009): 199–212 at 203–6). Rizzardi posits that scenes such as the resurrection of Lazarus could have been selected to portray the human nature of Christ. She also links the choice of scenes to Maximinus's *Sermo Arianorum*, one of the few Arian texts preserved, studied in depth by Meslin (Rizzardi, *Il mosaico a Ravenna*, 102; Michel Meslin, *Les Ariens d'Occident* (Paris: Editions du Seuil, 1967)).

18 It was built next to the Arian cathedral between the late fifth century and the early sixth century. See Maria Grazia Breschi, *La Cattedrale ed il battistero degli Ariani a Ravenna* (Ravenna: Istituto di antichità ravennati e bizantine, 1965); Bovini, *Edifici di culto*, 11–40. The Orthodox Baptistery, called Baptistery of Neon because of the renovation works carried out by Bishop Neon in the mid-fifth century, was built and decorated between the end of the fourth and the beginning of the fifth century. See Rizzardi, *Il mosaico a Ravenna*.

19 Bovini, *Edifici di culto*, 14.

ground of the Baptistery of Neon (although the central clipeus is gilded in both cases), and details in the personification of the Jordan and the figure of Christ, who appears beardless in the Arian building and bearded in the Orthodox Baptistery.[20] Although various theories have tried to explain most of these small differences on the basis of a variation of the cult, iconographies and compositions are so similar that scholars have reached the conclusion that the image of the Arian Baptistery was based on the decoration of the Orthodox Baptistery—in fact copied it—and, therefore, they show no obvious iconographic dissimilarities.[21]

The scene of the Ascension is not represented in these baptisteries.[22] We ignore which images could have been part of the lost decoration, but comparing these two buildings underlines the fact that spaces with similar functions do not seem to have featured elements that enable a distinction between Arian and Nicene iconography.

Sant'Agata dei Goti, one of the earliest documented Arian churches, sponsored by the Suevic warlord Ricimer,[23] underwent numerous modifications not only when it became a Catholic temple during the time of Gregory the Great, but also after the damage caused when the apse dome fell in 1589, and due to

---

[20] In the Orthodox Baptistery, the area around the head of Christ and the Holy Spirit was restored later, perhaps following the pattern of the previous image, but it is not clear whether the original figure of Christ was bearded and haloed nor whether St. John baptizes Christ by pouring water or by the laying on of hands (Rizzardi, *Il mosaico a Ravenna*, 72). Moreover, in the Arian Baptistery, all the apostles, except for the figures of Peter and Paul and the young heads of the apostles next to them, also appear to be the result of restorations (Breschi, *La Cattedrale ed il battistero*, 77, 81–83; Bovini, *Edifici di culto*, 22–23, 27).

[21] Bovini, *Edifici di culto*, 23. The direction of the procession of the apostles, Christ's beardlessness and other details have been interpreted in an Arian key. For further details see Deliyannis, "The Mosaics of Ravenna," 359, and Rizzardi, *Il mosaico a Ravenna*, 85–86. Rizzardi suggests that the Arian scene of the baptism was intended to enhance the historical character of the event. The Arian ritual was not performed in the name of the Holy Trinity but of the death of Christ, and prescribed a single immersion (Rizzardi, *Il mosaico a Ravenna*, 85).

[22] In the Orthodox Baptistery there are some inscriptions that can provide information about the missing scenes in the wall decoration of the building. As in the Dura-Europos Baptistery, these refer to themes related to salvation through water (Rizzardi, *Il mosaico a Ravenna*, 77–78). Thus, the Ascension of Christ may not have been a suitable iconography for a baptistery, which could explain its absence.

[23] This attribution is based on an inscription at the base of the apse first transcribed by Pietro Sabino at the end of the fifteenth century (Isaac Sastre de Diego, "La Iglesia de Santa Agata dei Goti: Reflexiones acerca de un caso único de edificio arriano en Roma," *Antigüedad y Cristianismo* 21 (2004): 77–100 at 79; Word-Perkins, "Where Is the Archeology," 267).

the remodellings carried out in the seventeenth and eighteenth centuries.[24] We only have knowledge of the decoration of the apse through the descriptions and drawings of Ciacconio, Cesare Baronio, and Pompeo Ugonio.[25] Apparently, it had a blue background with golden and purple clouds, which served as a backdrop for the figure of Christ standing among the twelve apostles, six on each side, dressed in white and blue robes, identified by their name at their feet and depicted in a lively and dynamic style. No distinctly Arian element is apparent in this description, apart from the absence of God's hand on Christ, and the lack of a cruciform halo.[26] Besides these details, the scene does not seem to stray from an iconographic programme that could be included in any Catholic church. As it is not possible to ascertain what the decoration beyond this space was, we do not know which episodes or figures were represented, whether any of them reflected attitudes closer to Arian views, or if among them there was a depiction of Christ's Ascension.

As for the church of La Daurade,[27] now no longer extant, we know much of the iconographic programme also thanks to sixteenth-century scholars.[28] The original building had already gone through different reforms when Dom Odon Lamothe described it, but it still preserved seven sides of its decagonal structure. Lamothe listed sixty-three figures framed between arches and distributed over three levels. In the lower level he described a cycle of the Nativity with scenes of the Massacre of the Innocents, Herod and the Magi, and the Adoration of the Shepherds, together with the Nativity itself, the Adoration of the Magi and, possibly, the Flight into Egypt. In the centre, the images of Christ the Saviour and the Virgin stood out among the figures of eight of the apostles, prophets, and the four archangels; in this case it seems that Christ was standing, wearing

---

[24] For an overview of the state of the art on the church, see Sastre de Diego, "La Iglesia de Santa Agata," 78–90.
[25] Ciacconio, Codex Vatican Latin 5407, 27r–72v and Codex Cartaceo Barberini, Vatican Library Lat. 2161.
[26] Sastre de Diego, "La Iglesia de Santa Agata," 98. It must be said that the absence of God's hand, and the fact that Christ does not wear a cruciform halo are present in similar iconographic programmes in Catholic churches such as Santa Pudenziana, to mention but one example.
[27] For a discussion of the function of the building, the description and analysis of the iconographic programme and its interpretation in an Arian key, see Helen Woodruff, "The Iconography and Date of the Mosaics of La Daurade," *The Art Bulletin* 13/1 (1931): 80–104; Ana María Jiménez Garnica, "El arte 'oficial' de Toulouse bajo la sobiranía visigoda," *Archivo español de arqueología* 61/157–158 (1988): 179–96.
[28] The most complete textual description is that of Dom Odon Lamothe preserved in manuscript Lat. 12680 of the Bibliothèque nationale de France, fols. 231v–235r, which Woodruff transcribed in graphic format (Woodruff, "The Iconography and Date," 97–99).

a cruciform halo, carrying a book in his left hand and making a blessing gesture with his right hand. In the upper level, Lamothe recorded the presence of different prophetic characters from the Old Testament: Jacob and four of his sons, Enoch, Elijah, the sacrifice of Isaac, Melchizedek, Noah, and the three Hebrews in the oven of Babylon with the figure of Gabriel in the middle. Jiménez Garnica links these scenes to the *Dissertatio Maximini contra Ambrosium*—a work by Maximinus, an Arian bishop exiled to Illyria in 381.[29] However, none of these actually clashed with what could be a pro-Nicene decoration. Although the programme in Lamothe's description is not complete, it seems unlikely that it included a depiction of the Ascension of Christ.

Studies such as those by Gwynn and Bager[30] have already suggested that Arian and Nicene art must not have been very different. They use Belisarius's entry and takeover of the city of Carthage from the Vandals in the Justinian era, as narrated by Procopius of Cesarea, to show that no major changes had to be made to liturgical spaces to make them suitable for Catholic ceremonies at the time of the city's conquest.[31] Something similar must have happened with the decorations, because Arians and Catholics were essentially Christians, and accepted the same episodes of Christ's life. The nuance was in the theological details of Christological debates.

Moreover, just as there was no one way of being a Christian, there was no one way of being an Arian. As Samuel Fernández rightly points out, our understanding of Arianism is largely based on the views of the great personalities who spoke out against it, for they promoted the destruction of the works of Arius and his acolytes. The version of Arianism presented by Alexander of Alexandria, Athanasius of Alexandria, and Augustine of Hippo focused on what probably were the most monolithic and radical of the postulates that Arius advocated.[32]

---

29 Following Woodruff's arguments, Jiménez Garnica sees links between the representations of La Daurade and the Arian monuments of Ravenna (Jiménez Garnica, "El arte 'oficial' de Toulouse," 189–96).
30 David Gwynn and Susan Bager, eds., *Religious Diversity in Late Antiquity* (Leiden: Brill, 2010). Word-Perkins, in particular, bases his work on the general hypothesis that Arian and Nicene art must not have had very marked differences at the iconographic level, and that the theological nuances that differentiated them were given by the texts that were read during liturgy (Word-Perkins, "Where Is the Archeology").
31 Word-Perkins, "Where Is the Archeology," 267; Procopius of Caesarea, *History of the Wars* 3.21–25.
32 In a very well documented article, Fernández explains that diversity was present within Arianism from the very beginning, as evinced by Arius's personal trajectory. He also describes the differences between the image of Arius that emerges from the letters and texts of his opponents and what can be gathered from the few preserved passages of *Thalia*, written by Arius

In fact, in the few examples of Arian works that have been preserved, we see how Arius changed his mind regarding the categorical way in which he denied the divinity of Christ, going so far as to state that he did not consider himself an adversary of Christ's divinity.[33]

The Arianism of the Germanic promoters of the buildings mentioned above came from the ideas of Ulfilas, and therefore was not very radicalized. As Homoiousians,[34] they believed that Christ the Logos was God but was subordinate to the Father, with a similar but different substance and engendered before time. They also believed in the Holy Spirit but not in the consubstantiality of the Trinity.[35] In fact, their doctrine was more national than theological.[36]

Therefore, it is not surprising that, beyond a few nuances and specific works, Arian and Nicene art were not extremely different. We do not have any evidence of a depiction of the Ascension in a documented Arian context, but in spite of this and even though the Ascension of Christ is related to the glorification of the figure of the Son, taking into account what has been said so far, we cannot affirm that it was avoided to vindicate the Arian faith.[37]

---

combining prose and verse and summarizing his views on the Logos (Samuel Fernández, "Arrio y la configuración inicial de la controversia arriana," *Scripta Theologica* 45 (2013): 9–40).

33 This is not against the divinity of the Logos but is a formula to mark the precedence of the Father and the distinction of the Son and to avoid the dictates of Sabellianism, a belief that exaggerated the unity of the three hypostases (Fernández, "Arrio y la configuración inicial," 36–37).

34 Homoiousians held the belief that God the Son was of a similar, but not identical, essence or substance with God the Father. As moderate Arians, they were closer to Nicene *homoousian* views, which described Jesus as "same in essence" with God the Father, than to the extreme Arian positions of Homoians, who thought it impossible to compare the Son and the Father.

35 Émilienne Demougeot, "Y eut-il une forme arienne de l'Art paléochrétien?," in *Atti del VI Congresso Internazionale di Archeologia Cristiana, Ravenna 23–30 settembre 1962* (Città del Vaticano: Pontificio Istituto di Archeologia Cristiana, 1965), 491–519 at 500–505; Word-Perkins, "Where Is the Archeology," 266.

36 Demougeot, "Y eut-il une forme arienne," 499.

37 In fact, in the examples we have seen, the image of a glorified Christ the Saviour is quite common in Arian decorations. It seems that it was associated with the idea of salvation reserved for believers of the true faith who had to suffer persecution, as Arians saw themselves. However, these images do not differ on a compositional level from Nicene depictions of the same iconographic motif; in other words, the difference is not visual but rather conceptual (Jiménez Garnica, "El arte 'oficial' de Toulouse"; Word-Perkins, "Where Is the Archeology," 266).

Art, Ascension, and Orthodoxy

As we have just discussed, it seems difficult to identify images that clearly express ideological dissidence in the Arian context. In contrast, Nicene art featured more iconographic elements that underlined dogmas; however, in general, these are compositional details in line with the views of each sponsor rather than iconographic themes.[38]

The image of the Ascension, associated with the ability to express the divine nature of Christ before the apostolate and manifest his glory, could be useful for ecclesiastical authorities to convey ideas that Arian dissidents did not share, namely the divinity of the Logos and his consubstantiality with the Father. However, in my opinion, the surviving depictions of the Ascension do not evidence this use, at least in a context of hostility to Arianism, for the iconography that best expresses the glory and divinity of Christ is that featured in the Eastern model,[39] and there are no examples of this type until well into the fifth century. The episode of the Ascension does not appear in the great iconographic cycles of Catholic monumental buildings contemporary with the Arian monuments analyzed above—that is, St. Peter in the Vatican, St. Paul Outside the Walls, St. Mary Major, and San Vitale in Ravenna, among others. The only example of this scene in this context can be found in the wooden doors of St. Sabina on the Aventine Hill in Rome, but this representation presents a complicated composition, closer to the Western model. In fact, recent studies have even questioned its identification as the Ascension of Christ.[40]

The Ascension does appear in the sixth and seventh centuries in relation to the pilgrimage to the Holy Land as well as in Egyptian monastic settings. Although these later dates make it impossible to relate its appearance to the Arian

---

38 This is evident in specific pieces such as the so-called Dogmatic Sarcophagus and the image of the three Christograms (Antonio Ferrua, *La polemica antiariana nei monumenti paleocristiani* (Vatican City: Pontificio Istituto di Archeologia Cristiana, 1991)).

39 The Western model, followed by the earliest surviving examples dated between the late fourth and the fifth century, depicts a more "realistic" account of the ascent to heaven, with compositional links to Roman art, and moves away from the Eastern model, which is linked to apocalyptic, prophetic, and theophanic perspectives that reinforce the image of the divine Christ in glory. For more details on this point, see Fernández Lahosa, "Transmissió de models iconogràfics"; Carles Buenacasa Pérez, Marta Fernández Lahosa, Carles Mancho Suárez, "Un ejemplo de apropiación semántica de la iconografía imperial en el siglo VI: El tema de la Ascensión de Cristo," *Hortus Artium Medievalium* 23/2 (2017): 686–92.

40 Foletti identifies the scene as Enoch's Ascension and links it to the catechetical use of the doors (Ivan Foletti, "Le porte lignee di Santa Sabina all'Aventino: Tra liturgia stazionaria e funzione iniziatica (Il nartece di Santa Sabina, II)," *Hortus Artium Medievalium* 2/2 (2014): 709–19).

controversy, it opens new research avenues in terms of the struggle of orthodoxy against other dissident movements.[41]

It is not easy to link the use of the Ascension of Christ as a pro-orthodoxy instrument with the extant artistic evidence, but a connection between the Ascension and orthodoxy is clearer in textual sources, which are the basis for this specific reading of the scene. Figures such as Leo the Great, Augustine of Hippo, and Cyril of Alexandria used the ascension to the right of the Father as an indisputable sign of the divinity of the Logos.[42] Thus, the Ascension could have had a pro-Nicene interpretation, asserting dogmas that were not accepted by the Arian mindset, but we do not know if the causes of the birth of this iconography are directly related to the fight against this dissidence. The question is still open. However, the fact that this iconography has its most representative examples in the East, and that the oldest evidence dates from around AD 400, could be linked to a campaign to establish the idea of Christ's divinity as a member of the Trinity initiated by the Eastern Church after the condemnation of the Arian faith at the First Council of Constantinople (381).

Conclusions

So, can we really speak of Arian art? I think so, at least in the most reductionist sense of the term, if only because Arians did exist and sponsored artistic expressions; and the same can be said for the case of Nicene art. What we should ask ourselves is whether there was any difference between the two. As we have seen, answering this question is not an easy task.

On the one hand, we must recall that Arians were obviously Christians, and therefore, as far as doctrine was concerned, they had more in common with pro-Nicene proponents than against them. The debates on the natures of Christ, the

---

41 For instance, the presence of the Virgin Mary among the apostles in the scene of the Ascension has been linked to the fight against Nestorianism. For more information on the Monza ampullae, see André Grabar, *Ampoules de Terre Sainte: Monza-Bobbio* (Paris: Librairie C. Klincksieck, 1958); on the chapels of Bawit, see Antonio Iacobini, *Visioni dipinte: Immagini della contemplazione negli affreschi di Bawit* (Rome: Viella, 2000).

42 To mention but a few examples, see Leo the Great, *Sermones et Epistolae I* 74.4 (PL LIV, col. 396); Augustine of Hippo, *Sermones* 265.8 (PL XXXVIII, col. 1225); Cyril of Alexandria, *Commentarium in Joannem librorum VII – IX* 9.14.2–3 (PG, col. 182). Following their general discourse, the sermons of Leo and Augustine use the celebration of the feast of the Ascension of Christ to convey their beliefs on the Christological problem to the faithful. We do not see a specific use of the Ascension to vindicate their ideas, but rather an incorporation of their doctrines, in line with orthodox views, into the celebration of the feast.

subordination to the Father, and the articulation of the Trinity were played out within the framework of shared Scriptures. Thus, everything that the Old and New Testaments contributed to the creation of Christian images influenced both sides. What gave meaning and intention to these representations was the interpretation made by those who contemplated them. Following the hypothesis of Word-Perkins, words were what differentiated Arian and Nicene images: the words of catechists educating neophytes, and the words of the sermons, epistles, and readings that accompanied these images in their liturgical context.[43] Words could turn the same episode into a representation of either Arian or Nicene faith. I find Rizzardi's theory on the Arian perspective of the episode of the Resurrection of Lazarus in Sant'Apollinare Nuovo particularly interesting.[44] The composition of this image differs little from those used by pro-Nicene art since the mid- third century, and the text that inspired the iconography is also the same (Jn 11:41–42), but in an Arian setting it was read as Christ asking the Father for help for the miracle of the resurrection of Lazarus, which showed that the figure of the Son was subordinate to that of God, thus illustrating one of the main points of Arian doctrine. Evidently, the same scene was also used in pro-Nicene art, but a single detail in the interpretation of the text changed its essence.

Another example of the proximity between the two doctrines is provided by the images of the aforementioned baptisteries of Ravenna. As noted above, both iconographies incorporate the figure of the Holy Spirit represented by a dove. It is striking that a doctrine that denied the consubstantiality between the three hypostases of the Trinity gave prominence to the Spirit at the culminating moment of Christ's baptism. This may be due to the fact that Germanic Arianism, rather moderate, accepted the existence of the Holy Spirit in spite of denying its consubstantiality. Thus, the Spirit is subordinated to the Son, his creator, who is at the same time subordinated to and created by the Father. In fact, in the liturgical celebration of the ritual of baptism, new initiates joined the Church (both the Arian and the Catholic Church) through the formula of Matthew (Mt 28:10), according to which Jesus commissioned his disciples to baptize his followers in the name of the Father, the Son, and the Holy Spirit. Liturgical forms were identical and the similarity of the baptismal ritual was such that a text by Eusebius (283–371), Bishop of Vercelli, shows concern for such similarity between Arian and Catholic rites. Eusebius warns against the dangers of false Arian baptism, which shares the same liturgy, and rebukes Arians for their lack of coherence,

---

[43] Word-Perkins, "Where Is the Archeology."
[44] Rizzardi, *Il mosaico a Ravenna*, 102.

as they deny the Trinity, but use its symbols during baptism.[45] Again we see that the difference, even in rituals, was minimal, almost confined to conceptual aspects. In Arian images of the Baptism of Christ, the presence of the Spirit would be justified by its mention both in the biblical text and in the ritual formulation of the act, which would render it a coherent iconography in this context.

We must also bear in mind that the theological debates that marked the difference between Catholics and Arians varied in intensity over the course of the fourth and fifth centuries. We have already seen how scholars have identified different stages of Arianism, with the Germanic period being the one with the most moderate opposition to Nicene positions. We do not have much information about what an earlier art promoted by more extreme Arians might have looked like, but what we do have has to do with this second phase, where Arianism had a "national" quality to it and doctrines closer to Nicene views.[46] An Arianism closer to orthodoxy could have generated an iconography so similar that it would be difficult to detect any nuances that might single it out.

As for Nicene art, there are enough extant examples to indicate that there was a certain use of images to emphasize beliefs that opposed those considered heretical.[47] However, as far as terminology is concerned, in my opinion it is per-

---

45 In his study on Western Arianism, Meslin translates some excerpts from *De Trinitate* into French (VII, 6, 16–17) (Meslin, *Les Ariens d'Occident*, 384–85). Meslin notes that in a second phase, some communities rejected the triple immersion and slightly changed Matthew's verse to "Je te baptise au nom du Père incréé, du Fils créé et de l'Esprit sanctifiant créé par le Fils créé" (Meslin, *Les Ariens d'Occident*, 386). Here the Trinitarian formula varies with regard to the relationship of the hypostases, that is, with regard to consubstantiality, but it does not eliminate the Holy Spirit and therefore, at least in reference to the examples preserved in Ravenna, it does not alter the iconography.
46 Meslin, *Les Ariens d'Occident*. Demougeot claims that the earliest Arian trends were aniconic, and justifies this by arguing that early forms of Syriac Christianity (which he claims influenced the foundations of Arianism) derived from Jewish attitudes of opposition to iconographic representations (Demougeot, "Y eut-il une forme arienne," 507–11); however, not everyone agrees (Urbano, "Donation, Dedication and Damnatio," 163).
47 In the aforementioned Dogmatic Sarcophagus, which dates from the early fourth century and is kept at the Vatican Museums, the three identical persons who intervene in the episode of the Creation of Eve provide an example of the use of artistic language to represent the involvement of the Logos in creation, and the equality between the persons of the Trinity. Additionally, three Christograms are depicted in a single image as a Trinitarian symbol (Roberto Giordani, "Probabili echi della crisi ariana in alcune figurazioni paleocristiane," *Rivista di Archeologia Cristiana* 54 (1978): 229–63; Ferrua, *La polemica antiariana*, 20–24, 37–62).

haps not entirely correct to speak of an "anti-Arian" art. It is true that the artistic production highlighted the Nicene beliefs in the Trinity, the divinity of the Logos, and consubstantiality, but images were meant to convey doctrinal positions, not to contribute to religious polemics, unlike, for example, in the disputes between iconoclasts and iconodules. Therefore, Catholic images were not a direct negation of Arian models.[48] Evidently, by emphasizing their ideas as true and unquestionable, they indirectly pointed to "the other," to the one who did not think as they did, to the dissident of the "rightful" faith. But these were not images expressly created to fight against the other, but to show what they believed to be the truth in a theoretical debate that was shaping the figure of Christ in all its dimensions for the first time. This creation of the theological, "theoretical" image of Christ, which was becoming increasingly detailed and complex, in turn enabled the artistic image of Christ to be outlined and enriched in ever greater depth.

But what role does the Ascension of Christ play in this whole framework? As noted, there are no preserved examples of this episode that support the views of Christe and Mathews. Even so, we can agree with Mathews's hypothesis justifying the appearance of the Ascension of Christ (and other episodes) in a context of development of the Christological figure.[49] At the same time that Christianity was setting its own limits, its dogmas, it conceptually shaped the features of the image of Christ.[50]

---

48 The debates against Arianism are more prominent in the written world of homilies and sermons, which do show a hostile attitude. For now, we cannot be sure whether this dispute pervaded artistic representations.
49 Mathews, *The Clash of Gods*, 51–53.
50 We must bear in mind that iconographic displays were gradually introduced in the early days of Christian art. In essence, an aniconic stage and the production of images that were indiscernible from those created in a pagan context gave way to the earliest depictions involving Old Testament characters and passages from the public life of Christ, especially those related to his thaumaturgical and healing activities. These images are almost signs that summarize the symbolism of the narrative. In spite of being based on texts, some of these iconographies are not a faithful transcription, which warns us of the danger and therefore the caution needed when relating the appearance of certain iconographic compositions and their meanings to written sources. From the fourth century onwards, especially after the promulgation of the Edict of Milan, a second shift in iconographic trends led to the emergence of new themes. Leaving aside the historiographic debate on the actual influence of the imperial world and the figure of the emperor on these new iconographies, these new images introduced scenes related to the Passion and Resurrection into the Christian artistic universe for the first time. This series of images vindicated the glory of Christ and the salvation of men through his sacrifice, and alluded to the central episode: the Crucifixion. But for a couple of exceptions, although this moment in the life of Christ had been key in the patristic writings of the second century, it did not appear in pictorial form

However, it is not possible to ascertain whether this iconography was created with the mission of expressing the ideas of the divinity of Christ and Trinitarian consubstantiality as such. It is true that the writings of some of the Fathers of the Church lent these meanings to the scene, but did Arian texts do the same? In spite of the significant dearth of Arian sources brought about by the destruction promoted by the adversaries of Arianism—who ultimately won the dispute and whose views became Christian orthodoxy—we preserve some of Maximinus's sermons expressing the importance of the celebration of the Feast of the Ascension for the communities he led in Illyria. Maximinus relates the Ascension to Pentecost, although he points out that these celebrations were carried out separately, and he uses this as a sign of the division and subordination of the persons of the Trinity. In a sort of correlation of events, first the Father sends the Son, and after his departure the Son sends the Holy Spirit; one person passes the mantle to the other, thus showing the separation of the hypostases.[51]

Thus, despite the lack of examples of this image, the episode of the Ascension could be interpreted as either Catholic or Arian depending on the eyes of the beholder. The link between Ascension and orthodoxy was not exclusive, at least in written texts. In an Arian key, Maximinus did not try to avoid this episode of Christ's life or to alter the evangelical narrative, but he used it to support his beliefs about the Trinity, just as Augustine or Leo the Great did.

In conclusion, we would like to suggest that, although the use of the Ascension in the disputes between Catholics and Arians is not certain, the relationship of this iconography with the disputes against Nestorianism does seem clearer. This dissidence challenged the true union between the two natures of Christ, distinguishing between Christ, the son of God, and Jesus, the son of Mary, and therefore denying the Virgin the title of *Theotokos*. Nestorianism was condemned

---

until the fifth century. Thus, in the mid-fourth century, this evolution of the images of the Passion and Resurrection that sought to emphasize Christ's victory over death, his kingship, glory and his salvific spirit, served as background for the appearance of the iconography of the Ascension; an appearance that, beyond the context of Christological debates, made sense in the visual context of the moment. Some fundamental works on the emergence of the earliest Christian iconography: André Grabar, *Las vías de la creación en la iconografía cristiana* (Madrid: Alianza, 1985); Mathews, *The Clash of Gods*; Robin M. Jensen, *Understanding Early Christian Art* (London and New York: Routledge, 2000); Fabrizio Bisconti, "Introduzione," in *Temi di iconografia paleocristiana*, ed. Fabrizio Bisconti (Rome: Pontificio Istituto di Archeologia Cristiana, 2000), 13–86; *Picturing the Bible: The Earliest Christian Art*, ed. Jeffrey Spier (New Haven: Yale University Press; Fort Worth: Kimbell Art Museum, 2007); *The Routledge Handbook*, ed. Jensen and Ellison).

51 In his study of these sermons, Meslin includes this passage and its Latin transcription, see Meslin, *Les Ariens d'Occident*, 404, and notes 103, 104.

at the Council of Chalcedon in 451, where Pope Leo the Great played a prominent role. In fact, in his sermon on the Ascension, he insists, as is usual in his writings, on the true union of the two natures of Christ, both of which ascended indivisibly to the right of the Father, thus glorifying human nature and making its salvation possible.[52] These ideas left their mark in iconography, more specifically in the representation of Christ's Ascension. Some of the ampullae from the Holy Land preserved in the treasuries of San Colombano of Bobbio and the Duomo of Monza exemplify this impact, as does the so-called reliquary of the Sancta Santorum of the Lateran Palace in Rome, preserved in the Vatican Museums. In these pieces, which feature the Eastern variant of the depiction of the Ascension,[53] the Virgin Mary appears vertically aligned with the figure of Christ. The presence of Mary in the image is significant, as she is not mentioned in the descriptions of the episode in the New Testament or its apocrypha. Therefore, it stands to reason that its addition was meant to provide a complementary meaning. The figure of Mary in these compositions is related to the idea of the Incarnation, and would underline the concept of the complete ascent of Christ, that is, body and soul, with his two natures completely united, from the very moment of the Incarnation, becoming also a vindication of Mary as Mother of God, in accordance with the canons resulting from Chalcedon.[54] In these instances, images do favour a reading along what would become orthodox lines in the face of the dissidence derived from Nestorius's ideas, thus showing the potential role played by images in the course of the doctrinal struggles within early Christianity.

---

52 Jordi Pinell, "Introducció," in *Lleó el Gran: Sermons* (Barcelona: Edicions Proa, 1995), 28–34. There are two very similar sermons for the feast of the Ascension of Christ written by Leo the Great and dated around 445.
53 Dewald, "The Iconography of the Ascension," 283–84.
54 In these images, the figure of the Virgin can be related to the Nativity, but also to the institution of the Church as intercessor between the faithful and Christ, and as true heir of the apostolic legacy. Schiller, *Ikonographie der christlichen Kunst*, 145–48; Christe, *Les grands portails romans*, 61, 73.

Stamatia Noutsou
Chapter 7
The Early Cistercian Order and the Persecution of Heresy: Bernard of Clairvaux's and Geoffrey of Auxerre's Attitudes Towards the Violent Persecution of Heretics

In his famous *Sermons on the Song of Songs*, Bernard of Clairvaux asked his audience "Quid faciemus his malignissimis vulpibus," a question he followed up by wondering how these *vulpes* could be caught.[1] In a similar vein, his disciple, Geoffrey of Auxerre, in his *Sermons on the Apocalypse*, also commented on the "foxes who ravage the Lord's vineyard."[2] Scholars have long argued that this image of the "little foxes" referred to individuals labelled as heretics by ecclesiastical authorities, for they posed a serious danger to Christianity in the eyes of churchmen.[3] Faced with the threat of religious "otherness," both Bernard and Geoffrey expressed in their writings their anxiety about this threat and its consequences for the Church and its people, while they discussed the most

---

[1] "What shall we do with these foxes, the most malicious of all?" in Bernard of Clairvaux, *Sermons On the Song of Songs III*, trans. Kilian Walsh and Irene M. Edmonds (Kalamazoo, MI: Cistercian Publications, 1979), 180. Bernard of Clairvaux, *Sancti Bernardi Opera*, ed. Jean Leclercq, Charles H. Talbot, and Henri Rochais, vol. II (Rome: Editiones Cistercienses, 1957–1977), 173. Hereinafter, Volumes II, III, VII, and VIII (published in 1958, 1963, 1974, and 1977, respectively) are cited as *SBOp* II, *SBOp* III, *SBOp* VII, and *SBOp* VIII.

[2] "Ad demoliendam vineam Domini vulpeculae prodierunt" and "vulpecalis, quae non cessant vineam Domini et eius sponsae nequiter demoliri," in *Goffredo di Auxerre: Super Apocalypsim*, ed. Ferruccio Gastaldelli (Rome: Edizioni di Storia e letteratura, 1970), 178 and 210. Geoffrey of Auxerre, *On the Apocalypse*, trans. Joseph Gibbons (Kalamazoo, MI: Cistercian Publications, 2000), 143: "These vixens went forth to ravage the Lord's vineyard," and 178: "little foxes of these times, who continue to wickedly destroy the vineyard of the Lord and of his bride."

[3] The image of the little foxes who destroy the Lord's vineyard was widely used in Cistercian anti-heretical writings. See Jean-Lous Biget, "'Les Albigeois': Remarques sur une dénomination," in *Inventer l'hérésie? Discours polémiques et pouvoirs avant l'Inquisition*, ed. Monique Zerner (Nice: Collection du Centre d'Études Médiévales de Nice, 1998), 219–55, and especially 236–37; Beverly Mayne Kienzle, *Cistercians, Heresy and Crusade in Occitania, 1145–1229: Preaching in the Lord's Vineyard* (York: York Medieval Press, 2001), 8; Lucy Sackville, *Heresy and Heretics in the Thirteenth Century: The Textual Representations* (York: York Medieval Press, 2011), 156–57.

effective way to deal with these "little foxes." Moreover, their writings show how these Cistercian abbots envisioned the different roles of clergy and laity in the fight against heresy. Thus, their encounter with this "religious edge" offers a privileged vantage point for the study of Cistercian ecclesiology, especially regarding its stance on societal order. This is the issue that serves as departure point for the present chapter, which will focus on the attitudes of these two Cistercian abbots towards the violent persecution of heretics.

Cistercians, Historiography, Violence

The Cistercian involvement in the fight against heretics in twelfth-century Europe has most certainly not been overlooked by modern scholarship. Quite the contrary, Cistercian anti-heretical writings have been the object of exhaustive rhetorical analysis by scholars addressing the role and the influence of the activities and writings of Cistercian monks on the centralisation of the efforts against heresy, which evolved from a mostly local matter to a challenge that demanded a response from the papacy.[4] Historians have traced the origins of the Cistercian response to heresy back to the order's understanding of the unity of Christendom and their dedication to the reform of the Church and Christianity as a whole.[5] For instance, Pilar Jiménez Sánchez sees Cistercian denunciation of heresy as a tool to impose Cistercian ecclesiology on the local population.[6] Moreover, the analysis of Cistercian anti-heretical attitudes has also been influenced by the overall study of the Church's strategies against heresy. It is not without controversy that some have posited the emergence of heresy in the twelfth century as a top-down process in which secular and ecclesiastical elites constructed heresy while they were seeking to establish their authority and accumulate power.[7] More specifically, Jean-Louis Biget has noted how the development of the Cistercian order and

---

[4] Raoul Manselli, "De la 'Persuasio' à la 'Coercitio'," in *Le Crédo, la morale et l'Inquisition* (Toulouse: Privat, 1971), 175–97 at 180–81; Robert Moore, *The Formation of a Persecuting Society: Authority and Deviance in Western Europe 950–1250* (Oxford: Blackwell Publishing, [1987] 2008), 24; Robert Moore, "The War against Heresy in Medieval Europe," *Historical Research* 81/212 (2008): 189–210 at 204; Kienzle, *Cistercians, Heresy and Crusade*, 8.

[5] Martha G. Newman, *The Boundaries of Charity: Cistercian Culture and Ecclesiastical Reform, 1098–1180* (Stanford: Stanford University Press, 1996), 219.

[6] Pilar Jiménez Sánchez, *Les catharismes: Modèles dissidents du christianisme médiéval (XIIe–XIIIe siècles)* (Rennes: Presses universitaires de Rennes, 2008), 263–76.

[7] For a discussion on developments in the historiography of medieval heresy, see Peter Biller, "Through a Glass Darkly: Seeing Medieval Heresy," in *The Medieval World*, ed. Peter Linehan and Janet L. Nelson (London: Routledge, 2003), 308–26.

the intensification of the problem of heresy happened more or less at the same time, and characterised the monks as the creators of heresy on an intellectual level.[8] Uwe Brunn in turn relates Bernard's preaching activities and the efforts for canonical reform to mentions of heresy in the area of Cologne.[9] Likewise, the connection between Cistercian anti-heretical efforts and political antagonism born from a struggle for power is also present in Robert Moore's works, especially in *The War on Heresy*.[10]

In contrast, as Beverly Kienzle points out, their views on the violent persecution of heretics has received only limited attention.[11] The historians who approached this topic seemed to be only interested in examining whether Bernard and, to a much lesser extent, Geoffrey, were in favour of the use of violence or against it. Jean Leclercq and Thomas Renna claimed that Bernard sought to place some limitations on the excessive use of violence, whereas Eoin de Bhaldraithe has presented a less "pacifist" image of the abbot of Clairvaux.[12] In sum, the prevalent conclusion among scholars is that Bernard contradicted himself when it came to violence, or at least was reluctant to condone the use of physical force. Kienzle links Bernard's ambivalence to his overall involvement in matters pertaining to the world outside the monastery. In fact, his fiery polemic could have paved the way for violent persecution.[13] Karen Sullivan adds that Bernard's reluctance should not necessarily be interpreted as evidence of disapproval, as he also advocated the occasional resort to violence.[14] Finally, Martha Newman argues that Bernard's portrayal of heretics as irrational or obstinate could have led to their violent oppression.[15]

I believe that the attitudes of Bernard and Geoffrey regarding the violent persecution of heretics can be reconsidered by shifting the focus from whether they

---

8 Biget, "'Les Albigeois': Remarques," 235–37.
9 Uwe Brunn, *Des contestataires aux "cathares": Discours de réforme et propagande antihérétique dans les pays du Rhin et de la Meuse avant l'Inquisition* (Paris: Institut d'études augustiniennes, 2006), 124–31.
10 Robert Moore, *The War on Heresy* (London: Profile, 2014), 146.
11 Kienzle, *Cistercians, Heresy and Crusade*, 106.
12 Jean Leclercq, "Saint Bernard's Attitude Toward War," *Studies in Medieval Cistercian History* 2 (1976): 1–39; Thomas Renna, "Early Cistercian Attitudes Towards War in Historical Perspective," *Cîteaux: Commentarii Cistercienses* 31 (1980): 119–29; Eoin de Bhaldraithe, "Jean Leclercq's Attitude Toward War," in *The Joy of Learning and the Love for God: Studies in Honor of Jean Leclercq*, ed. E. Rozane Elder (Kalamazoo, MI: Cistercian Publications, 1995), 217–37.
13 Kienzle, *Cistercians, Heresy and Crusade*, 106–8.
14 Karen Sullivan, *Truth and the Heretic: Crises of Knowledge in Medieval French Literature* (Chicago and London: The University of Chicago Press, 2005), 52.
15 Newman, *Boundaries of Charity*, 224.

favoured it or not to *how* they discussed the issue of violence specifically. This is indeed an important issue for several reasons. First, it will help us to better understand their role in the Church's strategy against heresy, especially as regards the process of legitimation and subsequent wider deployment of violence during the second half of the twelfth century.[16] Bernard was active at a time when the violent persecution of heresy was still a sporadic, smaller-scale endeavour carried out either by mobs or as a result of the decisiveness of secular authorities.[17] As for Geoffrey, his anti-heretical commitment first started when he accompanied Bernard in his preaching mission to southern France in 1145, but went on over a period in which violent persecution was becoming more prevalent. A mission led by another Cistercian abbot, Henry of Marcy, which was supported by secular arms, was an example of this tendency.[18] A close examination of the writings of Bernard and Geoffrey can help determine whether the idea of the use of force against heretics was unanimously endorsed. Secondly, violence was already present in the Cistercian vocabulary, as shown by Bernard's treatise *De laude novae militiae*, where he defended the Order of Knights Templar and presented his ideas on ideal knighthood and its duty to fight against Muslims and defend the Holy Land.[19] Moreover, violence was also present in his letters back-

---

[16] The literature on the Church's response to heresy in the twelfth century is quite extensive. See Bernard Hamilton, *The Medieval Inquisition* (New York: Holmes and Meier Publishers, 1981), 21–30; Moore, *Formation of a Persecuting Society*; Edward Peters, *Inquisition* (Berkeley: University of California Press, 1989), 44–52; Michael Frassetto, "Precursors to Religious Inquisitions: Anti-heretical Efforts to 1184," in *A Companion to Heresy Inquisitions*, ed. Donald Prudlo (Leiden: Brill, 2019), 41–72; Manselli, "De la 'Persuasio' à la 'Coercitio'," 175–97; Henri Maisonneuve, *Études sur les origines de l'Inquisition* (Paris: J. Vrin, 1960); Grado Giovanni Merlo, "Militare per Cristo contro gli eretici," in *Contro gli eretici: La coercizione all'ortodossia prima dell'Inquisizione* (Bologna: Il Mulino, 1996), 11–49.

[17] Robert Moore, "Popular Violence and Popular Heresy in Western Europe, ca. 1100–1179," in *Persecution and Toleration*, ed. William J. Sheils (Oxford: Blackwell, 1984), 43–50; Frassetto, "Precursors to Religious Inquisitions," 51.

[18] It is worth noting that despite Geoffrey of Auxerre's importance, his anti-heretical polemic in general and, in particular, his attitudes towards violence have not received as much attention as Bernard's. Scholars analysing the issue of violence have primarily focused on Bernard of Clairvaux and Henry of Marcy. I have decided to exclude Henry's polemic and involvement from the present study, as I believe he marked a turning point in the violent persecution of heresy. The missions of Henry of Marcy in 1178 and 1181, when he was accompanied by secular arms and a more violent crusade rhetoric entered anti-heretical polemics, were behind the legitimation of violence as a tool against heretics. See Yves Congar, "Henry de Marcy, abbé de Clairvaux, cardinal-évêque d'Albano et légat pontifical," *Analecta Monastica V, Studia Anselmiana* 43 (1958): 1–19 at 18; Kienzle, *Cistercians, Heresy and Crusade*, 109.

[19] Aryeh Grabois, "*Militia* and *Malitia:* The Bernardine Vision of Chivalry," in *The Second Crusade and the Cistercians*, ed. Michael Gervers (New York: St. Martin's Press, 1992), 49–56 at 49.

ing the Second Crusade and the expedition against the Wends.[20] The comparison of crusade polemics and anti-heretical writings will shed light on how Bernard

---

20 *Epistola* [hereinafter EP] 363, in *SBOp* VIII, 316–17: "Plane et gentiles, si essent similiter in fine futura subiugati, in eo quidem iudicio essent similiter expectandi quam gladiis appetendi. Nunc autem cum in nos esse coeperint violenti, oportet vim vi repellere eos, qui non causa gladium partant [Rom 13:4]"; Bernard of Clairvaux, *The Letters of St. Bernard of Clairvaux*, trans. Bruno Scott James (London: Burns Oates 1953), 463: "If the pagans were similarly subjugated to us then, in my opinion, we should wait for them rather than seek them out with swords. But as they have now begun to attack us, it is necessary for those of us who do not carry a sword in vain to repel them with force." EP 457, in *SBOp* VIII, 432–33: "quomodo suscitaverit spiritum regum Deus et principum ad faciendam vindictam in nationibus et exstirpandos de terra christiani nominis inimicos. … consilio domini regis et episcoporum et principum, qui convenerant Frankonovort, denuntiamus armari christianorum robur adversus illos, et ad delendas penitus, aut certe convertendas …. Illud enim omnimodis interdicimus, ne qua ratione ineant foedus cum eis, neque pro pecunia, neque pro tributo, donec auxiliante Deo, aut ritus ipse, aut natio deleatur"; Bernard of Clairvaux, *The Letters*, 466: "God has stirred up the spirit of kings and princes to take vengeance on the pagans and to wipe out from Christian lands …. We make known to you that at the council of the king, bishops, and princes who had come together at Frankfort, the might of Christians was armed against them, and that for the complete wiping out or, at any rate, the conversion of these people …. We utterly forbid that for any reason whatsoever a truce should be made with these peoples, either for the sake of money or for the sake of tribute, until such a time as, by God's help, they shall be either converted or wiped out."

The literature on Bernard's involvement in the Second Crusade is quite extensive. See Michael Gervers, ed., *The Second Crusade and the Cistercians* (New York: St. Martin's Press, 1992); John R. Sommerfeldt, "The Bernardine Reform and the Crusading Spirit," *The Catholic Historical Review* 86/4 (2000): 567–87. However, he strongly opposed any violent acts against Jews, as shown in EP 363, in *SBOp* VIII, 316: "Non sunt persequendi Iudaei, non sunt trucidandi, sed nec effugandi quidem. Interrogate eos qui divinas paginas norunt, quid in Psalmo legerint prophetatum de Iudaeis: Deus, iniquit Ecclesia, ostendit mihi super inimicos meos ne occidas eos, nequando obliviscantur populi mei [Ps 58:12]. Vivi quidam apices nobis sunt, repraesentantes iugiter Dominicam passionem. Propter hoc et in omnes dispersi sunt regiones, ut dum iustas tanti facinoris poenas luunt ubique, testes sint nostrae redemptionis. Unde et addit in eodem Psalmo loquens Ecclesia: Disperge illos in virtute tua, et depone eos, protector meus domine [Ps 58:12]. Ita factum est: dispersi sunt, depositi sunt; duram sustinent captivitatem sub principibus christianis. Convertentur tamen ad Vesperam, et in tempore erit respectus eorum [Ps 58:15]. Denique, cum introierit gentium plenitudo, tunc omnis Israel salvus erit [Sap 3:6], ait Apostolus [Rom 11: 25–26]. Interim sane qui moritur, manet in morte [1 Jn 3:14]"; Bernard of Clairvaux, *The Letters*, 462–63: "The Jews are not to be persecuted, killed or even put to flight. Ask anyone who knows the Sacred Scriptures what he finds foretold of the Jews in the psalm. Not for their destruction do I pray, it says. The Jews are for us the living words of Scripture, for they remind us always of what our Lord suffered. They are dispersed all over the world so that by expiating their crime they may be everywhere the living witnesses of our redemption. Hence the same psalm adds, only let thy power disperse them. And so it is: dispersed they are. Under Christian princes they endure a hard captivity, but they only wait for the time of

and Geoffrey envisioned their anti-heretical involvement, and on whether or not their sole purpose was punishing heretics. Lastly, the question of violence and, especially, of who had the right to exercise it and under what circumstances is closely related to issues of power and authority. The analysis of the attitudes of Bernard and Geoffrey towards the violent persecution of heresy offers the opportunity to examine aspects of their ecclesiology, their ideas on the structure of society, on the role of societal groups, and on the relationship of secular and ecclesiastical authorities. At the same time, and given that the texts also had a formative function, I will discuss the direct political implications of their writings, as they served to impose the ideas of these Cistercian abbots on their audience.[21]

The Violent Persecution of Heresy in Bernard's *Sermons On the Song of Songs*

In Sermon 64 of Bernard's commentary on the Songs of Songs, the abbot of Clairvaux argues against the use of violence, as heretics must be persuaded to return to the Church with arguments.[22] The reconciliation of heretics is presented as a part of the Church's salvific mission. Bernard was however aware that the efforts to convince heretics could be unsuccessful and opened the door to their exclu-

---

their deliverance. Finally we are told by the Apostle that when the time is ripe all Israel shall be saved. But those who die before will remain in death." The same arguments on Jews also appear in EP 365, in *SBOp* VIII 320–22. On Bernard's attitudes towards Jews, see David Berger, "The Attitude of St. Bernard of Clairvaux toward the Jews," *Proceedings of the American Academy for Jewish Research* 40 (1972): 89–108, where he compares the images of the subjugated and the docile Jew.

21 The idea that texts have not only an informative function but also a formative role comes from the field of discourse analysis. *Methods of Critical Discourse Analysis*, ed. Ruth Wodak and Michael Meyer (London: Sage Publications, 2001), 139–84; Louise Philips and Marianne Jørgensen, *Discourse Analysis as Theory and Method* (London: Sage Publications, 2002), 1–23.

22 *SCC*, in *SBOp* II, 170. "Capiantur, dico, non armis, sed argumentis, quibus refellantur errores eorum; ipsi vero, si fieri potes, reconcilientur Catholicae, revocentur ad veram fidem. Haec est enim voluntas eius [Jn 6:39–40], qui vult omnes homines salvos fieri et ad agnitionem veritatis venire [1 Tim 2:4]"; Bernard of Clairvaux, *Sermons On the Song of Songs* III, 175: "They are to be caught, I repeat, not by force of arms but by arguments by which their errors may be refuted. They themselves, if it can be done, are to be reconciled with the Catholic [Church] and brought back to the true faith."

sion using a scriptural reference, Titus 3:10.²³ This idea that heretics should be excluded for the sake of other Christians and the Church is repeated through Sermons 65 and 66.

Bernard returned to the issue of violence in Sermon 66, where he commented on a letter from Everwin of Steinfeld, the Praemonstratensian prior of a monastery close to Cologne, but his attitude there was entirely different. Everwin had appealed to the abbot of Clairvaux when heretical groups appeared in the Rhineland, expressing his anxiety and wonder, for a small group of heretics who had been apprehended by the people of Cologne—without ecclesiastical sanction—in 1143, had preferred death by fire to retraction and salvation.²⁴ In his response, Bernard appeared less surprised by this behaviour than Everwin. By connecting heresy to the devil and outlining the image of the stubborn and hypocritical heretic, Bernard concluded that these people were unable to understand arguments and incapable of recognising their mistakes.²⁵ Thus, it was no wonder that they

---

23 *SCC*, in *SBOp* II, 170. "Quod si reverti noluerit, nec convictus post primam iam et secundam admonitionem, utpote qui omnino subversus est, erit, secundum Apostolum, devitandus [Tit 3:10]. Ex hoc iam melius, ut quidem ego arbitror, effugatur, aut etiam religatur, quam sinitur vineas demoliri"; Bernard of Clairvaux, *Sermons On the Song of Songs* III, 176: "But if he will not be converted or convinced after a first and second admonition, then, according to the Apostle, he is to be shunned as one who is completely perverted. Consequently, I think it better that he should be driven away or even bound rather than be allowed to spoil the vines."
24 *Diversorum ad S. Bernardum et alios*, Epistola CDXXXII.2 (PL CLXXXII, col. 677): "cum per triduum essent admoniti, et resipiscere noluissent, rapti sunt a populis nimio zelo permotis, nobis tamen invitis, et in ignem positi, atque cremati. Et, quod magis mirabile est, ipsi tormentum ignis non solum cum patientia, sed et cum laetitia introierunt et sustinuerunt. Hic, sancte pater, vellem, si praesens essem, habere responsionem tuam, unde istis diaboli membris tanta fortitudo in sua haeresi, quanta vix etiam invenitur in valde religiosis in fide Christi." R. I. Moore, *The Birth of Popular Heresy* (London: Arnold, 1975), 75: "After they were urged for three days to come to their senses, and refused, and then were seized by the people, who were moved by great enthusiasm (though we were against it), put to the stake, and burned. The amazing thing was that they entered and endured the torment of the flames not merely courageously, but joyfully. I wish I were there with you, holy father, to hear you explain how such great fortitude comes to these tools of the devil in their heresy as is seldom found among the truly religious in the faith of Christ."
25 *SCC*, in *SBOp* II, 186: "Multa quidem et alia huic populo stulto et insipienti a spiritibus erroris, in hypocrisi loquentibus mendacium, mala persuasa sunt [Jn 20:30, Deut 32:6, Tim 4:11, Ps 5:7]; sed non est respondere ad omnia. Quis enim omnia novit? Deinde labor infinitus esset, et minime necessarius. Nam quantum ad istos, nec rationibus convincuntur, quia non intelligunt, nec auctoritatibus corriguntur, quia non recipiunt, nec flectuntur suasionibus, quia subversi sunt." Bernard of Clairvaux, *Sermons On the Song of Songs* III, 203–4: "Many other persuasive arguments are adduced by lying and hypocritical spirits to deceive the dull-witted and foolish people, but it is not necessary to answer all of them. For who can perceive all of them?

had not hesitated upon facing death. He continued by discussing the reaction of the people of Cologne.

> Itaque irruens in eos populus, novos haereticis suae ipsorum perfidiae martyres dedit. Approbamus zelum, sed factum non suademus, quia fides suadenda est, non imponenda. Quamquam melius procul dubio gladio coercentur, illius videlicet qui non sine causa gladium portat [Rom 13:4], quam in suum errorem multos traicere permittantur.²⁶
>
> [So people have attacked them, making new martyrs for the cause of godless heresy. We applaud their zeal, but do not recommend their action, because faith should be a matter of persuasion, not of force, though no doubt it is better for them to be restrained by the sword of someone who bears not the sword in vain than to be allowed to lead others into heresy.]²⁷

This passage has been the subject of much scholarly debate. Bernard's condemnation of mob violence has been examined in relation to the general framework of the Church's efforts to centralise justice against more traditional jurisdictions favoured by local communities.²⁸ Kienzle argues that Bernard's contradictory message opened the door to the violent persecution of heretics, whereas for Sullivan this passage indicates that Bernard understood the necessity for violent acts.²⁹ Leclercq points out that Bernard, recognising that violent acts were an unavoidable reality, sought to limit unrestrained violence by condemning the actions of mobs, "by imposing conditions as to its use and motivation."³⁰ Henri Maisonneuve argues that, following the Augustinian tradition, Bernard was prone to appeal for the assistance of secular leaders when preaching proved ineffective against heresy.³¹ According to Maisonneuve, Bernard's views on the use of force were related to his aims of disciplining and defending Christian society.³²

In my view, the above-mentioned passage shows how the violent persecution of heresy was organically related to issues of power and authority, as the

---

Besides, it would be an endless task and quite unnecessary. For these men are not to be convinced by logical reasoning, which they do not understand, nor prevailed upon by references to authority, which they do not accept, nor can they be won over by persuasive arguments, for they are utterly perverted."

26 *SCC*, in *SBOp* II, 186–87.
27 Bernard of Clairvaux, *Sermons On the Song of Songs* III, 204.
28 Robert Moore, *The First European Revolution ca. 970–1215* (Oxford and New York: Blackwell Publishing, 2000), 168–69.
29 Kienzle, *Cistercians, Heresy and Crusade*, 106–8; Sullivan, *Truth and the Heretic*, 52.
30 Leclercq, "Saint Bernard's Attitude," 1–39.
31 Maisonneuve, *Études sur les origines*, 104–5.
32 Maisonneuve, *Études sur les origines*, 104–5.

main point of interest was not the violent act itself, but rather the question of who had the right to exercise physical violence. Bernard appeared disturbed not by the burning of heretics but mostly because violence was committed by those who did not hold the authority to use it. The Cistercian abbot indeed sought to place strict limitations on violence by reminding his audience that only secular rulers had the right to employ force. Bernard quoted a passage from Paul's Letter to the Romans in which Paul deals with the relationship between Christians and the state of Rome and strongly advocates the need to submit to Roman rulers and to show obedience to those who have the right to execute God's wrath.[33] By commenting on a specific event, Bernard seized the opportunity to demonstrate his ideas on the relationship between the laity and secular leaders, which had to be predicated on the former's obedience to the latter. As "a man of order,"[34] he attempted to make a clear distinction between the role of secular elites and that of the laity at large on the basis of the legitimate use of force.

Moreover, in this passage, we can follow Bernard's ideas on the relationship between secular and ecclesiastical authorities, as he evoked the image of the two swords. This is not the only instance where this image appears in Bernardine writings, as it can also be found in Letter 256, written in 1150 to Pope Eugene III, as well as in *De Consideratione*, where he reminded the Pope that both swords belonged to the papacy but only secular leaders could use force whenever the Church demanded it.[35] The obligation of secular leaders to use the sword in order to assist ecclesiastical authorities is reiterated in Bernard's letters of cru-

---

[33] Robert Jewett, "Romans," in *Cambridge Companion to St. Paul*, ed. James D. G. Dunn (Cambridge: Cambridge University Press, 2003), 91–104 at 103–4.
[34] Gillian Evans, *Bernard of Clairvaux* (Oxford: Oxford University Press, 2000), 158.
[35] *EP 256*, in *SBOp* VIII, 163: "Petri uterque est, alter suo nutu, alter sua manu, quoties necesse est, evaginandus. Et quidem de quo minus videbatur, de ipso ad Petrum dictum est: Converte gladium tuum in vaginam [Jn 18:11]. Ergo suus erat et ille, sed non sua manu utique educendus"; Bernard of Clairvaux, *The Letters*, 471: "Both of Peter's swords must be drawn whenever necessary; the one by his command, the other by his hand. It seems that Peter was not to use one of these swords, for he was told 'put up thy sword into the scabbard.' Although they both belonged to him, they were not both to be drawn by his hand." *Csi*, in *SBOp* III, 454: "Uterque ergo Ecclesiae, et spiritualis scilicet gladius, et materialis, sed in quidem pro Ecclesia, ille vero et ab Ecclesia exserendus: ille sacerdotis, is militis manu, sed sane ad nutum sacerdotis et iussum imperatoris"; Bernard of Clairvaux, *Five Books on Consideration: Advice to a Pope*, trans. John Anderson and Elisabeth Kennan (Kalamazoo, MI: Cistercian Publications, 1976), 118: "Both swords, that is, the spiritual and the material, belong to the Church; however, the latter is to be drawn for the Church and the former by the Church. The spiritual sword should be drawn by the hand of the priest; the material sword by the hand of the knight, but clearly at the bidding of the priest and at the command of the emperor."

sading propaganda, where he urged knights to seize the sword that was entrusted to them,[36] as the clergy should not be actively involved in violent actions.[37]

The interpretation of the image of the two swords in Bernard's writings has been extensively discussed, mainly focusing on the nature of the relation between ecclesiastical and secular authorities.[38] This specific passage of Bernardine anti-heretical writings evinces how important it was for Bernard that secular authorities realised their obligations. Moreover, as the Church's Councils demanded—for instance the Second Lateran Council—he sought to enhance the collaboration between secular and ecclesiastical elites to combat heresy.[39]

The discussion of the episode of Cologne finishes with Bernard quoting Paul: "Dei enim minister ille est, vindex in iram ei qui male agit [Rom 13:4]."[40] The same quotation, albeit paraphrased, also appears in *On the Praise of New Knighthood*: "Miles, inquam Christi securus interimit, interit securior. Sibi praestat cum interit, Christo cum interimit. Non enim sine causa gladium portat: Dei enim minister est ad vindictam malefactorum, laudem vero bonorum [Rom 13:4]."[41] The use of the same quotation reveals that elements of crusading propaganda had entered anti-heretical polemics. By connecting the punishment of heretics with the image of the "servant of God," the Cistercian abbot gave a new dimension to the fight against heresy. His understanding of anti-heretical commitment bears a strong similarity to the way in which he understood the crusades: both acts are perceived as transformative, for the participant becomes a servant of God. John R. Sommerfeldt argues that in the crusades Bernard saw

---

36 *EP 363*, in *SBOp* VIII, 317: "Nunc autem cum in nos esse coeperint violenti, opportet vim vi repellere eos, qui non sine causa gladium portant [Rom 13:4]"; Bernard of Clairvaux, *The Letters*, 463: "But as they have now begun to attack us, it is necessary for those of us who do not carry a sword in vain to repel them with force."

37 James Brundage, "St. Bernard and the Jurists," in *Second Crusade and the Cistercians*, ed. Gervers, 25–33.

38 Elizabeth Kennan, "The 'De Consideratione' of St. Bernard of Clairvaux and the Papacy in the Mid-Twelfth Century: A Review on Scholarship," *Tradition* 23 (1967): 73–115; Alice Chapman, *Sacred Authority and Temporal Power in the Writings of Bernard of Clairvaux* (Turnhout: Brepols, 2013), 181–89.

39 Moore, *War on Heresy*, 144–45; Frasseto, "Precursors to Religious Inquisitions," 52–53.

40 *SCC*, in *SBOp* II, 187. Bernard of Clairvaux, *Sermons On the Song of Songs* III, 204: "Anyone who punishes a wrong-doer in righteous wrath is a servant of God."

41 *Ad milites Templi de laude novae militiae* [hereinafter Tpl], in *SBOp* III, 217. Bernard of Clairvaux, *In Praise of the New Knighthood: A Treatise on the Knights Templar and the Holy Places of Jerusalem*, trans. Conrad Greenia (Kalamazoo, MI: Cistercian Publications, 2000), 38: "The knight of Christ, I say, may strike with confidence and succumb more confidently. When he strikes, he does service to Christ, and to himself when he succumbs. Nor does he bear the sword in vain. He is God's minister in the punishment of evil doers and the praise of well doers."

an opportunity to carry out his ambition to reform society and, especially, secular leaders.⁴² The defence of Christianity would allow secular leaders to prove that, as a result of an internal reform, they had become servants of God and thus used their arms in God's service. Likewise, those who punished heretics were transformed into servants of God.

Letters 241 and 242

Bernard had the opportunity to directly appeal to secular authorities and to the laity for their assistance in the fight against heresy. Before and after his preaching mission of 1145 he wrote epistles to Count Alphonse Jourdain of Toulouse and to the people of that city. These sources show how certain key elements of Bernard's crusade ideology were also present in his anti-heretical writings. In his first letter, Bernard sought to emphasise the Count's duty to help in the fight against heresy as a result of the power that God had granted him.⁴³ Thus, just like the crusades, the combat against heretics became a duty of secular leaders.⁴⁴ Moreover, the collaboration between ecclesiastical and secular authorities, dominant in Bernard's crusade letters, also appears in his anti-heretical writings.⁴⁵ Finally, Bernard connected the fight against heresy with the Count's proper behaviour and honour.⁴⁶ In his crusade letter to the people of England, he made a similar point: if Christians continued to tolerate the presence of Muslims in the Holy Land, "verum id quidem omnibus deinceps saeculis inconsolabilis dolor, quia irrecuperabile damnumn, specialiter autem generatio-

---

42 Sommerfeldt, "Bernardine Reform," 569.
43 *EP 241*, in *SBOp* VIII, 127: "Tua interest, vir inclyte, honorifice suscipere illum et eos qui cum ipso sunt, ac ne tantus labor tantorum virorum, pro tua potissimum tuorumque salute susceptus, inefficax sit, secundum potestatem datam tibi desuper operam dare [Jn 19:11]." Moore, *The Birth*, 41: "It must be your concern, most excellent sir, to receive him honourably and those men who are with him; and, so that the good work which such a great man has undertaken on your behalf and on behalf of your people, shall not be in vain, give him all the help you can according to that power which you have received from above."
44 In addition, Ames has argued that the Cistercian abbot most probably knew that the Count's father, Raimon IV, had participated in the First Crusade; thus, as his father had defended his honour by taking part in the crusade, Alphonse could do the same by fighting heresy. Christine Caldwell Ames, *Medieval Heresies, Christianity, Judaism, and Islam* (Cambridge: Cambridge University Press, 2015), 151.
45 Maisonneuve, *Études sur les origines*, 124.
46 *EP 241*, in *SBOp* VIII, 126: "Quod tuone honori congruat, princeps illustris, ipse iudicato." Moore, *The Birth*, 40: "But whether or not this is in keeping with your honour, you alone must judge."

ni huic pessimae infinita confusio et opprobrium sempiternum."⁴⁷ In this manner, the response to heresy acquired a moral dimension; it was a matter of honour and of proving one's virtue.

Leaving aside the elements characteristic of crusade preaching, the issue of violence is totally absent from Bernard's letter to the Count of Toulouse. Discussing this absence, Raoul Manselli notes that Bernard most probably did not want secular forces assisting the preaching delegation, for otherwise he would have asked for them.⁴⁸ Bernard seemed indeed more interested in ensuring the Count's support than in the use of force. His anti-heretical commitment became another opportunity to demonstrate his societal ideas and force the Count of Toulouse to collaborate with the Church while accepting its primacy, as follows from his understanding of the image of the two swords.

In the letter to the people of Toulouse, written after his preaching mission was completed, he exhorted them to take action against heresy.⁴⁹ The responsibility to fight against heresy was thus extended and transformed into a matter that required wider mobilisation. As Christine Caldwell Ames argues, the consequences of this process were far-reaching, as it can be seen as an instance of the unfolding "monasticisation" of the laity. By becoming active defenders of Christianity, resembling the commitment of crusaders, Christians were obliged to obedience and proper behaviour according to the ideals of ecclesiastical authorities.⁵⁰ Furthermore, according to Bernard's letter, engaging in the fight against heresy had a transformative function for, as the crusading propaganda claimed, those who participated in such a fight could display their virtue and become servants of God.⁵¹ Bernard presented the hatred of heresy as a proof of the love for God.⁵² The same quotation appears later in one of his crusade letters,

---

47 *EP 363*, in *SBOp* VIII, 313. "Verily that would be an irremediable grief to all time, an irrecoverable loss, a vast disgrace to this most graceless generation, and an everlasting shame."
48 Manselli, "De la 'Persuasio' à la 'Coercitio'," 181–82.
49 *EP 242*, in *SBOp* VIII, 128: "Propterea, dilectissimi, persequimini et comprehendite eos [Ps 70:11], et nolite desistere, donec penitus depereant et diffugiant de cunctis finibus vestris, quia non est tutum dormire vicinis serpentibus." Bernard of Clairvaux, *The Letters*, 390: "And also, very dear friends, pursue them and seize them, until they have all gone, fled from your midst, for it is not safe to sleep near serpents."
50 Christine Caldwell Ames, "Crusade, Inquisition, and Monasticization" (unpublished paper presented at a conference, Kalamazoo, 2014), 6.
51 Yael Katzir, "The Second Crusade and the Redefinition of Ecclesia, Christianitas and Papal Coercive Power," in *Second Crusade and the Cistercians*, ed. Gervers, 3–11 at 8–9.
52 *EP 242*, in *SBOp* VIII, 128: "Nonne qui oderunt te, Domine, oderam, et super inimicos tuos tabescebam? Perfecto odio oderam illos, inimici facti sunt mihi [Ps 138: 21–22]." Bernard of Clairvaux, *The Letters*, 389–90: "Lord, do I not hate the men who hate thee, am I not sick at

but whereas in these letters it constitutes an open call to arms, it does not seem to serve the same function in the letter to the people of Toulouse, where violence is not mentioned. However, one specific word in the latter, the verb *depereant*, has attracted the attention of scholars. Leclercq claims that the use of this word was merely connected to the idea of good conduct and the prevention of wrongdoing and self-defence.[53] Maisonneuve argues that Bernard advised the people of Toulouse to persecute heretics and not to accept unauthorised preachers.[54] Eoin de Bhaldraithe points out that Bernard "said, not that the heretics should be killed, but that the territory should certainly be 'religiously' cleansed. Yet the word perish (*depereant*) is ambiguous, apparently allowing for some deaths in the purifying process," which paved the way for a future crusade against heretics.[55] However, in my view, the use of this word should not necessarily be interpreted as a call to arms. As noted above, in Sermon 66, Bernard condemned the use of violence against heresy when it was perpetrated by a mob, and appealed for obedience to secular leaders. It would have been out of character for Bernard to instigate violent acts if these acts did not fall within a specific framework, for instance a crusade. Bernard seems to be more interested in alerting the people of Toulouse about the dangers of heresy than in having them actively join the fight against it.

Geoffrey of Auxerre and the Violent Persecution of Heresy

Geoffrey of Auxerre's involvement in the anti-heretical endeavour began in 1145, when he accompanied Bernard in his preaching mission to the Midi, and continued throughout his life. He was an important figure in the early years of the Waldensian movement, as he and Henry of Marcy took the initiative to summon a council in Lyon where Valdes, its founder and leader, made a profession of faith.[56] Besides this active involvement, Geoffrey also wrote about heresy in

---

heart over their rebellion? Surpassing hatred I bear them, count them my sworn enemies." My argument here follows Sullivan's discussion; see Karen Sullivan, *The Inner Lives of Medieval Inquisitors* (Chicago: University of Chicaco Press, 2011), 44.
53 Leclercq, "Saint Bernard's Attitude," 19.
54 Leclercq, "Saint Bernard's Attitude," 19; Maisonneuve, *Études sur les origines*, 125.
55 Bhaltraithe, "Jean Leclercq's Attitude," 231–33.
56 Christine Thouzellier, *Catharisme et valdéisme en Languedoc à la fin du XIIe et au début du XIIIe siècle: Politique pontificale, controverses* (Louvain: Nauwelaerts; Paris: Béatrice-Nauwelaerts, 1969), 26–27; Moore, *War on Heresy*, 220–22; Michael Rubellin, "Au temps où Valdès n'é-

his *Vita prima Sancti Bernardi,* where he described the preaching mission of 1145. Heresy also appears twice in his commentary on the Apocalypse, a compilation of sermons originally delivered before a monastic audience, which Geoffrey reworked in the 1180s, during the last years of his life.[57] One of the main topics of Sermon 14 is unauthorised preaching by wandering laymen and laywomen. In turn, Sermon 18 refers to the conversion of two heretics as a result of Henry of Marcy's preaching in 1181.[58] Both Biget and Moore have underlined Geoffrey's importance for the development of the Church's strategy against heretics, especially in southern France, as in his writings he shaped the idea that this area was overrun by heresy.[59]

As noted above, Geoffrey's anti-heretical endeavour spanned a period during which the Church's response went through major changes. Although papal inquisitions were not yet established and would not be until the 1230s, in the last quarter of the twelfth century the Church's policy became more severe and far-reaching through the decisions of different councils. In 1179, the Third Lateran Council represented a milestone in the use of force against heresy and the idea of a crusade against heretics, strongly influenced by Henry of Marcy.[60] Some years later, in 1184, during the Synod of Verona, Pope Lucius III issued a bull in the presence of Emperor Frederick Barbarossa that has been deemed the de facto beginning of medieval inquisition.[61] Indeed, the declaration of *Ad abolendam* formally established a close collaboration between ecclesiastical and secular authorities for the persecution of heresy. Cistercian attitudes had also changed after Henry's campaign in southern France, when the castle of Lav-

---

tait pas hérétique: Hypothèses sur le rôle de Valdès à Lyon (1170–1183)," in *Inventer l'hérésie? Discours polémiques et pouvoirs avant l'Inquisition,* ed. Monique Zerner (Turnhout: Brepols, 1998), 193–218 at 199–200. Geoffrey mentions that "Abiuravit eiusmodi sectam primus inventor a loco nativitatis Wandesius": *Goffredo di Auxerre: Super Apocalypsim,* 179.

[57] Jean Leclercq, "Introduction," in *Goffredo di Auxerre: Super Apocalypsim,* 40–41.

[58] "Sermon 14," in *Goffredo di Auxerre: Super Apocalypsim,* 175–82; "Sermon 18," in *Goffredo di Auxerre: Super Apocalypsim,* 206–21.

[59] Biget, "'Les Albigeois': Remarques," 245; Moore, *War on Heresy,* 222.

[60] *Decrees of the Ecumenical Councils,* ed. Norman P. Tanner, vol. I (Washington, DC: Georgetown University Press, 1990), 211–25; Maisonneuve, *Études sur les origines,* 135–38; Jeffrey Burton Russel, *Dissent and Order in the Middle Ages: The Search for Legitimate Authority* (New York: Twayne Publishers, 1992), 55; Gordon Leff, *Heresy in the Later Middle Ages: The Relation of Heterodoxy to Dissent, 1250–1450* (Manchester: Manchester University Press; New York: Barnes & Noble, 1967), 36.

[61] Giovanni Domenico Mansi, *Sacrorum conciliorum nova et amplissima collectio,* vol. XXII (Venice: Antonio Zatta, 1778), 492; Maisonneuve, *Études sur les origines,* 153–55; Peters, *Inquisition,* 47–48; Moore, *War on Heresy,* 206–7.

aur was seized with the assistance of secular powers.⁶² In Sermon 18, Geoffrey commented on the conversion of two heretics during that mission, but he remained silent with regard to the violent seizure of the castle. Instead, he described the conversions in a more traditional monastic way; in line with Everwin and Bernard, he recounted how the capture of these two heretics was due to the zeal of the faithful rather than the result of a military action.⁶³

The issue of the violent persecution of heresy, or rather its absence, becomes even more significant in those instances when Geoffrey's writings bring up the matter of violent punishment. In Sermon 15, he posited that the role of punishment was to guide transgressors so that they became conscious of their behaviour: "He pretends to punish the faults of sinners to lead them to repentance. He reproves those who leave their offences and his patience unnoticed in order to bring them to consider both things. As a last resort he brings physical pain on them to make them realize their state."⁶⁴ Even bodily pain is legitimised as a last step when it is applied in order to prompt this internal change. In this passage we notice how much attention Geoffrey paid to the transformation of sinners and the positive role that corporal punishment could play in this process. Thus, he did not condemn the use of violence, especially as it could lead to positive results.

However, the question of the absence of violence in his anti-heretical writings remains. His approach can be better understood if we compare Geoffrey's anti-heretical polemic to other passages of his writings where he referred, albeit implicitly, to the use of violence. In Sermon 13 ("To the angel of the Church of

---

62 Congar, "Henry de Marcy," 36–37; Biget, "'Les Albigeois': Remarques," 244.
63 *Goffredo di Auxerre: Super Apocalypsim*, 210: "Denique super modernis eorum vulpeculis, quae non cessant vineam Domini et eius sponsae nequiter demoliri, inveteratos in eadem malitia et quorum sermo serpens ut cancer ad impietatem nimis profecerat, duos heresiarchas ante hos paucos annos in partibus Tolosanis cum oppido et in oppido, cui nomen est Vallis, ab exercitu zelo fidei congregato, comprehensos novimus et oblatos venerabili patri nostro domino Henrico Albanensi episcopo, apostolicae sedis in Aquitania tunc legato." Geoffrey of Auxerre, *On the Apocalypse*, 178: "Let us now say something about our little foxes of these times, who continue to wickedly destroy the vineyard of the Lord and of his bride. We know of two arch-heretics sunk in malice, whose talk spread like a canker and led to great impiety. They were caught a few years ago around Toulouse, in a town called Valence, by a zealous band of faithful, and were brought before our venerable father and lord Henry, Bishop of Alba, then legate of the Apostolic See in Aquitaine."
64 Geoffrey of Auxerre, *On the Apocalypse*, 154. *Goffredo di Auxerre: Super Apocalypsim*, 188: "peccantium culpas ulcisci dissimulat, ut adducat ad paenitentiam; dissimulantes suam offensionem et eius expectationem arguit, ad inspirandam eis utriusque rei considerationem; demum flagellat, ut perniciosam tollat impunitatem."

Pergamon"), Geoffrey criticised the clergy by making references to Nicholaism (interpreted as a breach of the vow of celibacy) and added:

> Would that today our priests may contend with tongues afire rather than with rigid iron swords! Would that they found armaments and shields fit for burning intolerable, and would prefer the dalmatic to the breastplate, the miter to the helmet, the pastoral staff to the military banner! The servants of God are to fight for God with spiritually powerful weapons, not with material and physical ones [2 Co 10:4], contending with prayer, preaching, supplication, and reproof [1 Tim 2:1]. Is there any wonder that unclean demons and wicked people have so little fear of the sword of their mouths when they put their confidence in material arms?[65]

In this passage, Geoffrey strongly condemned the use of violence by churchmen, as he believed that force was not a suitable "weapon" for the clergy. Accordingly, the violent persecution of heresy is absent from his anti-heretical writings for this same reason. However, this absence should not be interpreted as a moral condemnation of violence, and neither should Geoffrey be perceived as a "voice of tolerance," for he urged his audience to participate in the fight against heresy, as such a cause was the duty of any good pastor.[66] Rather, this omission needs to be associated with the post-Gregorian idea that churchmen, as a distinguished group in society, should avoid using material weapons and instead wield only spiritual arms, which were more powerful and important and thus granted them superiority.[67]

Generally, in his *Sermons on the Apocalypse*, Geoffrey of Auxerre appears preoccupied with the proper behaviour of the clergy. He criticised the churchmen's leniency towards heretics and their fondness for material goods. Moreover, in one of his sermons on the problem of Nicolaitism, he provided a definition of

---

65 Geoffrey of Auxerre, *On the Apocalypse*, 135. *Goffredo di Auxerre: Super Apocalypsim*, 170: "Utinam nostri hodie sacerdotes linguis potius igneis quam mucronibus ferreis, dimicarent, utinam comburenda igni arma et scuta non tollerent, loricas pro dalmaticis, pro mitris galeas, pro virgis pastoralibus vexilla militaria non praeferrent. Armis siquidem non materialibus, non corporalibus, sed spiritalibus et potentibus Deo, Dei ministro pugnandum; oratione, praedicatione, obsecratione et increpatione fuerat dimicandum. Quid miramur, quod gladius oris eorum ab immundis daemonibus vel iniquis hominibus minus metuitur, quandoquidem in materiali magis confiditur?"
66 *Goffredo di Auxerre: Super Apocalypsim*, 178: "Non est credendum quod arguere dissimulaverit, cuius ministeriu, approbatur." Geoffrey of Auxerre, *On the Apocalypse*, 143: "We are not to believe that he hesitated to give correction, for his ministry is applauded."
67 Peter Clarke, "The Medieval Clergy and Violence: A Historiographical Introduction," in *Violence and the Medieval Clergy*, ed. Gerhard Jaritz (Budapest: Central European University Press, 2011), 3–16.

heresy,⁶⁸ showing that for Geoffrey the line between inappropriate clerical behaviour and accusations of heresy was quite blurry, which demonstrates how the latter could be used in order to promote clerical reform. As Martha Newman points out, Geoffrey of Auxerre belonged to a generation that witnessed how Cistercians became the "dominant voice for clerical reform."⁶⁹ I believe that the absence of violence in Geoffrey's writings, in an era in which violent persecution was becoming more widespread, should be placed within the framework of his specific ideas on the clergy; that is, his contention that the clergy, as a distinguished social group, should not use violent means. With his *Sermons on the Apocalypse*, he was appealing to a monastic audience, seeking to remind them both of their duties and of their limitations. Using his anti-heretical writings, he tried to shape a specific monastic and clerical identity that included active commitment in matters like heresy but forbade the use of violence. At the same time, Geoffrey conveyed the idea of a strict societal divide between laymen and churchmen that entailed the superiority of the latter.⁷⁰

---

68 *Goffredo di Auxerre: Super Apocalypsim*, 136: "'Facta,' inquit, 'Nicolaitarum.' Cum haereticos faciat solus error vel obstinatio magis errandi circa articulos fidei, alios tamen in his decipi constat quae ad summam pertinent Trinitatem, vel alterutram naturam Christi, quosdam in sacramentis ecclesiae, nonnullos etiam super his quae in suis cuique moribus vel operibus eadem fides insectanda docet, vel sectanda commendat." Geoffrey of Auxerre, *On the Apocalypse*, 98: "The deeds, he says, of the Nicolaitans. Error alone, or rather the stubborn choice to continue to err in matters of faith, makes heretics. Some are deceived concerning the Trinity or the twofold nature of Christ, others regarding the church's sacraments. Some go astray over their behavior and actions, accepting norms that faith rejects or rejecting norms that faith accepts." The term "Nicholaism" refers here to clerical marriage and more generally to the sexual immorality of priests. It became an important issue during the Gregorian Reform and it is mainly associated with the efforts to morally redress the clergy. See also Jeffrey Burton Russell, *Dissent and Reform in the Early Middle Ages* (Berkeley and Los Angeles: University of California Press, 1965), 136–39; *Medieval Purity and Piety: Essays on Medieval Clerical Celibacy and Religious Reform*, ed. Michael Frassetto (New York and London: Garland Publishing, 1998), especially Paul Beaudette, "'In the World but not of It': Clerical Celibacy as a Symbol of the Medieval Church," 23–46, and H. E. J. Cowdrey, "Pope Gregory VII and the Chastity of Clergy," 269–302; Grado Giovanni Merlo, "Christian Experiences of Religious Non-Conformism," in *The Oxford Handbook of Medieval Christianity*, ed. John H. Arnold (Oxford: Oxford University Press, 2014), 436–54, especially 437–38.
69 Newman, *Boundaries of Charity*, 24–37.
70 *Goffredo di Auxerre: Super Apocalypsim*, 131–32: "Stellas angelos ecclesiarum et eorum ecclesias candelabra iam exposuerat, et necesse est eiusmodi stellas non ad sinistram inclinari ubi divitiae et gloria, sed in dextera stare ubi longitudo dierum. Alioquin non recte agitur, si sicut populus sic et sacerdos, et deorsum respicit, sicut grex ita etiam pastor." Geoffrey of Auxerre, *On the Apocalypse*, 94: "He has already stated that the stars are the churches' angels, and the lampstands their churches; stars of such a kind must never decline to his left hand, where are riches and glory, but must remain in his right hand, where there is long life. Otherwise the

Conclusion

A close analysis of the anti-heretical writings of Bernard of Clairvaux and Geoffrey of Auxerre confirms that it is very difficult to give a categorical answer when it comes to their views on the violent persecution of people accused of heresy. However, such an analysis does reveal how their polemics not only served to warn their audiences of the dangers of heresy but also had political implications. The elements of their ecclesiology present in their writings against heresy help us understand how these works sought to promote and impose their ideas. Bernard aimed to restrict the use of violence to those who had the authority and condemned uncontrolled violent acts. This idea of restricted violence is mainly related to his overall ideas on strict societal division, according to which the laity had to show obedience to secular authorities. Furthermore, the issue of violence shows that, for Bernard, the collaboration between secular and ecclesiastical authorities, based on the formula of the two swords, was a necessary condition for the defense of Christianity. For the abbot of Clairvaux, engaging the laity and their secular leaders in the common fight against heresy was of great importance; it was in fact much more important than the issue of violence itself.

In turn, Geoffrey was even less concerned with the use of force against heresy. Neither his accounts of the *Vita prima* nor the sermons from his commentary on the Apocalypse discuss the use of force at all. This omission suggests that, despite the decisions of the Church's Councils of the period, the process of legitimation of the violent persecution of heresy was still under way. Even within the Cistercian order there were different stances on this matter: whereas Henry of Marcy did not have any doubts about the legitimacy of violence, Geoffrey remained silent on this point. Especially in his sermons, the remarks on heresy could also have served the construction of a specific identity; churchmen should not use force even when they had to deal with a problem as serious as religious "otherness."

---

order of things would be reversed, as if we were to say, 'As with the people, so with the priest,' and 'As with the flock, so with the shepherd'." On the clergy's superiority, see *Goffredo di Auxerre: Super Apocalypsim*, 81: "quam sit dignior sacerdotalis unctio, quam regalis. A solis enim sacerdotibus reges unguntur, non a regibus sacerdotes." Geoffrey of Auxerre, *On the Apocalypse*, 41–42: "for the priestly anointing is worthier than the royal. Kings are anointed only by priests; priests are not anointed by kings."

Jordi Casals i Parés
Chapter 8
From Persecution to Exile: Jewish Views on Christians and Christianity in the Late Medieval Crown of Aragon

The following pages will analyse several Hebrew sources produced in the late medieval Crown of Aragon with the aim of delving into the life and perceptions of the Jews who lived there. My objective is not to reinforce the image of medieval Jews as victims of persecutions and edicts, or individuals excluded from society, but rather to bring to light some of the aspects of their way of living that transgressed the boundaries set up for them by the all-pervading Christian environment.

The society of the late medieval Crown of Aragon consisted of a Christian majority that coexisted with Jewish and Muslim minorities. Countless studies have been based on the wealth of archival documentation and religious works generated by this Christian society. These sources provide precious information about the life of Jewish communities, with special consideration to economic aspects and theological disputes, allowing us to learn about their history in that period and territory. In parallel, the Jews of the Crown of Aragon left numerous written sources that reveal much about the Christian society they lived side by side with. Among these writings, inter-religious disputations, literary and scientific works, and rabbinic *responsa* are particularly noteworthy. These sources convey vital details about the life of medieval Jews but they are also valuable tools for the study of this historical period.

In particular, the aim of the present chapter is to examine how medieval Catalan and Mallorcan Jewish communities and their religious leaders—namely rabbis such as Mosheh ben Nahman, Shlomoh ben Aderet, Isaac ben Sheshet Perfet, known as Ribash, and Simeon ben Tzemah Duran, known as Rashbatz—perceived the neighbouring Christian society both from a theological and a social perspective. For this purpose, I will focus on aspects such as the rejection of Christian religious ideas, the relationships between Jews and converts to Christianity, and also different social issues documented in the aforementioned sources. Furthermore, this chapter will consider whether these perceptions remained constant over time or varied depending on the changing political and social circumstances of the region.

The questions raised by the ways in which Jews saw Christians—and vice versa—are manifold; however, here I will only deal with the views of the Jews of the Crown of Aragon on Christians and Christianity, and with their feelings upon being forced to abandon their homeland and go into exile in 1391. What did they feel towards their Christian fellows when they had to leave their land: rejection or nostalgia? In contrast, I will not look into the objectives of Christian religious and secular powers, nor into Christian views on Jews, as these issues rely on the analysis of sources written either in Latin or in the vernacular languages of the different kingdoms of the Crown, which fall outside the purview of the present study.

A Few Initial Remarks

Judaism saw Christianity as a heresy, an error of dogma and an issue of wrongful habits. It was considered a heresy, among other reasons, due to what was deemed to be its idolatrous nature, which did not refer only to its division of the divinity in three persons, and will be discussed below. However, contrary to what could be expected from the medieval social context of Jewish life, extant Jewish documentation does not convey a hostile attitude towards Christians. In Hebrew, both Christians and Muslims were referred to as *goyim*, a term that is usually translated as "gentile," from the Latin term *gens* (plural *gentiles*), and which can be understood as "inhabitants of a foreign nation."[1] This was not meant to be a derogatory term, but rather a way of separating the people of Israel from the rest of the nations of the world. Accordingly, the non-Jewish inhabitants of the Crown of Aragon were described as *goyim* in Hebrew sources.

Although the Talmud, the main compilation of commentaries on the Oral Law of Judaism, has much to say about Christians, I will focus on Catalan and Aragonese Hebrew writings instead. In this regard it should be noted that the mere act of writing in Hebrew in a Christian society was a form of transgression, as religious authorities especially were likely to look negatively on opinions that fell outside their understanding. Thus, in order to analyse the theological and social perception of Christians among medieval Jews I will divide Jewish literary

---

[1] The *Online Etymology Dictionary* defines *gentile* as follows: "As a noun, gentiles (plural) might mean 'men of family; persons belonging to the same family; fellow countrymen, kinsmen,' but also 'foreigners, barbarians' (as opposed to Romans)." See https://www.etymonline.com/word/gentile.

sources into two groups that will help us understand the strategies of Jewish communities for surviving in an environment that constantly questioned their existence. The first group is made up of Hebrew sources that deal with Jewish-Christian disputations and controversies, and the second one covers rabbinic treatises, including the epistolary genre of *responsa* (sing. *responsum*)—that is, letters addressed to reputable rabbis by individuals who had problems applying Jewish Law to their everyday life.[2]

The present study revolves around the turning point of 1391, when persecutions against Jews arose in all the Iberian kingdoms. One of the points that makes this topic interesting is the abundance of nineteenth- and twentieth-century quotations mentioning the pleasant memories and emotions that the word "Sepharad" evoked among Sephardim—Jews of Iberian descent—who lived, for instance, in the Ottoman Empire.[3] Their words were filled with nostalgia, which is rather surprising, as it seems that the term "Sepharad" mostly inspired rejection from 1391 until at least the eighteenth century,[4] even if such negative emotion was aimed neither at Sephardim nor at their customs, but at the territory itself. Thus, the nostalgia conveyed by later documentation should instead be related to an ideal lost past of Jewish communities, to a sort of utopian world. Indeed, this idea shared by exiled Jews, especially after the expulsion of 1492, contains echoes of Messianism. According to the scholar of Jewish thought Ger-

---

[2] For an extensive online compilation of rabbinic *responsa*, see the Online Responsa Project hosted by Bar-Ilan University (Israel), https://www.responsa.co.il/home.en-US.aspx. Unless noted otherwise, all translations are mine.

[3] Marcos Caballero, who devoted his doctoral dissertation to the history of his family from the Middle Ages to the twenty-first century, described how his parents cried during their journey from Izmir to Buenos Aires as the ship neared the Spanish coast—according to him, because of a feeling of nostalgia. The transformation of rejection into nostalgia needs to be further explored. See Marcos Caballero (Mordechai ben Abir), "De Cervera a Be'er Seba: Genealogía de la familia judeocatalana Cavaller-Caballero y del cronista sefardí Bekor Eliyah Caballero, autor del Séfer-Zikrón-ha-Yammim (edición paleográfica, transliteración y análisis de un manuscrito inédito judeoespañol, Esmirna 1872–1928)" (PhD diss., Universitat de Barcelona, 2007). See also Pilar Romeu, "Sefarad ¿la 'patria' de los sefardíes?," *Sefarad: Revista de Estudios Hebraicos y Sefardíes* 71/1 (2011): 95–130.

[4] Although returning to settle in Sepharad has traditionally been considered as forbidden, there is no historical evidence of an actual Jewish ban or excommunication on Jews who wanted to go back issued after 1391. See Marc Shapiro, "The Herem on Spain: History and Halaka," *Sefarad: Revista de Estudios Hebraicos y Sefardíes* 4/2 (1989): 381–94; Simon Schwarzfuchs, "Herem Ha-yiyshuv (Ban of Settlement)," in *Routledge Revivals: Medieval Jewish Civilization: An Encyclopedia*, ed. Norman Roth (New York: Routledge, 2003), 329–30.

shom Scholem,[5] the forces that have guided rabbinic Judaism throughout history are three: the will to preserve the legal corpus of Judaism in exile, recreating the ideal conditions of the life of biblical ancestors, and a renewed vision of the future. The combination of these forces results in a vision of the past as a utopian world that is closely related to the apocalypse, a necessary aspect of Messianism. Both Messianism as future expectation and the fact that Jews needed to share the land of their exile with European Christian nations proved to be points of friction between Jews and Christians.

Christianity as Heresy

Since their exile from the Holy Land, Jews have had to share their destiny with other peoples who have hardly treated them as equals. Between the thirteenth and fifteenth centuries, when the Judeo-Christian controversy was at its peak, one of the main tasks of mendicant friars was the conversion of Jews and Muslims, especially in the Iberian Peninsula.[6] A bulky, almost encyclopaedic, Hebrew work written by Shem-Tov ben Isaac Shaprut and entitled *Eben Bohan* (The Touchstone) is in fact an anti-Christian treatise composed in Aragon between 1380 and 1385.[7] Moreover, the most significant examples of the controversy between Jews and Christians in Iberia written in Hebrew were composed in Catalonia, also in the second half of the fourteenth century. *Kelimmat ha-Goyim* (Shame of the Gentiles) was written by Profiat Duran (1345–1414) in 1397,[8] and *Bittul iqqare ha-notsrim* (Refutation of Christian Principles) was originally composed in Catalan in 1398—a version now lost—by Hasdai Crescas (1340–1410) and then translated into Hebrew by Joseph ibn Shem-Tov, with

---

[5] Gershom Scholem, *The Messianic Idea in Judaism and Other Essays on Jewish Spirituality* (New York: Schocken, 1995), 3.
[6] On the origin and the role of mendicant orders in the Crown of Aragon, see Prim Bertran Roigé, "Un nou impuls: L'arribada i l'expansió dels ordes mendicants," in *Arrels cristianes: Presència i significació del cristianisme en la història i la societat de Lleida*, ed. Prim Bertran Roigé and Francesc Fité, vol. 2 (Lleida: Pagès-Bisbat de Lleida, 2008), 139–58.
[7] Shem-Tov ben Isaac Shaprut, *La piedra de toque = Eben bohan: Una obra de controversia judeo-cristiana*, ed. José-Vicente Niclós (Madrid: Consejo Superior de Investigaciones Científicas, 1997).
[8] See an English translation of this work in Anne Berlin Blackman, "Shame of the Gentiles of Profiat Duran: A Fourteenth-Century Jewish Polemic against Christianity" (PhD diss., Harvard University, 1987).

the title in English *Refutation of the Cardinal Principles of the Christians*.⁹ The first of these three sources appeared just before the violent episodes of 1391, and the two others right after, but it is not clear whether these three works were known to Christians at the time of the so-called Disputation of Tortosa of 1412.

The Hebrew record of the Disputation of Barcelona of 1263 could indeed be understood as a trangression in the sense mentioned above, as there was a Latin version that could allow for a comparison of facts and phrasing between the two.¹⁰ The Hebrew record was written by Mosheh Ben Nahman—also known as Nachmanides, Ramban, and Bonastruc de Porta¹¹—and it is an invaluable source for the study of Jewish Messianic ideas in the thirteenth century and their confrontation with Christian religious principles. The Disputation of Barcelona was convened by King Jaume I of Aragon and was held in his palace to show that Jews were wrong regarding the figure of Jesus of Nazareth, whom Christians considered the true Messiah. The stipulations of the debate allowed for freedom of speech as long as nothing offensive was said against Christianity. The three main issues were whether or not the Messiah had already come, whether the Messiah's nature was divine or human, and who had truth on their side, Jews or Christians. Fortunately, a Latin and a Hebrew record of the disputation survive, the latter being far removed from political and religious Christian control.

According to the views of Rabbi Nahman on the first two of these three issues, the Messiah might have already been born and could be living among Christians, but he had not been anointed yet and therefore had not appeared, since the world had not achieved redemption and was still full of violence and dishonesty. The difference between the world of his time and a world governed by the Messiah would be the end of the governments of all nations. The

---

9 See Hasdai Crescas, *Sefer Bittul Iqqarei Ha-Nozrim*, ed. Daniel J. Lasker, trans. Joseph ibn Shem-Tov (Ramat-Gan: Bar-Ilan University, 1990). See also Hasdai Crescas, *The Refutation of the Christian Principles*, trans. Daniel J. Lasker, SUNY Series in Jewish Philosophy (Albany, NY: SUNY Press, 1992), and Carlos del Valle Rodríguez, ed. *La inconsistencia de los dogmas cristianos, de Crescas: Biṭṭul 'Iqqare ha-Noṣrim le-Rabbí Ḥasday Crescas* (Madrid: Aben Ezra, 2000).
10 See a Catalan translation of both texts in Nachmanides, *Disputa de Barcelona de 1263 entre Mestre Mossé de Girona i Fra Pau Cristià*, ed. Jaume Riera i Sans and Eduard Feliu Mabres (Barcelona: Columna, 1985). See also Nachmanides, *The Disputation at Barcelona*, ed. Charles Ber Chavel (New York: Shilo Publishing House, 1983).
11 This multiplicity of denominations was analysed by Jaume Riera who drew the conclusion that, despite the hundred-year debate on the actual name of the rabbi, he probably used both the Hebrew and the Catalan name. This was not a rare occurrence among medieval Jews, whose vernacular names were not always a direct translation of their Hebrew monikers. See Jaume Riera i Sans, "Moixè ben Nahman, Bonastruc de Porta," *Tamid* 10 (2014): 7–33.

Messiah would come to the defence of Israel, reconstruct the Temple, and gather exiles together. Nachmanides also claimed that the Messiah was not to be born until the End of Days was near. When his time arrived—in 1358, according to the rabbi—he would appear in Rome before the Pope and, in the name of God, he would say, "Let my people go"—just as Moses said to Pharaoh—and immediately destroy Rome; also like Moses, he would deliver his people from exile and guide them through the desert.[12]

Nachmanides believed that Judaism did not rely on the idea of the Messiah, and saw him as a king of flesh and blood. The Messiah had no power of resurrection, for he was just a human. In fact, Judaism maintains two different views on the Messiah, namely as the son of Joseph and as the son of David: whereas the former is a constructive and mortal Messiah—which does not imply that he has to be killed—the latter is a victorious Messiah. In either case, the Messiah suffers for his people because they are all in exile and he cannot do anything yet. This suffering is characteristic of being the son of man and woman. As for King David's ancestry (Is 11:1), the Messiah must be descended from David through the paternal line, as women could not inherit (which explicitly refers to Mary, who was the mother of Jesus and allegedly descended from the House of David).

As regards the issues of sin and reward, Nachmanides's account of the Disputation of Barcelona posits that the reward will be much greater for those who follow the precepts of the Law in exile, because these are much more difficult to observe under such circumstances.

The Coexistence of Jews and Christians

Through centuries of persecution, the fulfilment and observance of the 613 commandments of the Torah became an indispensable requirement for the salvation and redemption of the people of Israel.[13] It is in this context that rabbinic texts brought back the biblical writings from the first millennium before our era in which Israelites were distinguished from other peoples, who, as mentioned above, were called *goyim*. Indeed, the phrase "El derekh ha-goyim al tilmadu,"

---

[12] For a translation of the Hebrew record of the Disputation of Barcelona, see Nachmanides, *The Disputation at Barcelona*.

[13] Efraim Elimelech Urbach, "Redemption and Repentance in Talmudic Judaism," in *Types of Redemption*, ed. Raphael Judah Zwi Werblowsky and Claas Jouco Bleeker (Leiden: Brill, 1970), 190–206; Scholem, *The Messianic Idea*.

extracted from the Book of Jeremiah (Jer 10:2), which translates as "Don't follow the customs of those nations," encourages the Chosen People to make their own path, free from the influence of other cultures. Remarkably, to this day, certain groups of ultraorthodox Jews in Israel do not respect the minute of silence in memory of the victims of the Shoah because they see it as a "foreign custom."[14]

Returning to the Middle Ages, this biblical quotation is a clear example of how the relationship between Jews and Christians was understood. In the letters of Isaac ben Sheshet Perfet, a rabbi who lived in fourteenth-century Barcelona, we find a passage that conveys a similar message, "u-ve-huqqotehem lo telkhu" (and refuse their laws),[15] because as it is written, "minhag Israel Torà hi" (the custom of Israel is the Torah itself).[16] This is where the two main ideas presented so far came together among medieval Jews: do not imitate Christians and observe the laws of Judaism.

The aformentioned *Eben Bohan* (The Touchstone), written before the events of 1391, claims: "He (blessed be) will reward the righteous that keep His Law and His commandments. Through their righteousness, they will inherit the eternal life of the future world, the so-called 'Garden of Eden'; on the contrary, the wicked, who do not fulfill or keep His commandments, will die because of their wickedness, and will inherit hell."[17] As Christians ultimately aspired to replace the Old Testament—the Hebrew Bible that contains the Torah, the prophetic books, and other writings—with the New Testament, it made sense for them to be considered as part of "the wicked" whose goal was to lead Jews astray from the Torah. Therefore, the good Jew was the one who faithfully followed the precepts of the Torah and stayed well away from Christian customs.

Jewish views on Christianity are crucial to better understand the coexistence and the contrasts between cultures and societies in the territories of the medieval Crown of Aragon. Latin, Catalan, and Aragonese documents—Christian sources in general—provide many details about the history of Jewish communities in the kingdoms that made up the Crown, but they shed little light on the thoughts and feelings of the Jews who appear signing contracts, paying taxes, receiving interest or being granted a privilege, and neither do they say much about those whose freedom of residence was curtailed and who suffered persecution.

---

14 Ilene Prusher, "It's Complicated: The Jews Who Don't Stop for the Siren," *Haaretz*, May 6, 2014, https://www.haaretz.com/.premium-moment-of-silence-not-for-these-israelis-1.5247347.
15 Isaac ben Sheshet Perfet's *responsum* 158 quotes Leviticus (Lv 20:23), "Do not live by the regulations of the nation which I am expelling ahead of you."
16 Talmud Bavli (Menachot 20, b).
17 Chapter 1 of the First Book of the *Eben Bohan* (The Touchstone).

In contrast, these feelings can be gleaned from Hebrew sources, especially from rabbinic *responsa*—an epistolary genre consisting of questions and answers—which pose specific questions in need of concrete solutions. Both the question and the answer usually go beyond the legal sphere, as Talmudic law is at the same time secular and religious; in other words, it is a civil and criminal code, but also a religious canon.[18] The importance of *responsa* for the sociological study of Jewish communities and their views on "the other" lies in the fact that the legal questions behind them are always based on individual or local situations. Moreover, the answers themselves are usually accompanied by justifications or explanations that not only have legal value, but also social significance.[19]

The Talmud says, "dina de-malkhuta dina" (the law of the country is the law),[20] which constitutes a mandate for all Jews to abide by the political laws of the land they live in. Adding to this, the *responsa* of Catalan rabbis always praise the figure of the monarch using laudatory expressions such as *yarum hodo*, "may his glory be exalted."[21]

As far as religion was concerned, whereas these same rabbis likened Christianity to idolatry, *avodah zarah* (foreign worship), Nissim of Girona, also known

---

18 See a comprehensive definition of the Talmud in the *Encyclopaedia Judaica*, vol. 19 (2007): "Talmud," 469–70; "Talmud, Babylonian," and "Talmud, Jerusalem," 470–87.
19 The *responsa* are invaluable as historical sources because they constitute a reliable testimony of the way of life of Jews, their problems and the intervention of different characters linked to the community. There are numerous researchers who have studied *responsa* as a source for the medieval history of Iberian Jewries. See, for instance, Abraham Isaac Laredo, "Las 'Še'elot u-Tešubot' como fuente para la historia de los judíos españoles," *Sefarad: Revista de Estudios Hebraicos y Sefardíes* 5/2 (1945): 441–56; David Romano, "Responsa y repertorios documentales," *Sefarad: Revista de Estudios Hebraicos y Sefardíes* 26/1 (1966): 47–52; Yom Tov Assis, "Responsa Rabínicos y cartas reales: Fuentes para el estudio de la historia de los judíos en la Corona de Aragón," *Espacio, Tiempo y Forma. Serie III: Historia Medieval* 6 (1993): 363–76; José Ramón Magdalena Nom de Déu, "Aspectos de la vida de los judíos valencianos reflejados en los 'responsa' de Rabi Yiṣḥaq ben Šešet Perfet (segunda mitad del siglo XIV)," in *Juderías y sinagogas de la Sefarad medieval*, ed. Ana María López Alvárez and Ricardo Izquierdo Benito (Cuenca: Ediciones de la Universidad de Castilla-La Mancha, 2003), 145–57; Moisés Orfali, "Los responsa rabínicos y la vida interna en las aljamas aragonesas," *Aragón-Sefarad* 1 (2005): 161–75.
20 Talmud Bavli (Bava Batra 54, b; Gittin 10, b; Nedarim 28, a).
21 This praise probably stems from the belief that the monarch ruled by divine design. Thus, in the biblical tradition it is God who makes Saul rule over the people of Israel after they ask Him for a king (1 Sm 8:12).

as Nissim ben Reuben ha-Gerondi,²² Shlomoh ben Aderet,²³ and even the renowned Maimonides thought that Islam had to be considered an error, but not an act of idolatry.²⁴ Maimonides claimed that Ishmaelites were not idolatrous because they professed the unity of God. Rabbi Nissim, in turn, discussed the idea that Islam is idolatry in a commentary attributed to him, and known as *Hidushe Sanhedrin* (Innovations to the Treatise of the Sanhedrin). According to him, the fact that the faithful prostrate themselves before a man should not be considered as idolatry unless such man is deified. That is to say, both the cult of Christian saints and the veneration of Muhammad in Islam are not idolatrous rites because they are part of their customs and do not involve the deification of these figures. Rabbi Nissim insisted that it was lawful to prostrate oneself before a man, as Jacob did before Esau,²⁵ and Joseph before Jacob,²⁶ as long as it was not part of a ritual. *Hidushe Sanhedrin* conveys the fallacious idea—widespread among medieval Christians—that Muslims prostrated themselves before their prophet, which led to Islam being called Muhammadism. Likewise, as Christians prostrated themselves before a divinised man, their religion had to be interpreted as an act of idolatry.

Other *responsa* refer directly to Christian customs; however, unless it is to rebuke Jews who imitate such customs, for instance those who drink wine produced by Christians, *yayin nezekh* (wine for idolatry), their tone is not pejorative.²⁷ In fact, as a *responsum* by Shlomoh ben Aderet shows, the proximity between Christians and Jews—even in bed—is quite revealing.²⁸ As the following passage shows, it seems that Jews and Christians did not live as far apart as could be expected:

---

22 See the commentary attributed to Nissim, *Hidushe Sanhedrin*, fol. 61v, in Nissim ben Reuben ha-Gerondi, *Hidushe ha-Ran al ha-Shas*, eds. I. Saqler, S.B. Verner, H.S.F. Frank, and E. Lichtenstein (Jerusalem: Hotsaat Mossad ha-Rav Quq, 1991).
23 *Responsa* of Rashba, vol. 8 (New *responsum*), Manuscripts, no. 367.
24 See *Mishneh Torah, Book of Ha-Mada*, treatise Avodah Zarah, 9,4.
25 Gn 33:3: "Then he himself passed on ahead of them and prostrated himself on the ground seven times before approaching his brother."
26 Gn 48:12: "Then Joseph made his sons move away from Jacob's knees, and Joseph bowed down in front of him with his face to the ground."
27 The wine used in idolatrous rites could not be considered kosher, it is the *yayin nesekh*. It is written in the Mishnah (Avodah Zarah 29, b): "These things of the Gentile are forbidden: wine [...]." See David M. Freidenreich, *Foreigners and Their Food: Constructing Otherness in Jewish, Christian, and Islamic Law* (Berkeley: University of California Press, 2011) 214–17; Hayim Soloveitchik, *Ha-yayin bi-yeme ha-benayim: Yayin nesekh* (Jerusalem: Zalman Shazar Center for Jewish History, 2008).
28 *Responsum* heleq 1, number 1187.

Reuben came home at night holding a candle as his wife slept in bed. According to his words, he found a "Gentile" naked under the bed, only covered by a mantle and wearing sandals. The "Gentile" blew out Reuben's candle and jumped on him, and a fight ensued with much shouting. Some men who lived in the same household woke up and started looking for the "Gentile," but they could not find him; instead they found a shirt and breeches, while the woman exclaimed in dismay at her husband's words, claiming that the shirt and breeches were for her to mend, as that was her trade. Afterwards, the husband told some of the men that God forbid he doubted his wife, for the "Gentile" had probably entered with the intention of stealing, forcing her, or for some other reason.[29]

Shlomoh ben Aderet was considered an orthodox rabbi rather than an innovator. He was a staunch defender of Judaism against the constant attacks of Christian preachers, whose sermons focused on converting Jews. Aderet's *responsa* are a great source for the study of the economic and everyday relations between Jews and Christians. The full text of the aforementioned *responsum* makes it clear that, according to Jewish law, should a husband forbid his wife to leave the house, no rabbinic tribunal could force him to do otherwise. However, no Jew could be forced to present a *get*—a document effectuating a divorce—to his wife, especially not because of the acts of a Christian intruder.

The Turning Point: 1391

The underlying causes of the persecutions of 1391 resulted from the Castilian social and economic crisis that followed the Castilian Civil War in the second half of the fourteenth century. This situation worsened the devastating socioeconomic, political, and demographic consequences of the plague outbreak of 1348, which wiped out at least one-third of the European population of the time. Among other theories, the plague was thought to be a divine punishment on Christians for allowing the presence of Jews among them.[30] As the massive forced conversions of Jews to Christianity took place between 1391 and 1415, it

---

29 Eduard Feliu translated several *responsa* into Catalan, such as this one, on which I base my English translation. See Eduard Feliu, "Salomó ben Adret, mestre de la llei jueva," *Tamid* 4 (2002–2003): 35–109. A different English version can be found in Yom Tov Assis, "Sexual Behaviour in Mediaeval Hispano-Jewish Society," in *Jewish History: Essays in Honour of Chimen Abramsky*, ed. Ada Rapoport-Albert and Steven J. Zipperstein (London: Peter Halban, 1988), 25–59 at 47.
30 See Sílvia Planas and Manuel Forcano, *Història de la Catalunya jueva: Vida i mort de les comunitats jueves de la Catalunya medieval* (Girona: Ajuntament de Girona; Barcelona: Àmbit Serveis Editorials, 2009), 197.

is unreasonable to attribute the persecution of Judaism to the power of the inquisitorial institution, even if the Christian population already looked on *conversos* with suspicion. Assaults, fires, looting, and slaughter began in June in Seville, where Ferrand Martínez, archdeacon of Écija, taking advantage of the power vacuum created by the death of the archbishop of Seville, instigated Christians to act against Jews. Martínez, who had begun preaching in 1378, called on all Christians to demolish synagogues and seize Jewish prayer books. In January 1391, municipal authorities had managed to avoid a first attempt of assault on the Jewish quarter, but in June hundreds of Jews were assassinated, their houses were looted, and their synagogues were forcibly turned into churches. Some Jews managed to escape, while others, terrified, asked to be baptised.[31]

In the Crown of Aragon, on 5 August 1391, on the feast of Saint Dominic, the Jewish quarter of Barcelona, which at the time was said to house 15 percent of the total population of the city, was assaulted and ravaged, and between 300 and 400 Jews were murdered. In the aftermath of the attack, King Joan I sold the five synagogues of the Jewish quarter, along with all the assets of the Jewish community.[32] In the Kingdom of Castile, the Jewish *aljamas*—self-governing communities of Jews living under Christian rule—of Seville, Córdoba, Burgos, Toledo, and Logroño, and many others, were destroyed, and the same happened in Barcelona, Valencia, and other cities of the Crown of Aragon. Once the violent episodes died down, converted Jews could occupy positions that were previously forbidden to them because of their religion. Thus, these forced conversions became an instrument of social promotion.[33] However, the emergence of a large community of Jewish *conversos* resulted in what is known as the "converso problem," an ever-present issue throughout the Iberian Early Modern Period.[34]

After the attack on the Jews of Seville, anti-Jewish violence spread across Andalusia and Castile, finally reaching the Crown of Aragon. The Jews who managed to save their lives fled and many sought refuge in Navarre, Portugal, and France, while others left for North Africa. The total number of victims is difficult

---

31 Joseph F. O'Callaghan, *A History of Medieval Spain* (Ithaca and London: Cornell University Press, 2013), 536–37.
32 For the fate of the properties of the Jewish community of Barcelona after its destruction, see Francesc Caballé and Eloi Castells, *L'estructura urbana del call de Barcelona: Una aproximació* (Barcelona: MUHBA, Ajuntament de Barcelona, Institut de Cultura, 2015).
33 For a discussion of the role that conversion to Christianity played for some professionals, such as physicians, allowing *conversos* an easier access, see Clara Jáuregui, "Fisic e cirurgià juheu: La medicina hebrea a la Barcelona del segle XVI" (PhD diss., Universitat de Barcelona, 2017), 111.
34 See *After Conversion: Iberia and the Emergence of Modernity*, ed. Mercedes García-Arenal (Leiden and Boston: Brill, 2016).

to estimate, but by 1415 more than half the Jews of Castile and Aragon had renounced the Mosaic law and been baptised, including many rabbis and important personalities, such as the aforementioned Ribash and Rashbatz, that is, Rabbi Simeon ben Tzemah Duran.

Jews migrating from the Iberian Peninsula had a great influence over the Jewish communities of North Africa and brought about a cultural revival in the region. Among these Iberian emigrants to the Maghreb was Rabbi Isaac ben Sheshet Perfet—Ribash—a Talmudic expert and one of the main medieval Sephardic rabbinical authorities. After leaving Barcelona, he settled in Saragossa and later in Valencia, where he converted to Christianity after the massacre of 1391 and whence he fled to exile in Algeria.[35] This renowned rabbi and Talmudist left a series of *responsa*, written over a period of forty years, from 1368 to 1408. His writings were altered by their first publishers, who interspersed geographic and chronological references while editing the manuscripts. Thus, whereas the *responsa* written from Algeria between 1391/92 and 1408 are listed first (*response* 1 to 186), Ribash's earlier writings, composed in Barcelona and Saragossa between 1368 and 1385, appear last.[36]

Ribash's *responsum* 14 places us in the context that followed the attacks of 1391 on the island of Mallorca. It deals with the escape from the island and the problems of *conversos* after the attacks, an episode that in Hebrew sources is described as *gezerah*, which could be roughly translated as "decree of persecution":

> Before the decree in Mallorca, Reuben promised his underage daughter to the son of Simeon. Reuben agreed to give Simeon 500 *lliures* as dowry, and Simeon also agreed to provide his son with properties at the time of the marriage: 1,000 *lliures* and a house valued at more than 500 *lliures*. After the decree, Reuben and Simeon lost most of their properties, so that neither of them could fulfil the conditions they had previously agreed upon. After the edict of persecution, both of them decided to annul the engagement.
>
> After this, Reuben boarded a ship that was ready to sail to the land of the Ishmaelites to escape the decree, and left his wife and his family in Mallorca. But the ship was stranded in the port of Mallorca for a few days. In the meantime, Simeon reached a new agreement with Reuben's wife and his son to marry Reuben's daughter to the son of the said Simeon. They also had Simeon's son marry the girl immediately and in secrecy. Reuben was still in the harbour and they could have asked for his opinion. The witnesses of the wedding were two *conversos* who were relatives, that is, the wife of one of them was the cousin of the other. However, after the decree and before the wedding one of the witnesses profaned the Sabbath publicly. He even used to write on Sabbaths and feasts on behalf of other *conversos*, although no one forced him or coerced him to do it; he only did it for his personal

---

35 Jaume Riera i Sans, "El Baptisme de Rabí Ishaq ben Seset Perfet," *Calls* 1 (1986): 43–52.
36 See Abraham M. Hershman, *Rabbi Isaac ben Sheshet Perfet and His Times* (New York: Jewish Theological Seminary of America, 1943).

gain. The other witness ate forbidden meat with idolaters and frequented their company, they invited him and he ate their meat.

Afterwards, Simeon's son, the groom, boarded the same ship as Reuben and joyfully informed him that he had married his daughter. Reuben became very angry but remained silent, for he did not want to quarrel and raise his voice on the ship. He was afraid of making public that his daughter had been married without his consent before the idolaters on the ship, for fear that they would denounce the fact that they still observed the Jewish law. But secretly, he sent a letter to his son, scolding him for betrothing his sister without Reuben's consent and telling him that he would never accept this marriage.[37]

The researcher Dora Zsom, who studied the problems between Jews and *conversos*, quotes this *responsum* as an example of marriage issues. She claims that this marriage agreement was reached in a rush, in spite of the very young age of the girl, because of the riots and religious persecutions. Moreover, Zsom notes that the family was probably not travelling together either because they did not have enough money or because some of them refused to leave their land. But the fact is that the marriage was celebrated urgently without the father's permission, for he remained aboard the ship. According to Jewish law, an underage girl could not marry without her father's knowledge and consent, and this same law denied maternal relatives any authority in this regard.[38] Furthermore, the marriage could be annulled because both of its witnesses were *conversos* who had openly chosen to transgress Jewish law. They could only have been considered as valid witnesses if their conversion had been forced. In this *responsum*, despite the difficult situation of the protagonist, stranded on a ship, his greatest concern seemed to be the fulfilment of the commandments of the law. Thus, "new Christians" could influence the Jewish community negatively. He was not fleeing his land willingly but because he wanted to faithfully observe the Torah. When faced with an irregular marriage, he adopted a position that was in total accord with the dictates of orthodoxy, and remained unmoved by the exceptionality of the moment.

The Final Expulsion

A century later, in 1492, when Aragonese Jews were expelled from the Crown of Aragon, they followed exit routes that took them across Catalonia, while the Jew-

---

37 See another translation of this *responsum* in Dora Zsom, *Conversos in the Responsa of Sephardic Halakhic Authorities in the 15th Century* (Piscataway: Gorgias Press, 2014), 48–50.
38 Zsom, *Conversos in the Responsa*, 50–53.

ish community of Xàtiva, in Valencia, fled through the region of Morvedre. Although I have not analysed all the surnames of the Jews who left the Crown of Aragon, José Hinojosa Montalvo has studied the records of the procurator of the *aljama* of Xàtiva, who, on behalf of the Jews of Xàtiva and Morvedre, requested the services of the Genoese on 7 May 1492. As a result, between 20 June and 10 July of the same year, they sailed towards Pisa and Naples. Thus, they moved from the kingdom of Valencia to different Italian cities—Pisa, Naples, and Civitavecchia—either settling there or continuing on their way to the east and the Ottoman Empire.[39] Most of the Jews that were expelled from Sepharad settled in neighbouring territories, such as the Kingdom of Portugal, the Kingdom of Navarre, Italian cities, and North Africa, sometimes via Portugal. Likewise, in 1391, the massacres caused a great wave of emigration, both inside the Iberian Peninsula—initially, towards Portugal—and outside it, to North Africa and to Turkish and Greek cities such as Istanbul and Izmir.

In Salonica, a Catalan synagogue split in two—the Catalan Yashan synagogue, the Old one, and the Catalan Hadash synagogue, the New one—in the mid-sixteenth century. It seems that the reason for this separation was precisely a misunderstanding between old settlers and former *conversos* who returned to Judaism.[40] Isaac Molho quotes the introduction that Baruch ben Yaacob wrote to the medieval manuscript known as the Catalan Mahzor[41] mentioning the *minhag Catalunya* (the custom of Catalonia).[42] Recently, Idan Perez reconstructed and edited the *Siddur Catalunya*—the lost prayer book once used by the Jewish communities of Catalonia, Valencia, and Majorca—by compiling six manuscripts dating from the fourteenth to the sixteenth century. As a matter of fact, Eduard Feliu and other scholars have argued that Sepharad did not include medieval Catalo-

---

[39] José Hinojosa Montalvo, "Solidaridad judía ante la expulsión: Contratos de embarque (Valencia, 1492)," *Saitabi* 33 (1983): 105–24.
[40] Georgios M. Sariyannis, "From Catalonia and Aragon to Greece: The Saporta Family's Relations with Reomaniotes and Sephardim on Hellenic Territory," in *The Jewish Communities of Southeastern Europe: From the Fifteenth Century to the End of World War II*, ed. Ioannes K. Hassiotis (Thessaloniki: Institute for Balkan Studies, 1997), 473–93 at 479. The location of these two synagoges can be found in the map of the Jewish quarters of Salonica included in Cristina Pallini and Annalisa Riccarda Scaccabarozzi, "In Search of Salonika's Lost Synagogues: An Open Question Concerning Intangible Heritage," *Quest* 7 (2014): 1–29 at 8.
[41] The manuscript known as the Catalan Mahzor (MS Heb 6527, National Library of Israel) is a lavishly illuminated prayer book to be used by a cantor on the holy days of Rosh Hashana and Yom Kippur that was produced in Catalonia in the mid-thirteenth century.
[42] Isaac R. Molho, "Recuerdos y reminicencias catalanas y aragonesas de Salonica a traverso la historia," *Butlletí de la Reial Acadèmia de Bones Lletres de Barcelona* 24 (1952): 225–32 at 228–30.

nia: "the term 'Sephardic' (today's equivalent to 'Spanish' and too often opposed to 'Ashkenazi' with excessive ease), applied in modern times to all Mediterranean Jewish communities and some European communities to indicate a distant and mythologized Hispanic origin and implying certain liturgical, cultural and even common linguistic characteristics, deforms the history of Catalan medieval Judaism."[43] It must be noted that this theory has both followers and detractors.

The Disputations

At any rate, as mentioned above, two treatises written in Hebrew in Catalonia after 1391 are the most significant examples of the controversy between Jews and Christians, *Kelimmat ha-goyim* (Shame of the Gentiles), by Profiat Duran, and *Bittul Iqqare ha-Notzrim* (*Refutation of the Cardinal Principles of the Christians*), by Hasdai Crescas.

Whereas the earlier *Eben Bohan* focused on baptised Jews, their faith and conversion, and included a Hebrew translation of the Gospels into Hebrew with some commentaries, *Kelimmat ha-goyim* and *Bittul Iqqare ha-Notzrim* were written after 1391 and their purpose was accordingly different, as these two works were clear attacks against Christian dogmas and the Christian religion in general.

A few years later, in 1412, the Disputation of Tortosa was convened by Pope Benedict XIII at the request of Jerónimo de Santa Fe, a *converso* born Yehosua ben Yosef ha-Lorqui. The official Latin record of the disputation is extant, but, unfortunately, no Hebrew versions have survived. Regarding the tenor of the debate, according to the Latin record, Jews were delusional because they did not see that the Messiah had already arrived and refused to admit that the Talmud was full of errors. Other issues included whether it was mandatory or not to believe everything the Talmud said, the alleged heresies present in the Talmud, and whether the Law of Moses was eternal and perfect or not. Only two brief Hebrew abstracts of the disputation have been preserved. One is anonymous and the other one, a version of the first, was compiled in Shlomoh ibn Verga's *Shevet Yehudah* (The Scepter of Judah).[44] Since the Disputation of Barcelona in 1263,

---

43 Eduard Feliu, "Quatre notes esparses sobre el judaisme medieval," *Tamid* 2 (1998–1999): 81–122 at 81–87.
44 Antonio Pacios López, *La Disputa de Tortosa* (Madrid and Barcelona: Instituto Arias Montano-CSIC, 1957). See also, Jaume Riera i Sans, *La crònica en hebreu de la disputa de Tortosa* (Barcelona: Fundació Salvador Vives Casajuana, 1974); Ran Ben Shalom, "Vikuah Tortosa, Vincente

Jews had not delved into these subjects, and so they prepared for the debate using the same materials Nachmanides had used a century and a half before. In contrast, Christians had been studying Jewish literature. Taking advantage of this opportunity, Jerónimo de Santa Fe, the *converso*, used a wide variety of rabbinic literature, not to refute Jewish Messianic ideas, but to dismantle the Jewish religion as a whole. For instance, Christians built on Raimon Martí's work, *Pugio Fidei* (The Dagger of Faith). On the basis of the Talmud, *Midrashim*—compilations of rabbinic writings—and other Jewish sources, Raimon Martí tried to demonstrate that Jesus had already been announced in rabbinic literature as the Messiah and son of God, and that Jewish laws, despite being given by God, had been made unnecessary by the coming of Jesus.[45]

This depressing state of affairs was conveyed by Shlomoh ben Reuben Bonfed. This rabbi and poet from Saragossa, who was present at the Disputation of Tortosa, complained in his writings that the most prominent Jewish thinkers of the moment had not been able to pass the test of Tortosa, lamenting that he had seen friends of his and rabbis and other intellectuals converted to Christianity: "After this, misfortune spread and the hand of conversion grew strong, and I sent this collection of poems to a noble relative of mine, Nastruch Bonfed, while in mourning for the separation of many people and the most noble leaders of our communities."[46]

In his book *History of the Jews in Christian Spain*, Yitzhak Baer blames the disastrous consequences of the disputation on different factors: it is not that the Jews of that generation were less prepared than their predecessors, but they either failed to disprove the existence of dogmatic errors in Judaism or succumbed to social pressure. The end of the disputation resulted in the burning of the Talmud by Christian authorities and a massive campaign of Christian proselytism.[47] However, burning the Talmud was not a new practice, as the Disputation of Paris of 1240, which was considered a sort of inquisitorial trial against the Talmud, culminated in the burning of a staggering number of Jewish holy texts.

Ferrer u-be'ayat ha-anusim 'al-pi 'eduto shel Yitshaq Natan," *Zion: A Quarterly for Research in Jewish History* 56 (1991): 21–45.
45 Robert Bonfil, "The Nature of Judaism in Raymundus Martini's 'Pugio Fidei'," *Tarbits* 40/3 (1971): 360–75. See also, Philippe Bobichon, "Quotations, Translations, and Uses of Jewish Texts in Ramon Martí's Pugio Fidei," in *The Late Medieval Hebrew Book in the Western Mediterranean: Hebrew Manuscripts and Incunabula in Context*, ed. Javier del Barco (Leiden and Boston: Brill, 2015), 266–93.
46 Pacios López, *La disputa de Tortosa*, 77.
47 Yitzhak Baer, *A History of Jews in Christian Spain*, trans. Louis Schoffman, vol. 2 (Philadelphia: The Jewish Publication Society of America, 1966), 170–243.

This event marked a turning point in the relations between Christians and Jews, and offers further proof of the history of hostility that would end up triggering the persecutions of 1391 and others that followed.[48]

Beyond Iberia

In North Africa, the Mallorcan Simeon ben Tzemah Duran found a place to settle and became one of the most prominent rabbis of his time in Algeria and its region. One of his *responsa* conveys the drama of exile and the pride of those who suffered through it:[49]

> The wise men of Fez have asked me: "in our place of origin, we are used to adding broth from some other pot when the food dries out, whether the soup is hot or cold, and there are those who mix it with hot water. If the food dries, we add this water and we wonder about it, because we have not seen any justification for doing so in the Gemarah, or in the writings of Fassi, Rambam, ha-Rash, or the Baal ha-Turim. We have come to you to find out if there is a justification for this and if so, where it can be found."
>
> You must know that we are exiles from the land of Catalonia and, as our ancestors used to do when they were there, we too have the same custom in the places to which we have been scattered because of our sins. You know that the rabbis of Catalonia are the ones on whom all the customs of the communities [around the Mediterranean] are based, and they are Ramban, Rashba, ha-Raah, ha-Ran, and other great rabbis that each generation has had among them, but their comments have not been disseminated nor published.[50]

In the seventeenth-century epilogue added to the compilation of *responsa* of Rabbi Shlomoh ben Simeon ben Tzemah Duran, known as Rashbash and son of Rabbi Simeon ben Tzemah Duran, we find a passage that comments on the origins of the Jews who were expelled from their land:[51]

---

48 Ferran García-Oliver, a professor of Medieval History at the University of Valencia, has published a book devoted to these relations in which he tries to change the views on medieval Jews and show that, in spite of bouts of institutional and social violence, Jews and Christians lived in much closer proximity than was previously thought; see Ferran García-Oliver, *Els murs fràgils dels calls: Jueus i jueves dels Països Catalans* (Catarroja: Editorial Afers, 2019).
49 Rabbi Simeon ben Tzemah Duran, also known as Rashbatz or Tashbatz, *responsum* number 10.
50 The *responsum* adds that the custom of adding broth is written in the Gemarah (Shabat 145:72) and that a detailed explanation of it can be found in the writings of Rabbi Jonah ben Abraham Gerondi and Rabbi Nissim.
51 *Responsum* number 635, Epilogue of the *Responsa*.

> Until today He has helped me, He has rewarded me with His kindness. He has made me follow the path of righteousness. He has guided me down safe paths, and at the Gates of Wisdom He has gifted me with this precious book, helping me succeed in starting and completing this book, which is the book of *responsa* of our master and great rabbi, Rabbi Shlomoh, son of our master, the great rabbi Simeon ben Tzemah. I, the one who writes, am Seadia [...] son of rabbi David son of [...] Seadia son of [...] Yossef, a disciple of Rabbi [...] bar Yaakov son of [...] Yossef, also known as Zarafa, from the holy community of those who were expelled from Catalonia, from Barcelona and from the island of Mallorca, who were exiled here in Algeria. This book was completed in the month of Av of the year 5382 (1622) of the creation of the world.

These two passages reflect both the nostalgia of the exiles and the pride they took in their background as two faces of the same coin. This nostalgia was not for the land itself, but for the life they had led and the memory of their lost community.

Rabbinical Views on the Events of 1391: Exile or Conversion

Many of the witnesses and victims of the events of 1391 wrote about their decision to leave Sepharad as a way of protesting the Christian attacks and avoiding conversion. Among those who preferred exile to conversion—or rather exile after conversion—when given the chance, we find the great rabbis Ribash and Rashbatz. Some scholars have even argued that this migration followed an expulsion by decree, but the fact is that, unlike the absolute expulsion of 1492, this was rather a spiritual banishment. Like the aforementioned Rabbi Simeon ben Tzemah Duran and Isaac ben Sheshet Perfet, in 1391, most exiles chose Algeria as their destination. In the eighteenth century, Rabbi Haim Yosef David Azulai, commonly known as Hida, still recalled how Rashbatz had reached Algeria after the expulsion from Sepharad: "ki boreah hu mi-Sefarad me-ha-gerush" (because he escaped from Sepharad, from the expulsion).[52]

Scholars who argue in favour of the existence of a decree of expulsion in 1391, claim that it was issued by the aforementioned archdeacon of Écija, Ferrand Martínez, who arrogated to himself the powers of the Kingdom of Castile. However, the violence against Jews spread across the Iberian kingdoms, and, furthermore, it is unlikely that a member of the clergy could have such influence on a decision that would have pertained to kings. The fact is that, at the end of the

---

[52] Hayim David Azulay, *Shem ha-Gedolim*, letter Shin, number 24.

fourteenth century, religious authorities demanded the expulsion of Jews while royal authorities defended them. For instance, Joan I, King of Aragon was in Saragossa during the massacres of 1391 and no one laid hands on the Jews of that city.[53] However, Jews did flee Sepharad in 1391 feeling that they were no longer welcome. In fact, Ribash and Rashbatz were among the first to call on Jews to leave because of the danger, which was made apparent by the disappearance of the community of Mallorca.[54]

Faced with persecution, Jews took a stand and decided to escape, abandoning their possessions and what was beloved to them and crossing the sea to Italy or to the lands of the Ishmaelites across the Mediterranean. Ribash and Rashbatz, who left with the exiles in 1391, banned the return to Sepharad, emphasising the spiritual danger that such return posed for Jews. Ribash warned Jews about *conversos*: "those *conversos* who have remained for so long in the land of the decree and did not flee to another territory, as others did, both rich and poor, must be looked on with suspicion."[55] This is especially significant given that Ribash himself was a *converso* from 1391 to the time when he went into exile in Algeria.

In his *responsa*, Ribash recounted the case of a ship of *conversos* off the coast of Africa: "One day a ship arrived from Mallorca carrying forty-five *anussim* (*conversos*) from Mallorca, Valencia and Barcelona. The governor wanted them to enter the city, but someone tried to persuade the community to tell the governor to forbid them from entering and to return them to Mallorca instead. When I heard that some Jews complained about their arrival, I became angry."[56] It is important to recall that *conversos* were seen by Jews as brothers and sisters, as Jews who would always have the choice to return to Judaism, despite their deplorable customs and the harsh criticisms they received from rabbis such as Ribash and Rashbatz.[57]

---

53 Baer, *A History of Jews*, 97.
54 The community of Mallorca suffered the massacre of 1391 and was forced to accept Christianity in 1435; see Abraham Lionel Isaacs, *Jews of Majorca* (London: Methuen, 1936); Angela S. Selke, *The Conversos of Majorca: Life and Death in a Crypto-Jewish Community in XVII Century Spain* (Jerusalem: The Magnes Press, 1986).
55 Ribash, *responsum* number 4.
56 *Responsum* number 61.
57 On the Jewish perception of *conversos* based on the analysis of rabbinic sources, see Zsom, *Conversos in the Responsa*; and Moisés Orfali Levi, *Los conversos españoles en la literatura rabínica: Problemas jurídicos y opiniones legales durante los siglos XII–XVI* (Salamanca: Universidad Pontificia de Salamanca, 1982).

Conclusion

Despite the fact that Christianity was considered a heresy according to Judaism, Hebrew sources did not engage in attacks against it before 1391. However, even after that, Christianity was simply perceived as an error of dogma and a combination of bad habits. Hebrew texts do not take the aggressive tone towards Christians that could be expected from the social context. As for monarchs, who nominally ruled over Jews, their figure was never tarnished by these writings; on the contrary, they were always legitimised by Jewish authors, as Jews always remained compliant with the law of the land they lived in.[58] Regarding Christian social habits, *responsa* provide indirect information while warning Jews against certain actions such as adultery of Jewish women with Christians and sharing unclean wine with Christians. Although these cases are scarce, they can help us to better understand the coexistence between Jews and Christians.

The attacks of 1391 were an absolute tragedy for the Jews who lived in the Crown of Aragon, resulting not only in the disappearance of several major communities, but also in a hostile context that included episodes like the Disputation of Tortosa. In the aftermath of these attacks, the social and economic ties between Jews and Christians were forever severed.

Although the vicissitudes of the expulsion of 1492 certainly exemplify this rupture, the events of 1391 acted as a spiritual forerunner of what would happen a century later and were the turning point that led rabbis to start warning about the dangers of living in Sepharad. At the same time though, the Hebrew writings of the time convey that belonging to a community that had its roots in that particular area was a source of pride for the exiles; a sense of pride that was tinged with nostalgia, not for the land they had left behind, but for the community they had been forced to abandon.

Sasson Hai le-Bet Kastiel, a proud Sephardi who travelled Asia and Europe between the seventeenth and eighteenth century, added the expression *tehareb mehera*, "may it be soon destroyed," when he talked about Sepharad. According to him, this was a wicked kingdom where people hated Jews and delighted in burning them, while some Jewish souls, *conversos*, were very wealthy but

---

58 Thomas Barton, focusing on the *aljama* of Tortosa analysed the complex legal and jurisdictional mechanisms of control over minorities and their privileges granted to authorities in the Crown of Aragon in order to reestablish their rights over Jews: Thomas W. Barton, *Contested Treasure: Jews and Authority in the Crown of Aragon* (University Park: Penn State University Press, 2015).

suffered immeasurably because of their sins.[59] His ideas, which were not new, present a stark contrast to the views of the late nineteenth century, when Sepharad was seen by Jews through the prism of Romanticism, as the land of the three cultures, where their predecessors had lived in peace until the events of 1391 and the expulsion of 1492.

To conclude, the community they had left behind was much more important than the land itself. As we see in the *responsa* of Ribash, Rashbatz, and also Rashbash, they seem to have been proud of their origins, but their greatest source of self-regard was belonging to a community that had produced renowned rabbis, a community that was composed of souls, and had its own traditions, background, and customs.

---

[59] On Sasson Hai's writings, see Yitzhak Ben Zvi, "Massaʿot Śaśon Ḥay le-vet Qašti'el," in *Meḥqarim u-meqorot* (Jerusalem: Rubin Mass, 1966), 421–71; Naftali Ben Menahem, "Maʿaśe Nissim ʿal Abraham ibn ʿEzra mesupar ʿal yede Śaśon le-vet Qaśṭi'el," *Maḥberot la-Sifrut* 5 (1952–1953): 60–80; Yehuda Avida, "Maʿaśe Nissim le-Śaśon Ḥay le-vet Qašti'el," *Sefunot* 2 (1957–1958): 103–27.

Part III: **The Edge of Society**

Ivan Armenteros-Martínez
Chapter 9
Social Domination and Resistance: Slavery in the Medieval Christian Western Mediterranean

Over a century ago, the historian Foustel de Coulanges stated that "slavery was a primordial fact, contemporary to the origin of societies, rooted in an era of humankind where all inequalities had their raison d'être."[1] Slavery was indeed an institution known and practiced by the vast majority of past human societies, which, despite its various forms, was defined by some central elements: slaves were foreigners who were alien to the community into which they were brought, had been individualised from the moment of their enslavement, and had been subjected to the will of their owner. In the words of the anthropologist Claude Meillassoux, slaves were unborn, not yet deceased, but socially dead.

According to Meillassoux, slavery should be understood as a two-stage process. The first stage begins with a violent act, the capture that uproots the enslaved individual from his or her social and natural environment. This is essentially a process of social negation and depersonalisation through which this individual is isolated from his or her familial, social, and cultural background. The second phase involves the introduction of the slave into the owner's community, where he or she will forcefully become a sort of paradoxical non-being. Law, custom, and ideology become then necessary for the articulation of an intelligible dialogue between the slave and the community of free men and women. In short, Meillassoux maintained that slavery is a kind of "social death," an idea that, in a way, was also taken up by Orlando Patterson, who remarked that slavery is the social equivalent of a violent death.[2]

---

[1] This essay has been written within the framework of the project "Movement and Mobility in the Medieval Mediterranean: People, Terms and Concepts (MovMed)" (PGC2018–094502-B-I00) and the research group "La Corona de Aragón, el Islam y el mundo mediterráneo–CAIMMed" (2017 SGR 1092).
    Fustel de Coulanges, "Le colonat romain," in *Recherches sur quelques problèmes d'histoire* (Paris: Librairie Hachette et Cie, 1885), 1–186 at 3. All translations mine, unless noted otherwise.
[2] Claude Meillassoux, *Anthropologie de l'esclavage: Le ventre de fer et d'argent* (Paris: Presses Universitaires de France, 1986), 99–116; Orlando Patterson, *Slavery and Social Death, A Comparative Study* (Cambridge and London: Harvard University Press, 1982), 38–45.

The idea of slavery as a substitute for death was already considered by the jurists of classical antiquity. The etymology of the terms *mancipium* and *servus*, which designated the legal and social figure of the slave, is closely linked to Roman warfare. In Justinian's *Digest* of 533, the jurist Florentinus is credited with having explained both terms. *Mancipium* derives from the masculine noun *manceps*, which means "one who takes something with his hands" and claims possession of it ("mancipia vero dicta quod ab hostibus manu capiatur").[3] Thus, *mancipium* has a double meaning, namely "to take with one's hands" and "something that is fully owned," or more precisely, "slave," since slaves were captured with the force of hands. As for *servus*, Florentinus claims that it derives from the verb *servo*, "to save," "to ensure health or preservation," that is, what Roman officers did when they captured their enemies on the battlefield: enslaving and selling them and thereby preserving their lives from death ("servi ex eo appellati sunt, quod imperatores captivos vendere ac per hoc servare nec occidere solent").[4]

By the eighth century, the semantics of the word *servus* had become increasingly vague, especially under the influence of Christianity. From the time of the early Church onwards, Christian thinkers had embraced the stoic perspective on slavery, understood as the subjugation of the soul to the vices and passions of the body.[5] The dichotomy between freedom/slavery of the body and freedom/slavery of the legal and physical soul provided the perfect mirror in which to reflect the metaphysical link between God the Creator and all created beings. So much so that some bishops and civil rulers of Western Europe adopted the formula *servus servorum Dei* to refer to themselves,[6] as the Byzantine emperor had

---

3 Florentinus, *D.* 1.5.4.1. *Florentinus libro nono Institutionum:* "they are called *mancipia* because they have been taken by the enemy's hand."
4 Ibid.: "They are called *servi* because emperors are wont to sell their captives, and thereby save them, and not kill them." See, also, the entries *servus* and *mancipium* in Alfred Ernut and Antoine Meillet, *Dictionnaire étymologique de la langue latine: Histoire des mots* (Paris: Éditions Klincksieck, 1932; repr. 1979).
5 See Peter Garnsey, *Ideas of Slavery from Aristotle to Augustine* (Cambridge: Cambridge University Press, 1996), 14–19.
6 Although Gregory the Great (590–604) was the first to use this formula extensively, it was not until the twelfth century that it was definitely (and exclusively) adopted by the papacy. This expression was also used by civilian rulers: King Alfonso II of Castile, in 870, and the Holy Roman Emperor Henry III, in 1017. In fact, Gregory the Great himself employed this phrase as early as 587 while he was still a deacon; see the entry *"Servus servorum Dei,"* in *The Catholic Encyclopaedia*, at https://www.newadvent.org/cathen/13737a.htm.

embraced the Greek equivalent δουλειά (duty) to proudly convey his statesmanship.[7]

Over the same period, the Latin term *mancipium* seems to have been less problematic and referred to slaves in a more conventional sense. Of greater interest is the word *captivus:* if at first it designated a prisoner of war, in time it came to mean "slave."[8] For instance, in the eighth century, the biographer of Eligius of Noyon used the terms *mancipium* and *captivus* interchangeably when he wrote "with great passion and promptness, he [the Christian saint] went where he knew a slave [*mancipium*] was to be sold, and immediately paid the price and freed the slave [*captivum*]." In the same sentence he used both terms to refer to the same person.[9] Moreover, in the Early Middle Ages, slaves bound to the land or those who worked on the lord's fields were called *servi*, sometimes *servi casati*, but never *captivi*. In contrast, men and women subjugated by violence to be sold as slaves were described as *mancipia* and *captivi*. It seems clear, then, that there was some connection between these words and the notion of enslavement as an economic activity.[10]

It is clear that both Meillassoux and Patterson drew on the classical definitions of slavery to construct their analytical models. But both took these further when they substituted the physical non-death of the slave with social death, depersonalisation, and alienation. Turning back to the paradox Meillassoux referred to when he outlined the second phase of the enslavement process, slaves enter their owner's community as non-beings. As mentioned above, it is for this reason that law, custom, and ideology become a necessity in order to enable the dialogue between slavery and freedom.

---

7 Michael McCormick, *Orígenes de la economía europea: Viajeros y comerciantes en la alta Edad Media* (Barcelona: Crítica, 2005), 685.
8 *Captivus* ("prisoner, captive, slave") and *captor* ("the one who fastens," not documented before Augustine of Hippo) derive from the verb *capio* ("to take hold, to seize." Thus, *captivitas*—not documented before Seneca the Younger—is opposed to *libertas*, and the condition of captives is expressed through the term *servitium*; cf. Ernut and Meillet, *Dictionnaire étymologique*.
9 "Sane ubicumque venundandum intellexisset mancipium, magna cum misericordia et festinatione occurrens, mox dato praetio liberabat captivum"; *Vita Eligii Episcopi Noviomagensis* (Bibliotheca hagiographica latina 2474–76), ed. Bruno Krusch, Monumenta Germaniae Historica, Scriptores rerum Merovingicarum 4.667.4–6 (Hannover: Hahn, 1902) 3, 121.3–6. See a more detailed explanation in McCormick, *Orígenes de la economía*, 685–86 (also for the quotation and its interpretation, which I subscribe to).
10 For an overview of the debate on rural slavery in the European High Middle Ages, see, among others, Josep M. Salrach, "Els 'servi' de la gran propietat als segles VI–IX: Una panoràmica europea," *Butlletí de la Societat Catalana d'Estudis Històrics* 7 (1996): 9–23, and, especially, Alice Rio, *Slavery after Rome, 500–1100* (Oxford: Oxford University Press, 2017).

The aim of the present chapter is to address the development of slavery in the Christian western Mediterranean, paying special attention to the Catalan-Aragonese area from the early eleventh century to the irruption of Portugal into the interregional slave trade in the mid-fifteenth century. It will also define the characteristic features of slavery in Barcelona in the late medieval period and, finally, it will analyse slavery as a social and cultural event on the basis of a theoretical model built on late medieval Christian case studies.

From the Black Sea to Guinea

The Birth of a New Model

In her will of 1029, a woman named Trudgardis who lived in Barcelona left seven Muslim slaves to her inheritors.[11] This document situates us in a context far removed from the archaic forms of traditional rural slavery, the manifestations of which lasted until the first half of the eleventh century in most of Western Europe.[12]

Decades before Trudgardis signed her will, a series of geopolitical changes were set in motion that would prove fundamental to the future development of slavery in the Christian western Mediterranean. In fact, the turning point between the classical model and that which developed in Western Europe during the last medieval centuries occurred towards the end of the tenth century, when Italian maritime powers began to expand their trade networks across the Adriatic and eastern Mediterranean, and Iberian Christian kingdoms embarked on the conquest of the Iberian Peninsula, which put them on a collision course with Islamic powers. Thus, the two main elements of slavery in the late Middle Ages—namely the supply of slaves through commercial trade from the Balkans, the Black Sea, and the eastern Mediterranean, on the one hand, and the corsair war and border conflicts with Islamic states, on the other—began

---

11 José Balari Jovany, *Orígenes históricos de Cataluña*, vol. 2 (Sant Cugat del Vallès: Instituto Internacional de Cultura Románica, 1899; repr. 1964), 536; see also Joaquim Miret i Sans, "La esclavitud en Cataluña en los últimos tiempos de la Edad Media," *Revue hispanique: Recueil consacré à l'étude des langues, des littératures et de l'histoire des pays castillans, catalans et portugais* 41/99 (1917): 1–109 at 2, and Charles Verlinden, *L'esclavage dans l'Europe médiévale I, Péninsule Ibérique-France* (Bruges: De Tempel, 1955), 131–32.

12 See Pierre Bonnassie, "Supervivencia y extinción del régimen esclavista en el Occidente de la alta Edad Media (siglos IV–XI)," *Boletín de Historia Social Europea* 1 (1989): 53–107.

to develop in a process that consolidated approximately between the mid-twelfth and late thirteenth century.

In the Iberian Peninsula, al-Andalus became a centre of slave trade under the rule of the Umayyad Dynasty (756–1031). Conflicts with the Christian inhabitants of the northernmost part of the Iberian Peninsula, especially of the Cantabrian Mountains and the Pyrenees, and the activity of Jewish and Muslim traders supplied the markets of the Emirate—later Caliphate—of Córdoba with Breton, Irish, Frankish, Slavic, Germanic, and Iberian slaves. At the same time, from the early eleventh century onwards, the number of Muslim captives in Christian hands increased as the border war against Islam escalated. As the military balance between the two powers began to shift in favour of the Christians, Muslim slaves became part of the spoils of war.[13]

It is interesting to see how, after the campaign led by Almanzor against Barcelona in 985, the terms Saracen, Moor, captive, and convert began to appear in Catalan sources to refer to Muslim slaves, who were no longer classified as pagans. The slave came to be identified as a cultural foreigner, an enemy, while the terms that had designated European slaves, both Christian and pagan, such as *servus* and *mancipium*, were rarely used to refer to Muslim slaves.[14]

In Catalonia and Aragon, the expeditions for the redemption of captives were an important driving force behind the first contacts between Christians and Muslims. Several texts refer to pious foundations established for the release of Christian captives.[15] Conversely, in the case of Barcelona, we have already noted that in 1029 Trudgardis owned a minimum of seven Muslim slaves, and a few decades later, in 1062, the presence of slave-owning merchants is well documented.[16] In 1005, just twenty-four years before Trudgardis and her slaves were immortalised in writing, Armanno, son of the late Angelbert, sold the Burgundian slave Erkentruda in the Ligurian town of Noli.[17] However, whereas the sale of Erkentruda was one of the last instances of a type of slavery that was already waning, Trudgardis's slaves represented one of the new faces that the trade in human beings would take on during the last centuries of the Middle Ages.

Towards the mid-twelfth century, documentary evidence seems to indicate that Barcelona had become a key market for the introduction of Sudanese

---

13 Stephen P. Bensch, "From Prizes of War to Domestic Merchandise: The Changing Face of Slavery in Catalonia and Aragon, 1000–1300," *Viator* 25 (1994): 63–94 at 66–67.
14 Ibid., 65 and 68.
15 Ibid., 73–74.
16 Verlinden, *L'esclavage dans l'Europe*, 131–32.
17 Francesco Panero, *Schiavi, servi e villani nell'Italia medievale* (Turin: Paravia Scriptorium, 1999), 341.

gold and Muslim slaves into Christian Europe.[18] Towards the end of that century, this growing prosperity allowed the city to claim a space within the commercial maritime networks created in the wake of the Crusades.

In addition to cities such as Barcelona, large secular and religious estates were also slaveholders during this period. For example, from the late twelfth century onwards, the Cistercian abbey of Santa Maria de Poblet—in southern Catalonia—faced with the lack of alternatives for maintaining the yield of its estate in Torredà and in view of the relative ease with which Muslim slaves could be obtained, opted for acquiring enslaved people to aid its free and semi-dependent labourers. As time went by, and due to the difficulties Poblet had in attracting young peasants from the surrounding area—who were more interested in making a living in the burgeoning urban centres—the monastery found a way of coping with the lack of available agricultural manpower by acquiring and maintaining small slave crews.[19]

The case of Poblet was not unique. The Knights Templar used a similar strategy in their Catalan-Aragonese domains throughout the thirteenth century, especially after the conquests of Mallorca (1229) and Valencia (1239),[20] and the Catalan Benedictine abbey of Santa Maria de Montserrat, which in 1287, after the conquest of the island of Minorca, received eleven Muslim captives as a gift from King Alfons III of Aragon, also owned slaves.[21]

The fight against Islam soon provided a steady supply of slaves. Although the actual impact of the Christian campaigns of conquest in Mallorca (1229), Valencia (1239), Murcia (1266), and Minorca (1287) is still unclear, their effects were felt in the main markets of the Christian western Mediterranean. Slaves from the conquered territories arrived in Barcelona, Genoa, Sicily, Naples, and Marseille. Moreover, the impact of these conquests on the slave trade was also recorded in contemporary texts. According to the chronicler Ramon Muntaner (1265–1336),[22] once the conquest of Murcia was over, the then *infant* Pere, son of King Jaume I

---

18 As proposed by Jaume Vicens Vives, *Manual de Historia económica de España* (Barcelona: Editorial Vicens-Vives, 1959; repr. 1964), 139; see, also, Bensch, "From Prizes of War," 74–75.
19 Josep Maria Sans i Travé, "Els templers catalans, propietaris d'esclaus," in *De l'esclavitud a la llibertat: Esclaus i lliberts a l'Edat Mitjana*, ed. M. Teresa Ferrer i Mallol and Josefina Mutgé i Vives (Barcelona: Consejo Superior de Investigaciones Científicas, 2000), 309–25 at 314–15.
20 Ibid., 319–20.
21 Miret, "La esclavitud en Cataluña," 11.
22 Ramon Muntaner was a Catalan mercenary and the author of one of the four works known as the *Catalan Great Chronicles*. His *Crònica* covers the period between the conception of King Jaume I, known as the Conqueror (1207) and the coronation of Alfons IV of Aragon (1328). This text, full of historical references, is essential to analyse this period of the history of the Crown of Aragon.

of Aragon and future King Pere III, sent his father two thousand Muslim slaves—
a thousand women and a thousand men—to be offered as diplomatic gifts to the
Pope, to cardinals, to Emperor Frederick, to the King of France, and to counts
and barons who were among his friends.[23]

It was during this period that the foundations for the articulation of the Mediterranean slave trade of the fourteenth and fifteenth centuries were laid. However, the decisive moment only took place at the end of the thirteenth century, when Genoese and Venetian merchants expanded their commercial networks up to the main enclaves of the Black Sea, whence they vigorously traded slaves between the two shores of the Mediterranean. A few decades later, the demographic crisis left by the Black Death dramatically magnified the phenomenon of slavery in southern Western Europe.

From the Black Death to the Atlantic Slave Trade

The Italian commercial expansion towards the Black Sea and the Adriatic put both Eurasian and Balkan slaves into circulation. As time went by, Genoa and Venice became major slave markets, predominantly trading in Tatars, Cherkess from the North Caucasus, Serbs, and Bosnians. Meanwhile, Barcelona consolidated itself as the main entry point for Eurasian and Balkan slaves into the Iberian Peninsula.

The spread of the Black Death across Western Europe (1347) had a major impact on the dynamics of the Mediterranean slave trade: a few decades after the first great outbreak, the number of enslaved people arriving in the main cities of the region increased dramatically. Some authors have established an overly causal link between the 1348 population crisis brought about by the Black Death and the increase in slavery in the Christian western Mediterranean, which they regard as a mechanism of demographic compensation.[24] There is

---

[23] "mil catius sarraïns e altres mil catives sarraïnes [to be offered] qui al papa, qui als cardenals gran res, e a l'emperador Frederic, e al rei de França, e a comtes e a barons amics seus"; Ramon Muntaner, *Crònica*, vol. 3 of *Les quatre grans Cròniques*, ed. Ferran Soldevila (Barcelona: Institut d'Estudis Catalans, 2011), 43.

[24] See, for example, Maxime Kowalewsky, *Die ökonomische Entwicklung Europas bis zum Beginn der kapitalistischen Wirtschaftsform*, vol. 3 (Berlin: R. L. Prager, 1901–1914), 342; George Huppert, *After the Black Death: A Social History of Early Modern Europe* (Bloomington and Indianapolis: Indiana University Press, 1986), 113–14; Giovanni Marrone, *La schiavitú nella società siciliana dell'età moderna* (Rome: Salvatore Sciascia Editore, 1972), 11; Iris Origo, "The Domestic Enemy: The Eastern Slaves in Tuscany in the Fourteenth and Fifteenth Centuries," *Speculum* 30/3 (1955): 321–66 at 324, and Piero Guardicci and Valeria Ottanelli, *I servitori domestici della casa*

some truth to this argument, as this epidemic was certainly a major turning point. However, if we look at the history of slavery from a broader diachronic perspective—borrowing the concept of the "primordial fact" formulated by F. de Coulanges—it is clear that the increase in slave labour in Western Europe after the epidemic of Black Death was not a historical singularity. For instance, during the first decades of the eighth century, Mediterranean countries had to face the last onslaught of the so-called Plague of Justinian, which was especially prevalent in North Africa with an estimated mortality rate of 25 to 35 percent. In addition to this striking indicator, there are two consequences of this earlier pandemic that must be taken into consideration: first, its impact on the labour market, which led to a steep decline in the available labour force—that is, potential healthy workers—and a general rise in wages; and secondly, the concentration of economic means in the hands of the survivors. Both factors must have encouraged the acquisition of new workers from healthy populations such as those in Europe, which was not affected by this outbreak, leading to the establishment of an intense traffic of European slaves to the Maghreb and Ifriqiya countries in order to replenish the labour force and redress the wage tension.[25]

In the second half of the fourteenth century, two undated documents from Barcelona suggest that the proliferation of slave labour in the city after the Black Death crisis must also be analysed in these same terms. The first document justified the proliferation of male and female slaves from various ethnogeographical origins (*sclaus e sclaves de diverses nacions*) by claiming that it was difficult for the inhabitants of Barcelona to hire apprentices and free labourers, as young people were more willing to work as squires and servants than to carry out other jobs, given the better wages.[26] The second document, which linked the increase in escapes to the proliferation of slave labour, argued that the wage claims of farmers and labourers had driven those who held the bulk of the means of production to acquire slaves.[27] The pattern is similar to what we have seen for the

---

borghese toscana nel basso Medioevo (Florence: Salimbeni, 1982), 78. For a deeper analysis, see Ivan Armenteros-Martínez, "La esclavitud en Barcelona a fines de la Edad Media (1479–1516): El impacto de la primera trata atlántica en un mercado tradicional de esclavos" (PhD diss., Universitat de Barcelona, 2012), 150 ff.

25 See McCormick, *Orígenes de la economía*, 700.

26 Historical Archive of the City of Barcelona (hereinafter, AHCB), C, Miscel·lània, 13, C-V-13, ca. 1400.

27 AHCB, C, Miscel·lània, 13, C-V-13, ca. 1405. See also, for both documents, Roser Salicrú i Lluch, "Entre el reclam de les terres islàmiques i l'escapada septentrional: La institucionalització de la por a les fugues d'esclaus a la Catalunya tardomedieval," in *De l'esclavitud a la llibertat*, 87–134; Roser Salicrú i Lluch, "L'esclau com a inversió? Aprofitament, assalariament i rendibilitat del treball esclau en l'entorn català tardomedieval," *Recerques* 52/53 (2006): 35–71,

eighth century, namely a renewal of the labour force by incorporating slaves to contain the wage tension produced by the shortage of free workers.

Whatever the reasons, the increase in slave labour in southern Western Europe was a reality in the second half of the fourteenth century. Between 1355 and 1373, Barcelona passed the first by-laws regulating slave trading, which attempted to control the movement of slaves in order to curb what was perceived by society as a growing public order issue.[28] Of particular note among these by-laws were those relating to fugitive slaves, a rapidly escalating problem which, years later (1421), led to the imposition on the whole principality of Catalonia of a system of compulsory insurance against the escape of male slaves, the so-called *Guarda d'esclaus del General de Catalunya*.[29]

Over the years, the Iberian expansion along the West African coast set in motion the Atlantic slave trade, and the Turkish conquest of Constantinople (1453) and, later, of the whole Black Sea (1484), put an end to Latin commercial hegemony over the eastern and central Mediterranean. These events changed the direction of the trading routes and ushered in a new situation that ended up affecting the features of slavery in southern Western Europe and, more specifically, in the Iberian Peninsula. From the mid-fifteenth century onwards, the arrival of Eurasian and Balkan slaves began to decline at an increasingly rapid pace as the presence of West Africans gained ground. Following this trend, by the time the civil war broke out in Catalonia in 1462,[30] the majority of the newly arrived slaves were black men and women from West Africa.

---

especially 37–47; Josefina Mutgé i Vives, "Les ordinacions del municipi de Barcelona sobre els esclaus," in *De l'esclavitud a la llibertat*, 245–65 at 263–64, and Teresa M. Vinyoles i Vidal, "Integració de les llibertes a la societat barcelonina baixmedieval," in *De l'esclavitud a la llibertat*, 593–615 at 595.

28 Ivan Armenteros-Martínez, *L'esclavitud a la Barcelona del Renaixement: Un port mediterrani sota la influència del primer tràfic atlàntic* (Barcelona: Fundació Noguera, 2015), 44.

29 On this topic, see Roser Salicrú i Lluch, *Esclaus i propietaris d'esclaus a la Catalunya del segle XV: L'assegurança contra fugues* (Barcelona: Consejo Superior de Investigaciones Científicas, Barcelona, 1998), and Salicrú i Lluch, "Entre el reclam." The records produced by the *Guarda d'esclaus del General de Catalunya*, studied in depth by this author, are practically the only extant census of male slaves in the medieval Christian West. On the basis of the 1,379 slaves registered in the city of Barcelona in 1424, and considering the sex ratio proposed by Verlinden, *L'esclavage*, 453, Salicrú approximates a slave population of between 3,500 and 5,000 people out of a total population that some estimates place between 35,000 and 40,000 inhabitants; that is, slaves were between 8.3 and 14.3 percent of the total population: Salicrú i Lluch, "L'esclau com a inversió?," 37, n. 5.

30 On this conflict, see, among others, Alan Ryder, *The Wreck of Catalonia: Civil War in the Fifteenth Century* (Oxford: Oxford University Press, 2007); Santiago Sobrequés Vidal and Jaume Sobrequés i Callicó, *La guerra civil catalana del segle XV*, 2 vols. (Barcelona: Edicions 62, 1973).

The Impact of the Atlantic Slave Trade on the Iberian Peninsula: The Case of Barcelona

The European expansion in West Africa laid the foundations for the articulation of the Atlantic slave trade. The arrival of Portuguese ships on the coasts of Senegambia and the Gulf of Guinea set off a chain of events that, in a few years, would bring thousands of sub-Saharan men and women into slavery in the markets of southern Western Europe. This new form of slavery had the greatest impact on the Iberian Peninsula, specifically on its southern and eastern coastal cities, where black slaves, mainly from the region between present-day Senegal and Liberia, would soon end up being the main groups of the enslaved population.

As for Barcelona, between the end of the Catalan Civil War in 1472 and throughout the reign of King Ferran II (1479 to 1516), slaves represented an estimated 4.3 percent of the total population, that is approximately 1,200 people out of around 28,000 inhabitants by the end of the fifteenth century.[31] Whereas the largest group were sub-Saharan slaves, mostly from the west coast of Africa, the second largest group was made up of Muslim slaves from the Nasrid Kingdom of Granada, which was conquered in its entirety between 1481 and 1492, and from North Africa, although the latter were far fewer. Finally, besides slaves of unknown origin, there was also a small number of *llors*—a term used to describe people with dark skin[32]—Canarians, Turks, American Indians, and Eurasian slaves.[33]

The gender ratio, with a majority of male slaves (55.9 percent),[34] once again reveals a pattern that runs counter to the situation in Barcelona and other Christian western Mediterranean cities in the preceding decades, when female slaves had been far more numerous. However, the main feature of this new pattern of slavery in the Catalan city was a general decline in the number of slaves, especially if the numbers of the first quarter of the fifteenth century are taken into

---

31 Jaume Vicens Vives, *Els Trastàmares (segle XV)* (Barcelona: Edicions Vicens-Vives, 1956; repr. 1988) 187; Josep Iglésies i Fort, *El fogatge de 1497: Estudi i transcripció*, 2 vols. (Barcelona: Rafael Dalmau Editor, 1992).
32 The Catalan word *llor*, *loro* in Spanish, derives from the Latin *laurus*, laurel. Due to the dark colour of the leaves and fruits of this tree, in medieval sources the term was also used to describe not only people of mixed race, but also the inhabitants of the Canary Islands and North Africa.
33 Armenteros-Martínez, *L'esclavitud a la Barcelona*, 109 ff.
34 Ibid., 97, fig. 15.

account, when enslaved men and women reached up to 14 percent of the total population of the city.³⁵

The relatively low number of slaves documented in Barcelona stands out when compared with the figures for other Iberian cities during this same period. Thus, for example, the aforementioned 1,200 slaves registered in Barcelona between 1472 and 1516 contrast with the over 7,300 registered in Valencia between 1489 and 1516,³⁶ and the 3,300 slave trade transactions closed in notaries' offices in Seville between 1472 and 1516.³⁷

This situation is somewhat striking, especially taking into account Barcelona's history in the slave trade. It also raises the question of why the Catalan city took on the role of a secondary market at a time when the supply of sub-Saharan slaves was particularly intense. It could be argued that its geographical distance from the main commercial circuits that were consolidating in the mid-Atlantic, mainly in Atlantic Andalusia and southern Portugal, was a limiting factor. Furthermore, the economic depression following the Catalan Civil War caused a contraction in productive capacity and, consequently, a drastic drop in the demand for new workers, which would in theory have had a negative impact on the arrival of new slaves.

However, these two arguments fall rather short. On the one hand, in the years following the civil war, Barcelona's merchants built up solid trade relations with other ports in the western and eastern Mediterranean and, especially, in the mid-Atlantic. Some Catalan mercantile companies even achieved a relatively significant position in the trade of Atlantic sugar and sub-Saharan slaves.³⁸ On the other hand, although the military conflict had wrecked the Catalan economy, it is also true that things started to look up from the second half of the 1480s onwards and over the next decade.

In addition, it is also necessary to bear in mind that the civil war and a series of successive outbreaks of plague had caused a considerable demographic decline, reducing the estimated population of the city to the aforementioned 28,000 inhabitants.

---

35 See note 29.
36 These figures are calculated on the basis of the data in Vicenta Cortés Alonso, *La esclavitud en Valencia durante el reinado de los Reyes Católicos (1479–1516)* (Valencia: Publicaciones del Archivo Municipal de Valencia, 1964), 58–61, figs. 1 and 2.
37 Alfonso Franco Silva, *La esclavitud en Sevilla y su tierra a fines de la Edad Media* (Sevilla: Publicaciones de la Excma. Diputación Provincial de Sevilla, 1979), 133–37.
38 On this issue, see Ivan Armenteros-Martínez, *Cataluña en la era de las navegaciones: La participación catalana en la primera economía atlántica (c.1470–1540)* (Lleida: Editorial Milenio, 2012).

All these factors put together would suggest that, contrary to what actually happened, the conditions were right for Barcelona and its hinterland to absorb at least as many slaves as other cities. A shortage of labour power and possible upward pressure on wages, the accumulation of capital and means of production in the hands of those who had survived the war and the epidemics, and the opportunity of accessing the supply of black slaves from the Atlantic trade would certainly lead to that conclusion. Yet this was not the case. In fact, these variables, especially the shortage of potential workers that could cover the demands of the labour market, only intensified within the Catalan area, subjected as it had been to the effects of the civil war. In other words, the population of Barcelona and some areas of Catalonia had decreased, but not that of other relatively nearby regions.

In Barcelona, over the same period in which the aforementioned 1,200 slaves can be documented, there is also evidence of the formalisation of almost 3,000 apprenticeship contracts for young workers from southern France, Castile, Portugal, the rest of the peninsular territories of the Crown of Aragon, and the main islands of the western Mediterranean.[39] In short, considering these figures, the labour market of Barcelona was capable of absorbing a significant number of workers including both young apprentices and slaves.

Slavery, Ideology, Law, and Custom

The considerations presented above make it sufficiently clear that slavery responds first and foremost to a demand for workers. The institution seems to have traditionally been intertwined with the balance between supply and demand of labour forces that is characteristic of any productive system. From a male slave who worked as a stevedore, longshoreman, or tanner, to a female slave who was assigned to household tasks, all of them fulfilled an undeniable economic-productive function. However, this economic need was not the only one that shaped the institution of slavery, as socio-cultural aspects were also major elements in the dialectic between enslaved people and the dominant community.

In classical antiquity, the Roman agronomist Marcus Terentius Varro argued that a slave was little more than an animal with a soul and no *logos*—that is, no capacity for reasoning—or a tool that could articulate words, an *instrumentum vocale*. According to this author, slaves were commodities to be exchanged, a

---

[39] See Armenteros-Martínez, *L'esclavitud a la Barcelona*, 88, fig. 12.

work force that only differed from animals because they could articulate words, albeit without meaning.⁴⁰ However, whether willingly or inadvertently, he did not incorporate into his reflections the main quality that defines every enslaved person: humanity. Slaves never ceased to be human beings with a will and a capacity for action, with feelings and emotions, beliefs, and resolve. Obviously, the contemporaries of Varro were fully aware of this, as would be their medieval descendants. It is precisely for this reason that dominant societies created norms and rules to fit the "primordial fact" of slavery into their daily lives.

Although analysing legislative and regulatory systems is a good way of grasping the momentum of slavery in a given case study, this is not the place to undertake such an exercise. Instead, I would like to return to the paradox defined by Claude Meillassoux in reference to the arrival of the slave in the owner's community as a non-being, an individual who had been dissocialised, depersonalised, and alienated. This same idea had already been expressed by classical thinkers when they described slaves as dehumanised beings. However, slavery implied the violent domination of one group of individuals by another, all of whom were human beings with unquestionable capacities for socialisation.

Socialisation, as well as the mechanisms of formation of individual identity, is essentially a dynamic process. In particular, socialisation is a process by which individuals adopt the socio-cultural elements of their environment and integrate them into their personality in order to adapt to society. Hence, individuals constantly build up their social and cultural references from birth.⁴¹ On this basis, it can be argued that from the moment they are subjugated, slaves experience an abrupt change in the context in which they develop socially, in their socialisation environment. But this process is never interrupted, as slaves can adapt to new contexts by building new references. Moreover, on many occasions individuals entered the community of their owner, the society where they would "permanently" live as slaves, after having undergone a journey that might have taken them to places where they lived through the same experiences as other individuals, not all of whom shared their same circumstances. In other words, a slave, as a social individual, came into contact with new sectors of his or her uni-

---

40 Marcus Terentius Varro, *De re rustica*, ed. William Davis Hooper (London: Harvard University Press, 1974), 225; see also, among others, Moses I. Finley, *Esclavitud antigua e ideología moderna* (Barcelona: Crítica, 1982), 92; Garnsey, *Ideas of Slavery*, 23–26 and 35; Ángel Muñoz García, "Esclavitud: Presencia de Aristóteles en la *polis* colonial," *Revista de Filosofía* 55/1 (2007): 7–33 at 12–15.
41 See, for example, John A. Clausen, *Socialization and Society* (Boston: Little Brown and Company, 1968).

verse of relationships, with partial realities that contrasted with the basic sociocultural references acquired in the first stages of socialisation.[42]

The image conveyed by late-medieval archival sources seems to reinforce this same idea. The registers known as *Presentacions i Confessions de captius*, kept in the Archives of the Kingdom of Valencia, collect the interrogations to which slaves were subjected upon their arrival in Valencia, and as such are an exceptional source of information.[43] This administrative formality was also adopted in other western Mediterranean cities, such as Barcelona, where despite being imposed in 1433 by order of the municipal government, it has unfortunately left no extant records.[44] Its aim was to declare "just-war slaves" (*esclaus de bona guerra*); in other words, to confirm the legality of their enslavement and then to estimate their value in order to calculate the tax due to the Crown. Thanks to these records we can learn about the background of many of these slaves, their capture, their relatives, and their fate, whether they arrived alone or accompanied to Valencian lands; we can also learn about the languages they spoke and their personal journeys. In short, these unique testimonies do not portray dissocialised or depersonalised individuals, but men and women who had suffered the violence of enslavement and a process of dehumanisation imposed by the dominant society.

As an individual, the capture itself marked the beginning of a new phase in the socialisation process of a slave. From then onwards, there were three main vectors on the basis of which a slave would build his or her identity within the dominant society: linguistic learning, the first contact with the new religious universe—in other words, the first contact with a new symbolic interpretation of

---

[42] This question has been discussed in greater detail in Ivan Armenteros-Martínez, "L'identité culturelle et sociale des esclaves avant leur affranchissement (Barcelone, XVe–XVIe siècle)," in *Sortir de l'esclavage: Europe, Afrique et Amériques (XVe–XIXe siècle)*, ed. Dominique Rogers and Boris Lesueur (Paris: Karthala, 2018), 59–78.

[43] According to Debra Blumenthal, these interrogations "were formal hearings explicitly designed to make public arguments justifying an individual's capture and sale into slavery": Debrah Blumenthal, *Enemies and Familiars: Slavery and Mastery in Fifteenth-Century Valencia* (Ithaca and London: Cornell University Press, 2009), 22; see, also, José Hinojosa Montalvo, "Confesiones y ventas de cautivos en la Valencia de 1409," *Ligarzas* 3 (1971): 113–27; Cortés Alonso, *La esclavitud en Valencia*, 68–70; Armenteros-Martínez, *L'esclavitud a la Barcelona*, 55, n. 94.

[44] Ivan Armenteros-Martínez, "Regular las declaraciones de buena guerra en un centro del comercio interregional de esclavos: Barcelona, 1433," in *A l'entorn de la Barcelona medieval: Estudis dedicats a la doctora Josefa Mutgé Vives*, ed. Manuel Sánchez Martínez, Ana Gómez Rabal, Roser Salicrú i Lluch, and Pere Verdés Pijuan (Barcelona: CSIC. Institució Milà i Fontanals, 2013), 25–38. This procedure can also be found with identical question lists in some Italian republics; Cortés Alonso, *La esclavitud en Valencia*, 69, n. 5.

reality—and the recognition and comprehension of social hierarchies. The adaptive response of a slave could well determine his or her future.⁴⁵

Learning a new language was a fundamental stage in the process of inserting slaves into late-medieval society. But not everyone achieved the same linguistic mastery, a process that could depend on several factors, such as the degree of relationship with free people or with other slaves of the same or different origin. Language skills thus became a distinctive feature of slaves, a unique quality that was used, for example, to identify escaped slaves.

Slaves also made their first contact with the symbolic interpretation of reality of the dominant group through forced baptism, an act that staged their entry into late-medieval Christian society under a new formal identity. Baptism itself and the explicit will to administer this sacrament to those slaves who were not yet Christians when they arrived in the city reveal the intention of the dominant group to impose their religious beliefs over those of the slaves, whether they were Muslims or pagans. Baptism was therefore considered the first step towards the salvation of a slave's soul, a metaphor for liberation, as, in the end, and according to the Christian worldview, it was thanks to this sacrament that the soul was redeemed and the slave was transformed into a new human being who, from then onwards, was included in Christian society as a valid actor.

After the sale in the city market, the establishment within the productive family unit initiated the next phase in the socialisation process. The influence that the owner and his or her family exerted over a slave, the representation of society that they conveyed, and the strictness, or lack thereof, with which they demanded the slave's adaptation were probably the main elements that favoured a more or less intense degree of socialisation within the owner's family environment or instead enabled the emergence of alternative paths.

The labour exploitation of slaves is another vector that allows us to track their socialisation process. Since female slaves normally remained in the family home, for they were mostly assigned to domestic service and to caring for the owner's children, they were better placed to establish emotional ties with the family, which could in turn lead to a process of intense assimilation. In the case of male slaves, however, the fact that their labour force was exploited in a variety of ways often meant that they were rented out or leased to third parties. Thus, male slaves not only interacted daily with their owner, the members of the family unit, and its neighbourhood, but also, and possibly more intensely, with

---

45 These factors have been extensively addressed in Armenteros-Martínez, *L'esclavitud a la Barcelona*, 362–69.

apprentices and day labourers. With them they shared efforts, but also leisure activities, as some municipal by-laws seem to suggest when they forbid bachelors, young non-specialised workers, and slaves alike to throw stones, oranges, fireworks, and other objects around the city.[46]

The high turnover in the slave market and the renting out and temporary leasing of slave labour foreshadowed the problem of the lack of labour specialisation of freedmen and made it difficult to establish stronger ties between slave and owner. The capacity of the latter to pave the way for the understanding of social norms, as well as to facilitate the adoption of certain behaviours typical of the socio-professional sphere to which their family belonged, was replaced by the social stratum occupied day labourers, porters, and apprentices. In this way, this labour context became the slave's means of socialisation, and the negativity often associated with these precarious environments became the slave's main model of social integration. Ultimately, both male and female slaves lived in ideal, albeit substantially different, environments for the enhancement and reinforcement of the adoption of socio-cultural elements that would add to the shaping of their identities.[47]

One last phase of the socialisation process to which it is necessary to dedicate a few lines is access to freedom. First of all, it should be noted that, according to the documentation, everything seems to indicate that manumission was not a widespread practice. On the contrary, for every hundred slave sale contracts documented in Barcelona between 1472 and 1516, the *alforries* or manumission documents are less than fifteen, a figure similar to those documented in other Iberian cities, such as Malaga, Granada, and Lisbon.[48]

However, it is still true that access to freedom symbolised what was probably the most significant episode in the process of socialisation of slaves. Leaving aside other forms of liberation, such as escape or rescue, it is interesting to consider two specific modalities, direct manumission and conditional access to freedom.[49] Most cases of unconditional manumission respond to the liberation of

---

46 See, for instance, AHCB, CC, Registre d'ordinacions, IV-7, 26 June 1451, fol. 65r–v; AHCB, CC, Ordinacions originals, XXVI-5, 6 June 1452; AHCB, CC, Registre d'ordinacions, IV-7, 11 June 1452, fol. 85r; IV-13, 17 June 1514, fols. 93v–94r.
47 Armenteros-Martínez, *L'esclavitud a la Barcelona*, 368–69.
48 Raúl González Arévalo, *La esclavitud en Málaga a fines de la Edad Media* (Jaén: Universidad de Jaén, 2006), 386–87; Aurelia Martín Casares, *La esclavitud en la Granada del siglo XVI: Género, raza y religión* (Granada: Universidad de Granada, 2000), 437, fig. 42; A. C. de C. M. Saunders, *A Social History of Black Slaves and Freedmen in Portugal, 1441–1555* (Cambridge: Cambridge University Press, 1982; repr. 2010), 61.
49 On this matter, see Armenteros-Martínez, *L'esclavitud a la Barcelona*, 369–72.

slaves who were close to the owner's family circle or slaves born in the owners' house, which seems to indicate that this type of manumission was granted to people who had experienced an intense process of assimilation. But it is also true that, in some cases, those who obtained their freedom did so at an advanced age, which may suggest that there was an economic factor at play—that is, the low productivity of a person who was no longer young could force his or her liberation.[50]

As regards conditional manumission, its analysis is a priori more complex. First, it is necessary to address the factors that made possible the existence of a type of contract with which the owner committed to freeing a slave if he or she fulfilled certain conditions. These stipulations could be monetary, such as the payment in instalments of a ransom that typically doubled or even tripled the price paid for the slave on the market,[51] or labour-related, that is, the provision of a service during a certain period of time. Besides these conditions, however, a promise of manumission usually demanded certain moral standards from the slave, such as not drinking or gambling, not engaging in procuring, not stealing or blaspheming, not fighting, and not disobeying the owner, for absolute loyalty was definitely a must.[52]

From an economic perspective, it can be argued that the owner, through the promise of freedom, sought to increase the productivity of the slave or to secure an income either from the payment in instalments of the slave's freedom or from the lease of his labour force to third parties. But the fact that slaves were branded

---

[50] As Miguel de Cervantes illustrated when he made Don Quixote speak of a reality that was surely quite commonplace: "los ahorran y dan libertad a sus negros cuando ya son viejos y no pueden servir, y, echándolos de casa con título de libres, los hacen esclavos del hambre, de quien no piensan ahorrarse sino con la muerte" (*El Quijote*, II, Chap. XXIV): "they set free their black slaves when they are old and useless, and, turning them out of their houses under the pretence of freeing them, make them slaves to hunger, from which they cannot expect to be released except by death."

[51] This way of accessing freedom was called *talla* in Catalan sources and *coartación/coartação* in the Castilian and Portuguese tradition, both in Iberia and the Americas (see, among others, José Andrés-Gallego, *La esclavitud en la América española* (Madrid: Ediciones Encuentro / Fundación Ignacio Larramendi, 2005), 275 ff., and Eduardo França Paiva, "Coartações e alforrias nas Minas Gerais do século XVIII: As possibilidades de libertação escrava no principal centro colonial," *Revista de História* 133 (1995): 49–57). It was relatively common in Barcelona during the fourteenth century (Josep Hernando, *Els esclaus islàmics a Barcelona: Blancs, negres, llors i turcs. De l'esclavitut a la llibertat (s. XIV)* (Barcelona: Consejo Superior de Investigaciones Científicas, 2003), 203–31), but mostly residual by 1500 (Armenteros-Martínez, *L'esclavitud a la Barcelona*, 250).

[52] Notarial records, especially sales and promises of manumission, are full of this sort of references.

as drinkers, violent, and disobedient should not be overlooked, nor can it be simply assumed that these were patterns of behaviour typical of the precarious contexts in which many of them had been socialised.

Let us recall for a moment the idea of the animated tool advocated by the thinkers of classical antiquity. This concept legitimised slavery and reinforced the belief that slaves were inferior to free men. But this way of understanding slavery was challenged on a daily basis by voluntary and organised acts of slave resistance. In order to make sense of this contradiction, slave owners pointed out the alleged natural defects of slaves, such as laziness, gluttony, a tendency to steal and drink, and to the immoderate practice of sex. In their opinion, slaves were inclined to cause problems due to their abject nature. For instance, Lucius Junius Columella advised that the *vilicus*—that is, the slave foreman who organised the crews of non-free labourers in agricultural estates—be accustomed from childhood to work in the fields, because otherwise a foreman, "apathetic and sleepy [...], accustomed to leisure, to the arena, the circus, the theatre, gambling, and the taverns and brothels" of the city could prove a disaster for the economy of the *villa*.[53]

Centuries later, the aforementioned document written towards the end of the fourteenth century that connected the wage demands of labourers with the increase in the slave population of Barcelona described slaves as follows:

> irrational and voluptuous people, [who] have sown in this city many and various vices to which they were already accustomed in their lands, where they lived voluptuously and where their life was bestial, such as [...] drunkenness, lust, procuring, larceny, poisons and many other enormous crimes, of which this city had been free before that time.[54]

The author was repeating the same idea expressed by classical thinkers. The resistance of slaves was interpreted as clear evidence of their inferiority, justifying a contempt that could only be corrected—this was the aim of the document—through corporal punishment. The text insisted, shortly afterwards, on this last idea by stating that,

---

[53] Lucio Junio Moderato Columela, *De los trabajos del campo*, ed. Antonio Holgado Redondo (Madrid: Siglo XXI, 1988), 10.

[54] "axí com a persones brutes e voluptuoses, [que] han sembrats en la dita ciutat molts e diverses vicis, que havien acostumats stant ja en lurs terres, hon vivien voluptuosament e siguent lur vida bestial, axí con són [...] embriagueses, luxúries, alcavoteries, ladornicis, metzines e molts altres crims enormes, dels quals, abans d'aquest temps, era quítia aquesta ciutat." AHCB, C, Miscel·lània, 13, C-V-13, ca. 1400.

> these male and female slaves are given to vice, and by themselves they have no virtues or good manners, so they must be redressed and, by force, brought back to the proper way of living, insofar as it is possible, for words alone would never correct them. For it is written that *servus durus non emendabitur verbis* [an indomitable slave will not be corrected by words].[55]

The biblical aphorism could not be more explicit. This Latin maxim, extracted from the Book of Proverbs (Prov. 29:19), also appeared in Cassian's *Collationes* in the fifth century, and directly opposed the theory held by Varro and Columella that slaves should be treated kindly and brought to heel by talking to them. Instead, it is aligned with the practices of harsh treatment of slaves advocated by Marcus Porcius Cato over 1,500 years earlier.[56]

That said, it is necessary to look into the factors that led to the existence of the promise of manumission in late medieval Barcelona. Regardless of the economic incentives that could make the owner agree, the slave's own agency was a powerful resource that could help him or her out of the slave system. This agency took many forms, namely passive resistance—that is, poor execution of assigned tasks, more or less prolonged absences—disobedience and other forms of internal opposition to slavery, all of which questioned the principle of authority, broke the relationship of subjugation, and damaged productivity. This is what this same document seems to indicate when it unambiguously states that,

> many of the said slaves have managed by force to purchase their freedom or enfranchisement by serving badly, because their masters and mistresses, fearing the scandal and the danger to their persons, have removed them from their service.[57]

To sum up, however rare such emancipations were, they preserved and perpetuated the slave system. The slaves that were "chosen" to be freed were conflictive individuals, elderly people, or women and children close to the owner's family who had earned their trust. These manumissions did not question the existence of the slave system itself and were balanced out by the establishment of new

---

55 "los dits sclaus e sclaves són enclinats a vicis, e de sí mateixs no han virtuts ne bones costums, perquè és mester que sien corregits e, per força, tornats a bona retgla de viure, aytant quant sia possible, car ab paraules null temps se corregirien. Car scrit és que *servus durus non emendabitur verbis*," Ibid.
56 Marcus Porcius Cato, *De re rustica*, ed. William Davis Hooper (London: Harvard University Press, 1974), 13 ff.
57 "molts dels dits sclaus e sclaves [...] per força han obtenguda taylla o franquea ab mal servir, en tant que lurs senyors e dones, tement scàndol e perill de lurs persones, els han hauts a foragitar de si mateixs," AHCB, C, Miscel·lània, 13, C-V-13, ca. 1400.

forms of dependency, such as patronage. They allowed the system to get rid of those elements that were less useful or more difficult to subjugate, and they did not endanger the stability of the slave society, as the rupture they brought about was remedied, on the one hand, by acquiring new servile individuals and, on the other, by inserting emancipated slaves into the free community after a more or less extended period.

From the moment emancipated slaves gained access to freedom and "recovered," at least *de iure*, their condition of *ingenui*—men and women born free—their life was conditioned by the process of socialisation they had undergone during their time in slavery. Reconstructing the life experience of an individual from his or her arrival in the city as a slave to the drafting of his or her will as a freedman or freedwoman is only possible in a handful of cases. The extant examples, however, show a great variety of personal stories, most of which speak of precarious and impoverished socio-professional environments. Some individuals reached what we could call a certain degree of "successful socialisation," which even culminated in the acquisition of citizenship, a process that was not merely formal, as it implied the social recognition of the individual and his or her equal status with the free community, at least in terms of reputation and honourability.[58] In contrast, some freedwomen ended up engaging in prostitution and procuring. On the whole, these were the stories of men and women who, after having suffered enslavement and uprooting, culminated different processes of socialisation until they were inserted into the universe of late medieval Christian society.

To conclude these pages by recalling the ideas with which we started, it might be more appropriate to speak not so much of the social death of slaves, as Patterson and Meillassoux do, but of social resurrection in a new context in which the slave's agency, but also external conditioning factors, led the process of socialisation in multiple directions.

---

[58] On this matter, see Carolina Obradors Suazo, "Council, City and Citizens: Citizenship between Legal and Daily Experiences in 15th Century Barcelona," *RiMe: Rivista dell'Istituto di Storia dell'Europa Mediterranea* 10/1 (2013): 371–418.

Anna M. Peterson
Chapter 10
Diverging Views of the "Leper" in Legal, Literary, and Doctrinal Texts from Thirteenth-Century Western Europe

When we think about marginalised people in the Middle Ages, lepers are among the first to come to mind. The visibility of both lepers and their illness—marked, in its advanced stages, by knobby fingers, raspy voice, and bandaged limbs—turned them into a shorthand for the consequences of sin in religious and literary texts. However, the lepers that lived within the margins of these pages should not be confused with their real-world counterparts, and they certainly were not at the time.

Unfortunately, neither nineteenth-century scholarship nor popular perception of the historical leper succeeded in making this distinction; instead, they conflated allusion with reality, portraying lepers as repellent, leprosy as a sin, and leprosaria as places of exile. Recently, the works of François-Olivier Touati and Carole Rawcliffe, among others, have challenged the view that lepers were forcibly excluded from society.[1] The extant evidence points to a more symbiotic relationship between leprous and healthy populations whose expressions varied across Christian Europe as well as over time. As Touati notes, from the 1230s and 1240s onwards, changes in the social and medical rhetoric resulted

---

Note: I would like to thank Dr. Delfi Nieto-Isabel for accepting my chapter, Courtney Krolikoski for presenting alongside me at the conference that lay the foundations for this chapter, and the anonymous reviewers for their comments. I am indebted to Dr. Fernando Arias Guillén for his wonderful insights. This chapter is part of the project "Hermenéutica del cuerpo visible: Conceptualizaciones y prácticas en la medicina medieval de tradición latina" funded by Spain's Agencia Estatal de Investigación (PID2019–107671GB-I00 / AEI / 10.13039/501100011033).

1 François-Olivier Touati, "Les léproseries aux XIIème et XIIIème siècles, lieux de conversions?," in *Voluntate Dei Leprosus: Les lépreux entre conversion et exclusion aux XIIème et XIIIème siècles*, ed. Nicole Bériou and François-Olivier Touati (Spoleto: Centro italiano di studi sull'alto medioevo, 1991), 1–32; Carole Rawcliffe, *Leprosy in Medieval England* (Woodbridge: Boydell and Brewer, 2006). See also: François-Olivier Touati, *Maladie et société au Moyen Âge: La lèpre, les lépreux et les léproseries dans la province ecclésiastique de Sens jusqu'au milieu du XIVe siècle* (Brussels: De Boeck Supérieur, 1998); Luke Demaitre, *Leprosy in Premodern Medicine: A Malady of the Whole Body* (Baltimore: Johns Hopkins University Press, 2007); Elma Brenner, *Leprosy and Charity in Medieval Rouen* (Woodbridge: Boydell Press, 2015).

in lepers being seen less and less like benign intercessors and more as a potential source of contagion.² Thus, the rise in regulations restricting the freedom of movement of lepers from the mid-thirteenth century onwards was far from coincidental.

The emergence of stricter controls on lepers and their place in society was woven into the preexisting framework of protection and valorisation of their communities. Specifically, I will be using five diverse texts from France, Italy, and Iberia to provide a more nuanced understanding of how lepers were conceptualised by their neighbours. To this end, I will compare the depictions of lepers in three legal texts, namely, *Las Siete Partidas*,³ the 1262 *Constituto* of Siena,⁴ and the *Coutumes de Beauvaisis*,⁵ with those featured in two literary works, the *Roman de Jaufré*⁶ and an exemplum from Jacques de Vitry's *Sermones Vulgares*⁷ (1180–1240).

To understand how and why these texts portray lepers, especially those that seem to take an exclusionary stance on the topic, we need context. Let us begin with Canon Twenty-Three of the Third Lateran Council (1179), which established lepers as a community that should be protected and included as part of society. Specifically, the canon chastises "certain ecclesiastics" who would turn away

---

[2] François-Olivier Touati, "Contagion and Leprosy: Myth, Ideas and Evolution in Medieval Minds and Societies," in *Contagion: Perspectives from Pre-Modern Societies*, ed. Lawrence I. Conrad and Dominik Wujastyk (Aldershot: Ashgate, 2000), 194–97.

[3] *Las Siete Partidas*, ed. Robert I. Burns, trans. Samuel Parsons Scott, 5 vols. (Philadelphia: University of Pennsylvania Press, 2001) (hereafter: Burns, *Partidas*). I am using both Burns's edition and *Las siete partidas del Rey Don Alfonso el Sabio: Cotejadas con varios códices antiguos por la Real Academia de la Historia*, ed. La Real Academia de la Historia, 3 vols. (Madrid: Imprenta Real, 1807) (hereafter: *Partidas*).

[4] *Il Constituto del Comune di Siena dell'anno 1262*, ed. Lodovico Zdekauer (Bologna: Arnaldo Forni, 1983), only covers the first four *distinctiones*, the fifth has been published in Lodovico Zdekauer, "Il frammento degli ultimi due libri del più antico Constituto senese, 1262–1270," *Bullettino Senese di Storia Patria* 1 (1894): 131–35, 271–84; 2 (1895): 137–44, 315–22; 3 (1896): 79–92.

[5] Philippe de Beaumanoir, *Coutumes de Beauvaisis*, ed. Amédée Salmon, 2 vols. (Paris: Libraires des Archives nationales et de Société de l'École des Chartes, 1899–1900) (hereafter: Salmon, *Coutumes*); Philippe de Beaumanoir, *The Coutumes de Beauvaisis of Philippe de Beaumanoir*, ed. and trans. Frank R. P. Akehurst (Philadelphia: University of Pennsylvania Press, 1992) (hereafter: Akehurst, *Coutumes*).

[6] *Jaufré: Roman Arthurian du XIIIe siècle en vers Provençaux*, trans. Clovis Brunel, 2 vols. (Paris: Société des Anciens Textes Français, 1943) (hereafter: Brunel, *Jaufré*); *Jaufre: An Occitan Arthurian Romance*, trans. Ross G. Arthur (New York: Garland Publishing, 1992) (hereafter: Arthur, *Jaufre*).

[7] Jacques de Vitry, *The Exempla or Illustrative Stories from the Sermones Vulgares of Jacques de Vitry*, ed. and trans. Thomas Frederick Crane (New York: Lenox Hill Publishing, 1890).

lepers, and grants the latter their own churches, cemeteries, and priests.[8] As we will see, these norms took hold in legal texts, wherein the secular authorities—kingdoms and municipalities alike—codified the protection and support of lepers. This legislation was further bolstered by what has come to be known as the Charitable Revolution of the thirteenth century, which manifested in a rise in vocations and donations of money and properties to leprosaria and other similar institutions.

The outpouring of wealth and support not only legitimised these communities but also provided the sick with protection, as long as they remained within these houses. As we will see, the sick who were not part of these communities became a source of anxiety for the healthy, which helped to inspire the stereotype of the rogue, sexually voracious leper in fiction. In the aforementioned five texts, inclusion came with certain stipulations. Rawcliffe uses the labels "tame" and "wild" to denote the binary categorisation of medieval lepers. Tame lepers existed within the textual prescriptions set out by these sources. They served as models for other leprosy sufferers. A wild leper, therefore, would operate outside the boundaries of these regulated behaviours.[9] The idea of the "tame" leper reminds us that there were legal and social norms governing the disease, which largely stemmed from the Third Lateran Council. These texts directly and indirectly interacted with the citizenry—both sick and healthy—for example, by outlining the rights of proven lepers, the benefits of supporting those affected by leprosy, and the fate of virtueless men. While these texts are diverse in nature, they all viewed lepers as individuals who suffered due to their illness and, therefore, had to be cared for by the wider community.

The Texts

The five sources used in this chapter can be divided into two categories based on their depiction of lepers: normative and metaphorical. The first group of texts, which consists of the *Constituto*, the *Partidas*, and the *Coutumes*, impacted lepers living within their respective communities. These works, which date from the sec-

---

[8] *Decrees of the Ecumenical Councils*, ed. and trans. Norman Tanner, vol. 1 (London: Georgetown University Press, 1990), 222–23.

[9] Rawcliffe, *Leprosy in Medieval England*, 284. This is similar to the "good leper," as found in Daniel Le Blévec, "Les lépreux peuvent-ils vivre en société? Réflexion sur l'exclusion sociale dans les villes du Midi à la fin du moyen âge," in *Vivre en société au Moyen Âge: Occident chrétien VIe–XVe siècles*, ed. Claude Carozzi, Daniel Le Blévec, and Huguette Taviani-Carozzi (Aix-en-Provence: Presses de L'Université de Provence, 2008), 290.

ond half of the thirteenth century, drew on prevailing norms in canon and secular law and custom to provide regulatory tenets for kingdoms and municipalities. The earliest extant *Constituto* of Siena was compiled in Latin in 1262 by the city's Commune and underwent many revisions, including a vernacular version from 1309.[10] *Las Siete Partidas* were commissioned by King Alfonso X of Castile (r. 1252–1284) around 1265 and written in the vernacular. The *Partidas* are more of an ideological statement regarding royal authority than a traditional law code.[11] They were revised from the mid-thirteenth to the late fourteenth century, and the first full printed edition dates from the late fifteenth century.[12] Although they are an outstanding example of medieval law, they were not officially given legal force until 1348, when King Alfonso XI of Castile (r. 1312–1350) commissioned an edition for personal use.[13] Finally, the *Coutumes de Beauvaisis* are the only law code with an identifiable author. The *Coutumes* were written in the vernacular by Philippe de Beaumanoir (ca. 1247/52–1296), who became the *bailli* (the king's local agent) for Clermont, in northeastern France, in 1279.[14] The text was completed in 1283; a testament to Louis IX's (r. 1226–1270) widespread bureaucratisation of France.[15] Additionally, both the *Constituto* and the *Coutumes* were influenced by local cases brought before their respective governing bodies.[16]

The themes in these three law codes evince that they drew heavily on both Roman and canon law, especially the Decretals of Pope Gregory IX, and the Third and Fourth (1215) Lateran Councils.[17] For instance, the *Constituto* is divided into

---

10 See *Il Costituto del Comune di Siena, volgarizzato nel MCCCIX – MCCCX*, ed. Mahamoud Salem Elsheikh, 3 vols. (Siena: Fondazione Monte dei paschi di Siena, 2002).
11 Regarding the conceptualisation of law in the *Partidas:* Daniel Panateri, "La ley en *Las Siete Partidas*," *eHumanista* 31 (2015): 671–87.
12 Joseph F. O'Callaghan, "Alfonso X and the *Partidas*," in Burns, *Partidas*, xxx–xl at xxxiv.
13 O'Callaghan, "Alfonso X and the *Partidas*," xl.
14 Frank R. P. Akehurst, "Introduction," in *Coutumes*, xiii–xxxii at xiii.
15 For instance, Beaumanoir's section on *baillis* is based on Louis's reforms regarding that office: Akehurst, "Introduction," xv–xix; William Chester Jordan, "Anti-Corruption Campaigns in Thirteenth-Century Europe," *Journal of Medieval History* 35 (2009): 204–19 at 211–12.
16 Akehurst, "Introduction," xxiii; Alessandro Dani, *Gli statuti dei Comuni della Repubblica di Siena (Secoli XIII–XV): Profilo di una cultura comunitaria* (Siena: Editrice Il Leccio, 2015), 161–66.
17 José Giménez y Martínez de Carvajal, "El decreto y las decretales fuentes de la primera partida de Alfonso el Sabio," *Anthologica Annua* 2 (1954): 239–45; O'Callaghan, "Alfonso X," xxxvii–xxxviii; Michele Pellegrini, "La norma della pubblica pietà: Istituzioni comunali, religione e *pia loca* nella normativa statutaria senese fino al Constituto volgare del 1309," in *Siena nello specchio del suo Constituto volgare del 1309–10, Atti del convegno di studi (Siena,*

five *distinctiones:* Church and charity, civil procedure, communal jurisprudence, citizen's conduct, and penal code.[18] The 1262 version includes a total of 1,415 statutes, with only nine—in the first and fifth *distinctiones*—governing the lepers and leprosaria of San Lazaro and Corpo Santo respectively.[19] A similar thread is found in the *Partidas*. They are divided into seven parts: God and religion, the governance of the kingdom, law, domestic life, commerce, wills and inheritance, and finally, crime and punishment. These are further subdivided into 182 titles, totalling 2,802 laws, only five of which refer to lepers. The structure of the *Coutumes* is far more distinctive, with seventy chapters arranged in no particular order, and 1,982 entries, twelve of which refer to lepers in some capacity. According to Amédée Salmon's edition, in the original each chapter was headed by a long title, such as Chapter 61: "Those who should not hold property, and of the leprosaria, and of the hospitals." Oddly enough, Frank Akehurst's recent translation succinctly entitles this chapter "Incompetents," although it also includes the descriptive title.[20] While this may be a useful summation for the modern reader, it is an inaccurate translation that colours the reading.

Regarding the literary sources mentioned above, the first one is the *Roman de Jaufré*, which has been dated to the first third of the thirteenth century and survives in two complete manuscripts and several fragments.[21] The text circulated widely in Languedoc and northern Iberia, especially in the Crown of Aragon, which it explicitly mentions.[22] I will focus on the chapter in which the eponymous hero encounters a distraught mother who entreats him to chase after a leper who has kidnapped her baby with the intention of exsanguinating it.[23]

28–30 aprile 2010), ed. Nora Giordano and Gabriella Piccinni (Pisa: Pacini, 2013), 240–44; Akehurst, "Introduction," xiv.

18 Lodovico Zdekauer, "Sugli Statuti del Comune di Siena fino alla redazione del 1262," in *Il Constituto del Comune di Siena dell'anno 1262*, ed. Lodovico Zdekauer (Bologna: A. Forni, 1983), lxxxxvii.

19 San Lazaro, located near Porta Romana in the south, first appears in a land sale on 25 August 1229, and Corpo Santo, near Porta Camollia in the north of the city, was first mentioned in the *Constituto* of 1262. Anna M. Peterson, "Beyond the City's Walls: The Lepers of Narbonne and Siena before the Black Death," in *Tracing Hospital Boundaries: Integration and Segregation in South Eastern Europe and Beyond, 1050–1970*, ed. Jane L. Stevens Crawshaw, Irena Benyovsky Latin, and Kathleen Vongsathorn (Leiden: Brill, 2020), 28.

20 "de ceus qui ne doivient pas tenir eritages, et des maladeries et des osteleries," Salmon, *Coutumes*, vol. 2, 326. *Ostelerie* can be translated as "hospital" or "poor house"; I have chosen the former.

21 Ross G. Arthur, "Introduction: Manuscripts, Editions, Translations," in Arthur, *Jaufre*, ix–liii at ix–xvii.

22 Arthur, *Jaufre*, 4.

23 Brunel, *Jaufré*, ll. 2180–3016; Arthur, *Jaufre*, 43–56.

The story features three lepers who end up suffering fates that mirror the binary categorisation—the "wild" and the "tame" leper—discussed above. The text is purposefully evocative in its descriptions, in the same way hagiographies are, in an effort to juxtapose the actions of the hero and damsel with those of the villains.

The second literary work I will analyse is an exemplum from Jacques de Vitry's (1180–1240) *Sermones Vulgares*, also known as *ad status* or *ad omne hominum genus*.[24] This work is undated, but it is believed that it was compiled between 1226/1228 and Vitry's death in 1240.[25] The exemplum in question tells the story of Count Theobald, who was known for his piety and devotion to lepers, in the same vein as other prominent figures such as Elizabeth of Hungary and Bishop Hugh of Lincoln.[26] Specifically, it extolls Theobald the Great (1093–1152), who was count of Blois and Chartres from 1102 and count of Champagne from 1124, as Theobald II. Theobald's exemplum was used in Vitry's *Sermo ad hospitalarios et custodes infirmorum thema sumptum ex psalmo* [Sermon to the hospital staff and administrators of the sick on a theme selected from the psalms]; focused on the hardships and benefits of serving the poor and sick, and it was delivered to the *familia* (staff) of hospitals and leprosaria.[27] Theobald founded two leprosaria, one in Provins, which is mentioned in chapter 29 of Jacques de Vitry's *Historia occidentalis*,[28] and the leprosarium of Grand-Beaulieu in

---

[24] Two other exempla in the collection mention lepers: one uses the symptoms of the disease to illustrate what happens to a gluttonous priest (*Exempla*, 5); the other recounts the tale of a noble woman who takes in a leper and allows him to sleep in her and her husband's bed. When the husband returns home, the leper, who was actually Christ in disguise, approves of her charity by disappearing and leaving behind a sweet smell. This is expertly analysed in Sharon Farmer, "The Leper in the Master Bedroom: Thinking through a Thirteenth-Century Exemplum," in *Framing the Family: Narrative and Representation in the Medieval and Early Modern Periods*, ed. Rosalynn Voaden and Diane Wolfthal (Tempe: Arizona Center for Medieval and Renaissance Studies, 2005), 79–100.

[25] Thomas Frederick Crane, "Introduction," in *Exempla or Illustrative Stories*, xv–cxvi at xxxviii–xl.

[26] Carole Rawcliffe, "Learning to Love the Leper: Aspects of Institutional Charity in Anglo-Norman England," in *Anglo-Norman Studies XXIII, Proceedings of the Battle Conference, 2000*, ed. John Gillingham (Woodbridge: Boydell Press, 2002), 231–50 at 239–40.

[27] Jessalynn Bird, "Texts on Hospitals: Translation of Jacques de Vitry, *Historia Occidentalis* 29, and Edition of the Jacques de Vitry's Sermon to Hospitallers," in *Religion and Medicine in the Middle Ages*, ed. Peter Biller and Joseph Ziegler (York: York Medieval Press, 2001), 109–34 at 113–22.

[28] Theobald's inclusion should not be surprising, as Vitry himself was born near Provins. Translation is Bird's: Bird, "Texts on Hospitals," 112.

Chartres.²⁹ In the text, Theobald personally delivers alms to a leper who lives near the town of Sézanne and/or in a hut in front of the castle. On one of his visits, Theobald talks to the leper and inquires about his health, although, unbeknownst to him, the leper had beeen dead for a month. When Theobald later learns about this, he returns to the house to find it empty except for a sweet scent signifying God's approval of his pious works.

Given their varied backgrounds, all these sources based their treatment and portrayal of lepers on their own context.

Categorisation and "Exclusion"

The exclusion narrative, which, until recently, was a historiographical cornerstone, relied heavily on the ritual of the so-called Leper Mass.³⁰ These "masses" were taken as evidence that lepers were publicly removed from society by being symbolically declared dead. While they were actually a fifteenth-century fabrication, the process of *separatio leprosorum* (the separation of the lepers) did exist to some degree, but was neither as public nor as absurd as the Leper Mass. This is best exemplified by the *Coutumes* wherein Beaumanoir described the status of lepers in Beauvaisis using the very evocative phrase: "il est mors quant au siecle" (they are dead to secular society).³¹ Out of context, this has the sinister overtones of expulsion and social death. However, this phrase should not be detached from its context. Lepers were expected to divest themselves of their property to support their stay in a leprosarium and ensure that the needs of the individual did not drain the house's resources; this was tantamount to an "entrance fee." In turn, the house's staff, whether they were lay people or professed religious, had

---

29 Elma Brenner, "Outside the City Walls: Leprosy, Exclusion, and Social Identity in Twelfth- and Thirteenth-Century Rouen," in *Difference and Identity in Francia and Medieval France*, ed. Meredith Cohen and Justine Firnhaber-Baker (Farnham: Ashgate, 2010), 139–55 at 153.
30 Secondary sources use Édouard Jeanselme's collection of rituals from seventeen dioceses in France and the Crown of Aragon. Most of these are undated, aside from publication dates, which makes it difficult to determine the context surrounding their development and dissemination. The only dated rituals are from Alençon (1446), Vienne (1478), Amiens (1497), and Reims (1583). Ironically, these date from a period when leprosy had begun to disappear in Europe; see Édouard Jeanselme, "Comment l'Europe, au Moyen Age, se protégea contre la lèpre," *Bulletin de la Société Française d'Histoire de la Médecine* 25 (1931): 1–155 at 63–65.
31 Salmon, *Coutumes*, vol. 2, 327; Akehurst, *Coutumes*, 589.

to do the same in order to work there.³² Indeed, Beaumanoir uses "ne pueent pas revenir au siecle" (they cannot return to secular society) when discussing their status.³³ In the absence of living relatives, all these properties reverted to their respective lords rather than remain unclaimed.³⁴ To put it simply, control over one's patrimony was what anchored a person to the "living" or, more accurately, to the secular world. Being considered as dead was not a punishment, but a means of distinguishing lepers, the sick, the disabled, and ecclesiastics who depended on a non-secular institution from those beholden to the municipality.

The fact that many of these texts were read into the exclusion narrative in the nineteenth and twentieth centuries speaks to the complex and vexing conceptualisation of the "leper" from the mid-thirteenth century onwards. In most instances, leprosaria were the product of preexisting communities of lepers who chose to live together and, coincidentally, were located *extra muro* (outside the wall). This trend shifted in the thirteenth century, when healthy individuals of means founded leprosaria to bolster their social and spiritual prestige, as in the cases of Count Theobald and Pope Alexander III (r. 1159–1181) who, in 1170, established a leprosarium in Veroli, Italy.³⁵ The *Coutumes*, the exemplum from the *Sermones Vulgares*, and the *Constituto* mention expelling or at least distancing lepers. The *Coutumes* explicitly state that leprosaria are located outside the city because of the risk of contagion: "li sain en pueent devenir mesel" (the healthy could become lepers).³⁶ In Siena, the link is not as explicit; however, it is evident from Statute 121 that there were some concerns about proximity. According to this statute, from January 1262 onwards, lepers were no longer allowed to live within the city walls, and three men, one from each *terzo* (district), were appointed to remove (*expellere*) them. This was likely done in an effort to ensure that family members did not continue to care for their afflicted kin in their homes, instead encouraging them—by penalising the family with a fine—to move the sick to one of the leprosaria, all of which were exempt from any kind of penalty.³⁷ The statute does not specify that foreign lepers were not to

---

32 Staff took vows of poverty and obedience, but not chastity. The terms used to describe staff vary and their roles were not strictly defined (Charles de Miramon, *Les "donnés" au Moyen Âge: Une forme de vie religieuse laïque v. 1180–v. 1500* (Paris: Cerf, 1999), 340–41, 368–69).
33 Salmon, *Coutumes*, vol. 2, 320; Akehurst, *Coutumes*, 589.
34 Salmon, *Coutumes*, vol. 2, 329–30; Akehurst, *Coutumes*, 591–92.
35 Brenda Bolton, "The Absentee Lord? Alexander III and the Patrimony," in *Pope Alexander III (1159–81): The Art of Survival*, ed. Anne J. Duggan and Peter D. Clarke (London: Routledge, 2012), 153–80 at 178–79.
36 Salmon, *Coutumes*, vol. 2, 329; Akehurst, *Coutumes*, 591.
37 Zdekauer, "Più antico constituto," 137–38. This statute was in place since the 1240s, see Anna M. Peterson, "Public Health and Hospitals in Medieval Siena before the Black Death,"

be admitted, but, as we will see in the *Coutumes*, it is likely that they were ordered back to their birthplace. We have evidence of the Sienese Commune paying for a leper's entrance fee, something they would not have done for a foreigner.[38] That said, all lepers, including foreigners, were allowed to enter the city during Holy Week.[39]

Theobald travelled to the outskirts of Sézanne in order to visit the leper, an individual—and location—other townspeople were well aware of. The leper's house, which would have been located on a major road, mirrors the locations of leprosaria in both Beauvaisis and Siena, which were easily accessible to those who wished to support the sick. The exemplum illustrates the universality of lepers' dwelling places—in reach of a town or city—and the pious person's desire to gain the social capital that came with being seen caring for lepers.

Both the *Constituto* and the *Coutumes* are clear that the legislation was only to benefit the lepers in their respective cities. Being a member of a local leprosarium had its benefits. Perhaps this stemmed from the notion of the "wild" leper who moved from place to place, or perhaps the city did not find it necessary to care for foreigners. Again, this is where categorisation matters. For example, the Ospedale di Santa Maria della Scala, Siena's main hospital, catered to pilgrims passing through Siena on their way to Rome. By definition, these people were outsiders; however, the city and the citizenry welcomed the opportunity to assist them because of their status as pilgrims. It should also be noted that both the *Constituto* and the *Coutumes* allowed for some exceptions. The *Coutumes* authorised widows and wives of residents to enter the leprosarium, otherwise lepers who had no ties to the city—whether familial or linked to properties—were expected to return to the town of their fathers.[40] In Siena, there were no regulations that afforded similar safeguards, but the *Constituto* extended its protection over the leprosaria and their patrimony, as well as the aforementioned benefits of membership.[41]

In *Jaufré* the location of lepers is also noteworthy, albeit for different reasons. In this case the house and the three lepers who lived there—a lord, a giant, and an unwilling accomplice—and by extension their disease, were associated with wealth, vice, and violence, juxtaposed with the beauty of the landscape, the maiden, and the child they kidnapped. Their house is described as

---

in *A Companion to Late Medieval and Early Modern Siena*, ed. Santa Casciani and Heather Richardson Hayton (Leiden: Brill, 2021), 191–92.

38 For the case of Pierzivallus, see Peterson, "Public Health," 191.
39 Zdekauer, "Più antico constituto," 138; *Il Constituto del Comune*, 51.
40 Salmon, *Coutumes*, vol. 2, 327; Akehurst, *Coutumes*, 590.
41 *Il Constituto del Comune*, 51.

"spacious and beautiful" (*bela e grans*), but readers were aware that this welcoming façade harboured murderers and a would-be rapist.[42] Not only were they trying to spoil beauty, they were also exsanguinating children, for the lord believed his leprosy would be cured once he bathed in their blood.[43] The house itself was enchanted and would have imprisoned Jaufré for a hundred years had the third leper not traded the key to its destruction in exchange for mercy.[44] The house and the lepers' appearance and actions were used by the author to comment on spiritual leprosy, a trope used in literary and religious texts as a cautionary tale.[45] Sin corrupted body and soul, a concept that was codified in Canon 22 of the Fourth Lateran Council, which states that the soul should receive treatment first as it would undoubtedly cure the ills of the body.[46] In *Jaufré*, people who had committed horrible crimes hid in a beautiful house where they were either punished for their misdeeds through death—in the cases of the lord and the giant—or confessed and found mercy in God, as did the third leper. Additionally, this story echoes the concerns regarding "wild" lepers, who were seen as both exhibiting and perpetuating sinful behaviours. The sexual violence displayed by the leper in *Jaufré* not only speaks to the fear that male lepers were sexually voracious—a claim Vitry himself dispelled in his exemplum about the faithful wife allowing a leper to sleep in the marital bed[47]—but also presents an inversion of the hagiographical trope of kissing lepers. Saints, such as Catherine of Siena (1347–1380), often kissed or touched lepers as a means of expressing their devotion and vicariously experiencing their disability.[48] Unlike the actual disease, spiritual leprosy could be cured through redemption and penance, just as the "wild" leper could become "tame" should they join a leprosarium.

In a similar vein, Jaufré laments, "a base man in rich clothing looks good on the outside, but on the inside he's totally corrupt and stuffed with dishonesty [...] so puffed up with it he can't keep it all inside, and it has shown up on the outside."[49] The beautiful house never really existed. Instead it was an illusion, one that ultimately could not contain the wrongdoings of those who lived in it. The

---

42 Brunel, *Jaufré*, l. 2297; Arthur, *Jaufre*, 45.
43 Brunel, *Jaufré*, ll. 2706–12; Arthur, *Jaufre*, 51.
44 Brunel, *Jaufré*, ll. 2720–21, 2749–52; Arthur, *Jaufre*, 52.
45 I have rehabilitated this expression from Saul Brody, *The Disease of the Soul: Leprosy in Medieval Literature* (Ithaca: Cornell University Press, 1974), 133–38.
46 *Decrees of the Ecumenical Councils*, 245–46.
47 Farmer, "The Leper in the Master," 84–85.
48 Julie Orlemanski, "How to Kiss a Leper," *Postmedieval* 3 (2012): 142–57 at 143–51.
49 Brunel, *Jaufré*, 92–93; Arthur, *Jaufre*, 50.

idea of one's actions having a physical manifestation is also echoed in the *Partidas*.

Treason is framed as "so wicked that they compared it to leprosy; for just [like] leprosy [it] is a disease which attacks the entire body, and after it had once been contracted cannot be removed or treated by medicines."[50] Just as lepers were marked by their sores, so too were the individuals who betrayed their king. The preamble warns that treason affected, or corrupted, not only the perpetrators, but also those who came into contact with them, in a manner akin to the spread of a disease.[51] This hinted at the contagious nature of leprosy, a concept put forth by Ibn Sina, also known as Avicenna (ca. 980–1037) in his *Canons*, which would have been known to physicians in Castile. Despite a Latin translation of the Arabic text being available from 1187, it was not until the late fourteenth century that the benefits of segregation were discussed.[52] In both cases, there is a push for exclusion not because of leprosy as a disease, but because these people committed an action so villainous that it manifested and impacted those around them in the same way leprosy did those who were proven to be lepers.

Moreover, throughout Jaufré's interaction with the lepers, including the narrator's interruption, there is not a single mention of concerns about contagion. The battle between the knight and the giant leper is bloody and yet neither Jaufré nor the narrator express any fear that the hero may contract the disease, nor does this seem to be an issue for the maiden, who was sexually assaulted, or the children who were being held hostage at the house. It is true that women were believed to be immune, likely due to the uterus being considered a cold, hard organ, but their sexual partners were not similarly protected.[53] The characters do not fear infection because they are victims of corrupted individuals. Jaufré is only afraid of the first leper because of his appearance and the fact that he has a very large club that he uses to incapacitate the hero. There is, however, a modicum of plausibility to the story, as the giant leper, who is described in visceral detail as having "gnarled arms and puffy hands, crooked teeth and stinking gums, a face covered with monstrous swellings [...] dark menacing pupils, staring, bloodshot eyes surrounded by red," exhibits the hallmarks of leprosy.[54] In

---

50 *Partidas*, vol. 3, 540; Burns, *Partidas*, vol. 5, 1318.
51 Burns, *Partidas*, vol. 5, 1318.
52 Touati, "Contagion and Leprosy," 194–97.
53 Brenner, *Leprosy and Charity*, 61–62.
54 "E d'espatlas doas brassadas,/ Gros los brasses e mans enfladas,/ Els dentz corbs e totz desnozatz,/ E fu per la cara bosatz ... E ac las prunelas escuras,/ Els ueils trebles e grepellatz,/ tot entorn de vermeil orlatz," Brunel, *Jaufré*, ll. 2315–18, 2322–24; Arthur, *Jaufre*, 45. The whole

truth, it would have been difficult for someone at this stage of the illness to attack anyone, never mind a trained knight. The description serves to highlight Jaufré's goodness as a hero and justify him killing a sick person; just as the sweet smell was a reward for Theobald, whose piety allowed him to "endure" the smell and sight of a leper. In contrast though, the leper in the exemplum is not there as a foil for the count, rather as a token of his virtuousness.

The exclusion seen in these literary sources should not be taken at face value. The lepers in both *Jaufré* and the exemplum are metaphorical and their disease served either as a warning or to highlight the goodness of other characters. By employing the trope of spiritual leprosy, the authors warned their audience that without immediate intervention their actions—be it murder or treason —would corrupt them and those around them. When someone was proven a leper, their status changed, much like in the case of those who chose to take the veil. They remained tethered to their city through their families and their newfound role as "tame" lepers. In this way, they were expected to live in separate communities that were accessible and visible, even though they were located beyond the city's walls.

Lepers and the Wider Community

The regulations concerning freedom of movement and the protection of lepers and leprosaria were intrinsically linked. We know from the Third Lateran Council that lepers were entitled to their own priests and churches, and exempt from paying tithes on their gardens and animals.[55] It is still unclear why Pope Alexander III took such an interest in the condition of lepers, but he was particularly concerned about their access to *viaticum*—that is, the Eucharist administered as part of Extreme Unction—which led to the composition of Canon 23.[56]

However, lepers were not necessarily required to join a leprosarium: in some contexts, this was intended to be a choice. That said, lepers who had no family would have had little recourse but to enter one of these houses, especially as their illness took a toll on their bodies resulting in the need for palliative care, which was only available in a leprosarium. The *Partidas* clearly illustrate these circumstances. Married lepers, along with other sick or disabled persons, were

---

manuscript is beautifully illustrated, see Bibliothèque nationale de France, MS Français 2164, fols. 27r – 36r (https://archivesetmanuscrits.bnf.fr/ark:/12148/cc48716h).
55 *Decrees of the Ecumenical Councils*, 222 – 23.
56 Joseph Avril, "Le IIIe concile du Latran et les communautés de lépreux," *Revue Mabillion* 40 (1981): 21 – 76 at 32 – 35.

permitted to remain in their homes because marriage vows superseded concerns about infection. This directly echoes Pope Alexander III's decretals regarding leprosy and marriage, in which he, writing to Richard, Archbishop of Canterbury, in the wake of the Council of Westminster in 1175, reasoned that marriage vows remained valid regardless of illness. He even went so far as to recommend abstinence (*vivente continentiam*) should a spouse be unable to fulfil their conjugal obligations.[57] It should be noted that while the *Partidas* did not view leprosy as grounds to dissolve a marriage, it was a reason to break a betrothal contract.[58]

Much in the same way that lepers existed within fixed categories, so too did sex, at least in regard to the fourth book of the *Partidas*. Marriage involved consent given by two sane and healthy people, as advocated by Peter Lombard, Bishop of Paris,[59] or sealed through intercourse, as prescribed by Gratian. Alexander III merged these two ideas, arguing that marriage could only be dissolved if it remained unconsummated.[60] The idea was that spouses became one, a notion that is reinforced by the text, wherein the married coupled were "serien amos como una carne" (they are like one flesh) just as Eve was made from Adam.[61]

Spouses were prohibited from "deserting" (*desamparar*) their partner. Lepers were allowed to move into another room in the house, but the healthy partner was expected to be their care giver and comply with marital obligations, including having sex.[62] Should a spouse end up in a leprosarium, then their partner was required to go and care for them. Any children that resulted from the union, prior to the illness, were to remain with the healthy parent to prevent exposure. Finally, they could not take religious vows if they still engaged in "carnal intercourse" (*allegados en uno carnalmiente*), or unilaterally decide to enter into a chaste marriage.[63] In the *Coutumes*, family only mattered if the individual was

---

57 *Corpus Iuris Canonici: Editio Lipsiensis secunda post Aemilii Ludouici Richteri*, ed. Aemilius Friedberg (Graz: Akademische Druck- u. Verlagsanstalt, 1959), 691; Philip Jaffé, *Regesta Pontificum Romanorum*, vol. 2 (Graz: Akademische Druck- u. Verlagsanstalt, 1956), 13794; Bolton, "The Absentee Lord?," 177.
58 *Partidas*, vol. 3, 7; Burns, *Partidas*, vol. 4, 883.
59 Peter Lombard, *Liber IV Sententiarum*, vol. 2 (Florence: Ex Typographia Collegii S. Bonaventurae, 1916), 917–18.
60 Marilyn Stone, *Marriage and Friendship in Medieval Spain: Social Relations According to the Fourth Partida of Alfonso X* (New York: Peter Lang, 1990), 43.
61 *Partidas*, vol. 3, 13; Burns, *Partidas*, vol. 4, 887; Esteban Martínez Marcos, *Las causas matrimoniales en Las Partidas de Alfonso el Sabio* (Salamanca: Consejo Superior de Investigacíones Cientificas, 1966), 71; Stone, *Marriage and Friendship*, 43.
62 *Partidas*, vol. 3, 15; Burns, *Partidas*, vol. 4, 889.
63 Ibid.

illegitimate, one of the spouses was a foreigner, or in times of war. This meant that lepers were exempt from taking part in wars between families, and the opposing side could not use the ensuing conflict as an excuse to hurt them.[64] Neither the *Coutumes* nor the *Constituto* allowed lepers to physically remain with their kin, while in the *Partidas* lepers, despite their changed status, still belonged to and were protected by their family.

The Voice of the Leper

This chapter has discussed the religious and legal conceptualisation of lepers, but what did they have to say for themselves? Sadly, outside of being given a voice as literary characters or allegories, they are rarely heard. Very few, if any, narrative sources focusing on lepers were produced during the thirteenth century; they often appeared in hagiographies as background actors with very little agency. Conversely, normative sources provide a sterile understanding of their experience, although they do offer a glimpse into the lives of those who chose to enter a leprosarium. That is not to say we do not have instances of lepers speaking for themselves; however, these are rare and often speak to us through intermediaries, namely representatives or the indirectness of administrative documents.

The presence or, more likely, the absence, of the leper's voice is apparent in all these texts. In the case of *Jaufré*, lepers can speak. For instance, the one wielding the menacing club is described as having a "voice so hoarse that he could barely speak."[65] In contrast, when the third leper begs Jaufré for mercy, there is no comment on his voice. He speaks like any penitent man; however, when the time comes for him to recount his encounter to King Arthur he is not even mentioned and the maiden is the only one who speaks.[66] The bacterium that causes leprosy often damages the vocal cords, which left the afflicted with rough or raspy voices. This is why we see depictions of lepers with clappers or bells. These tools were intended to speak for the sick, so that the healthy could hear them and seek them out to give them alms.[67] This is clear in the *Con-*

---

[64] Salmon, *Coutumes*, vol. 2, 364; Akehurst, *Coutumes*, 617.
[65] "El polset, e fo rauculos/ Si qe a penas pot parlar," Brunel, *Jaufré*, ll. 2332–33; Arthur, *Jaufre*, 45.
[66] Brunel, *Jaufré*, ll. 2927–98; Arthur, *Jaufre*, 55–56.
[67] Rawcliffe, *Leprosy in Medieval England*, 14, 199; Touati, "Contagion and Leprosy," 184–85. See also: Luke Demaitre, "The Clapper as 'vox miselli': New Perspectives on Iconography," in *Leprosy and Identity in the Middle Ages: From England to the Mediterranean*, ed. Elma Brenner and François-Olivier Touati (Manchester: Manchester University Press, 2021).

stituto of Siena, wherein the Commune mandates that the lepers who live at San Lazaro be permitted to use a bell when they are within the city walls. No other leper was allowed to ring a bell.[68] The *Coutumes* in turn forbade them from testifying because "they should be excluded from conversation with other people." Additionally, lepers could use their status to say they were beyond *la loi mondaine* (secular law) in order to avoid a "wager of battle" (*gages*); conversely, if a leper asked for *gages* then their healthy opponent could deny them due to their illness.[69] That said, bastards, serfs, individuals suffering from mental illness or intellectual disabilities, persons who intended to harm the defendant, and women—with the exception of cases regarding childbirth—were also banned from testifying.[70] It is clear from this list that membership in society was rather restrictive, with only legitimate, able-bodied men being afforded all legal rights, including a voice.

As for Vitry's exemplum, the purpose of the voice of the leper in Theobald's story is twofold: it serves to reinforce the image of the count as a holy and charitable man, as well as an outlet for Christ's approval. The leper's voice is not his own, but is co-opted in order to glorify Theobald. He only speaks after he is dead, and has consequently found freedom from his illness, saying "Well, by the grace of God never was I better."[71] Perhaps this is a cynical view, but the sick man only serves to reinforce the idea that lepers, by virtue of their status as intercessors, only exist in some capacity to benefit the healthy. Similarly, in the exemplum involving a leper and a married woman, the leper speaks once, in order to gain entry to her home, "[b]ehold, the heat of the sun is torturing me; I can't eat or drink or receive any service unless you bring me inside." His suffering is meant to play on her compassion—for her husband "abhors" lepers—as well as to highlight the corporal acts of mercy. She is the only one who can relieve his pain, and he is a tool for her own salvation, which culminates in the leper disappearing and leaving behind a sweet smell. The result of the whole interaction leads the husband to mirror his wife's pious lifestyle.[72] Beaumanoir makes this clear when he notes that leprosaria were created to serve the "public good of towns" (*le commun pourfit des viles*).[73] The *Partidas*, however, allude to the sick having a say in the manner in which they deal with their

---

[68] *Il Constituto del Comune*, 51.
[69] Salmon, *Coutumes*, vol. 2, 420; Akehurst, *Coutumes*, 665.
[70] "qu'il soient debouté de la conversacion d'autre gens," Salmon, *Coutumes*, vol. 2, 107–8; Akehurst, *Coutumes*, 426–27.
[71] Translation in Crane, *The Exempla or Illustrative*, 174.
[72] Translations in Farmer, "The Leper in the Master," 81–82.
[73] Salmon, *Coutumes*, vol. 2, 328; Akehurst, *Coutumes*, 590.

illness, which also appears in the *Constituto*. Nevertheless, in terms of their actual voices these texts remain silent.

Conclusion

We should not take the idea of the exclusion of lepers at face value. The norms fostered by the Third Lateran Council are sown throughout these five works, which exhibit signs of a binary categorisation of lepers. That is not to say that the concept of "leper" was not multifaceted, but there is a clear through line that suggests that lepers who conformed to the norms were rewarded with the municipality's or the king's protection and care. The sources presented here are a diverse grouping with a wide array of audiences, nonetheless their representation of lepers remains largely consistent. The *Coutumes* and the *Constituto* provided practical legislation for governing lepers, whereas the *Partidas*, which were also heavily influenced by Roman and canon law, extended similar protections to lepers by regulating their conduct within the context of marriage. Vitry's exemplum reinforces the role of lepers as intercessors, by rewarding Theobald's charity with a divine encounter. All of the works discussed here continue to challenge the exclusion narrative, even *Jaufré*, which uses the visuality of leprosy to warn of the dangers of vice while also showing that there was always an opportunity to return to a virtuous path. For the most part, whereas the sick portrayed in these texts are "tame" lepers with family or ties to the locality, "wild" lepers are outsiders who posed a risk to others by travelling and existing outside the community of their peers. The inclusion of lepers in literary and legal texts demonstrates their importance within the social fabric of medieval Europe.

Angana Moitra
Chapter 11
On the Margins of Society: Exclusion through Exile as a Structuring Motif in *Sir Orfeo*

Medieval romance narratives are typically associated with the primary foundational motif of the quest. The brave and industrious knightly hero sets forth on a journey, prompted either by the need to successfully perform a task assigned by a superior (who may be another, more senior knight, a feudal lord, or even the king himself), as a response to a challenge devised by an opponent, as a concrete realisation of the chivalric ethos of proving one's mettle, or, as one of the most programmatic agents of causation, in order to rescue and retrieve a purloined object of great value or an individual (typically the heroine) who has been abducted.[1] The motif of the quest tethers this act of venturing forth and functions as the catalyst which sparks the series of adventures that usually lend momentum to the romance narrative. There is, however, yet another motif which, although it paradoxically temporarily arrests the narrative's trajectory of motion, nonetheless contributes crucially to the wider thematic and hermeneutic framework of the romance text: the motif of exile. Although Erich Auerbach has observed that the fundamental organising principle of the romance is the creation of a chivalric world predicated upon "a practically uninterrupted series of adventures," it is also important to bear in mind that episodes which revolve around the temporary cessation of such adventures are also crucial to the plot.[2] The trope of exile thematises the hero's disengagement from the ordinary rhythms of heroic life and the normal cycles of knightly activity. The exilic state, which enacts the hero's removal from the centre to the margins of society, can be either an imposition or a voluntary decision and is typically intimately involved with the arc of self-amelioration, moral improvement, and spiritual

---

[1] For a brief discussion of the standard literary motifs adopted by romance authors, see Corinne Saunders, "Introduction," in *A Companion to Romance: From Classical to Contemporary*, ed. Corinne Saunders (Oxford: Blackwell, 2004), 1–10 at 1–4, and Helen Cooper, "Quest and Pilgrimage: 'The adventure that God shall send me'," in *The English Romance in Time: Transforming Motifs from Geoffrey of Monmouth to the Death of Shakespeare* (Oxford: Oxford University Press, 2003), 45–105.
[2] Erich Auerbach, "The Knight Sets Forth," in *Mimesis: The Representation of Reality in Western Literature* (Princeton: Princeton University Press, 2003), 123–42 at 136.

growth which is a hallmark of the hero's development of character. The rigours of exile function simultaneously as a test of the hero's endurance and fortitude as well as a ritual of purification whereby the hero is stripped (both physically and mentally) of the trappings of worldly attachment, bodily longing, and the extraneous markings of social and communal life. Freed from the earthly bonds which fetter and constrain human existence, the hero can come to terms with himself and with the things that really matter. In the fourteenth-century Middle English romance *Sir Orfeo*, the trope of exile acts as an episodic fleshing-out of the protagonist's journey of self-improvement. However, the romance's treatment of exile is interesting because although a self-willed act, it is provoked not by personal transgression on the part of the hero but by an external act of persecution engendered by, and upon, secondary characters. Orfeo exiles himself to the wilderness following the abduction of his wife Heurodis by the sinister and threatening Fairy King, and the hero's experience of exile appears at the median point of the narrative. *Sir Orfeo*'s episode of exile is thus both literally and figuratively central. Positioned at the central cusp of plot complication and narrative resolution, the episode lends symmetry to the structure of the text, and as an indispensable part of Orfeo's pattern of character development, the trope of exile adds semiotic meaning to wider thematic concerns of the romance. It is to an examination of the ways in which the trope of exile works in the poem that this essay is devoted.[3]

The Romance of *Sir Orfeo*

Sir Orfeo is a medieval retelling in verse of the classical story of Orpheus, and the romance is currently extant in three manuscripts (Auchinleck MS Advocates' 19.2.1, Harley MS 3810, and Ashmole MS 61) of which the version contained in the Auchinleck manuscript, presently housed in the National Library of Scot-

---

[3] The trope of exile in *Sir Orfeo* has been examined by scholars before, most significantly in Kenneth R. R. Gros-Louis, "The Significance of Sir Orfeo's Self-Exile," *Review of English Studies* 18/71 (1967): 245–52. Although I am largely in agreement with Gros-Louis's reading, I do feel that he has a tendency to somewhat overstate the sentimental import of Orfeo's state of exile, viewing the king's decision as a conscious "sacrifice." In my reading of the poem, the motif of exile is simultaneously consistent with the testing mechanism frequently employed by medieval romances to demonstrate the worth of the hero as well as a tool of narrative structuring that balances the two halves of the poem; it has, that is, both an ontological as well as a structural function.

land, seems to be the earliest and the most complete.⁴ The Middle English *Sir Orfeo* is believed to have descended from an Old French or Anglo-Norman intermediary which was itself a translation of the *Lai d'Orphey*, a Breton lay which is no longer extant but references to which have been found in three other works: *Le Conte de Floire et Blanchefleur*, the *Lai de l'Espine*, and the *Prose Lancelot*.⁵ The term "Breton lay" is applied to poetic works produced between approximately 1150 and 1450 which claim to be literary versions of lays sung by ancient Bretons usually to the accompaniment of the harp.⁶ The credit for codifying the genre goes to the twelfth-century Anglo-Norman writer Marie de France who composed twelve lays as a sort of tribute to the Breton tradition of musical storytelling. The lays of Marie de France typically catered to a multilingual, aristocratic audience, were usually set in Brittany, Wales, or Normandy, and dealt with

---

4 The Auchinleck MS is believed to have been compiled around 1330–1340, whereas the versions of the poem belonging to the Harley and the Ashmole MSS are conjecturally dated to the early and late fifteenth century respectively. For more information about the Auchinleck MS, see the introduction by Derek Pearsall and I. C. Cunningham in *The Auchinleck Manuscript: National Library of Scotland Advocates' MS. 19.2.1* (London: Scholar Press, 1977).

5 The standard textual history of *Sir Orfeo* is usually taken to be Alan J. Bliss's work on the romance, and it is he who contends that the Middle English *Orfeo* is a derivative text, based on an Old French/Anglo-Norman intermediary text. For an iteration of these views, see Alan J. Bliss, "Introduction," in *Sir Orfeo*, ed. Alan J. Bliss, 2nd ed. (Oxford: Clarendon Press, 1966), ix–li. Recent research conducted by Patrick Joseph Schwieterman has, however, modified Bliss's conclusions, positing that the Middle English *Sir Orfeo* was not so much a translation (through an intermediary) of a now-lost Breton lay as a conscious literary endeavour written in response to references to the *Lai d'Orphey* (itself the product of a collaborative literary fiction rather than an actual text which formerly existed) contained in other works. Schwieterman has also argued that the Harley and Ashmole texts of the poem derive from a common antecedent copied from the Auchinleck version after its prologue had been excised. For a detailed discussion, see Patrick Joseph Schwietermann, "Fairies, Kingship, and the British Past in Walter Map's *De Nugis Curialium* and *Sir Orfeo*" (PhD diss., University of California, Berkeley, 2010), 32–119.

6 For a more detailed discussion of the Breton lay, its form and literary conventions, and the cultural context within which it flourished, see Anne Laskaya and Eve Salisbury, "General Introduction," in *The Middle English Breton Lays*, ed. Anne Laskaya and Eve Salisbury (Kalamazoo: Medieval Institute Publications, 1995), 1–8, http://d.lib.rochester.edu/teams/text/laskaya-and-salisbury-middle-english-breton-lays-general-introduction. A thorough recent examination of the structure of the Breton lay, its interconnections with the genre of romance, as well as a study of the common motifs that characterise it is the subject of Claire Vial, *"There and Back Again": The Middle English Breton Lays, A Journey Through Uncertainties* (Paris: Presses Universitaires de France, 2013). The nomenclature is, however, not without its problems, especially since critics continue to debate what is exactly meant by the constituent terms "Breton" and "lay." For an overview of these problems, see the introduction in Leah Jean Larson, "Love, Troth and Magnanimity: The *Weltanschauung* of the Breton Lay from Marie de France to Chaucer" (PhD diss., University of Southwestern Louisiana, 1996).

themes of courtesy, chivalry, and courtly love. Old French imitations of Marie's lays probably influenced the composition of the Middle English lays usually regarded as belonging to the generic framework of the Breton lay. These lays, which include (apart from *Sir Orfeo*) *Sir Degaré, Lay le Freine, Erle of Tolouse, Emaré, Sir Gowther,* and *Sir Launfal*, are all believed to have been composed between the late thirteenth or early fourteenth and the early fifteenth century.

The narrative trajectory of *Sir Orfeo* is simple and straightforward: Orfeo is the king of Winchester and his court is presented as an idyllic political landscape where both ruler and ruled, lord and subject are united by bonds of harmony, concord, and felicity. The happiness of the kingdom is, however, marred by a personal tragedy when Orfeo's beloved wife Heurodis is abducted on a balmy May morning by the tyrannous and diabolical King of the Fairies. Heartbroken at the loss of his queen, an inconsolable Orfeo withdraws from society and exiles himself to the woods where he spends ten years in a state of penitent contrition. One morning, Orfeo comes across a lavish hunting party and is astonished to find Heurodis as part of the company. Determined to ascertain the whereabouts of his kidnapped wife, he follows the group through an opening in the hillside to discover that he has entered Fairyland, the nefarious domain of the Fairy King, whose glittering exterior seems to belie an unsettling and horrifying reality. Adopting the disguise of a minstrel, Orfeo is granted access to the Fairy King's palace where he surveys with mute horror the gallery of the Fairy King's former victims, a grisly exhibition of tortured bodies in suspended animation. Upon meeting the Fairy King, Orfeo offers to entertain him with the music of his harp and when the king, well pleased with Orfeo's musical artistry asks him what he would like as his reward, requests that his wife be returned to him. The Fairy King reluctantly agrees, and Orfeo returns with Heurodis to Winchester where, following Orfeo's test of the fidelity of the steward upon whom he had entrusted the administration of his kingdom during his exile, the conventional happy ending of the romance takes place as the English court celebrates the homecoming of its king and queen.

Volition in Orfeo's Exile

Orfeo's self-imposed exile is of vital importance since it serves as a preparatory interlude before the poet can initiate the final chain of events which will culminate in Orfeo's successful recovery of Heurodis. This voluntary abdication is directly provoked by the abduction of the queen by the Fairy King, and although it is an immediate, emotionally involved, and affective response, it is not a knee-jerk reaction but rather one which is well thought out. Orfeo will quit his kingdom to live the life of a hermit, but not before he has made arrangements to ensure the smooth functioning of the court in his absence:

> He cleped to-gider his barouns,
> Erls, lordes of renouns,
> & when þai al y-comen were,
> "Lordinges," he said, "Bifor 30u here
> Ich ordainy min hei3e steward
> To wite mi kingdom afterward;
> In mi stede ben he schal
> To kepe mi londes ouer-al,
> For now ichaue mi quen y-lore,
> Þe fairest leuedi þat euer was bore,
> Neuer eft y nil no woman se.
> In-to wilderness ichil te,
> & liue þer euermore
> Wiþ wilde bestes in holtes hore;
> & when 3e vnder-stond þat y be spent,
> Make 3ou þan a parlement,
> & chese 3ou a newe king
> —Now doþ 3our best wiþ al mi þinge."
>
> [He called together his barons, earls, and lords of renown, and when they had all gathered, he said, "Lords, before you here I ordain my steward to rule the kingdom in my absence; in my place he shall administer all the lands, for now that I have lost my queen, the fairest lady that ever was born, I shall never again see another woman. I will go to the wilderness and live there evermore with the wild beasts in the grey woods, and when you understand that I have passed away, summon a parliament and choose a new king—now do the best you can with all my possessions."][7]

While it is certainly true that, unlike the conventional knightly hero of romance, Orfeo does not embark upon a quest to seek Heurodis, choosing the life of a pariah instead, it is nevertheless important to note that this decision is not imposed but very clearly self-willed.[8] Orfeo's choice of exile also reveals another aspect of

---

7 Bliss, *Sir Orfeo*, 19–20, ll. 201–18. All subsequent references are to this edition by line number. The excerpts quoted are drawn from the Auchinleck text. All translations of quoted passages are my own. In my translation, I have aimed at capturing the essence of the words and the overall meaning conveyed. It is, thus, a loose translation rather than one which is scholarly rigorous and metrically consistent.

8 The quest was a characteristic extension of the code of chivalry upon which much romantic literature was based. This ideology, which was predicated upon a codification of behaviour and comportment proper to a knight, developed in tandem with the elaboration of the code of *fin' amor* or courtly love which prescribed the rules to be observed during interpersonal interactions between aristocratic men and women. Accordingly, romance representations of the quest fre-

his character: his steadfastness and single-minded pertinacity. Despite the anguished cries and protestations of his subjects and the royal household imploring him to revoke his decision, Orfeo is not dissuaded; his iron will cannot be overturned, and he alone must bear the burden of his self-imposed banishment:

> Þo was þer wepeing in þe halle,
> & grete cri among hem alle:
> Vnneþe miʒt old or ʒong
> For wepeing speke a word wiþ tong.
> Þai kneled adoun al y-fere
> & praid him, ʒif his wille were,
> þat he schuld nouʒt fram hem go
> —"Do way!" quaþ he, "It schal be so!"
> Al his kingdom he for-soke,
> Bot a sclauin on him he toke.
> He no hadde kirtel no hode,
> Schert, [no] no noþer gode,
> Bot his harp he tok algate
> & dede him barfot out atte ʒate;
> No man most wiþ him go. (ll. 219–33)

[Then there was much weeping and crying in the hall, so much so that both old and young could scarcely speak a word for it. They kneeled down before him and begged him that, should it be his will, he should not go away from them. "Stop!" exclaimed Orfeo, "I shall do as I have determined!" He departed from his kingdom, renouncing everything save a pilgrim's mantle which he took with him. He took with him no coat or hood, no shirt nor any other article of clothing or possession except his harp. Proceeding barefoot out of the palace gate, Orfeo embarked upon his exile alone—no man might go with him.]

Orfeo is not only willing to embrace the life of exile but is also resolute in his determination to see it through. This perseverance will help him in the future when he makes up his mind to seek his wife and win her back by following

---

quently took the form of attempts by the knight to secure the affections of the lady and to safeguard her from harm, especially in cases of abduction of the heroine. Given Arthurian literature's particular affinity for the chivalry-courtly love complex, knights of Arthur's court were typically given to undertaking such quests, of which the most programmatic was that of the hero Lancelot. For a succinct summary of these relations, see Robert Rouse, "Historical Context: The Middle Ages and the Code of Chivalry," in *Handbook of Arthurian Romance: King Arthur's Court in Medieval European Literature*, ed. Leah Tether and Johnny McFadyen (Berlin: De Gruyter, 2017), 13–24. For a detailed overview of the sociohistorical milieu that informed the processes through which the chivalric code and courtly love dovetailed with each other, see Richard W. Kaeuper, "Knights, Ladies, and Love," in *Chivalry and Violence in Medieval Europe* (New York: Oxford University Press, 1999), 209–30.

the fairy train of hunting women.⁹ Calling the narrative arc featuring Orfeo's exile the "subplot," Mary Hynes-Berry has argued in favour of reading Orfeo's autonomy in a positive light and the motif of exile as the pivotal arena where negative determination—unsuccessfully seeking to prevent Heurodis's abduction through military fortification, surrendering the kingdom to the hands of his appointed delegate—turns to positive resolution—Orfeo's decision to follow the hunting party—which eventually leads to restoration.¹⁰

Exile as a Narrative Motif: Provenance and Deployment

Exile, writes Robert Edwards, "means separation, banishment, withdrawal, expatriation, and displacement; its emotional expression is loss, usually manifested as sorrow, sometimes as nostalgia"; it is a break "not simply with space or location but with the cultural and social continuities of place and with a collective history."¹¹ The reality of exile was often encountered in the classical world, where it was a part of the civic emphasis of a republican state, a kind of imperial adjudication to punish transgressors and dissidents. Within the purview of Christian thought, however, exile took on a more spiritual significance. The scriptural imagination refashioned exile from a legal edict issued by royal authority to an

---

9 Anna Elizabeth Dow offers an interesting explanation for Orfeo's decision to exile himself. According to her, Orfeo recognises the liminal nature of both the fairy otherworld as well as the space of the wilderness itself and consequently comes to the conclusion that his best chance of retrieving his wife is to sequester himself in the forest. The forest as a space of alterity is thus both literally and metaphorically "marginal"; to quote Dow, "whilst Orfeo remains in the forest he becomes part of the marginal landscape, and his integration into that transitional space draws him closer to the faerie otherworld." See Anna Elizabeth Dow, "Distorted Boundaries: The Marginal Spaces of the Preternatural in *King Horn* and *Sir Orfeo*" (Master's thesis, University of Alberta, 2012), 65.
10 Mary Hynes-Berry, "Cohesion in *King Horn* and *Sir Orfeo*," *Speculum* 50/4 (1975): 652–70 at 664. Unlike Hynes-Berry, however, I see the episode of exile as belonging quite definitively to the main plot of the romance (insofar as divisions typically characteristic of dramatic works can be applied to a verse romance). Structurally positioned after the complication (Heurodis's abduction) and just prior to the dénouement (Orfeo's confrontation with the Fairy King) and the resolution (retrieval of Heurodis and return to Winchester), the episode of exile furnishes the ground of character growth that is fundamental both to romance's generic project of effecting the hero's intellectual, spiritual, and ethical advancement as well as to the establishment of the setting within which the climactic phase (the successful rescue mission) can be achieved.
11 Robert Edwards, "Exile, Self, and Society," in *Exile in Literature*, ed. María-Inés Lagos-Pope (London: Associated University Presses, 1988), 15–31 at 15–16.

interiorised condition of being, a state of mind associated with the denial of the self and the rewards of renunciation promised by Christ to his disciples. Viewed this way, exile can be an act of volition, consciously chosen and deliberately adopted; as Edwards remarks, "Exile can also involve withdrawal as a means to gain or learn something, and such retreat is often the prelude to change."[12] The motif of exile played a prominent part in the literature of Anglo-Saxon England, a literature which, perhaps by virtue of being produced in an insular environment geographically separated from continental Europe, frequently dealt with themes of loss, abandonment, mutability, and transience.[13] Contemporary historical and political circumstances are equally likely to have influenced the development of the trope of exile (together with its concomitant motif in romance, the return). Rosalind Field has persuasively argued that the exile-and-return trope enjoyed its heyday in literary works that post-dated the Norman Conquest, a phenomenon that could be explained as an offshoot of both the cultural reorganisation of society in the feudal pattern as well as the establishment (and subsequent enforcement) of the law of primogeniture which accorded supreme importance to agnatic succession.[14] It is within this sociocultural and literary context that Orfeo's exile should be read.

The *Orfeo*-poet provides a poignant description of the rigours of exile, employing a combination of repetition and contrast to highlight the drastic change in Orfeo's fortunes, an account which is all the more moving in view of the fact

---

12 Edwards, "Exile, Self, and Society," 18.
13 For a discussion of Anglo-Saxon attitudes towards their own insularity, see Daniel Anlezark, "The Anglo-Saxon World View," in *The Cambridge Companion to Old English Literature*, ed. Malcolm Godden and Michael Lapidge (Cambridge: Cambridge University Press, 2013), 66–81, and Christine Fell, "Perceptions of Transience," in *The Cambridge Companion to Old*, 180–97.
14 Rosalind Field, "The King Over the Water: Exile-and-Return Revisited," in *Cultural Encounters in the Romance of Medieval England*, ed. Corinne Saunders (Cambridge: D. S. Brewer, 2005), 41–53. See also Liliana Worth, "'Exile-and-Return' in Medieval Vernacular Texts of England and Spain ca. 1170–1250" (PhD diss., University of Oxford, 2015). Laura Ashe has, however, argued that the roots of this influence can be traced not only to the Norman Conquest but further back to historical developments (and their literary representations) that occurred in Anglo-Saxon England. See Laura Ashe, "'Exile-and-return' and English Law: The Anglo-Saxon Inheritance of Insular Romance," *Literature Compass* 3/3 (2006): 300–17. Talking specifically about the exile episode in *Orfeo*, Dominique Battles shares a similar line of argument in reading the trope of exile as belonging to a distinctively Anglo-Saxon heritage. In fact, Battles goes further to contend that the motif of exile highlights conflicting attitudes between Orfeo and the Fairy King apropos of their treatment of the exilic space of the wilderness, whereby Orfeo's attitude is reminiscent of a pre-Conquest "Anglo-Saxon" mentality while the Fairy King's attitude is evocative of a post-Conquest "Norman" context. For an illustration of these views, see Dominique Battles, "*Sir Orfeo* and English Identity," *Studies in Philology* 107/2 (2010): 179–211 at 196–204.

that this is an experience not inevitable but entirely discretionary. Orfeo's exilic state is marked throughout by absence, not only of marital companionship and the sense of *communitas* which binds society together, but also of past comforts and the luxuries of royal living. His only link to his former existence is through a material object, the harp, an instrument he is particularly adept at playing. This somewhat long section merits quoting in full:

 Þurth wode & ouer heþ
 In-to þe wildernes he geþ.
 Noþing he fint þat him is ays,
 Bot euer he lieuþ in gret malais.
 He þat hadde y-werd þe fowe & griis,
 & on bed þe purper biis
 —Now on hard heþe he liþ,
 Wiþ leues & grasse he him wriþ.
 He þat hadde had castels & tours,
 Riuer, forest, friþ wiþ flours
 —Now, þei it comenci to snewe & frees,
 Þis king mot make his bed in mese.
 He þat had y-had kniʒtes of priis
 Bifor him kneland, & leuedis
 —Now seþ he no-þing þat him likeþ,
 Bot wilde wormes bi him strikeþ.
 He þat had y-had plenté
 Of mete & drink, of ich deynté
 —Now may he al-day digge & wrote
 Er he finde his fille of rote.
 In somer he lieuþ bi wild frut,
 & berien bot gode lite;
 In winter may he no-þing finde
 Bot rote, grases, & þe rinde.
 Al his bodi was oway duine
 For missays, and al to-chine.
 Lord! who may telle þe sore
 Þis king sufferd ten ʒere & more?
 His here of his berd, blac & rowe,
 To his girdle-stede was growe.
 His harp, where-on was al his gle,
 He hidde in an holwe tre,
 & when þe weder was clere & briʒt
 He toke his harp to him wel riʒt
 & harped at his owhen wille.
 In-to alle þe wode þe soun gan schille,
 Þat alle þe wilde bestes þat þer beþ
 For ioie abouten him þai teþ,
 & alle þe foules þat þer were

> Come & sete on ich a brere,
> To here his harping a-fine
> —So miche melody was þer-in;
> & when he his harping lete wold,
> No best bi him abide nold. (ll. 237–280)

[Through wood and over heath he went into the wilderness. He did not find anything to comfort him but lived in great malaise. He who had worn variegated furs and lain on beds of fine purple linen, now lay on hard ground wrapped only in grass and leaves. He who had had castles and towers, rivers, forests, and woodlands with flowers in bloom, now made his bed on moss when it began to snow and the ground to freeze. He who had had knights of renown kneeling before him and ladies of worth, now found nothing of value except wild worms which crawled about him. He who had had food and drink in plenty would now dig and grub all day before he could find his fill of wild root. In the summer he lived on wild fruits and a few berries, but in winter he would find nothing except roots, grass, and husk. His body began to waste away from the discomfort and he was shrivelled and broken. Lord! Who may tell the misfortunes this king suffered for ten years and more? The hair of his beard, black and rough, had grown to his girdle. His harp, on which was bestowed all his happiness and glee, was sheltered in the hollow of a tree, and when the weather was clear and bright, he took his harp and played it at his own will. The sound would resound shrilly throughout the woods, and all the beasts would approach him in joy and all the birds would nestle on the branches and twigs to hear his harping—such melody was there in it. And when he would cease harping, no beast would abide by him.]

The privations suffered by the romance hero through his estrangement (voluntary or otherwise) from society and/or his former mode of life are in keeping with the narrative requirements of the genre.[15] This alienation is imperative to bringing about the final return which typically concludes the narrative arc of the romance since this trope becomes the arena in which important, life-altering lessons are learnt and fundamental changes are wrought in the personality and psychological make-up of the protagonist.[16] The motif of alienation-through-

---

[15] Helen Cooper sees such suffering as a necessary prelude to expiation and regards it as a characteristic trait of what she terms the "romance of atonement." The suffering was necessary for the knight to atone for past failings, a motif which could be construed as a literary embodiment both of the Church's emphasis on the forgiveness of sin as well as the sacramental nature of penance itself (viewed as a tangible outward expression of an inward, invisible grace). See Cooper, *The English Romance in Time*, 86–90. I shall have more to say on the religious overtones of this motif shortly.

[16] The separation of the hero from his familiar sociocultural milieu to strange and alien surroundings which usually double as the battleground for testing the hero's tenacity is a common structural pattern in the folktale, as pointed out by Vladimir Propp in *The Morphology of the Folktale*. For a Proppian reading of the romance in general, see Alexandra Hennessey Olsen,

exile is also a helpful tool in the romance poet's arsenal since it enables him to telescope time. Large swathes of time are passed over quickly, thereby enabling the poet to focus on what is of true significance, that is, the development of the romance hero; through the truncation of time, dramatic action becomes secondary to character maturation.

Exile and Christianity

An unmistakable religious impulse informs the *Orfeo*-poet's crafting of the trope of exile, a tendency informed by the ethos of Christianity itself. Helen Cooper has observed that the ostensibly linear pattern of the quest motif in romance narratives would often double back upon itself when the protagonist would return to his own society. Although such a doubling back is a symmetrical process that restores equilibrium within the world of the romance, there are privations to be suffered before such balance is restored. These interludes of conflict, complication, and ordeal which constitute the heart of the mythic quest parallel the crises suffered by mankind within Christian history itself. Viewed in such a way, the hero's overcoming of trials and his re-joining of society mirrors both the sacrifice of Christ as well as his resurrection.[17]

The severe shortage of nourishing food and the inclement conditions of life in the wilderness chip away at Orfeo's health. Adopting Cooper's line of reading, this is his confrontation with death, and his (metaphoric) resurrection is only brought about once he has regained his wife and returned to his kingdom. The severity of his contrition is almost monastic, based as it is on the total abnegation of the indulgences of monarchical existence. The trope of self-exile is not an invention of the *Orfeo*-poet; the classical Orpheus too had consigned himself to the woods to mourn the loss of Eurydice following his jeopardising of the pact entered into with the lord of the Underworld. The artistic achievement of the *Orfeo*-poet lies in the fact that, unlike his classical forbears, he has transposed Orfeo's exile to the period of time *prior* to the rescue of Heurodis, a strategy probably borrowed from the Orpheus episode related by King Alfred in his Anglo-Saxon translation of Boethius's *Consolation of Philosophy*.[18] The biblical echoes

---

"Loss and Recovery: A Morphological Reconsideration of *Sir Orfeo*," *Fabula* 23/3 (1982): 198–206.
17 Cooper, *The English Romance in Time*, 57–58.
18 Alfred's work was not simply a translation of Boethius but also an expansion of the Latin original, an augmentation clearly visible in Alfred's treatment of the Orpheus episode. For a more comprehensive discussion of the Alfredian influence on the *Orfeo*-poet, see Jonathan

apparent in the passage are not merely fortuitous, but were probably deliberately crafted into the narrative. The pagan Orpheus, for instance, had often been compared with Christ by virtue of his peaceful nature, his power to bring harmony and concord through music and eloquence, as well as by his tragic death at the hands of his followers.[19] The harp, in view of its divine associations as an instrument of celebration, deification, as well as penance, had allied Orpheus with the figures of David and Apollo.[20] The wildness of Orfeo's appearance in exile together with the intractable and hostile nature of his surroundings are also reminiscent of early Christian legends of the hairy anchorite.[21] The forest itself becomes symbolic of the eremitic tradition, recalling the penitence of Nebuchadnezzar.[22]

The eschatological parallels are not simply gratuitous embellishments designed to exhibit the breadth of the poet's scriptural knowledge but serve to underscore a vital point. By presenting Orfeo in terms paralleling the sufferings of Christian saints, hermits, and martyrs, the poet seems to suggest that Orfeo too undergoes a kind of spiritual purification akin to those of his ecclesiastical counterparts. It is his resigned acceptance of his fate together with the drive to cast off all material attachment that makes Orfeo succeed where his classical progenitor

---

Burke Severs, "The Antecedents of Sir Orfeo," in *Studies in Medieval Literature: In honor of Professor Albert Croll Baugh*, ed. MacEdward Leach (Philadelphia: University of Pennsylvania Press, 1961), 187–207 at 188–92.

19 For a detailed overview of the parallels drawn in the medieval mind, especially in medieval iconography, between Orpheus and Christ, see John Block Friedman, "Orpheus-Christus in the Art of Late Antiquity," in *Orpheus in the Middle Ages* (Syracuse: Syracuse University Press, 2000), 38–85.

20 David Lyle Jeffrey, "The Exiled King: Sir Orfeo's Harp and the Second Death of Eurydice," *Mosaic* 9/2 (1976): 45–60 at 50–51.

21 Patrizia Grimaldi, "*Sir Orfeo* as Celtic Folk-Hero, Christian Pilgrim, and Medieval King," in *Allegory, Myth, and Symbol*, ed. Morton W. Bloomfield (Cambridge, MA, and London: Harvard University Press, 1981), 147–61 at 155–58. Grimaldi notes the biblical features in association with what she calls the "second" level of meaning enshrined within the poem: the "allegorical and moral" meaning in which Orfeo becomes the literary embodiment of the Christian pilgrim. The other two levels of meaning she discerns are the "literal" and the "anagogic" or "social" levels which correspond respectively to the apparatus of Celtic mythology and folklore and to the theme of political education of the king. The unkempt nature of Orfeo's appearance also seems to have been constructed as a mirror to the tradition of the Wild Man of the Woods, a figure well established in medieval art and iconography and with which contemporary audiences would most likely have been familiar. For more on this figure, see the introduction in Timothy Husband, *The Wild Man: Medieval Myth and Symbolism* (New York: Metropolitan Museum of Art, 1980), 1–18.

22 Corinne Saunders, *The Forest of Medieval Romance: Avernus, Broceliande, Arden* (Cambridge: D. S. Brewer, 1993), 138.

had failed. In the versions of the legend popularised by the Augustan poets Virgil and Ovid and subsequently by Boethius in late antiquity, Orpheus had, by flouting the decree of the gods, displayed both inconstancy and immoderate emotion, excesses which condemned him to failure; Orfeo, by contrast, not only embraced his lot but also embarked upon a programme of personal and spiritual amelioration by relinquishing the material trappings of secular existence. In his state of self-willed expulsion, Orfeo physically strips himself of royal finery, renounces all the appurtenances of monarchical rule, and isolates himself from civilisation. Having been relegated, quite literally, to the margins of society and having surrendered all earthly possessions, Orfeo learns how little it means to be king. He refuses to be mired within the illusory world of sensory pleasure and earthly splendour, choosing atonement through repudiation and self-abasement. His unconditional and voluntary surrender to forces both divine and natural is rewarded when he is finally allowed, in what is intended to be read at least partially as an act of heavenly dispensation, to view Heurodis and thereby undertake the journey which concludes in her successful recovery and their mutual return.[23]

---

[23] While the religious significance of Orfeo's exile is undoubtedly an important part of the poem's larger thematic concerns, I would argue that scholarship has tended to overstate the extent to which the *Orfeo*-poet intended the episode to function as a romance equivalent of an exemplum. Critics such as Gros-Louis and Grimaldi have read Orfeo's exile as concrete testaments to the hero's sacrificial prostration before the awful power of Christian grace as well as an allegorical illustration of the soul's redemption from sin. In such readings, Orfeo's subsequent encounter with Heurodis in the fairy hunting party is thus directly and exclusively a gift of divine benediction. However, such an argument ignores the crucial part played by chance in almost all encounters with fairies in medieval texts. Etymologically deriving from the Fates of classical mythology, fairies were by nature liminal beings, unassimilable within any of the available registers of interpretation. The capriciousness and unpredictability of their character went hand in hand with the coincidental nature of most fairy encounters. The motivations of *Orfeo*'s fairy denizens are similarly inscrutable: we may conjecture, but it is not explicitly known why the Fairy King singles out Heurodis for abduction, nor why Heurodis just happens to be among the train of hunting women on that particular day and not during the ten years of Orfeo's exile, a period during which he had often witnessed the Fairy King with his retinue. Thus, Orfeo's meeting with Heurodis can at best be partially explained as a reward for penance done; the element of chance cannot be ruled out. I read the episode of exile as a mélange of different traditions, informed by the poet's syncretistic assimilation of Christian motifs, insular Celtic mythology, as well as the classical, pagan heritage of the Orpheus myth. Above all, I see the episode as an instance of deft structuring, constructed within the standard romance mechanism of testing the hero's worth and one which by virtue of its central positioning lends the poem an admirable equipoise. For more on the etymological basis of *fairy*, see Noel Williams, "The Semantics of the Word *Fairy:* Making Meaning Out of Thin Air," in *The Good People: New Fairylore Essays*, ed. Peter Narváez (New York and London: Garland Publishing, 1991), 462–72, and for an in-depth discussion of the un-

The trope of exile is thus invested with a dual function in the poem. On one level, it acts as a structuring device of narrative arrangement by means of which the psychological maturation of the protagonist, so crucial to the trajectory of character development of romance heroes, is articulated. With a deftness of versification that is at once pithy and evocative, the *Orfeo*-poet conveys both the passage of time as well as the spiritual edification of Orfeo while temporarily arresting dramatic action. At the same time, the poet also enriches the semantic field of exile with associations drawn from Scripture and Christian theology which were already well established in the medieval mind. I should mention here that I do not wish to imply that *Sir Orfeo* is a biblical poem composed by a theologian; rather, I read the poem as a multifaceted text produced by a skilled versifier who made exile into one of the narrative's pivotal thematic concerns and deftly exploited all the denotative possibilities of the field in his representation of it: exile as a kind of spiritual abnegation, as a politico-legal instrument, as a well-established literary formula. Exile in *Sir Orfeo* becomes a sign with a negotiated referent; it constitutes an "edge" that is at once literal and ontological, epistemic and hermeneutic. The boundaries of this edge are porous and unknowable—Orfeo is shunted to the margins, to the nebulous and mysterious realms of the wilderness that lie beyond the edge of his court at Winchester, and he returns to society after having travelled to the inscrutable kingdom of Fairyland, yet another space of liminality that exists on the precipitous edge of the human and the fairy worlds. The literal consignment of Orfeo to the margins of society via the trope of exile is not only a significant aspect of the poem's narrative and artistic apparatus but also an eloquent testimony to the world-making powers of the poet.

---

assimilable nature of fairies, see James Wade, *Fairies in Medieval Romance* (New York: Palgrave Macmillan, 2011).

Estela Estévez Benítez

Chapter 12
Defying Containment: The Use of the Frame in Depictions of Monstrous Peoples in Monte Cassino Rhabanus Maurus Codex

In the medieval period, "monstrous races"[1] were, broadly speaking, the peoples with features that differed from those of Western Europeans and who were located in the unknown places of the *oecumene*—the habitable world—usually in India or Africa, at least according to medieval authors and the classical thinkers that preceded them.[2] Those differences have led scholars to consider "monstrous peoples" as an example of alterity: they were "Other" for they could be used as a negative mirror image that embodied the idea that "they are what we are not." One of the definitions of alterity that feels particularly appropriate when discussing these beings is the one suggested by Zygmunt Bauman, who proposed that the "Other" is materialised in the figure of the stranger. The stranger is used in the formation of collective identity through a differential logic of opposition between the in-group and the outgroup, but with a small nuance, and that is that when we are dealing with a "cultural other," the limits become porous and unstable.[3] This idea of the "cultural other" fits "monstrous peoples" perfectly well,

---

[1] "Monstrous races" is the conventional expression used to refer to these peoples, but they are also commonly known as "Plinian races," as most of them were described by Pliny the Elder. Some scholars, such as Asa S. Mittman, have argued that the word "race," which these two labels share, should no longer be used, because "it would have either carried no meaning for their creators, depicters and original audiences, or would have meant something radically different from what modern readers associate with the term." See Asa S. Mittman, "Are the 'Monstrous Races' Races?," *postmedieval: a journal of medieval cultural studies* 6/1 (2015): 36–51, esp. 48. Accordingly, throughout this chapter I will give preference to the expressions "monstrous peoples" and "monstrous nations." See also Debra H. Strickland, "Monstrosity and Race in the Late Middle Ages," in *Research Companion to Monsters and the Monstrous*, ed. Asa S. Mittman and Peter J. Dendle (London: Ashgate, 2012), 365–86.
[2] The earliest documented reference to these people is the mention of Pygmies in *The Iliad*: Homer, *The Iliad* III.3.6, trans. Anthony Verity (Oxford: Oxford University Press, 2011).
[3] Vincet Marotta, "Zygmunt Baumann: Order, Strangerhood and Freedom," *Thesis Eleven* 70 (2002): 42. See also Michael Hviid Jacobsen and Poul Poder, *The Sociology of Zygmunt Baumann: Challenges and Critique* (London and New York: Routledge, 2008).

for, as Jeffrey Jerome Cohen argued, monsters are "pure culture."[4] Therefore, they would neither belong to the in-group nor to the outgroup, but to an intermediate space, breaking with the binary social constructions of belonging.

This discussion is especially relevant given that, over the medieval period, these peoples became part of different textual traditions that encompassed encyclopaedic texts, such as *De natura rerum* of Thomas of Cantimpré and Bartholomeus Anglicus's *De proprietatibus rerum*,[5] different versions of the *Alexander Romance*,[6] and travel books,[7] and they were even featured in several world chronicles such as the *Konstanzer Weltchronik*. As will be shown below, such interest in turn gave rise to questions regarding their humanity. Furthermore, the presence of "monstrous people" was not restricted to the literary field; they were also part of the visual culture, including both sculptural and pictorial representations, such as the Cynocephali—dog-headed figures—of the tympanum of the central portal of Vézelay Abbey, the Blemmyae—headless men—carved in the choir stalls of Ripon Cathedral, and the Sciapod or Monopod depicted in the lower margin of the *Breviary of Renaud de Bar*.[8]

Unquestionably, miniatures were the preferred means used to represent "monstrous peoples," especially in encyclopaedic works, where these depictions were particularly numerous.[9] The earliest medieval encyclopaedic text where we can find an illustration featuring these beings is Manuscript 136 of Monte Cassino Abbey, which contains *De universo* by Rhabanus Maurus. The singularity of the illustration in folio 84v (p. 168, Fig. 1) lies in the fact that it is the only one in the whole codex where figures are depicted within a thick frame divided into

---

[4] Jeffrey Jerome Cohen, "Monster Culture (Seven Theses)," in *Monster Theory: Reading Culture*, ed. Jeffrey Jerome Cohen (Minneapolis: University of Minnesota Press, 1997), 3–25 at 4.

[5] Thomas of Cantimpré devoted the third book of his encyclopaedia to these beings. Likewise, several chapters of Book XV of Bartholomeus Anglicus's *De proprietatibus rerum* focus on them, for instance Book LXXII, where we can find a description of the peoples of India.

[6] "Monstrous peoples" are featured, among many others, in the *Roman d'Alexandre en prose*, the *Roman de toute chevalerie* written by Thomas of Kent, and in Jean Wauquelin's *Livre des conquestes et faits d'Alexandre le Grand*.

[7] See, for instance, *The Travels of Sir John Mandeville* and Marco Polo's *Il Milione*.

[8] London, British Library, Yates Thompson 8, fol. 250v.

[9] Twenty-six of the seventy-five manuscripts that form the main corpus on which my research is based, are encyclopaedic works. The second most illustrated group, with twenty-three manuscripts, is made up of volumes containing the history and battles of Alexander the Great. For an in-depth study of these manuscripts, see Estela Estévez Benítez, "*De monstruosis gentibus*: Los pueblos monstruosos en la tradición textual y visual en la Edad Media (siglos XI–XV)" (PhD diss., Universidad de Santiago de Compostela, 2020), 243–326.

several registers. As this is the only miniature that presents this structure, this could suggest that including a frame was not incidental, but rather the result of a careful decision. Thus, in this case, the frame would be much more than a mere decorative element. As Asa S. Mittman and Susan M. Kim argued in their paper "Anglo-Saxon Frames of Reference," "the violence of framing, generically speaking, is the segregation of this from that, one from the other."[10] This statement summarises the ideas that we think underlay the decision to include a frame in the aforementioned miniature, namely isolation and order. Moreover, the frame holds a deeper meaning related to the concept of containment, the need for which will be discussed in the first part of the present chapter on the basis of the analysis of the text that accompanies the miniature, that is, the chapter entitled "De portentis," based on Chapter III of Book XI of Isidore of Seville's *Etymologies*. Understanding the text is crucial, but grasping the problems, doubts, and theological explanations that arose surrounding these "monstrous peoples" is just as important. Thus, the way in which they are depicted in the Monte Cassino codex is connected with the type of text they illustrate and with its theological content. The second part of the chapter is in turn devoted to the analysis of the miniature depicting "monstrous peoples" in MS 136 of Monte Cassino Abbey. To this purpose, it will be compared to other illustrations included in the same manuscript and also to a miniature from Codex Pal. Lat. 291 from the Vatican Library, which is the only other extant copy of Rhabanus Maurus's *De universo* that includes a depiction of "monstrous nations." To fully understand the meaning of the frame, the analysis will also include the Carolingian ivory relief sculpted on the back of a leaf of one of the diptychs of Consul Areobindus. This piece features an image based on Isidore's *Etymologies*, and, by extension, on Rhabanus's *De universo*, organised in a composition that is quite similar to that of the illustration under discussion.

Between Two Realms: The Humanity of "Monstrous Peoples"

As noted above, the tradition of the "monstrous peoples" can be traced back to ancient times, when they were described as inhabitants of the distant and less well-known parts of the world, such as India and Africa. The establishment of

---

10 Asa S. Mittman and Susan M. Kim, "Anglo-Saxon Frames of Reference: Framing the Real in the *Wonders of the East*," *Different Visions: A Journal of New Perspectives on Medieval Art* 2 (2010): 1–25, esp. 12.

Figure 1: Monstrous people. Montecassino Abbey Library, Cod. Casiniensis 132, fol. 84v / p. 168 (detail). Photo: © Montecassino, Archivio dell'Abbazia.

Christianity led to a transformation in the ways in which these peoples were seen, that is, to an attempt to adapt them to the ideals and precepts of the new religion. Most of them—particularly Blemmyae, Cynocephali, Cyclops, and Sciapodes, all of whom became widespread in the medieval period—had specific features, usually some physical trait, that made them different in the eyes of medieval Western Europeans,[11] as is evident in Augustine of Hippo's comment in his work *De Civitate Dei*, where he mentions "the stories about the divergent features of those races, and their great difference from one another and from us."[12] Those "differences" raised ontological questions about their existence, their origins, their relationship with humanity, and their potential conversion to Christianity. These concerns are apparent in the *Epistola de cynocephalis*, written by Ratramnus of Corbie, a monk of the monastery of Corbie, in northern France, to his friend Rimbert. In this letter, Ratramnus writes about the existence of Cynocephali and the different reasons that could be argued both in favour of them having human nature and against it.[13]

This notion of difference was based on one specific feature, namely their non-normative body. In fact, this connection with the body ran parallel to the development of a Christian discourse on "monstrous peoples" that is already apparent in Augustine's work. According to Genesis, God created humankind in His own image (Gn 1:27); thus, people born with just one eye or no head were seen as different because they had a body that deviated from the normative. Chapter XVI of *De Civitate Dei* begins by introducing the "monstrous peoples" whose monstrous features were precisely their bodies: Cyclops, Antipodes, Hermaphrodites, Astomi, Pygmies, Sciapods, Omophtalmi, and Cynocephali—the only exception are Calingian women, also introduced in the same chapter.[14] Augustine starts by describing monstrous births—that is, infants born with a body that is significantly different from that of their parents—to create an analogy with "monstrous peoples": "The same account which is given of monstrous births in individual cases can be given of monstrous races."[15] In Augustine's view, these

---

11 The analysis of 876 figures from different manuscripts, which forms the basis of my doctoral research, reveals that Cynocephali, Cyclops, Sciapodes, and Blemmyae were the most frequently depicted "monstrous peoples": Cynocephali appear fifty-two times, Cyclops fifty, Sciapodes thirty-nine, and Blemmyae on fifty-two occasions.
12 Augustine of Hippo, *City of God* XVI.8, trans. John O'Meara (London: Penguin, 2003).
13 For an in-depth study of this letter see E. Ann Matter, "The Soul of the Dog-Man: Ratramnus of Corbie between Theology and Philosophy," *Rivista di storia della filosofia* 61/1 (2006): 43–53.
14 Calingian women bore children at the age of five and did not live past eight years old. Pliny is the only author who gave a name to these people: Pliny, *Natural History* VII.2.30.
15 Augustine of Hippo, *City of God* XVI.8.

births demonstrate that if such deformed humans could be born, God could also have created nations formed by people with monstrous bodies. Moreover, the argument works in reverse too, because the existence of such nations could prove that God is not wrong when He allows monstrous births.[16] However, as Maaike van der Lugt notes, although Augustine seems to argue in favour of the acceptance of monstrous beings as part of humankind, his stance is ultimately not clear ("[il] ne se prononce finalement pas su ce point").[17] The humanity of monstrous people is therefore surrounded by doubts and constraints rather than a well-established fact.

Isidore of Seville also discusses the dilemma of "monstrous peoples" in his *Etymologies*, and by extension, so does Rhabanus in *De universo*. Specifically, Isidore addresses this issue in Book XI, entitled "De homine et portentis." As their humanity had already been considered by Augustine, Isidore simply follows his lead: "Just as, in individual nations, there are instances of monstrous people, so in the whole of humankind there are certain monstrous races."[18] However, he actually goes one step further by creating a whole new set of categories that relied on the manner in which their bodies were shaped: superfluous members or missing parts; size of members or differences in their shape; partial mutations, that is, *heteromorphia*, or complete transformations or changes in the position of some features; *connaturatio* or premature development, and so on.[19] After introducing these various categories, and following the structure of *De Civitate Dei*, Isidore goes on to list "monstrous peoples" whose singularities lie in their physical appearance. Other characteristics, like their eating habits—only mentioned in the description of Cyclops and in that of the people who eat through a straw—and the ability to speak—in the case of Cynocephali and speechless peoples—are relegated to the background. Besides the aforementioned categories, Isidore creates a new division for portents based on the actuality of their existence: "Other fabulous human monstrosities are told of, which do not exist

---

[16] "What if God has seen fit to create some races in this way, that we might not suppose that the monstrous births which appear among ourselves are the failures of that wisdom" (Augustine of Hippo, *City of God* XVI.8).

[17] Maaike van der Lugt, "L'humanité des monstres et leur accès aux sacrements dans la pensée médiévale," in *Monstres, humanité et sacrements dans la pensée medievale*, ed. Anna Caiozzo and Anne-Emmanuelle Demartini (Paris: Créaphis, 2005), 135–61 at 139.

[18] Isidore, *Etymologies*, ed. Jose Oroz Feta and Manuel A. Marcos Casquero (Madrid: Biblioteca de Autores Cristianos, 1994), XI.3.12: "Sicut autem in singulis gentibus quaedam monstra sunt hominum, ita in universo genere humano quaedam monstra sunt gentium." Isidore, *The Etymologies of Isidore of Seville*, trans. Stephen A. Berney, W. J. Lewis, J. A. Beach, and Oliver Berghof (Cambridge: Cambridge University Press, 2006), XI.3.12.

[19] Isidore, *Etymologies* XI.3.28.

but are concocted to interpret the causes of things."²⁰ If beings such as Sirens or Gorgons are explicitly categorised as pure fantasy, it stands to reason that "monstrous peoples" should be considered as real.

Even though Isidore presents these peoples as part of humankind, we can find glimpses of a different interpretation in his work. One of these discrepancies is apparent in his description of Cynocephali, whose lack of articulate language would place them closer to beasts than to humans: "And their barking indeed reveals that they are rather beasts than humans."²¹ The problem posed by Cynocephali is in fact related to their hybrid body, given that when Isidore describes the human body, he claims that the head is one of its fundamental parts, and Cynocephali are dog-headed beings.²² Furthermore, other "monstrous peoples" are also afflicted by a similar problem, as Blemmyae and Omophtalmi have no head and no neck, another part present in the human body according to the Isidorian text.²³ In the case of Artibatirae, who walk on all fours like animals, their body does not match another Isidorian statement about humanity: "And the human stands erect and looks toward heaven so as to seek God, rather than look at the earth, as do beasts that nature has made bent over and attentive to their bellies."²⁴ Likewise, Hippopodes also have a hybrid body. All these divergences from the human norm make it necessary to reconsider the humanity of these beings, which ultimately depends on the presence of a rational soul. However, Isidore does not go into this topic, nor does he discuss why they should be included in the human category.

In these early encyclopaedic texts, "monstrous people" lived within a categorical limbo because their humanity was mentioned and discussed but, at the same time, it was not established beyond doubt. This duality made it possible to ascribe them to the human realm, but also to that of animals and beasts. In the following centuries, the debate about their humanity was a recurring argument in different encyclopaedic works, such as *De naturis rerum* of Thomas of Cantimpré. In Book III, *De monstruosis hominibus Orientes*, Cantimpré settled this issue by arguing that the closer their physical appearance was to the human body, the closer they were to this category; in contrast, the lack of a fully organ-

---

20 Isidore, *Etymologies* XI.3.28: "Dicuntur autem et alia hominum fabulosa portenta, quae non sunt, sed ficta in causis rerum interpretantur."
21 Isidore, *Etymologies* XI.3.15: "quosque ipse latratus magis bestias quam homines confitetur."
22 Isidore, *Etymologies* XI.1.25.
23 Isidore, *Etymologies* XI.1.61.
24 Isidore, *Etymologies* XI.1.5: "Qui ideo erectus caelum aspicit, ut Deum quaerat, non ut terram intendat veluti pecoram, quae natura prona et ventri oboedienti finxit."

ised body would prevent the presence of a rational soul.²⁵ It was for this reason that, according to him, "monstrous people" could not be considered as fully fledged humans.

Although we have discussed the problems connected with the body, this is not the only characteristic that was taken into account when determining which of these peoples should be seen as monstrous. The great medieval encyclopaedias of the twelfth and thirteenth centuries made additions to the lists of "monstrous peoples" proposed by Augustine and Isidore. In general, there was an increase in the number of peoples included in these works, as shown in the *Historia Orientalis* of Jacques de Vitry—in which he describes thirty-three nations —and in the *Speculum Historiale* of Vincent of Beauvais—who mentioned sixty-one.²⁶ The escalation in the number of monstrous peoples implied the addition of beings whose monstrosity could not be simply justified by means of a "different" body, and thus customs, habits, and religion became part of their defining features. The majority of these "new" peoples were already present in the works of Pliny and Solinus, but they were given little attention in earlier encyclopaedic works.

The Issue of the Frame: The Representation of Monstrous People in MS 136 of Monte Cassino

The earliest medieval encyclopaedic text featuring a depiction of "monstrous peoples" is *De universo*, written by the Carolingian author Rhabanus Maurus, specifically, Manuscript 136 of Monte Cassino Abbey, which was produced between 1022 and 1023. The main goal of the present study is in fact to analyse the miniature that illustrates Chapter VII, "De portentis," of Book VII, which appears in the inner and lower margins of the folio (Fig. 1). The image is framed by a twenty-six-line-high gilded rectangle, divided into four horizontal registers. In-

---

25 Thomas of Cantimpré, *Liber de natura rerum* III.1, ed. Helmut Boese (Berlin and New York: Walter de Gruyter, 1973).
26 Jacques de Vitry, *Orientalis et occidentalis historia*, ed. F. Moschi (Douai: Ex oficina typographica Balthazaris Belleri, 1596), 92; Vincent of Beauvais, *Speculum historiale* II.64, 69, 76, 77, 86–90, 92, 93. I have used the edition of Anton Koberger (Nuremberg, 1483), which belongs to the "He" family (University Library of Würzburg, I.t.f., 471b). For more information on the main families of this encyclopaedia and their characteristics, see Laurent Brun, "Le Miroir Historial de Jean de Vignay: Edition critique du livre I (Prologue) et du livre V (Histoire d'Alexandre le Grand)" (PhD diss., University of Stockholm, 2010), 38.

side this frame, the fifteen figures that represent monstrous people are organised in groups of four, except for the lower register, where there are only three.

Faced with the task of translating their monstrous appearance into an image, the miniaturist closely followed the descriptions provided by the text. In the top register we can find the representation of a Hermaphrodite, showing the right breast of a woman and the left side of the chest of a man, a dog-headed Cynocephalus, a one-eyed Cyclops, and a headless Blemmyae with the face on its chest. The second register depicts an Omophtalmus, with its eyes on its shoulders, a four-legged Artibatirae, a Satyr with a brownish body and hoofs instead of feet, and a Panotii, whose ears reach to its feet.[27] The first figure depicted in the third register is a Sciapod, who holds its single foot above its head to shade itself from the sun. Next to it there is an Antipode, with eight toes in each foot and its feet pointing forward instead of backwards, a Hippopod with horses' hooves, and, finally, two Pygmies depicted as bearded men sitting under a tree. This iconography of Pygmies is unique and based on Rhabanus's interpolation from *De Verborum Significatione*, written by Sextus Pompeius Festus: "There is also a nation of ulnar stature, which the Greeks call pygmies, whom the common people call *septemcaulinos*, because seven can rest under a stem."[28] In the last register, which features no lower border, there are three hybrid creatures holding branches in their hands: a Minotaur, an Onocentaur, and a Hippocentaur. These last three characters are called by Isidore and Rhabanus "fabulous human portents," that is, made-up fictions and, therefore, they are not considered as part of any "monstrous people."[29]

It is also worth noting that despite the text's silence on the matter, all the figures are depicted naked. The miniaturist might have decided to portray them without clothes to evoke a savage or primitive state.[30] The representatives of each "nation" are depicted in diverse positions and displaying a variety of ges-

---

[27] The figure of the Panotii is the only one that does not follow the sequence provided by the text, according to which it should be placed after the Omophtalmus.
[28] Rhabanus Maurus, *De universo* VII.VII: "Est et gens ibi statura cubitalis quos Græci a cubito Pygmaeos vocant, quos vulgus septemcaulinos vocant, eo quod septem sub uno caulerequiescunt, de qua supra diximus." See Guglielmo Cavallo, ed., *Rabanus Maurus, De rerum naturis: Cod. Casin. 132, Archivio dell'Abbazia di Montecassino* (Turin: Priuli & Verlucca, 1994), 124.
[29] Isidore, *Etymologies* XI.3.28: "Dicuntur autem et alia hominum fabulosa portenta, quae non sunt, sed ficta in causis rerum interpretantur." The reasons why they do not belong to the category of "monstrous peoples" will be discussed later on.
[30] The use of clothes is linked with human nature and the lack of them is a sign of wildness. On this subject, see John Block Friedman, *The Monstrous Races in Medieval Art and Thought* (New York: Syracuse University Press, 2000), 31; Emily Kovatch, "Defining the Indefinable: The Cultural Role of Monsters in the Middle Ages" (PhD diss., Ball State University, 2008), 11–13.

tures, giving the impression that they are engaged in conversation. Examples of this dialogue between figures can be found in the first register, where the Cynocephalus—with his mouth open—and the Cyclops reach out their arms to each other, and in the third register, where the Antipode and the Hippopod also seem to address each other. Some authors, such as Marianne Reuter and John Block Friedman, use terms such as "rigidity" and "statism" when discussing this same miniature, but I believe that the insertion of these gestures and stances can be interpreted as an attempt to grant some movement or dynamism to the illustration.[31]

A. Goldschmidt (1923–24), Paul Lehmann (1927), Fritz Saxl (1939), Erwin Panofsky (1967), Rudolf Wittkower (1942), and Diane O. Le Berrurier (1967), among others, have analysed the iconographic programme of this codex.[32] Their works put forward two main theories: the first one, held by Saxl, Panofsky, and Wittkower, defends the existence of a Carolingian illuminated manuscript of *De universo* based on a copy of the *Etymologies* that would have been illuminated shortly after Isidore completed his work; the second thesis, sustained by Goldschmidt, Lehmann, and Le Berrurier, accepts the existence of a Carolingian archetype, but rejects the idea that it could have been based on a copy of the *Etymologies*, as none of the surviving manuscripts of the latter feature a group of images similar to the ones illustrating Rhabanus's work. Le Berrurier delves deeper into this subject by conducting an iconographic study of the mythological and scientific images in *De universo* in order to discover their potential sources. She puts forward two possible hypotheses for the origin of the depictions of "monstrous peoples": they could draw either on a Carolingian archetype formed by seventeen or fifteen figures—instead of the nineteen proposed by Panofsky—or on two separate Carolingian archetypes that would ultimately have used the same pictorial sources.[33] This last theory could explain the differences between the manuscript held at Monte Cassino Abbey and the one at the Vatican Library, which, as noted above, is the only other copy that features a miniature depicting "monstrous peoples." Regarding the specific sources for each of them, Le Berrurier narrows them down to two: an illustrated manuscript of Solinus's *Collecta-*

---

31 Marianne Reuter, *Metodi illustrativi nel Medioevo: Testo e immagine nel codice 132 di Montecassino "Liber Rabani de Originibus Rerum"* (Naples: Liguori, 1993), 17; Friedman, *The Monstrous Races*, 132.

32 For a summary of the theories on the iconographic programme of MS 136 predating Le Berrurier, see Diane O. Le Berrurier, *The Pictorical Sources of Mythological and Scientific Illustrations in Hrabanus Maurus "De rerum naturis"* (New York: Garland, 1978), 4–7.

33 Le Berrurier, *The Pictorial Sources*, 116.

nea and a version of the *Wonders of the East*. Let us now turn to the reason why the illuminator decided to present the reader with "monstrous peoples" inside a gilded frame resembling a table.

The representation of a frame that surrounds figures and scenes is commonplace in different types of medieval manuscripts. What calls attention to the image in folio 84v (p. 168) is not just its arrangement, as if it was a table, but also the fact that it is the only one out of the 335 miniatures that form the iconographic programme of the manuscript that features this kind of composition.[34] The first question that springs to mind regarding the thick frame is whether it was part of the original miniature of the archetype from which the iconography seems to derive, or whether it is instead an addition of Manuscript 136 of Monte Cassino. To try to answer this question, it is necessary to compare it to the miniature in the Vatican manuscript. In folio 75v of Codex Pal. Lat. 291, in the "De portentis" chapter, we can find miniatures decorating the inner margin of the left text column and the top margin of the right column. In the first image, the figures of "monstrous peoples," which appear arranged in groups of four in horizontal registers, are depicted against a rectangular ultramarine blue background. The second smaller miniature only depicts two figures, namely a female Hippocentaur and a Chimaera. Despite the fact that the image in the Vatican codex does not feature dividing lines between registers, the horizontal layout in groups of four is the same in both manuscripts. The idea that the blue background could be a reinterpretation—or a remnant—of the framed table in Manuscript 136 should be dismissed, as the Vatican codex uses this same pattern in other images. For instance, the illuminations in folios 86r and 86v, which illustrate the chapter entitled "De bestiis," feature pairs of animals over the same blue background. This same scene appears in folio 191 of the Monte Cassino manuscript, but there the animals are depicted more haphazardly all over the folio. Comparing the composition of the depiction of "monstrous peoples" in these two manuscripts leads to three possible scenarios, all of them related to the hypothesis formulated by Le Berrurier: (1) the archetype on which both manuscripts are based featured a frame, but only MS 136 of Monte Cassino reproduced it; (2) the miniature of the archetype did not have a frame, and therefore it was an addition of MS 136; and (3) the two codices were based on different archetypes, one of which had a framed image while the other only had figures arranged in horizontal registers.

---

[34] Giulia Orfino, "Per una filologia delle illustrazioni del *De rerum naturis* di Rabano Mauro," in *Rabanus Maurus, De rerum naturis, Cod. Casin. 132, Archivio dell'Abbazia di Montecassino* (Turin: Priuli & Verlucca, 1994), 99–175, esp. 101.

The miniature of "De portentis" in the Monte Cassino manuscript and the illuminations in the two sources suggested by Le Berrurier, namely Codex 246 of the Biblioteca Ambrosiana in Milan, which contains Solinus's *Collectanea* and is based on an earlier ninth-century manuscript, and the insular Nowell Codex held in the British Library (Cotton Vitellius A XV), which includes the *Wonders of the East*, feature quite different types of frames. Regarding the three extant manuscripts containing the *Wonders of the East*, the frames in Cotton Vitellius A XV (Fig. 2) are "consistently represented as partial"; in contrast, the frames in the other two codices—British Library Cotton Tiberius B. v and Oxford Bodleian 614—are fully outlined, but only enclose individual "nations."[35] The Ambrosiana codex does contain framed group representations, for instance in folios 24r and 57r, and, in addition, the different "monstrous nations" seem to be arranged in horizontal registers. However, unlike in the case of the Monte Cassino manuscript, this composition might be due to an attempt to make the most of the space left for the image and not so much to a deliberate decision to display a specific classification.

The consular diptych of Areobindus contains an image from the Carolingian period that is actually much more similar to the one in Monte Cassino's MS 136. On the back of one of the diptych leaves there is an ivory plaque known as "The Earthly Paradise."[36] The plaque depicts the different beings created by God arranged in seven horizontal registers, with Adam and Eve in the top register, followed by hybrid beings—that is, two Sirens, two Centaurs, three Cynocephali, and two Satyrs—in the second and third registers. Again, it is worth noting the manner in which these figures are organised, as they are separated from the wide ornamented border by a thin line while wavy lines decorated with plant motifs separate the different horizontal sections. This plaque was meant to illustrate the text of Isidore's *Etymologies* or, maybe, depending on its date, the text of Rhabanus's *De universo*.[37] At any rate, although it does not depict the same

---

35 Mittman and Kim, "Anglo-Saxon Frames," 4.

36 Following the work of Wolfgang Fritz Volbach, Jacqueline Leclerq-Marx dated the plaque to the beginning of the ninth century; see Jacqueline Leclerq-Marx, "La Sirèneé dans la pensée et dans l'art de l'Antiquité et du Moyen Âge: Du mythe païen au symbole chrétien," *Koregos*, last modified 2 October 2014, http://www.koregos.org/fr/jacqueline-leclercq-marx-la-sirene-dans-la-pensee-et-dans-l-art-de-l-antiquite-et-du-moyen-age/4622/#chapitre_4622. The website of the Musée du Louvre, where the plaque is kept, dates the plaque to circa 870–875; see Marie-Cécile Bardoz, "Plaque Known as The Earthly Paradise," Musée du Louvre, accessed 14 June 2019, https://www.louvre.fr/en/oeuvre-notices/plaque-known-earthly-paradise.

37 Rhabanus Maurus composed his work around 842–847. Were we to accept the date proposed by Leclerq-Marx and Volbach, the plaque would then be illustrating Isidore's *Etymologies*. How-

Figure 2: Donestre. The British Library, Cotton Ms Vittellius A XV, fol. 103v (detail). Photo: © British Library Board.

passage represented by the miniature of the Monte Cassino codex, the evident similarities between the two works go beyond the presence of a framed table, including a short-haired bearded Centaur holding a branch in his hand, a Cynocephalus depicted in profile and looking up, and the body language of certain figures, such as Eve and the Hermaphrodite. Without going so far as to suggest that

---

ever, the date suggested on the Louvre's website would allow for the plaque to have been based on Rhabanus's work. See previous note.

this plaque could have been a source for the Carolingian archetype of MS 136—or vice versa—this piece should be considered as an example of the presence of a framed table in association with the text of "De portentis."

The "Earthly Paradise" ivory divides space into different levels or registers to organise the figures it portrays, but this system also serves to present characters in descending order of precedence. As Leclerq-Marx argued:[38] first comes humanity, represented by Adam and Eve; in the second register we find hybrid beings with the upper body of a human; in the third register, we find Cynocephali and Satyrs, whose animality is much more marked; and, finally, the lower registers are reserved for various quadrupeds. The different levels are thus used to indicate different natures: human, hybrid, and animal. Moreover, even hybrids are classified according to two categories depending on their degree of humanity or animality. Therefore, the frame acquires symbolic value in connection with the different essences and orders of nature. However, this interpretation falls short in the case of the miniature of MS 136, for the idea of a divide based on the respective natures of the figures can only be applied to the lower register, which includes the depiction of the three equine hybrids that belong to a different category of portents. In spite of being represented in different registers, the rest of the "monstrous peoples" are part of the same realm. Then, why present them to readers inside a frame? The answer, in my opinion, is linked to their nature: it is not that it changed between registers, as occurred in the ivory plaque, but rather that it set them apart from the rest of humankind.

As for the debate on the presence of a frame in the image of the original archetype manuscript, it lies outside the purview of the present chapter. The disposition of the figures and the differences between the images of the Monte Cassino manuscript and the Vatican Library codex seem to lead to the conclusion that these two codices belonged to two different families that were based on two different archetypes, a thesis put forward by Le Berrurier. Bearing in mind the example of the "Earthly Paradise" ivory plaque, if the manuscript of Monte Cassino indeed had an earlier Carolingian source, it is likely that this featured a frame surrounding the illustration of the "De portentis" chapter.

Conclusion: A Frame that Organises and Contains

The miniature in folio 84v (p. 168) of the Monte Cassino manuscript and the function of the frame featured in it can only be fully understood against the

---

38 Leclerq-Marx, "La Sireneé dans la pensée."

backdrop of the theological discussion on "monstrous peoples" and in connection with the type of text the image illustrates, that is, an encyclopaedic work. This two-pronged analysis reveals the double function of the frame, namely ordering and containing.

As for its first function, the frame allows for the display of the different characters in an orderly manner within the space left for the miniature, in the same way that Isidore presented the knowledge of his time arranged in themes in each book and chapter. Nevertheless, this order imposed by the frame is also linked to Isidore's focus on creating categories. Just as each category is used to isolate certain beings from others, establishing an order within the Creation and rationalising their place in it, the frame allows us, the readers, to do the same on a visual level. Furthermore, this type of representation, where the different figures appear organised, isolated from nature, and arranged in a sequence, is also connected with how they were introduced in encyclopaedic texts. In this type of work, "monstrous peoples" were simply listed along with only the most basic details about them. These lists would grow longer in later centuries. As John Block Friedman argued:

> The point of view that develops from Pliny's way of treating the Astomi or Panotii or Pygmies isolates these races from one another; they exist in the abstraction of the list rather than in a defined geographic space. [...] When illustrated encyclopaedias such as the Monte Cassino Rhabanus Maurus codex make their appearance, the separation of the monstrous races from true geographic and naturalistic space is complete.[39]

The idea of creating an order would be consistent with what we have said about the ivory plaque of the "Earthly Paradise," where the variety of natures are arranged in descending order through the registers of the frame. However, organising the different characters was not the only purpose of this frame, for, if that were the case, the miniaturist would have surely used a similar frame in other miniatures of MS 136, such as the one depicting the animals in the "De Bestiis" chapter. Therefore, we have to consider the possibility that the frame could have also symbolised containment. The works of Augustine, Isidore, Rhabanus, and, later, Cantimpré show the quandary surrounding "monstrous peoples," which stemmed from their uncertain human nature. For Augustine, the human condition of these beings was guaranteed as long as their existence and rationality could be proven. For Isidore, as their humanity had already been addressed by Augustine, the goal was to create a series of categories that defined these "human portents" according to their physical appearance and to their actual

---

39 Friedman, *The Monstrous Races*, 132.

or fictional existence. This cataloguing process presented and explained these peoples to readers, in an attempt to rationalise their nature and to make them comprehensible. However, this nature did not fit neatly into categories that were based on a system that understood the world in terms of dualities and opposing concepts: human/inhuman, people/beasts, real/fiction. In the words of Jeffrey J. Cohen, "the monster always escapes because it refuses easy categorization."[40] In spite of this attempt, Isidore's text is full of contradictions regarding what we can understand as "human," and whether Sciapods or Pygmies could belong to this group. If, as noted above, the frame was an adaptation of the encyclopaedic language to images, in a symbolic sense it would also serve as a kind of reinforcement of the categories used by Isidore and Rhabanus, into which "monstrous peoples" did not quite fit because, as stated above, they were "cultural others" who belonged to an intermediate space. The frame was thus a visual element that tried to succeed where categories had failed, that is, containing these beings and their ambiguous nature.

Therefore, in Isidore's work, the theological problems created by the existence of beings such as Cynocephali and Artibatirae were solved through the creation of categories into which the author attempted to classify them. On a visual level, this idea is recreated in the Monte Cassino manuscript by including a frame that formally served as a structure that ordered and organised figures according to the reasoned language of encyclopaedias, and symbolically helped to contain beings that challenged the conception of the world in binary terms.

---

40 Cohen, "Monster Culture," 6.

Notes on Contributors

Ivan Armenteros-Martínez is a Tenured Scientist at the Milà i Fontanals Institution for Research in the Humanities (Spanish Council for Scientific Research—CSIC, Barcelona). He is a member of the research group CAIMMed—The Crown of Aragon, Islam and the Mediterranean. His research focuses on slavery in the Medieval and Early Modern Western Mediterranean as well as on the Iberian expansion in Africa and the Americas during the early sixteenth century.

Jordi Casals Parés holds degrees in Hebrew Philology (2007) and Arabic Philology (2013), and a Master's Degree in Medieval Cultures (2009) from the University of Barcelona, from which he received a PhD in Linguistic, Literary, and Cultural Studies (2016). He works as a part-time lecturer in the Greek, Latin, and Romance and Semitic Languages Department of the University of Barcelona, where he teaches Medieval Hebrew Literature and Language, and Jewish History.

Laura Cayrol-Bernardo is a Marie Skłodowska-Curie postdoctoral fellow at the University of Bergen (Norway) and research associate at the Centre d'Études Historiques of the École des Hautes Études en Sciences Sociales—EHESS (Paris). Her PhD dissertation focused on ideas, materialisations, and lived practices regarding older women in Late Medieval Iberia. She is currently developing a research project on the ageing female body in fifteenth-century Florence at the intersection of art, art theory, and natural history. She has also worked extensively on Iberian women religious during the High Middle Ages.

Mireia Comas-Via is a Lecturer in Medieval History at the University of Barcelona. She has published works on widowhood and women's writings in the Middle Ages. Among these, she is the author of *Entre la solitud i la llibertat: vídues barcelonines a finals de l'Edat Mitjana* (Viella, 2015). Her current research project deals with ageing and elderly people in Catalonia between the thirteenth and the fifteenth century.

Rachel Ernst is a Senior Lecturer at Georgia State University. She received her PhD in Medieval Studies from the University of Reading in 2015 for her dissertation, "The Church of Heresy: Early Clerical Perceptions on the Cathar Heresy." She has designed multiple courses that incorporate her research in dissent and persecution in the medieval Church. Her pedagogical interests have expanded to embrace a global approach to the Middle Ages to reflect the interests and cultural backgrounds of Georgia State's diverse student body. In 2020, she published *Creating History*, a pre-modern World History textbook for her students.

Estela Estévez Benítez holds a PhD in Medieval Studies from the University of Santiago de Compostela (Spain), which she received for her doctoral dissertation "*De monstruosis gentibus:* Los pueblos monstruosos en la tradición textual y visual en la Edad Media (siglos XI–XV)." Her research interests focus on the depiction of monstrous peoples in medieval miniature, the relation between images and texts, the notion of monstrosity in the Middle Ages, and the representation of female monstrous nations.

Marta Fernández Lahosa holds a BA in Art History, and a Master's Degree in Medieval Cultures from the University of Barcelona (Spain), where she received her doctoral degree in Medieval Cultures. Her dissertation, entitled "The Origins of the Theme of the Ascension of Christ in Early Christian Art," focused on the creation and transmission of iconogographic programmes. She currently combines her work in cultural heritage management, documentation, and dissemination with teaching.

Courtney Krolikoski is Assistant Professor of History at Jacksonville University (Florida, USA). Her research explores the status of lepers in Bologna (Italy) in the High Middle Ages with attention to the interaction between contemporary social, political, religious, and medical aspects of leprosy. She was one of the founders and organizers of the recurring conference "Leprosy and the 'Leper' Reconsidered" and is co-editing the volume, *Leprosy from the Medieval to the Modern World: A Global Interdisciplinary Approach*.

Laura Miquel Milian completed her dissertation, entitled "The Catalan Civil War and the Financial Crisis of Barcelona during the Reign of Joan II, King of Aragon (1458–1479)," within the framework of a doctoral programme jointly developed by the University of Girona and the Milà i Fontanals Institution—CSIC, under the supervision of Dr. Pere Orti Gost and Dr. Pere Verdés Pijuan. She holds a Juan de la Cierva Formación Fellowship and is a member of the Society, Power, and Culture (14th–17th centuries) Research Group at the Euskal Herriko Unibersitatea (Spain). Her main research interests focus on public debt and fiscality in fifteenth-century Barcelona, as well as on the study of this Mediterranean metropolis during that period.

Angana Moitra is Assistant Professor at O.P. Jindal Global University (India). She completed her PhD in 2020 on the Erasmus Mundus TEEME (Text and Event in Early Modern Europe) Joint-Doctoral Programme, defending a thesis entitled "A Spirit of Another Sort: The Evolution and Transformation of the Fairy King from Medieval Romance to Early Modern Prose, Poetry, and Drama." Her research interests span the length and breadth of the literary, religious, and political culture of the European medieval and early modern periods, and she is particularly interested in exploring the continuities and correspondences between the two. She is currently exploring the representation of fairies in witchcraft trials and revising her doctoral thesis for publication.

Delfi I. Nieto-Isabel is a Marie Skłodowska-Curie Fellow and Lecturer in History at Queen Mary University of London, where she carries out her research project ILLITTERATAE on the role of illiterate women in the spread of alternative religious knowledge. She is a former Research Associate and Visiting Lecturer in the Women's Studies in Religion Program at Harvard University and an Associate Researcher of the Institute for Research on Medieval Cultures (IRCVM) of the University of Barcelona. She holds a BSc in Physics, a BA in History, an MA, and a PhD in Medieval Cultures from the University of Barcelona, which she received for her dissertation, "Communities of Dissent: Social Network Analysis of Religious Dissident Groups in Languedoc in the Thirteenth and Fourteenth Centuries."

Stamatia Noutsou holds a BA in History from Thesalonikis University (Greece) and an MA in History from Copenhagen University (Denmark). In September 2021, she received her PhD from Masaryk University in Brno (Czech Republic) for her dissertation on medieval religious persecution. Her research focuses on the role of the Cistercian Order in the Church's anti-heretical efforts, and particularly on Cistercian attitudes towards violence against heretics between 1145 and 1190.

Anna M. Peterson is an adjunct at the Universidad Europea Miguel de Cervantes. In 2017, she was awarded her PhD in medieval history from the University of St Andrews. Her thesis, "A Comparative Study of the Hospitals and Leprosaria in Narbonne, France and Siena, Italy (1080–1348)," analysed the development of assistive institutions in these cities, focusing on their relationship with religious and secular bodies as well as responses to corruption. She was awarded a Mellon Fellowship at the Pontifical Institute of Mediaeval Studies (Toronto) from 2018 to 2019. She is also the co-organizer of the recurring conference "Leprosy and the 'Leper' Reconsidered" along with Courtney Krolikoski. Currently, she is a member of the project "Hermenéutica del Cuerpo Visible: Conceptualizaciones y Prácticas en la Medicina Medieval de Tradición Latina/Hermeneutics of the Visible Body: Conceptualisations and Practices in Medieval Medicine in the Latin Tradition" (PID2019-107671GB-I00).

Sergi Sancho Fibla is a researcher at UCLouvain (Belgium) since 2020, when he won a "Fonds Spéciaux de la Recherche" contract with his project "Transferring Knowledge in the Nunnery." He received a PhD from the Pompeu Fabra University, in Barcelona. His dissertation focused on the study of the writing and spiritual practices of a medieval mystic writer, Marguerite d'Oingt (*Escribir y meditar*, Siruela 2018). Later, he worked as a postdoctoral researcher at the University of Aix-Marseille (2016–2018) and at the École des Hautes Études en Sciences Sociales in Paris (2018–2019). He currently works on female spirituality of the Late Middle Ages: reading and writing practices, monasticism, and devotion.

Justine Trombley is a Leverhulme Early Career Fellow in the Department of History at the University of Nottingham. She received her M.Litt and PhD in Medieval History from the University of St Andrews and was later a Mellon Fellow at the Pontifical Institute of Mediaeval Studies in Toronto. Her work focuses on the condemnation and circulation of heretical texts in the fourteenth and fifteenth centuries.

Index

Acta Archelai 137
Acts of the Apostles 142
Ad abolendam 172
Ad Nostrum 34–36
Adriatic Sea 204, 207
Aelred of Rievaulx
– *Genealogia regum anglorum* 65
Africa 135, 137, 209f., 251, 253
– North Africa 187f., 190, 193
Agnellus of Ravenna 146
Agnès, daughter of Antònia 88
Agnès, widow of Francesc Plaensa 83
Agnès Vigouroux 45
Aix-en-Provence 25
Akehurst, Frank 225
Albanell, Joan 88
Albanès, Joseph-Hyacinthe 23f., 47–50, 52
Albertí, Arnau, knight 82, 88f.
Albi 16
Albigensian Crusade 119, 135
Albini, Giuliana 90
Alençon 227
Alexander III, Pope 5, 228, 232f.
Alexander IV, Pope 5
Alexander of Alexandria 150
Alexander Romance 252
Alexander the Great 252
Alfons III, King of Aragon 206
Alfons IV, King of Aragon 206
Alfonso II, King of Castile 202
Alfonso X, King of Castile 224
Alfonso XI, King of Castile 224
Alfred, King of the West Saxons and of the Anglo-Saxons 247
Algeria 188, 193
Almanzor, Abu ʿĀmir Muḥammad ibn ʿAbdullāh ibn Abi ʿĀmir al-Maʿafiri, *called* 205
Alphonse Jourdain, Count of Toulouse 169f.
Ames, Christine Caldwell 170
Amiens 100, 227
Amorim Goskes, Juliana 59
Andalusia 211

Andrew II, King of Hungary 69
Antònia *la Begura*, wife of Joan Albanell 88
Apollinaris of Ravenna 146
Aragon 205
Aragon, Crown of 17, 111, 177f., 180, 183, 187–190, 196, 212, 225
Arius 150
– Thalia 150
Armanno, slave owner 205
Armenia 138
Armenteros-Martínez, Ivan 18
Arnauda de la Mota, accused of heresy 5
Arnold, John H. 15
Artigues, Bartomeu, tailor 83
Ashe, Laura 244
Athanasius of Alexandria 150
Atlantic Ocean 207, 211
Auerbach, Erich 237
Augustine of Hippo 8, 123–135, 137, 139f., 144, 150, 153, 157, 255f., 258, 265
– *Confessiones* 131
– *Contra adversarium legis et prophetarum* 134
– *Contra Faustum* 132
– *Contra Felicem manichaeum* 125, 131
– *De Civitate Dei* 255f.
– *De haeresibus* 124–126, 129, 132, 135
– *De natura boni contra manichaeos* 133
Avicenna, Ibn Sina, *also known as* 231
– *Canons* 231
Avignon 37

Baer, Yitzhak 192
Bager, Susan 150
Balkans 119–121, 204, 207, 209
Barcelona 75, 182f., 187f., 194f., 204–212, 214, 216, 218f.
– *Carrer* d'En Roset 83
– *Carrer* Petritxol 83
– Hospital de la Santa Creu 86
– Jewish *Call* 82
– *Quarter de la Mar* 79, 81, 84f.
– *Rec Comtal* 82

– Santa Maria del Mar 79, 82
– Santa Maria del Pi 82 f.
Barjols 49
Baronio, Cesare 149
Bartholomea, beguine 30
Bartholomeus Anglicus
– *De proprietatibus rerum* 252
Barton, Thomas 196
Baruch ben Yaacob 190
Battles, Dominique 244
Bauman, Zygmunt 251
Bavarian National Museum, Munich 143
Beauvaisis, county of 229
Begura, Bernat 88
Belisarius 150
Belpech 6
Benedict XIII, Pope 191
Bernard Gui 5 f., 14
– *Liber sententiarum inquisitionis Tholosanae* 6
– *Practica inquisitionis heretice pravitatis* 6, 14
Bernard of Clairvaux 8, 159, 161–171, 173, 176
– *De Consideratione* 167
– *De Laude Novae Militiae* 162, 168
– *Sermons on the Song of Songs* 159, 164
Bernat de Na Jacma, Franciscan tertiary 6, 16 f.
Bernat Fenàs, accused of heresy 16
Bhaldraithe, Eoin de 161, 171
Biget, Jean-Louis 160, 172
Black Death 207 f.
Black Sea 204, 207, 209
Blanca, daughter of Clara 83
Bliss, Alan J. 239
Block Friedman, John 260, 265
Blumenthal, Debra 214
Bobbio 158
– San Colombano, Abbey of 158
Bodleian Library, Oxford 262
Boethius 247, 249
– *Consolation of Philosophy* 247
Bonastruc de Porta. *See* Nachmanides
Bonaventura de Bagnoreggio 42
– *Legenda maior* 30
Boniface VIII, Pope 33

Bonnet, Marie-Rose 56
Boquet, Damien 41
Bosnia 207
Boyer, Jean-Paul 37
Breviary of Renaud de Bar 252
British Library, London 262
Brittany 239
Brunet Psalter 42
Brunn, Uwe 123, 161
Buenos Aires 179
Burgos 187
Burgundy 84, 205
Buzet-sur-Tarn 6
Bynum, Caroline Walker 61

Caballero, Marcos 179
Cabrera, Sança Ximenis de 83
Caesarius of Heisterbach 67 f.
Cantabrian Mountains 205
Carozzi, Claude 30, 37
Carthage 124 f., 128, 131, 133 f., 137 f., 150
Casals i Parés, Jordi 17
Cassian
– *Collationes* 219
Castile 187, 194, 231
Catalan Civil War 209–211
Catalan Mahzor 190
Catalonia 189, 205, 209
Caterina, widow of Mateu Gual 87
Caterina, widow of Pere Garraf 83
Caterina, widow of Pere Vidal 81
Catherine of Siena 230
Cato, Marcus Porcius, *called* the Elder 219
Caucasus 207
Cayrol-Bernardo, Laura 14
Cecilia de Volta 25, 30, 52 f., 56
Chalcedon 158
Charles II, King of Naples 48
Charles of Anjou 49
Chartres 227
Chichester 66
Christe, Yves 141, 144, 156
Ciacconio, Alfonso 149
Clapers, Joan, labourer 90
Clara, widow of Guillem Comes 83
Classe 146
Clement V, Pope 34 f.

Clermont, county of 224
Clermont-Ferrand 142
Climent, Joan de, illuminator 88
Codex Theodosianus 124
Cohen, Jeffrey Jerome 266
Cohn, Norman 8
– *The Pursuit of the Millennium* 8
Collection Doat 5f., 16
Cologne 161, 165f., 168
Columella, Lucius Junius 218f.
Comas-Via, Mireia 14
Comes, Guillem, house builder 83
Conrad of Marburg 69–71, 73
– *Summa vitae* 69
Constantine the Great 136, 144
Constantinople 144f., 153, 209
Constituto of Siena 222f., 228f., 234–236
Cooper, Helen 246f.
Corbie Abbey 255
Córdoba 187
– Caliphate of 205
– Emirate of 205
Córdoba, Joan de, armourer 88
Cotxí, Ramon 88
Coulanges, Foustel de 201, 208
Council of Trent 33
Council of Vienne 33f., 40, 48, 56
Council of Westminster 233
Coutumes de Beauvaisis 222–225, 227–229, 233–236
Coyle, J. Kevin 134
Crenshaw, Kimberlé 93
Crusades 206
Cugada, Elisenda, widow 90
Cum de quibusdam 34f., 56
Cyril of Alexandria 153
Cyril of Jerusalem 134, 137
– *Catechesis* 133

David I, King of Scotland 65
Delphine de Puimichel 25, 42
Demaitre, Luke 60
Demougeot, Émilienne 155
Diocletian 135
Disputation of Barcelona 181, 191
Disputation of Paris 192
Disputation of Tortosa 181, 191f., 196

Domenja, daughter of Antònia 88
Douce Vivaud 45, 56
Douceline, daughter of Felipa Porcelleta 49
Douceline de Digne 23–31, 36–57
Dow, Anna Elizabeth 243
Drogo of Metz 143
Dura-Europos 148
– Baptistery 148
Durante Borda 45
Dyptich of Areobindus 253, 262

Écija 187, 194
Eckbert of Schönau 123
– *Sermones contra catharos* 124
Edict of Milan 7, 136, 156
Edwards, Robert 243f.
Egeria 144
Egypt 136, 138, 152
Eligius of Noyon 203
Elizabeth of Hungary 60, 68–74, 226
Emaré 240
England 169, 244
Enríquez, Juana 87
Epiphanius of Cyprus 125, 137
Epistle to Titus 165
Erkentruda, slave 205
Erle of Tolouse 240
Ernst, Rachel 7
Estévez Benítez, Estela 11
Eugene III, Pope 167
Euphemia of Chalcedon 146
Eusebia, Manichean 126, 128
Eusebius of Caesarea 125
Eusebius of Vercelli 154
Everwin of Steinfeld 165, 173

Falcó, Pere 87
Farmer, Sharon 83
Faustus, Manichean bishop 131
Felipa Porcelleta 45, 48f., 53–55
Felipa Porcelleta, young beguine, daughter of Bertrand 45, 49, 56
Feliu, Eduard 190
Ferran II, King of Aragon 210
Fernández, Samuel 150
Fernández Lahosa, Marta 7

Ferrand Martínez, archdeacon of Écija 187, 194
Ferrer, Friar, *known as* the Catalan, inquisitor 5
Ferrer, Guillem 85
Festus, Sextus Pompeius
– *De Verborum Significatione* 259
Fez 193
Field, Rosalind 244
Field, Sean 38, 47
Fish, Stanley 11f.
Florence 78, 80, 84
Florentinus 202
Florus, Praetorian Prefect of the East 136
Foletti, Ivan 152
Foucault, Michel 130
Fourth Council of the Lateran 10, 32, 224, 230
France 11, 187, 222, 255
– southern France 40, 135, 162, 171f., 212
Francesca *Na Mingueta* or *la de les tauletes*, widow of Minguet de Renda 88
Francis of Assisi 26–29, 36–38, 41f., 44, 55
Frederick I, Holy Roman Emperor, *called* Barbarossa 172
Frederick II, Holy Roman Emperor 207

Galharda Fabre, accused of heresy 6
García-Oliver, Ferran 193
Garraf, Pere 83
Gaul 133
Genesis, Book of 255
Genoa 190, 206f.
– Poor Clares 24, 31
Geoffrey of Auxerre 8, 159, 161f., 164, 171–176
– *Sermons on the Apocalypse* 159, 172, 174–176
– *Vita prima Sancti Bernardi* 172, 176
Gesta episcopalia 126
Giovanni di Andrea 34
Goldschmidt, A. 260
Gout, Raoul 23
Granada 216
– Nasrid kingdom of 210
Gratian 136, 233
Gregorian Reform 174

Gregory I, *called* the Great, Pope 148
Gregory IX, Pope 69
– *Decretals* 224
Grimaldi, Patrizia 248f.
Gros-Louis, Kenneth R. R. 238, 249
Grundmann, Herbert 9
– *Religiöse Bewegungen im Mittelalter* 9
Gual, Mateu, wheat dealer 87
Guarda d'Esclaus del General de Catalunya 209
Guilhem Garcias, Franciscan friar 16
Guillaume de Montolieu 40
Guinea, Gulf of 210
Gwynn, David 150

Haim Yosef David Azulai, *also known as* Hida 194
Hasdai ben Abraham Crescas 180, 191
– *Bittul iqqare ha-notsrim* 180, 191
Hedwig of Silesia 60, 66–69, 72–74
Henry III, Holy Roman Emperor 202
Henry of Marcy 162, 171f., 176
Henry the Bearded, Duke of Silesia 67
Hinojosa Montalvo, José 190
Hippolytus of Rome 129
Holy Land 144, 152, 158, 162, 169, 180
Hugh of Lincoln 226
Hugonette Bertrande 37f.
Hugues de Digne 24–26, 30–33, 37–39, 43f., 54f.
Huneycutt, Lois L. 65
Hyères 25, 30, 32, 36, 38, 41, 52
Hynes-Berry, Mary 243

Iberian Peninsula 11, 93, 180, 188, 190, 194, 204f., 207, 209f., 222, 225
Illyria 150, 157
India 251–253
Isaac ben Sheshet Perfet, *also known as* Ribash 177, 183, 188, 194
Isabel, daughter of Francesca *Na Mingueta* or *la de les tauletes* 88
Isentrud, handmaid 69
Isidore of Seville 256–260, 265f.
– *Etymologies* 253, 256f., 260, 262
Israel 178, 182f.
Istanbul 190

Italian Peninsula   135, 137, 222
Italy   11, 190, 195
Izmir   190

Jacma Lauret, accused of heresy   6
Jacobi, copyist   50
Jacques de Vitry   68, 72, 226, 230, 235f., 258
– *Historia occidentalis*   72, 226
– *Historia orientalis*   258
– *Sermones Vulgares*   222, 226, 228
Jaume I, King of Aragon   181, 206
Jaume I of Urgell   88
Jean Wauquelin
– *Livre des conquestes et faits d'Alexandre le Grand*   252
Jeanselme, Édouard   227
Jerome, Saint, *also known as* Jerome of Stridon   8
Jerónimo de Santa Fe   191f.
Jerusalem   144
Jesus of Nazareth   181
Jiménez Garnica, Ana María   150
Jiménez Sánchez, Pilar   160
Joachim of Fiore   37
Joan I, King of Aragon   187, 195
Joana, *called* the Valencian, wife of Joan de Córdoba   88
Joana, widow of Joan Clapers   90
Johan of Breyssan, accused of heresy   6
John, Gospel of   142
John Mandeville
– *The travels of Sir John Mandeville*   252
John of Parma   37f., 55
John XXII, Pope   17, 32–35, 37, 42f.
Jonah ben Abraham Gerondi   193
Joseph ibn Shem-Tov   180
Josselin d'Orange   37, 44
Juana de la Cruz   56
Julian, Proconsul of Africa   135
Justinian   150
– *Digest*   202

Kienzle, Beverly Mayne   161, 166
Kim, Susan M.   253
Klaniczay, Gábor   15
Knights Templar   162

Koberger, Anton   258
Konstanzer Weltchronik   252
Krolikoski, Courtney   15

La Guiche en Charolais, convent of   52
Lai de l'Espine   239
Lai d'Orphey   239
Lamothe, Dom Odon   149f.
Landes, Richard   8
Languedoc   5, 15f., 18, 225
Las Siete Partidas   222, 223–225, 231–236
Lavaur   173
Lay le Freine   240
Lazarus   147
Le Berrurier, Diane O.   260–262, 264
Le Conte de Floire et Blanchefleur   239
Leclercq, Jean   161, 166, 171
Leclerq-Marx, Jacqueline   262, 264
Lehmann, Paul   260
Leo I, *called* the Great, Pope   129, 137, 139, 153, 157f.
Letter to the Romans   167f.
Libellus de dictis quatuor ancillarum   70
Liberia   210
Lisbon   216
Lleida   89
Llull, Jaume   85
Lodève   6
Logroño   187
Lucius III, Pope   172
Ludwig IV, Landgrave of Thuringia   69f.
Lugt, Maaike van der   256
Luke, Gospel of   142
Lyon   84, 171

Mabila, daughter of Felipa Porcelleta   49
Maghreb   188, 208
Maimonides, Moses ben Maimon, *also known as*   185
Maisonneuve, Henri   166, 171
Makowski, Elizabeth   33, 35
Malaga   216
Malcolm III, King of Scotland   65
Mallorca   188, 194f., 206
Mani   137
Manselli, Raoul   170
Maragda Porcelleta   48f., 53

Marco Polo
– *Il Milione* 252
Marcos de Lisboa 43
Margaret of Scotland 64f., 72f.
Margarida, widow of Bartomeu Artigues 83
Margarita, young girl 126, 128, 135, 139
Marguerite d'Alon, beguine 56
Marie de France 239f.
Marita, beguine 40
Mark, Gospel of 142
Marseille 24f., 30, 32, 35–37, 43, 49, 51, 206
Martin of Tours 147
Mathews, Thomas F. 141, 144f., 156
Matilda of Scotland 60, 64–66, 69, 73f.
Matthew, Gospel of 142, 154f.
Maximinus, Arian bishop 147, 150, 157
– *Dissertatio Maximini contra Ambrosium* 150
– *Sermo Arianorum* 147
Meillassoux, Claude 201, 203, 213
Melucci, Alberto 11
Merkelbach, Rebecca 4
Meslin, Michel 147, 155, 157
Mesopotamia 138
Meyer, Paul 47
Michaud, Francine 40, 44f.
Michel de Pech-Rodil, accused of heresy 5
Milan 156, 262
– Biblioteca Ambrosiana 262
Mills, Vivian 59
Minorca 206
Mîrşanu, Dragos 147
Mittman, Asa S. 251, 253
Moitra, Angana 10
Molho, Isaac R. 190
Montauban 5
Monte Cassino Abbey 251–253, 258, 260–266
Monza
– ampullae 143, 153
– Duomo 158
Moore, Robert I. 8, 119, 121, 161, 172
– *The Origins of European Dissent* 8
– *The War on Heresy* 161
Morató, Guillem 76
Morella, Francina 76

Morgan, Christine 59
Moses 182, 191
Muhammad 185
Mulder-Bakker, Anneke B. 61
Muntaner, Ramon 206
Murcia 206

Nachmanides, Mosheh ben Nahman, *also known as* Ramban, *commonly referred to as* 177, 181f., 192
Naples 190, 206
Narbonne 5
Nastruch Bonfed 192
Navarre 187, 190
Nestorius 158
Neumarkt 67
Newman, Martha 161, 175
Nicaea 144
Nicodemus, Gospel of 142
Nissim of Girona, Nissim ben Reuben ha-Gerondi, *also known as* 185
– *Hidushe Sanhedrin* 185
Nogués, Joan, tanner 82
Noli 205
Normandy 239
Noutsou, Stamatia 8
Nowell Codex 262
Nuper ad audientiam 33

Omnis utriusque sexus 10
Osrhoene 138
Ottoman Empire 179, 190
Ovid 249

Panofsky, Erwin 260
Paphlagonia 133
Paris 24, 29, 84
– Bibliothèque nationale de France 5, 24, 149
– Louvre, Musée du 262f.
Patterson, Orlando 201, 203
Pegg, Mark Gregory 119
Peire Fabre, husband of Galharda 6
Peire Garcias, accused of heresy 16
Peiró, Joan 89
Pellegrin Repelin 48
Pere III, King of Aragon 206f.

Pere IV, King of Aragon   78, 88
Perez, Idan   190
Pergamon   174
Periculoso   33
Persia   138
Peter, Gospel of   142
Peter Lombard, Bishop of Paris   233
Peterson, Anna M.   11, 59
Petrus Iohannis Olivi   40
Philastrius of Brescia   125, 137
Philippe de Beaumanoir   227 f., 235
Phillips, Claire   59
Pilate, Acts of   142
Pisa   190
Plaensa, Francesc   83
Pliny the Elder   251, 255, 258, 265
Poimenia   144
Poitiers
– Abbey of the Holy Cross   59
Poland   67
Portugal   187, 190, 204, 211 f.
Presentacions i Confessions de captius   214
Procopius of Cesarea   150
Profiat Duran   180, 191
– *Kelimmat ha-Goyim*   180, 191
Propp, Vladimir   246
Prose Lancelot   239
Provence   23, 25, 32 f., 36–38, 40 f., 49
Proverbs, Book of   219
Provins   226
Puyloubier   25
Pyrenees   205

Qocho   134
Quodvultdeus of Carthage   124–126, 128, 131 f.

Rabbula Gospels   143
Radegund, Frankish queen   59
Raimon Martí   192
– *Pugio Fidei*   192
Raimon IV, Count of Toulouse   169
Raimon VII, Count of Toulouse   5
Raimundeta, widow of Joan Nogués   82
Rainier Sacconi   5
– *Summa de Cathari*   5
Ramban. *See* Nachmanides

Rashbash   197, Shlomoh ben Simeon ben Tzemah Duran
Rashbatz   188, 194 f., 197, *See* Simeon ben Tzemah Duran
Ratramnus of Corbie   255
– *Epistola de cynocephalis*   255
Ravenna   145 f., 150, 152, 154
– Arian Baptistery   145, 147 f., 154
– Baptistery of Neon   147 f., 154
– San Vitale   152
– Sant'Apollinare Nuovo   145–147, 154
Rawcliffe, Carole   60, 221, 223
Reims   100, 227
Renda, Minguet de, royal hunter   88
Renna, Thomas   161
Reuter, Marianne   260
Rhabanus Maurus   251 f., 256, 258 f., 262, 265 f.
– *De universo*   252 f., 256, 258, 260, 262 f.
Rhineland   165
Ribash   188, 194 f., 197, *See* Isaac ben Sheshet Perfet
Ribelles, Lluís   87
Richard of Dover, Archbishop of Canterbury   233
Ricimer   148
Riera i Sans, Jaume   82, 181
Rifà, Guillem, weaver   83
Rimbert   255
Ripon Cathedral   252
Riu i Riu, Manuel   80
Rizzardi, Clementina   147 f., 154
Roach, Andrew P.   8
Roman d'Alexandre en prose   252
Roman de Jaufré   222, 225, 229 f., 232, 234, 236
Rome   136–138, 145, 152, 158, 182, 229
– Aventine Hill   152
– Civitavecchia   190
– Lateran Palace   158
– Saint Paul Outside the Walls   152
– Saint Sabina   152
– Sant'Agata dei Goti   145, 148
– Santa Pudenziana   149
Rosa, of the parish of Santa Maria del Pi   82
Roseline de Villeneuve   25

Roubaud 12, 23, 25, 33, 35f., 39f., 42–46, 50, 52, 57

Sackville, Lucy 119f.
Salimbene de Adam 24, 31f.
– *Cronica* 24, 31
Salmon, Amédée 225
Salonica 190
Sança, widow 89
Sança de Mallorca, Queen of Naples 36, 38
Sancho Fibla, Sergi 12
Santa Maria de Bélem 42
Santa Maria de Montserrat Abbey 206
Santa Maria de Poblet, Royal Abbey of 206
Saragossa 188, 195
Sardinia 83
Sassari 83
Sasson Hai le-Bet Kastiel 196
Saxl, Fritz 260
Scholem, Gershom 180
Schwieterman, Patrick Joseph 239
Second Council of Lyon 32f.
Second Council of the Lateran 168
Seneca the Younger 203
Senegal 210
Senegambia 210
Sennis, Antonio 121
Sentmenat, Joan Pere de 87
Sepharad 179, 190, 194–196
Serbia 207
Serra, Bernardó 85
Servanes 142
Seville 187, 211
Sézanne 227, 229
Shem-Tob ben Isaac Shaprut 180
– *Eben Bohan* 180, 183, 191
Shlomoh ben Aderet 177, 185f.
Shlomoh ben Reuben Bonfed 192
Shlomoh ben Simeon ben Tzemah Duran, also known as Rashbash 193
Shlomoh ibn Verga 191
– *Shevet Yehudah* 191
Sicily 206
Siena 228f., 235
– Corpo Santo 225
– Ospedale di Santa Maria della Scala 229
– San Lazaro 225, 235

Simeon ben Tzemah Duran, *also known as* Rashbatz or Tashbatz 177, 193f.
Simon of Trebnitz
– *Vita Maior Beate Hedwigis* 68, 73
Sir Degaré 240
Sir Gowther 240
Sir Launfal 240
Sir Orfeo 10, 238
Solà, Jaume 84
Solinus, Gaius Julius 258
– *Collectanea rerum memorabilium* 261f.
Sommerfeldt, John R. 168
Stock, Brian 9
Sullivan, Karen 161, 166
Synod of Verona 172

Tarí, Caterina *na Trialles*, widow of Bernat Trialls 88f.
Tarrant, Jacqueline 34
Tashbatz. *See* Simeon ben Tzemah Duran
Theobald II, Count of Champagne 226–229, 235f.
Theodoric the Great 146
Theodosius, Manichean 132
Theodosius I 136
Théry-Astruc, Julien 130
Third Council of the Lateran 5, 172, 222–224, 232, 236
Thomas Eccleston 32
Thomas of Cantimpré 252, 257, 265
– *De natura rerum* 252, 257
Thomas of Kent
– *Roman de toute chevalerie* 252
Toledo 187
Torredà 206
Tortosa 196
Touati, François-Olivier 60, 221
Toulon 32, 36
Toulouse 5, 16, 145, 169–171
– Sainte-Marie de la Daurade 145, 149f.
Trebnitz 67
Trialls, Bernat 89
Trudgardis, slave owner 204f.
Turfan 132f., 138

Ugonio, Pompeo 149
Ulfilas 151

Umayyad Dynasty   205
Urbano, Arthur   146
Úrsula, daughter of Joana the Valencian   88
Úrsula, granddaughter of Raimundeta   82
Ursus, procurator   125

Valdes, *also known as* Waldo   171
Valencia   187f., 190, 195, 206, 211, 214
– Morvedre, region of   190
Valentinian I   136
Valentinian III   137
Van Oort, Johannes   130, 133f.
Varro, Marcus Terentius   212f., 219
Vatican City
– Saint Peter in the Vatican   152
– Vatican Library   253, 260f., 264
– Vatican Museums   155, 158
Vauchez, André   64
Venantius Fortunatus   59
– *Vita Sanctae Radegundis*   59
Venice   78, 207
Vercelli   154
Veroli   228
Vézelay Abbey   252
Viator, Manichean   126
Vida de la benaurada Sancta Doucelina mayre de las donnas de Robaut   12, 23–25, 28, 30f., 35–38, 40–57
Vidal, Pere, house builder   81
Vienne   227
Vincent of Beauvais   258
– *Speculum Historiale*   258

Vinyoles Vidal, Teresa   88, 90
Virgil   249
Vita Margaretae   65
Volbach, Wolfgang Fritz   262

Wales   239
Wallis, Faith   59
Wartburg Castle   69
Wends, Slavic people   163
Westminster
– Hospital of St. James   66
widow of Bernardó Serra   85
widow of Guillem Ferrer   85
widow of Jaume Llull   85
widow of Jaume Solà   84
widow of Joan Pere de Sentmenat   87
Winchester   240, 243
Wittkower, Rudolf   260
Wolf, Kenneth Baxter   63
Wonders of the East   261f.
Woodruff, Helen   150
Word-Perkins, Bryan   146, 150, 154

Xàtiva   190

Yehosua ben Yosef ha-Lorqui   *See* Jerónimo de Santa Fe
Yitzhak Baer
– *History of the Jews in Christian Spain*   192

Zbíral, David   120
Zsom, Dora   189

www.ingramcontent.com/pod-product-compliance
Lightning Source LLC
Chambersburg PA
CBHW050518170426
43201CB00013B/1997